Current Perspectives in Forensic Psychology and Criminal Justice

Editors

Curt R. Bartol
Castleton College, Vermont

Anne M. Bartol
Castleton College, Vermont

 SAGE Publications
Thousand Oaks ■ London ■ New Delhi

For information:

Sage Publications, Inc.
2455 Teller Road
Thousand Oaks, California 91320
E-mail: order@sagepub.com

Sage Publications Ltd.
1 Oliver's Yard
55 City Road
London EC1Y 1SP
United Kingdom

Sage Publications India Pvt. Ltd.
B-42, Panchsheel Enclave
Post Box 4109
New Delhi 110 017 India

Printed in the United States of America

Library of Congress Cataloging-in-Publication Data

Current perspectives in forensic psychology and criminal justice /
edited by Curt R. Bartol, Ann M. Bartol.
    p. cm.
Includes bibliographical references and index.
ISBN 1-4129-2590-8 (pbk.)
  1. Criminal psychology. 2. Forensic psychology. 3. Police psychology. 4. Correctional psychology. 5. Criminal investigation—Psychological aspects. 6. Criminal justice, Administration of—Psychological aspects. I. Bartol, Curt R., 1940- II. Bartol, Anne M.
HV6080.C87 2006
614'.15—dc22   2005019685

This book is printed on acid-free paper.

05   06   07   08   10   9   8   7   6   5   4   3   2   1

Acquisitions Editor:	Jerry Westby
Editorial Assistant:	Laura Shigemitsu
Typesetter:	C&M Digitals (P) Ltd.
Cover Designer:	Michelle Lee Kenny

CONTENTS

Current Perspectives in
Forensic Psychology and Criminal Justice

PREFACE

The articles in this book are offered as supplementary readings to accompany the main text in a variety of undergraduate courses, such as Introduction to Forensic Psychology, Criminology, Psychology and Criminal Justice, Psychology and Law, and similar courses. While most articles were originally published after 2000, a few were first published in the mid-1990s but have been well cited in the forensic literature. Included in the more recent articles are some that provide a different perspective on crime victims or on common or attention-getting crimes. Finally, three articles were written especially for this book of readings, and one—"Overview of Forensic Psychology"— is a revision of an earlier textbook chapter.

In the interest of space we have taken the liberty of editing most of the original works. When substantial portions of an article have been omitted, we have indicated that in a footnote at the beginning of the article. In addition, all abstracts, notes, and some figures and tables have been removed. References now appear in a master reference list at the end of the book. Complete citations are included for those readers who wish to review the original publication.

The articles are introduced and are grouped in accordance with our view of forensic psychology as a specialty that has relevance to a wide range of both criminal and civil settings. Nevertheless, due to the vast amount of research on crime-related topics and the fact that this reader is a supplement to crime-related courses, the great majority of the articles relate to criminal matters.

We are grateful for the encouragement and support of Jerry Westby, and our reviewers: Amy Thistlewaite of Northern Kentucky University, Chandrika Kelso of National University, Trina Cyterski at the University of Georgia, Don Mohr at Purdue University, Robyn Diehl Lacks at Virginia Commonwealth University, and Sara Broaders at Northwestern University.

UNIT 1

INTRODUCTION

1

OVERVIEW OF FORENSIC PSYCHOLOGY

ANNE M. BARTOL
CURT R. BARTOL

The term "forensic" refers to matters that pertain to courts or to law, both civil and criminal. Forensic *science* involves the application of scientific knowledge to legal problems. Today, virtually all branches of the natural and social sciences have made this application. Psychology, the science of behavior, is no exception.

The forensic sciences as a whole have become popular career choices among students, and many scientific professions now have forensic specialties. In addition to forensic psychology, we have, for example, forensic engineering, forensic medicine, forensic pathology, forensic anthropology, forensic archaeology, forensic psychiatry, and forensic social work. Non-scientific professions, such as accounting and linguistics, also have forensic specialties.

The focus of each discipline is evident from the terms. Forensic anthropology, for example, refers to the identification of skeletal, badly decomposed, or otherwise unidentified human remains. Forensic linguistics is concerned with the in-depth evaluation of language-related characteristics of text, such as grammar, syntax, spelling, vocabulary and phraseology, either to profile an offender or to determine whether specific writing samples are from the same author (Black, 1990). Forensic pathology is the branch of medicine concerned with diseases and disorders of the body that relate to questions that might come before the court. The forensic pathologist examines the bodies of crime victims for clues about the victim's demise. Popularized in such television shows as CSI, the work of the pathologist is actually quite non-glamorous, though of course crucial. "While the TV world of forensic science provides instant gratification, the real world is tedious and slow" (Hempel, 2003, p. 14). Forensic social workers, as well as other mental health practitioners, may conduct child custody evaluations, and forensic psychiatrists and psychologists evaluate juveniles and criminal defendants. These are but a few of the many tasks performed by forensic professionals.

Editors' Note: Adapted from Bartol, C.R. & Bartol, A.M. (2004). "Forensic Psychology: Introduction and Overview," in C. R. Bartol & A. M. Bartol, *Introduction to forensic psychology* (pp. 3–29). Thousand Oaks, CA: Sage.

Psychologists have long been conducting research and providing services in the legal arena. J. McKeen Cattell conducted the first experiment on the psychology of testimony in 1893, and an American psychologist testified as an expert witness in a courtroom in 1921. In 1917 and 1918, respectively, psychologists used psychological tests to screen law enforcement candidates and developed the first inmate classification system. William Marston was appointed a professor of legal psychology in 1922, and Martin Reiser became the first full-time police psychologist in 1968.

It was not until the 1970s, however, that the term "forensic psychology" emerged. In 1971, the disciplines of psychology and psychiatry each established organizations that, according to Grisso (1996, pp. 98–99), "set the stage for developments that would identify forensic assessment as a specialty and would promote the quality of mental health evaluations for the courts." These organizations were the American Psychology-Law Society (AP-LS) and the American Academy of Psychiatry and Law (AAPL). In 1974, an interdisciplinary program in psychology and law was initiated at the University of Nebraska, and in 1978 the AP-LS created the American Board of Forensic Psychology. This became the examining board for certifying diplomates in forensic psychology, under the auspices of the American Board of Professional Psychology. (Although we do not discuss them here, parallel developments occurred in the field of psychiatry.) A diplomate is a professional with extensive knowledge of and expertise in his or her area. Following this initial activity in the 1970s, forensic psychology developed very rapidly over the next two decades and embraced not only practitioners but also a large body of research literature. In 2001, the Council of Representatives of the American Psychological Association voted to recognize forensic psychology as an applied specialty within the field, joining clinical, counseling, school, and industrial/organizational psychology.

There are two major approaches to defining forensic psychology—the narrow and the broad. In the narrow sense, forensic psychology refers to the application and practice of psychology in the legal system, particularly the courts. This narrow definition focuses heavily on clinical practice. A broader conception of forensic psychology covers a wider landscape of psychology's involvement with legal matters, as will be discussed below. It is probably accurate to note that the narrow term is the more favored within psychology. For example, Ronald Roesch (cited in Brigham, 1999, p. 279) notes that "(m)ost psychologists define the area more narrowly to refer to clinical psychologists who are engaged in clinical practice within the legal system." Additionally, in recognizing forensic psychology as a specialty in 2001, the APA Council of Representatives endorsed a narrow rather than broad definition. "(I)t was ultimately decided that the petition for specialization should define forensic psychology narrowly, to include the primarily clinical aspects of forensic assessment, treatment, and consultation" (Otto & Heilbrun, 2002, p. 8).

Nevertheless, we prefer a broader definition, and the readings in this text reflect this breadth. "We view forensic psychology broadly, as both (1) the research endeavor that examines aspects of human behavior directly related to the legal process . . . and (2) the professional practice of psychology within, or in consultation with, a legal system that embraces both civil and criminal law" (Bartol & Bartol, 1987, p. 3). This broad definition includes not only clinicians (also called practitioners) but also social, developmental, counseling, cognitive, experimental, industrial-organizational, and school psychologists, some—but not all—of whom are clinicians. The common link is their contribution to the legal system. Thus, the social psychologist who conducts research on eyewitness testimony, the psychologist who offers workshops to police on interviewing child witnesses, and the clinician who initiates a sex offender treatment program in a prison setting are all engaging in forensic psychology, broadly defined. The field also includes research and theory building in criminology; the design and implementation of intervention, prevention, and treatment for youthful offenders; and counseling of victims of crime.

The readings in this book, then, are organized to reflect the division of forensic psychology into five subspecialties: (1) police psychology; (2) psychology of crime and delinquency; (3) victimology and victim services; (4) psychology applied to the courts; and (5) psychology applied to corrections. While we separate these subspecialties for organizational purposes, it is important to note that there is considerable overlap among them. The correctional psychologist, for example, is well versed in the psychology of crime and delinquency. The police psychologist may offer services to victims as well as to police. All of the above may testify in court, and all of the above may be conducting research in more than one subspecialty area. The point here is to emphasize that the various sub-areas of forensic psychology are not mutually exclusive.

POLICE PSYCHOLOGY

Police psychology is the research and application of psychological principles and clinical skills to law enforcement and public safety (Bartol, 1996). Included in the term "police" is a range of primarily public agents, such as sheriffs and their deputies, fish and wildlife officers, airport security personnel, marshals, constables, and many types of other state and federal agents.

The relationship between psychology and law enforcement has waxed and waned over the years. Overall, though, we have seen an increase in the services provided by psychologists to the police community. This is partly because law enforcement agencies have become more professional and their administrators and agents better educated, and partly because the public has demanded more accountability on the part of police. Psychologists today perform pre-employment psychological assessment and evaluations for a variety of special situations, including fitness-for-duty, assignment to special units (e.g., SWAT teams), and deadly-force incidents. Some provide counseling or therapy to officers and their families, assist in hostage negotiations, and conduct workshops on stress management. Forensic psychologists are also increasingly asked to do investigative-type activities, such as criminal profiling, psychological autopsies, handwriting analysis, and eyewitness (or earwitness) hypnosis. Larger police departments usually hire full-time, in-house police psychologists, while the smaller departments usually use psychological consultants.

CRIMINAL AND DELINQUENT BEHAVIOR

The psychology of crime and delinquency, sometimes referred to as criminal psychology, is the *science* of the behavioral and mental processes of the adult and juvenile offender (Bartol, 2002). It is primarily concerned with how criminal behavior is acquired, evoked, maintained, and modified. Recent research has focused on the offender's cognitive versions of the world, especially his or her thoughts, beliefs and values and how they can be changed. It assumes that various criminal behaviors are acquired by daily living experiences, in accordance with the principles of learning, and are perceived, coded, processed, and stored in memory in a unique fashion for each individual. Criminal psychology examines and evaluates prevention, intervention, and treatment strategies directed at reducing juvenile delinquency and criminal behavior.

Criminal psychologists also are interested in research on specific crimes as well as the perpetrators of these offenses. The focus has been violent crimes, particularly murder, sexual assault, and aggravated assault, such as that associated with hate crimes or domestic violence. For example, psychological concepts and principles associated with aggression, reinforcement, and deindividuation can help us understand causes and aid in the prevention of these violent offenses. Nevertheless, criminal psychologists also have addressed causes and prevention of drug abuse, theft, fraud, and other nonviolent crimes.

The topic that has caught considerable attention of psychologists in recent years has been criminal psychopathy. A psychopath is a person who demonstrates a discernible pattern of psychological, cognitive, interpersonal, and neurophysiological features that distinguish him or her from the general population. The term "criminal psychopath" is reserved for those psychopaths who persistently engage in a wide variety of antisocial behaviors that are harmful to others. As a group, criminal psychopaths tend to be "dominant, manipulative individuals characterized by an impulsive, risk-taking and antisocial life-style, who obtain their greatest thrill from diverse sexual gratification and target diverse victims over time" (Porter et al., 2000, p. 220). Porter and his associates go on to say that, "Given its relation to crime and violence, psychopathy is arguably one of the most important psychological constructs in the criminal justice system" (p. 227).

More recently, attention has been directed at "juvenile psychopaths." There is considerable debate over whether such a label can be applied to children and adolescents, however. Specifically, attempts at diagnosing youths as psychopaths "raise several conceptual, methodological, and practical concerns related to clinical/forensic practice and juvenile/criminal justice policy" (Edens, Skeem, Cruise, & Cauffman, 2001, p. 54). Can characteristics of adult psychopathy be applied to children in the first place? And, if it is discovered that psychopathy is a meaningful term for youth, what are the ethical issues of labeling a child a psychopath? A third debate centers on how accurate the assessment instrument must be before it should be used in courts. After all, a clinical diagnosis may destine the child to be considered dangerous and incorrigible throughout life. There is also concern that a diagnosis of psychopathy may be used to justify decisions to transfer juvenile offenders to the adult criminal justice system. A fourth debate examines whether psychopathy can be prevented or treated effectively. So far, the results have not been encouraging, but much more work needs to be done in this area before conclusions can be reached.

Female psychopathy and differences in psychopathic behavior due to ethnic, racial, and cultural factors have not received much research attention. These issues and the many questions concerning juvenile psychopathy will be the topics of greatest concern in future research on psychopathy.

It should be noted that developmental psychologists are becoming increasingly involved in the study of crime and delinquency. Although it is generally agreed that crime and delinquency has many causes that involve both individual and environmental factors, and that it takes many forms, developmental psychologists have discovered that there are many developmental pathways or trajectories to crime. Some offenders start in early childhood, while others start in early adolescence or later. Moreover, these developmental trajectories appear to differ as a function of cultures, subcultures, and sociodemograhic environments. Overall, developmental

psychologists have been instrumental in shifting the psychological study of crime away from personality traits as sole or even major determinants of criminal and delinquent behavior and more toward an interactive cognitive and social focus as they relate to developmental changes across the life span.

One of the most exciting developments on the criminal psychology front is the current interest in applying research and principles from positive psychology. Traditionally, the field of psychology has focused on mental disorders, abnormality, and maladjustment. Positive psychology—a field that has emerged over the last decade—focuses instead on human strengths and what makes individuals emotionally healthy (Seligman, 2002). A primary illustration of positive psychology is the recent interest in resilience in children and adolescents who are exposed to adversity in their lives and have been assumed to be good candidates for delinquency. Resilience research indicates, on the contrary, that many become productive, pro-social adults. Positive psychology also helps us to understand how victims of crime can become survivors and how prisoners can benefit from treatment programs.

VICTIMOLOGY AND VICTIM SERVICES

Victimology is the study of persons who have experienced either actual or threatened physical, psychological, social, and/or financial harm as the result of the commission or attempted commission of crime against them. The harm may be direct or primary (against those who experience it and its consequences firsthand) or indirect or secondary (against family members, relatives, survivors, or friends who experience the harm because of their closeness to the victim) (Karmen, 2001). This latter group is often referred to as the covictims of the crime.

Violent victimization of children, such as terrifying abductions, school shootings, and sexual attacks, can disrupt the course of child development in very fundamental ways and can be associated with emotional and cognitive problems over the course of the life span (Boney-McCoy & Finkelhor, 1995). In adults, there is strong evidence that the effects of criminal victimization—such as assault, robbery, and burglary—are both

As a group, the readings in this section provide a sampling of what police psychologists do and how psychological research can be applied to police work. Many areas, though, are not represented in the readings. For example, psychologists conduct research on police lineups, offer stress-management workshops to officers and their spouses, accompany police on domestic violence calls, perform fitness-for-duty evaluations, and screen detainees held in police lockups for mental illness. The extent to which interested psychologists work directly with police—either consistently or as needed—is limited primarily by the willingness of the police to call upon them for service.

2

POLICE PSYCHOLOGY

Then, Now, and Beyond

CURT R. BARTOL

My involvement in psychological services to law enforcement began in 1973 when I was asked to teach a course in abnormal psychology at a police academy. Shortly thereafter, law enforcement agencies began seeking my help in dealing with various psychological issues, such as job stress, interactions with the mentally disordered, and pre-employment screening. I soon found myself sliding into longer and longer hours consulting and training. I became a certified academy instructor in crisis intervention, interviewing and interrogation, hostage negotiation, and criminal psychology. I was appointed to a statewide Criminal Justice Training Council, where I helped establish standards for the screening and selection of law enforcement officers. It wasn't long before I was asked to evaluate and make recommendations concerning the police academy curriculum, with the idea of moving it from a paramilitary format to a human relations one. I also was asked by agencies nationwide to offer workshops on screening and selection or to participate in the training of police recruits.

At this point, I began to believe I was quite good and that I even possessed a tinge of charisma. It did not dawn on me then that it was more a case of being in the right place at the right time. The Law Enforcement Assistance Administration (LEAA), created by Congress in 1965, was in full swing, disbursing substantial funds to encourage law enforcement agencies to become more human sensitive. I began to realize that I simply happened to be one of the few psychologists in the area willing to work with law enforcement. Since this early propitious beginning, I have continued to provide many psychological services to a variety of law enforcement agencies. I also have conducted large-scale, longitudinal research projects by following the careers of officers in small-town police and sheriff's departments in an effort to identify potential predictors of success. Not surprisingly, I follow avidly developments in the emergence of police psychology.

The term *police psychology* is discomfiting, however, because it appears to preclude other law enforcement agents, such as deputy sheriffs, marshals, or constables. Blau (1994),

Editors' Note: This article first appeared in *Criminal Justice and Behavior*, Vol. 23, No. 1, March 1996, pp. 70-89.

a psychologist and deputy sheriff in the Manatee County (Florida) Sheriff's Department, may have felt the same way when he called his book *Psychological Services for Law Enforcement*. The term law enforcement also has its critics, however, particularly those who argue that police enforce the law selectively and minimally. The real work of police is maintaining order, keeping the peace, or being co-producers, with citizens, of public safety. Rather than weigh in heavily in favor of one or the other term, I will opt for the less cumbersome. Police psychology here will encompass all law enforcement agencies and agents, with the caveat that they do much more than—and sometimes much less than—enforce the law. In the remainder of the article, I shall sketch the development of police psychology, describe its current status, and try to predict its future.

THEN: 20 YEARS AGO AND EARLIER

When did police psychology begin? Some have said that the profession was launched formally at the National Symposium on Police Psychological Services (NSPPS) held at the FBI Academy on September 17, 1984 (Chandler, 1990; McKenzie, 1986). The proceedings of this meeting were published in a monograph (Reese & Goldstein, 1986) titled, like Blau's work, *Psychological Services for Law Enforcement*. The NSPPS was antedated by a number of symposia, conferences, and workshops on police psychology, however. The Society of Police and Criminal Psychology, for example, has had annual conferences and symposia on topics pertaining to police psychology since 1971. To set 1984 as the date for the origin of police psychology seems unjustified, given the amount of conference activity over a decade before that. Another important date in the history of police psychology was December 1968, when Martin Reiser was hired by the Los Angeles Police Department as a full-time psychologist. Soon afterward, in 1969, Reiser (1972) presented a paper at the Western Psychological Association Convention, Vancouver, titled "The Police Department Psychologist." Chandler (1990) referred to this presentation as the informal birth of the profession of police psychology.

Here, too, my own opinion differs. There is no doubt that Reiser's contributions to the field have been invaluable. In the early 1970s, he was clearly the most prolific writer on police psychology. In 1972, in cooperation with the California School of Professional Psychology, he helped establish an internship in police psychology in the Los Angeles Police Department. To conclude, as Chandler did, that Reiser's paper marked the informal beginning of the profession is problematic, however. Psychologists were working in various capacities in law enforcement settings long before the 1970s. Reiser (1982) himself, in a collection of published papers, noted that he was not at all sure he was the first full-time police psychologist in the country. Reese (1986, 1987), a historian on psychological services to law enforcement, estimated that only six police agencies in the United States had full-time psychologists by 1977.

Before we become too myopic in our proclamations of historical firsts, we should realize that our international colleagues may have been ahead of us. Viteles (1929) reported that police departments in Germany were using psychologists in a variety of capacities as early as 1919. Chandler (1990) noted that, in 1966, the Munich (Germany) police were employing a full-time, in-house psychologist to train officers to deal with various patrol problems, such as crowd control. The informal origin of police psychology probably goes back more than 50 years, but I leave it to others to propose a more specific date. I much prefer to discuss the developmental stages of police psychology. A review of the literature suggests that police psychologists have pursued four distinct, although overlapping, trends, beginning with an affinity for cognitive assessment and proceeding through personality assessment, a clinical focus, and an organizational approach.

The first trend was concerned with the cognitive functioning of police officers, specifically intelligence and aptitude. This track probably began in this country with Terman's (1917) testing (using the Stanford-Binet) of applicants for several fire fighter and police officer positions for the city of San Jose, California, in 1916. His results, which suggested police applicants were not a very intelligent lot, appeared in the first issue of the *Journal of Applied Psychology*. Five years after the Terman report, the intelligence of police officers still was being debated, particularly in the work of Thurstone (1922,1924) and Telford and Moss (1924).

The cognitive approach, although never wholeheartedly subscribed to, had very little competition until the mid-1960s. Moreover, involving psychologists in policing seems to have been the exception rather than the rule. In a survey of 90 police departments (Oglesby, 1957), only 14 reported that they used some type of psychiatric or psychological input in their screening procedures. Only two departments said that they used a psychologist for the screening, with the rest preferring to use a psychiatrist. Interestingly, one department reported dropping the services of its psychiatrist because he rejected none of the 1,500 applicants. A subsequent survey by Narrol and Levitt (1963) to discover the extent of selection testing used by major police departments in the United States found an increase in the use of psychological testing. Specifically, they found that 100% of the departments used some kind of selection test, usually a standardized intelligence test (40%) or non-standardized aptitude test (87%) that usually was developed by the department itself. Only 22% were using any kind of personality inventory or psychiatric interview. However, only 6 of the 55 cities surveyed indicated that they employed qualified psychologists in connection with their selection procedures.

In the mid-1960s, interest shifted to assessing the personality attributes of police officers. Some of the shift from cognitive appraisal to personality assessment was probably due to widespread concerns directed at "IQ tests" and the danger of adverse impact on minority groups. The major impetus, however, was the report by the President's Commission on Law Enforcement and the Administration of Justice (1967) recommending widespread use of psychological tests to determine the emotional stability of all potential officers. Specifically, the commission asserted:

Screening out candidates whose emotional stability makes them clearly unfit for police work—through psychological tests and psychiatric interviews— should also improve the capacity of police forces to improve community relations. . . . While there is no one psychological test which can reliably identify all candidates who are emotionally unfit for police service, a combination of tests and oral psychiatric interviews can pinpoint many serious character defects. (pp. 164–165)

The commission hoped that departments would reject police candidates who demonstrated racial and ethnic prejudice prior to being hired. Similarly, the 1968 National Advisory Commission on Civil Disorder called for screening methods that would improve the quality of the law enforcement officers hired (Scrivner, 1994).

In keeping with commission recommendations, Congress provided LEAA funds for law enforcement agencies to retain the services of mental health professionals. Many of us currently working in some capacity in law enforcement started our work with the help of some variant of LEAA funding. LEAA, which became President Johnson's centerpiece in his war on crime, also funded technical assistance, materials, training, college education (through LEEP, the Law Enforcement Education Program), and research, including searches for selection procedures that would identify emotionally suitable police officers. Because the funding was intended to identify the emotional stability and prejudices of law enforcement officers, psychologists were required to become more clinical and personality/psychopathology-based in their work with law enforcement organizations. In 1973, the Police Task Force Report of the National Commission on Criminal Justice Standards and Goals encouraged the establishment of a behavioral sciences resource unit or consultant for all law enforcement agencies.

By the early 1970s, personality assessment had increased, but it certainly was not the norm. In a survey, Murphy (1972) found that only 44% of large municipal police departments used some kind of psychological test or inventory in evaluating applicants, most commonly the Minnesota Multiphasic Personality Inventory (MMPI). Murphy also found that only 13% of state agencies used psychological instruments for screening purposes.

Murphy (1972) concluded that general psychological testing for screening had not changed significantly over the 8 years since the Narrol and Levitt (1963) survey. However, he did notice an increase in the use of personality assessment. For example, the MMPI was the instrument of choice for nearly 50% of the agencies indicating that they used psychological testing in their screening and selection procedures.

The personality assessment trend had two research offshoots, the first being a search for the "police personality" (Lefkowitz, 1975). Agencies began to ask, Does law enforcement draw a certain type of person? Some psychologists obliged them by trying to answer. The question has yet to be answered satisfactorily, however, and researchers today have shifted their interests to other issues.

The second research offshoot involved an effort to identify instruments that could select in, as well as screen out. Selecting-in procedures are intended to identify those attributes (almost invariably personality) that distinguish one candidate over another as being a potentially more effective officer. Implicit in this assessment is the ability to rank order applicants, allowing agencies to select the top candidates from a pool who passed the initial screening procedures. This approach assumes that there are traits, habits, reactions, and attitudes that distinguish an outstanding cop from a satisfactory one. To the best of my knowledge, there is little evidence that psychologists can accomplish this goal in any satisfactory manner. For more than 20 years I have tried, unsuccessfully, to develop an instrument or instruments that would help identify applicants who would become above-average or superior officers in the field.

Screening-*out* procedures, on the other hand, try to eliminate those who demonstrate significant signs of psychopathology or emotional instability, or who lack the basic ability or mental acuity to perform the job in a safe and responsible manner (Meier, Farmer, & Maxwell, 1987). On average, about 15% of candidates are screened out through personality assessment. We have been far more successful in our screening-out than in our screening-in determinations. Research on officers who did not succeed in law enforcement, for example, has suggested that warning signs were present on MMPI measures (Bartol, 1991), rendering them "true negatives." The "false negative" picture is much more difficult to obtain, however, because agencies generally heed the MMPI warning signs pointed out by the police psychologist.

The third trend is best represented by the word stress, which became the overriding theme from the mid-1970s to the early 1980s. More than ever before, clinicians were called upon to identify and dissipate stress, which presumably— if left unmanaged or untreated—would result in an array of psychological and physical health problems for the officer and potentially put the public at risk. *Stressors, burnout, posttraumatic stress disorder,* and *critical incident trauma* became standard terms in the police psychologist's vocabulary. Whether police officers actually experienced more stress than people in other high-risk occupations (e.g., air traffic controller) remained highly debatable (Yarmey, 1990), however. Nevertheless, there was little doubt that stress played a major role in the lives of law enforcement officers at all levels within the organization. The focus on stress was significant because it propelled police psychologists away from their traditional testing functions and into a much larger realm of opportunity and services. Consequently, psychologists began to offer not only stress management, but also crisis intervention training, hostage negotiation training, domestic violence workshops, and substance abuse treatment.

The fourth trend reflects a discernible move into industrial/organizational kinds of issues and a drift away from exclusively clinical and mental health ones. During the mid-1970s, a trend developed toward looking more closely at the law enforcement organization rather than emphasizing—sometimes to the exclusion of other factors—the person. There were moves, of course, in that direction earlier. Bard's work (Bard, 1969; Bard & Berkowitz, 1969) promoted a closer look at training and the police organization from a psychological perspective, for example. We will examine this organizational trend in more detail later in the article, when the future of psychological services to law enforcement is discussed.

During the 1980s, the development of police psychology seemed to reach a plateau. Federal funding to state, municipal, and county agencies became limited, and law enforcement agencies were inclined not to require or seek additional psychological services unless absolutely necessary.

Although psychologists continued to consult with law enforcement agencies, give workshops, provide screening services, and offer therapy and counseling, there is no indication that the decade of the 1980s was one of significant growth. However, police psychologists did continue to refine their profession through conferences, professional meetings, and publications.

Now: Who, What, and How Much

Perhaps the best way to describe the present work of police psychologists is to ask police psychologists themselves what they are doing. The following data are taken from an unpublished nationwide survey of 152 police psychologists conducted by the author during the spring of 1994. Respondents were members of the Police and Public Safety section of the American Psychological Association's Division of Psychologists in Public Service, the Council on Police Psychological Services (COPPS), the police psychology section of the International Association of Chiefs of Police, and the Society of Police and Criminal Psychology. The survey had a return rate of 74%, representing a good cross-section of the psychologists engaged in providing services to law enforcement. The respondents were asked to indicate whether they were a full-time in-house police psychologist, a full-time consultant to law enforcement, or a service provider to law enforcement as part of their professional activity. Therefore, much of the discussion will be based on these three major professional groupings. Forty respondents were full-time in-house psychologists, 36 were full-time consultants, and the remainder ($n = 76$) indicated that they worked with law enforcement as psychologists in some part-time capacity.

The respondents tended to be a rather senior group, with an average age of 48.7 ($SD = 5.5$) and an average experience of 11.8 years ($SD = 4.8$) in services to law enforcement. The age and experience data were highly similar to Scrivner's (1994) data on 65 psychologists employed in large-city police departments. No significant age differences were found between in-house psychologists and consultants, or between those employed full- and part-time. The average age of psychologists working in

law enforcement underscores the point made above about the influence of LEAA funds on careers in police psychology.

Most (89%) of the respondents had Ph.D. degrees, followed by Ed.D. degrees (4.5%), master's degrees (3.6%), and Psy.D. degrees (2.7%). Most obtained their terminal degrees in clinical (60.7%), counseling (17%), or industrial/organizational (8%) psychology. Interestingly, the terminal degree-granting institution most frequently mentioned by the respondents was the California School of Professional Psychology (CSPP) (6.3%), probably reflecting the LAPD internship program started by Reiser. All but one of the CSPP graduates were working full-time in providing psychological services to law enforcement.

The average salary for psychologists employed full-time in psychological services to law enforcement was $77,412 (median = $64,000). However, psychologists who considered themselves full-time consultants in law enforcement made considerably more than individuals employed as full-time, in house police psychologists (mean = $102,192, compared to $57,133; median = $80,000, compared to $53,000). About 25% of the respondents ($n = 36$) were women. However, only 3 were employed as in-house psychologists. On the other hand, 14 of the 36 full-time police consultants were women. There were no significant differences in salary or age between the men and women.

Participants in the nationwide survey were requested to indicate the type of services they provided specifically to law enforcement during a typical month, as well as the amount of time they usually spent on each activity. As expected, the respondents, as a whole, indicated that pre-employment screening consumed the largest percentage (34.3%) of their time. However, psychologists who engaged in full-time police services, particularly in-house psychologists, spent less time at this activity. In-house psychologists reported that only about 15% of their time involved pre-employment screening. A greater portion (28.7 %) of their time was occupied working directly with the officers in such services as counseling and treatment. Full-time consultants, on the other hand, spent about 27.5% of their professional time in pre-employment screening and 23.2% in the counseling of officers.

Interestingly, full-time consultants were more involved in providing various services to the family members of police personnel and were more engaged in fitness-for-duty evaluations. This pattern probably reflects a tendency for departments to contract out sensitive issues for more objective appraisals, thereby avoiding criticism about conflict of interest.

Unfortunately, little time in a typical month was spent dealing with victims. It is interesting to note, however, that Delprino and Bahn (1988) reported that police departments saw a great need for this service. Apparently, few departments are able to provide it because of the more immediate, pressing demands of agency personnel.

One surprising finding of the survey was the amount of time consumed by criminal or psychological profiling of offenders. Criminal profiling refers to the process of identifying personality traits, behavioral tendencies, and demographic variables of an offender, based on characteristics of the crime (Bartol & Bartol, 1994). On average, 2% of the total monthly work time of in-house psychologists and 3.4% of the monthly workload of part-time consulting psychologists were directed at criminal profiling. Although this may not seem to be a dramatically high percentage, the finding is surprising, considering that a majority of the surveyed police psychologists (70%) did not feel comfortable profiling and seriously questioned its validity and usefulness. This skepticism was especially pronounced for the in-house psychologists (78%). One well-known police psychologist, with more than 20 years of experience in the field, considered criminal profiling "virtually useless and potentially dangerous." Many of the respondents wrote that much more research needs to be done before the process becomes a useful tool.

Several of the questions on the survey focused on the best way to prepare for police psychology as a career. Although 61% of the respondents had doctorates in clinical psychology, most indicated that, because of the rapid expansion of the psychological services requested by law enforcement agencies, a broad graduate education in psychology with a strong research focus was critical. Nearly 20% of the respondents felt that course work or background in industrial/organization psychology was highly desirable. Specific graduate coursework most recommended by all respondents was assessment (38%), testing (37%), counseling (33%), and crisis intervention (23%).

The psychologists appeared to be extremely satisfied with their careers. About 54 percent indicated that they were extremely satisfied, and 39% were moderately satisfied; only 3% were neutral or dissatisfied. Women were especially satisfied with the profession, with all female respondents indicating they were either extremely (65%) or moderately satisfied (35%).

The police psychologists also were asked about their perceptions of the current, as well as the future, job market in police psychology. Full-time and part-time police psychologists perceived the market similarly. About two thirds of both groups saw both the current and future job market as either *good* (defined as a balance between available positions and qualified psychologists), *very good* (more positions available than qualified psychologists), or *excellent* (many more positions than qualified psychologists). These data suggest that police psychologists, as a whole, perceive good opportunities in the field and see room for expansion in the future.

BEYOND: SANGUINE PREDICTIONS

I am usually as cautious predicting trends in the field as I am predicting human behavior. . . . Some of what follows . . . falls into the category of what *should* happen without being optimistic that it *will*. Psychologists should, for example, address issues of diversity, multiculturalism, and discrimination. I am not so sure we will.

In reality, police psychology in the United States depends greatly on political, economic, and social pressures, ultimately reflected in executive, legislative and, to a lesser extent, judicial decision making. The LEAA and a variety of presidential commissions had enormous influence on policing and police psychology during the late 1960s and 1970s. The media also have played a prominent role. Televised events focus public attention on police behavior, as they did during the 1968 Democratic

Convention in Chicago. More recently, the videotape documenting Rodney King's beating by Los Angeles police officers, as well as the conviction of two officers by a federal jury, created a nationwide concern about the use of excessive force. As a result, Scrivner (1994), a police psychologist, was encouraged to conduct an extremely useful study examining the many psychological factors involved in excessive force and suggesting strategies for monitoring and preventing it. The recently completed Mollen Commission Report (July, 1994), detailing widespread police corruption in New York City, should prompt police psychologists to address this disturbing behavior. In the relationship among crime, fear of crime, and the public perceptions of policing, the media are exerting a more powerful influence than ever before (Manning, 1994).

In an attempt to control police deviance, pre-employment screening (of the screening-out variety) will continue to be an important service provided by police psychologists. Although organizational factors are relevant to explaining police behavior, the effort to identify potentially problematic officers should and will continue. Pre-employment screening, however, will be affected increasingly by legislation and judicial decision making. It is quite clear to me, for example, that police psychologists who continue to resist using the MMPI-2 in favor of the MMPI do so at their own risk, in light of *Soroka et al. v. Dayton Hudson Corporation* (1991).

Target Stores (owned and operated by the Dayton Hudson Corporation) administered a battery of psychological tests to candidates for security officer positions. The battery, called *Psychscreen,* was a combination of the MMPI and the California Psychological Inventory (CPI). Plaintiff Soroka argued, among other things, that MMPI questions probing religious attitudes and sexual orientation were invasive and offensive. The California Court of Appeals ultimately ruled that invasive psychological tests violated both the constitutional right to privacy and statutory prohibitions against improper inquiries into a person's sexual orientation and religious beliefs. Although the defendants could have attempted to justify continued use of the test, they chose instead to settle out of court and to stop using the test.

I have been disturbed by the reactions of some of my colleagues to this case. First, they believe that the case does not relate to them because the plaintiff was applying to a private security firm rather than a public police agency. This observation misses the point, because the court's decision struck a fatal blow to the content of the test, regardless of the context. Second, some colleagues believe that this case should have been played out in the courts, rather than settled. They argue that, despite the Appeals Court's objections to the MMPI items, a case could be made for continued usage of the test if it could be shown to be job validated. Why the insistence on retaining an instrument that has so often made us uncomfortable and alienated professionals in other disciplines? As one who has been faced for many years with the task of justifying offensive items on the original MMPI to students, police chiefs, and candidates, I am very happy that the court in this case forced the issue.

The MMPI-2 is a vast improvement over its predecessor and addresses many of the legal concerns about standardization and item content. Again, my opinion is not shared; some colleagues, even workshop presenters, proclaim that the revised test is nothing but a marketing gimmick. Those psychologists who wish to reduce their potential time in court, however, should use the MMPI-2 in place of the MMPI and validate it the best way possible on the population being evaluated. Screening instruments—including the MMPI-2—will continue to be tested in the courts on validation issues. Just as surely will they be tested on offensive item content, however.

One piece of recent legislation that may affect the work we do is the Americans with Disabilities Act (ADA), which became fully effective in July 1992. The ADA is the most far-reaching public law since the Civil Rights Act of 1964, affecting all levels of state and local governments, about 5 million private businesses, and some 43 million people defined by law as physically or mentally disabled (Bartol & Bartol, 1994). The law prohibits employers from discriminating against any people with disabilities who can perform the essential functions of the jobs they hold or desire to hold. It specifically prohibits oral questions or questionnaire items pertaining to past medical history or otherwise eliciting information about disabilities. It is unclear at this time how the law will affect screening and selection procedures, but if police psychologists validate their methods in relation to effective performance measures, the overall effect of the ADA on police psychology is apt to be minimal.

Psychologists seeking to expand their contributions beyond the traditional screening, therapy, training, and crisis intervention areas may be drawn to the current zeitgeist of community policing. Its primary philosophy is straightforward: It attempts to form a coalition between the community and the police to solve community problems. In application, the concept is not that clear, however.

***

Moreover, proponents of community policing sometimes ignore segments of communities that do not feel that the police represent them. This current interest in community policing, then, challenges social and community psychology to give valuable input concerning attitudes and attitude change, as well as neighborhood and group dynamics. It should be an exciting area for police psychologists; at this point, however, I see little indication that these contributions are being made.

One area needing far more attention, by both practitioners and researchers, is the rural and semi-rural community. Police psychologists—at least those with high visibility—have studied and consulted with large, metropolitan police departments or state police agencies, to the neglect of small-town and rural law enforcement. Approximately 80% of the 17,000 local police agencies in this country are located in small towns (i.e., having fewer than 50,000 people) and rural communities. The current interest in community policing may shift some attention to small-town and rural policing, but it would be optimistic to think that they ever will be the center of research focus. Nevertheless, the need for psychological services is great. Small-town policing generates its own unique stress, for example, and some crimes, such as domestic violence, are believed to be more hidden. Therefore, psychologists involved in police training programs in small towns and rural areas are faced with challenging tasks.

The composition of police forces will continue to change significantly in the future, which, in turn, will affect the nature of police psychology. The two decades ahead will see greater attention to gender issues in policing, an important trend that is beginning to emerge. Research demonstrates that women and men are equally capable—cognitively, emotionally, and behaviorally—of doing law enforcement work (Bartol, Bergen, Volckens, & Knoras, 1992). There are some indications that women may have a more "gentling effect" on law enforcement, using communication and interpersonal skills more effectively. This may be a crucial variable for policing in the future, especially as policing evolves into increased community involvement.

Women going into law enforcement still encounter sexual harassment and attitudinal resistance, primarily from their male supervisors. However, I anticipate a growing and substantial influx of women into both law enforcement and police psychology in the near future. In 1972, for instance, women constituted 4.2% of police officers employed in urban departments. By 1988, the figure had more than doubled to 8.8% (Manning, 1994; Martin, 1990). I fully expect that women will comprise at least 25% of the police forces within the next two decades. If these predictions are borne out, they will produce significant changes in police training and the prioritization of services. The needs of victims, for example, are more likely to be attended to with a better gender balance, both on police forces and among police psychologists.

The percentages of African Americans and members of other minorities will continue to increase, especially in the large metropolitan departments. At this writing, 58% of the officers in the Detroit Police Department are African American, and it is anticipated that the percentages in other major cities will begin to approximate that of the minorities within their community. It also is highly likely that the composition of police psychology will change. One glaring aspect of the police psychology survey described above is that only 3 of the 152 respondents were from minority groups.

The future also should see a shift from the counseling/clinical orientation to more non-mental health-oriented psychological services.

This shift will be consistent with and accompany the overall changes occurring in policing. For example, there are clear indications that policing is moving away from the professional crime fighting model to a more corporate strategy model, where policing resembles a corporate business rather than a public service agency (Manning, 1994; Moore & Trojanowicz, 1988). Manning (1994) observed: "The currently fashionable language of economics and management used by command personnel to describe police functions, command obligations, and planning creates a picture of policing as a business" (p. 2). Problem-solving strategies and strategic decision-making models are likely to predominate in the near future. Industrial/organization, community, and social psychology will be called upon to make many major theoretical and practical contributions to police psychology. These contributions will be especially notable in human resource management, police management skills, mediation, organizational psychology, community policing, human factors, and operations research. Psychological research on how to deal effectively with turnover rates, personnel dissatisfaction, and lowered morale in reactions to budget cuts and cycles of hiring blitzes and freezes will become critical.

During the personality trend of police psychology, a group of political and social scientists argued that police behavior was not the result of some personality characteristic that existed prior to entry into law enforcement, but rather of the culture found within each department. Presumably, the rough edges of individual differences were sanded and polished by the social and political forces of the organization. Wilson (1968), for example, developed a departmental typology, consisting of various policing styles. He argued that the preexisting personality of the individual really did not matter. The department promoted specific policing styles, with differences in policing being explainable by differences among organizations. Wilson's perspective has merit. As I have found in my own consulting work, it is not uncommon for an individual to be regarded as a failure in one agency but a success in another. Nevertheless, individual attributes of some officers preclude them from being a success in any law enforcement setting. It is becoming increasingly apparent, therefore, that the study of police behavior requires a careful examination of all the systems involved, such as the individual or infrasystem, the organization, the family, the culture, and the community. We need to be more sensitive to the interactions among these systems rather than to assume that one law enforcement organization is like any other.

Police psychology increasingly will become international in scope, with psychologists across the globe sharing ideas, research, and programs. Although this exchange takes place now, it will increase substantially within the next decade.

Traditionally, law enforcement has used psychologists on an "as needed" basis rather than for systematic human resource development and prevention (Scrivner, 1994). The growing array of available psychological services, therefore, has not been integrated systematically into law enforcement. For this to be accomplished, psychologists themselves must articulate what it is they have to offer; we cannot expect the police community to know how we can help. Psychological services directed toward prevention and proaction will, in the long run, bring more benefit to policing than the reactive activity that has been expected in the past.

More than anything else, police psychologists need to become better and more skillful researchers and evaluators of programs, including their own. One of the things that was most emphasized by practicing police psychologists in our survey was that aspiring police psychologists must be better equipped with research skills. In her survey, Gettys (1990) also found an unfortunate lack of research involvement by police psychologists. Chandler (1990) strongly recommended that future police psychologists become well versed and much more active in conducting research. He said this within the context of acknowledging that law enforcement agencies are highly prone to act on "hot" issues without the benefit of good research and evaluation. These hot issues have included missing children campaigns, voice stress analysis, use of psychics, ritualistic crimes, and satanic cults. Good research, he stated, eventually brings fad-like behavior in check.

***

Finally, we need a broad-based graduate program in police psychology that will encompass not only clinical areas but also will prepare aspiring police psychologists in the many areas described here. . . . With the exception of a master's degree in forensic psychology offered by the John Jay College of Criminal Justice and various internships sponsored by some universities, I know of no academic graduate programs that prepare future police psychologists for the enormously diverse demands that they will encounter in the future. . . . A majority of the respondents in our survey thought that a graduate program in police psychology was an excellent idea, but they also strongly recommended that the program be diverse and academically broad. Several of the respondents believed that most traditional graduate programs are too narrow and circumscribed for training police psychologists. Therefore, with confidence, I predict that police psychology will have several graduate programs exclusively devoted to the field within the next decade.

In conclusion, police psychology has an extremely promising future. Professions rarely develop along a continuum of steady growth but usually expand and contract in a cyclical fashion. Police psychology is about to experience another upward swing, perhaps equal to the growth seen during the 1970s. Legislatures and much of the public continue to be convinced that the best way to deal with the crime problem is by improved and expanded policing, as demonstrated by the Crime Control Act of 1994. Although the law provides for preventive programs, it gives more support to law enforcement efforts, particularly those of the community policing variety. It is highly likely that this prioritization of policing will welcome the skills and knowledge of police psychologists. This anticipated growth in police psychology will be sustained, however, only if we engage in high-quality research designed to test the effectiveness of various programs, policies, methods, and innovations.

3

PSYCHOLOGICAL TESTING AND THE SELECTION OF POLICE OFFICERS

A National Survey

ROBERT E. COCHRANE
ROBERT P. TETT
LEON VANDECREEK

Personnel selection practices have become more widely used over the years, particularly with law enforcement candidates. This increased use has included more sophisticated methods of evaluating potential police officers. One reason for greater emphasis on selection procedures is the negative impact of having unqualified employees. Financial costs are one way police agencies are affected. For example, the Los Angeles Police Department spends approximately $100,000 to train each new police officer. Furthermore, it was estimated that the average new police recruit was required to undergo nearly 1,000 hours of training (U.S. Department of Justice, 1996). Obviously, if hires later prove unable to perform their duties, substantial resources have been wasted. Although several factors influence the potential success or failure of police recruits, agencies are largely concerned about the emotional or psychological adequacy

of recruits. Hibler and Kurke (1995) defined this as "psychological suitability," or the presence of personal factors that contribute to human reliability and the absence of those that create unreliability.

Shusman, Inwald, and Landa (1984) reported several purposes for preemployment screening of police officers. First, employers want to weed out lateness and absenteeism, which result in understaffing, excessive overtime pay, and a breakdown in trust among officers. Second, disciplinary interviews increase department expenses and use up valuable administrative time. Third, screening helps to avoid potential harm to citizens or fellow officers. Last, poor publicity and court litigation may result from reckless or irresponsible officer behavior. In at least one case, a plaintiff won a large settlement due to a department's negligence in conducting psychological evaluations

---

Editors' Note: This article was originally published in *Criminal Justice and Behavior*, Vol. 30, No. 5, October 2003, pp. 511-537. We have deleted findings related to differences on the basis of department size.

of its officers (*Bonsignore v. City of New York,* 1981). Considering the duties of a police officer, there is little room for error. Besides the military, there is perhaps no other profession that has the authority to use force on others if necessary and invade the privacy of citizens. The consequences of officers' behavior can result in negative effects for the department, individuals, and the community.

The purpose of properly selecting a candidate is rather obvious. However, employee selection is more difficult to conduct than other personnel decisions (e.g., promotion) because little is known about the individual and there is no in-house record of previous performance for the candidate. Because recruiters cannot evaluate applicants based exclusively on their observed performance, other measures must be utilized. Determining persons' abilities from their past performance and behavior would probably be ideal. Unfortunately, this information is often unavailable for a new recruit. Lester (1983) argued that the most valuable information comes from observing officers in training and during a probationary period. This may be true, but many resources (e.g., money, time) will be depleted if all applicants go through the training process. Furthermore, not all determinants of job performance, such as cognitive ability and personality variables, can be acquired or altered via training (Reiss, Ones, & Viswesvaran, 1996). Also, if well-designed selection is used during the recruitment phase, less socialization will be needed in terms of social control, disciplinary procedures, and ongoing supervision (Hancock & McClung, 1984).

THE SELECTION AND ASSESSMENT PROCESS

In 1973, the National Advisory Commission on Criminal Justice Standards and Goals recommended that every police agency follow a formal selection process that includes (a) a written test of mental ability or aptitude, (b) an oral interview, (c) a psychological examination, and (d) a background investigation. Even earlier, the President's Commission on Law Enforcement and the Administration of Justice (1967) recommended the screening of all potential officers. It was believed that introducing greater screening and standardization to the selection process would result in a more qualified police force. More recently, the International Association of Chiefs of Police developed several guidelines for preemployment psychological evaluations (1998). These recommendations address such issues as validation of testing instruments, compliance with legislation (e.g., Americans With Disabilities Act [ADA]), using qualified psychologists who are familiar with the relevant research, and content of the written reports.

Over the years, countless measures for screening candidates have been used to predict officer performance; these have shown varying levels of success. One of the best predictors of future work performance has been ability to perform duties similar to those required on a job (Guion & Gibson, 1988). For example, Schmidt, Hunter, McKenzie, and Muldrow (1979) compared job performance for employees selected with an ability test (e.g., situational exercise) and those without the test and found on average that those selected with the test were 0.487 standard deviation units better in job performance.

Hunter and Hunter's (1984) meta-analysis showed that when artifacts such as statistical error and small sample size were removed from research studies for entry-level jobs, the best predictor of job performance was ability, which had a mean validity of .53. Assessment centers have a long history of evaluating candidates based on how well they perform job-related activities in simulated settings. These centers are typically private agencies that design evaluation instruments and assess candidates on numerous variables before providing feedback to the employers. However, as of 1990, less than one fourth of police departments reported using assessment centers (Ash, Slora, & Britton, 1990). Although still controversial, the polygraph is frequently cited as a tool used in selection (e.g., Ben-Shakhar & Furedy, 1990; Lykken, 1981; Saxe, 1994). Of the municipal agencies responding to the Ash et al. (1990) survey, 73% indicated using the polygraph in preemployment screening. The Civil Service Examination (CSE) is a multiple-choice exam designed for the selection of civil servant employees, including police officers (Cortina, Doherty, Schmitt, Kaufman, & Smith, 1992). However, there is no indication as to how extensively the CSE is used. The National Police Officer Selection Test (POST), a less well-known skills-based instrument, has also shown decent reliability and criterion-related validity in several studies (Henry & Rafilson, 1997; Rafilson & Sison, 1996). The POST assesses mathematics, reading, grammar, and incident report writing. Certain information derived from the interview, application blank, and background investigation has also been used to select police officers even though much of this data is not subject to predictive validity studies like other variables. For example, many departments will deny an applicant further consideration if he or she has a history of a reckless driving conviction. In this case it would be impossible to validate the predictive or concurrent validity of this measure without danger to the public. Cognitive measures have also been used to predict job performance across various occupations. However, intelligence and cognitive ability are not highly predictive of on-the-job performance, despite showing some promise in predicting police academy performance (Aylward, 1985; Henderson, 1979; Spielberger, Ward, & Spaulding, 1979).

Two large meta-analytic studies have demonstrated the usefulness of personality measures in predicting job performance using the "big five" personality dimensions (conscientiousness, agreeableness, extraversion, neuroticism, and openness to experience) (Barrick & Mount, 1991; Tett, Jackson, & Rothstein, 1991). Other studies have also established the ability of personality tests and inventories to predict job performance (e.g., Inwald, 1988; . . . McDaniel & Frei, 1994 . . .).

Traits from the Neuroticism, Extraversion, and Openness (NEO) Personality Inventory–Revised, which was based on the five factor model of personality, have also shown to be predictive of police performance. In fact, conscientiousness added incremental validity to cognitive testing in one study with 284 police recruits (Black, 2000).

The Minnesota Multiphasic Personality Inventory–2 (MMPI-2) and the Inwald Personality Inventory (IPI) have been shown to be effective in predicting several job criteria for police officers, as well (e.g., Bartol, 1991; Inwald & Knatz, 1988; Scogin, Schumacher, Howland, &

McGee, 1989 . . .). Various inventories and psychological measures have also been used to assess the degree to which applicants present excessive socially desirable responses, because applicants may have a tendency to minimize their flaws or weaknesses (e.g., Borum & Stock, 1993; Grossman, Haywood, Ostrov, Wasyliw, & Cavanaugh, 1990).

Between 1979 and 1988, there was enormous growth in the use of psychological services in police departments, assessment being the primary service used (Delprino & Bahn, 1988). In their 1988 nationwide survey, Delprino and Bahn found that 52% of responding police agencies were conducting psychological screening on police recruits and 90% perceived a need for its use in their department. Similarly, Behrens (1985) found that 50% of police agencies responding to a nationwide survey were doing psychological screening. Bartol (1996) surveyed 152 police psychologists and found that preemployment screening consumed the largest percentage of their time (34.3%), again suggesting this activity's importance to police departments.

The psychological tests most frequently used in departments throughout the United States are personality measures (Hancock & McClung, 1987). Hartman (1987) reported that most agencies use the MMPI and the clinical interview along with one or more of the following: the California Psychological Inventory (CPI), the Sixteen Personality Factor Questionnaire (16PF), Edwards Personal Preference Schedule, and the Inwald Personality Inventory. An earlier survey found the most commonly used personality instruments were the Rorschach, MMPI, CPI, and Eysenck Personality Questionnaire (EPQ) (Spielberger, 1979). However, a more recent finding (Ash et al., 1990) suggested that Rorschach use has declined among police departments (only 4.4% using it).

Clearly, numerous different psychological tests are used to screen officers, yet little is known about the degree of variability among departments in the United States. Understanding the psychological tests and procedures used today to select officers may help us understand whether departments are using those instruments shown to be most effective in selecting police officers. This information will also allow us to take a look at possible reasons why different departments use different measuring devices. Examining selection practices will also inform us about how police agencies use collected data to make decisions and how much attention they give to various measures and outcomes.

Other important questions that have not been adequately addressed to date are the extent to which police departments are following public policy guidelines regarding selection procedures and the extent to which selection practices have been affected by policy changes. Various agencies have put in place several policies and guidelines including *Standards for Educational and Psychological Tests* (American Psychological Association, 1985), *Principles for the Validation and Use of Personnel Selection Procedures* (Society for Industrial and Organizational Psychology, 1987), *Enforcement Guidance: Preemployment Disability–Related Inquiries and Medical Examinations Under the Americans With Disabilities Act of 1990* (Equal Employment Opportunity Commission, 1995), and the *Civil Rights Act of 1991*. These guidelines address such issues as inappropriate inquiries during selection, cutoff scores on standardized tests, and the use of norms. Also, the Equal Employment Opportunity Commission focuses much attention on selection procedures that may discriminate or have an adverse impact on certain racial and gender groups.

In addition to examining current selection practices and adherence to guidelines, this study examines how police departments differ based on their size and degree of selectivity of applicants. Knowledge gained from this study will help determine if changes are needed in how police officers are selected as well as provide important feedback to police agencies regarding how well they are performing their selections relative to accepted standards and normative practices. We gathered information to help answer these questions via a survey developed specifically for this study.

Although this study was intended to primarily be exploratory in nature, the following hypotheses are offered: (a) Police departments would use psychological evaluations to a higher degree than has been found in prior studies (Behrens, 1985; Delprino & Bahn, 1988); (b) larger police departments (those that served larger areas and had more employees) and more selective departments (those with higher applicant to selection ratios) would use a greater number of selection devices as well as more sophisticated procedures because these agencies tend to have more options and greater resources (sophistication was defined as the use of psychological assessment, development of norms, conducting a job analysis, using a greater number of selection procedures, and making conditional offers of employment); and (c) larger departments would use a pass-fail approach to psychological assessment and a minimum cutoff score approach to the selection process, based on the belief these approaches require less judgment and lend themselves to quicker decision making, which is especially important for larger and busier departments.

Method

Participants

We mailed the survey to personnel departments of municipal police agencies located throughout the United States. We chose municipal police departments because they are the most widely recognized law enforcement agencies and they represent the largest number of police or safety personnel in the United States. Currently, more than 12,000 municipal agencies exist in this country. Of the 355 departments randomly selected based on geography and population size served (stratified random sample), 155 agencies returned completed surveys (43%). To facilitate the analyses and illustration of the data, we categorized each department into one of three groups based on the size of the population served. Departments were considered *large* if population size served was greater than 100,000, *medium* if between 25,000 and 100,000, and *small* if less than 25,000. The source used to select departments and determine population size was *The National Directory of Law Enforcement Administrators and Correctional Agencies* (National Police Chiefs and Sheriffs Information Bureau, 1996).

Survey

We developed 20 survey questions that were intended to cover the content relevant for this study. . . . These questions encompassed several topics such as background about the department, selection procedures utilized, the selection process, public policy issues, and use of norms and job analyses.

Procedure

We asked four reviewers (psychologists) with experience in the criminal justice system, police selection, or test construction to review the survey questions for clarity, content, and ease of response. We revised item content based on feedback from these sources. Then we showed the revised survey to two personnel managers at local police departments. They reported no difficulties in reading or understanding the questions on the survey and invested approximately 10 to 15 minutes in completing the survey.

We analyzed survey results to identify selection practices and procedures among police departments. In the first sets of analyses, descriptive statistics were computed (i.e., percentages) comparing the procedures and psychological tests used among small, medium, and large departments. We then utilized chi-square analyses to discern statistically significant differences among these departments.

We implemented further analysis to compare departments based on their number of employees, population size, and degree of selectivity in hiring. We completed Pearson correlation coefficients to show relationships between these continuous variables and several procedures related to sophisticated methods utilized by departments (e.g., use of job analysis, use of norms).

Results

Selection Procedures

Table 3.1 lists the diverse procedures used by departments serving different population sizes as well as the percentage of departments that use each procedure. Results show that the median number of procedures reported by departments to select officer candidates was nine, indicating that respondents use a package of tools to select employees.

More than 90% of departments use the background investigation along with a medical exam, interview, application, and psychological assessment. More than half of the agencies also reported utilizing drug testing, measures of physical fitness, and the polygraph.

One interesting finding is that more than 27% of police departments use procedures other than those listed. Also, 36 different procedures were reported by responding agencies. Of these 36 procedures, not one was utilized by more than six departments. Clearly, a wide variety of selection tools is used by police

Table 3.1   Percentage of Departments that Use Selection Procedures

	Department Size			
Procedure	*Small (n = 35)*	*Medium (n = 53)*	*Large (n = 67)*	*Combined (n = 155)*
Background investigation	100.0	98.1	100.0	99.4
Medical exam	97.0	98.1	100.0	98.7
Interview	100.0	98.1	97.0	98.1
Application blank	97.0	90.5	98.5	95.5
Psychological assessment	73.5[a]	94.3[b]	98.5[b]	91.6
Drug testing	70.5[a]	90.5	95.5[b]	88.4
Physical fitness	64.7	81.1	86.5	80.0
Polygraph	26.4[a]	69.8[b]	82.0[b]	65.8
Civil Service Exam	32.3	50.9	56.7	49.7
Recommendation letters	50.0	35.8	53.7	46.5
Knowledge, skills, abilities	47.0	49.0	44.7	46.5
Other	20.5	26.4	31.3	27.7

NOTE: Figures within a row that do not share subscripts differ at $p < .001$ by the chi-square test.

agencies. Although there is conformity among agencies in using the major selection procedures, departments also utilize many unique methods.

Additionally, there were a few differences in selection procedures used by departments of different sizes. Small departments reported using psychological assessment less frequently than medium . . . and large departments. . . . . Small agencies also reported less use of drug testing than large departments . . . and they used the polygraph less than medium . . . and large departments . . .

Psychological Assessment

Survey results indicate that approximately 91% of respondents reported they required psychological assessment for all new police recruits. This figure compares with 52% in 1988 (Delprino & Bahn, 1988) from a study that used a fairly similar sample (287 municipal agencies and 49 state police agencies). Although a large percentage of departments require a psychological evaluation, the amount of weight or consideration reportedly given to the evaluation in the overall selection process is modest. Almost one third (31.9%, $n = 44$) of the 155 agencies in our final sample reported they weighted the evaluation in comparison to other selection procedures used, whereas the remaining 68.1% of agencies ($n = 94$) viewed data from the psychological evaluation in terms of passing or failing for the candidate. In other words, the majority of respondents see candidates as either passing or failing the psychological evaluation with those who fail no longer being considered for a position. However, of these departments, psychological assessment is given a median weight of 30.0% (range 15 to 100), a fair degree of emphasis. The percentage of applicants ultimately rejected solely on the basis of psychological assessment is small (median = 5.0%, $n = 111$, range 0 to 75).

Table 3.2 lists the psychological tests most frequently used by police departments. Consistent with results from the late 1980s (Hartman, 1987), the most widely used testing instrument is the MMPI-2. The clinical interview and the CPI also continue to be used by a large number of agencies (57.4% and 24.5%, respectively), whereas the EPQ and the Rorschach

have decreased in use. The Personal History Questionnaire was used by a large number of departments (52.9%). This tool is useful for collecting information that can be used to rule out job candidates and to verify information obtained through other means (e.g., background check).

The only significant difference in psychological tests used by departments of different sizes was with the MMPI-2. Small departments reported less use of the MMPI-2 . . . than large agencies.

Public Policy Issues

Conditionally offering employment to potential employees is one way for departments to avoid soliciting medical information prior to hiring, which would violate public policy guidelines (i.e., ADA, 1990). In this study, 87% of municipal police departments reported using conditional offers in their selection process. The median year these departments began this procedure was 1992. This may be a response to the 1990 ADA which prohibited medical inquiries prior to job offers. Medical information can include information from such sources as medical examinations, psychological tests that measure psychopathology, drug testing, and physical fitness tests. . . .

Overall, most departments resist medical inquiries until after offers of employment have been made. However, medical exams are conducted prior to offers in 12.3% of departments, whereas pathology-based psychological testing (testing to assess mental illnesses or disorders) is done prior to offers in 17.4% of departments.

Municipal police departments also appear to comply fairly well with other mandates regarding selection of potential employees. However, a small portion of police departments utilize different norms for racial groups or genders (13.3%, $n = 113$). This practice violates guidelines in *Standards for Educational and Psychological Testing* (American Psychological Association, 1985). However, virtually all departments that use cutoff scores on various procedures do not use different cutoff scores when selecting members of different races or genders (95.0%, $n = 61$), suggesting a very high level of compliance in this area.

Table 3.2   Percentage of Departments That Use Psychological Tests

Psychological Test	Department Size			
	Small (n = 35)	Medium (n = 53)	Large (n = 67)	Combined (n = 155)
Minnesota Multiphasic Personality Inventory–2	52.9[a]	67.9	83.5[b]	71.6
Clinical interview	50.0	52.8	64.1	57.4
Personal History Questionnaire	50.0	49.0	56.7	52.9
California Psychological Inventory	17.6	20.7	29.8	24.5
Other	5.8	20.7	31.3	21.9
16 Personality Factor Questionnaire	14.7	13.2	23.8	18.7
Inwald Personality Inventory	2.9	13.2	14.9	11.6
Mental status exam	11.7	16.9	4.4	10.3
Rorschach/inkblot	2.9	7.5	5.9	5.8
Hilson Safety/Security	2.9	9.4	1.4	4.5
Eysenck Personality Questionnaire	5.8	0.0	1.4	1.9

NOTE: *Figures within a row that do not share subscripts differ at p < .001* by the chi-square test.

Level of Sophistication of Selection Procedures

Several authors have made suggestions regarding the procedures and processes of selecting police officers (e.g., Beutler, Storm, Kirksih, Scogini, & Gaines, 1985; Hiatt & Hargrave, 1988; Meier, Farmer, & Maxwell, 1987). However, police agencies are under no obligation to follow these recommendations and there may be times or circumstances when a department should follow other procedures not suggested.

Nonetheless, one point this study was designed to address is the level of sophistication of police departments' selection procedures and the extent to which agencies follow recommendations offered by available research.

Conducting job analyses to determine the essential job functions, duties, and work skills needed for police officers involves a great endeavor and investment by police departments. Performance of job analyses suggests a high level of sophistication in the selection process.

Prior to this study, it was not expected that many agencies would utilize job analyses, given this high degree of investment. Surprisingly, 74.5% of departments surveyed reported having completed a job analysis or systematic evaluation of essential job functions at their agencies. Furthermore, an additional 7.4% of departments reported using job analysis information from other sources. Results show that the median year agencies last conducted a job analysis was 1995 (n = 98), and on average a job analysis is updated every 2.8 years (SD = 2.4).

For the evaluator to properly determine whether an applicant will be capable of performing the required duties of an officer the evaluator needs to know what those duties are and the kind of environment in which the officer will be working. Agencies that request psychological assessment to cover more than just "rule outs" for mental disorders should provide or make sure the evaluator has access to job analysis results. When asked whether job analysis or job description information was provided to the evaluator(s), 78.8% (n = 108) of police departments reported providing this material. This suggests the majority of evaluators are aware of job requirements and duties of officers when conducting the evaluations.

Another question examined was whether police departments review applicant results on a procedure-by-procedure basis or with a more global outlook where performance on all selection procedures is considered together. The majority of agencies used a minimum cutoff score approach (62.9%, $n = 83$) where applicants who do not achieve a certain predetermined score on a particular measure are no longer considered for a position. A more global approach where performance is evaluated together for all measures was reported by 15.9% of departments, whereas 21.2% used both a minimum cutoff score and a global approach.

In terms of procedures used to select officers, it was of interest to determine how frequently formal assessment centers were used by police departments. Assessment centers can be a costly means of assessing police candidates, and the benefits they reap may or may not outweigh the costs. In response to the survey, only 8.1% of the police departments reported using a formal assessment center. The low use of this selection procedure may reflect the belief by police personnel that the costs do indeed outweigh the gains, or they may simply not know how to use them. Whatever the reasons, many authors (e.g., Ash et al., 1990; Coulton & Field, 1995; Dunnette & Motowidlo, 1976) would argue that assessment centers are currently being underutilized.

DISCUSSION

Municipal police departments throughout the country have given increasing attention to procedures for selection of police officers. One reason for greater emphasis on selection of new recruits is the high costs associated with poor officer performance. These costs are incurred through such means as greater supervision, dismissals, lawsuits, and low morale. The primary purpose of this study was to identify the selection procedures used by municipal police departments, paying particular attention to the psychological assessment process. It appears that greater emphasis on selection can be seen in the increased use of selection procedures, particularly psychological assessment procedures. In fact, comparing this study's results with that of prior research (Delprino & Bahn, 1988), psychological assessment of police candidates has increased dramatically over the past 10 years, with 52% of agencies using psychological screening in 1988 compared to more than 90% in this study.

The Selection Process and Psychological Assessment

Large attention given to selection is also reflected in the high number of procedures used by departments to evaluate candidates. On average, police agencies use nine different procedures when selecting new recruits. And although most departments reported using similar procedures (i.e., background investigation, medical exam, interview, application, and psychological assessment), great variability existed. This diversity among departments may reflect an appropriate application of selection techniques because departments differ to some degree in terms of specific duties and the amount of time invested in performing different tasks. These wide differences could also be the result of a lack of awareness by municipal agencies or their consulting psychologists regarding the most effective selection procedures. The high degree of variability found in this study may also be due to each department utilizing different selection criteria. The measures used and the conclusions drawn depend to a large degree on the police department's criteria. For example, some departments may consider abuse of an officer's power and early termination as highly important, whereas other agencies may place greater emphasis on tardiness and poor supervisory evaluations.

Despite the fact that no unified criteria or selection procedures exist at this time and there is great variability in procedures used, many agencies use a core set of similar selection measures. In fact, the typical department reported using the following measures when selecting officers: an application, background investigation, medical exam, oral interview, psychological assessment, drug test, physical fitness measures, and polygraph test. It also makes conditional offers of employment to those candidates they are interested in and then conducts the medically related tests following this offer.

The typical department also uses approximately three or four different psychological tests or procedures, with the MMPI-2, clinical interview, Personal History Questionnaire, and the CPI being the most common.

Although psychological assessment appears to be valued in the selection process (median weight = 30.0%), very few individuals are rejected based solely on the results (median = 5%). This contrasts with a previous finding reported by Meier, Farmer, and Maxwell (1987) that approximately 15% of candidates were screened out through personality assessment. The reason for this difference is not clear. One possible explanation could be that, more recently, qualified candidates are pre-selected through other procedures prior to the psychological evaluation. Therefore, once the psychological evaluation is completed, few individuals are found to be outright unqualified. At a first glance, this would seem to make psychological assessment essentially irrelevant. However, although a 5% rejection rate based on psychological assessment results does not appear high, if only half of these candidates (2.5%) would eventually prove to be problematic, this could cost a police department a tremendous amount of difficulty including loss of money, potential harm to others, and negative publicity.

Whereas the typical agency did not report using norms for most of their procedures (many of which are not conducive to developing normative data), a large percentage did use norms for psychological testing.

Also, the average agency conducted its own job analysis and provided this information to the person(s) conducting the psychological evaluation. Overall, the average municipal police department appears to have a relatively thorough and professional selection process. Almost 25 years ago, the National Advisory Commission on Criminal Justice Standards and Goals (1973) recommended that police agencies use written tests of mental abilities (i.e., tests of Knowledge, Skills, and Abilities [KSAs]), an interview, psychological assessment, and a background check on all police officer candidates. With the exception of KSAs, this study found that police departments are following these suggestions at a relatively high rate.

Public Policy Issues and Testing Recommendations

A significant minority of agencies failed to follow public policy guidelines and other recommendations. For example, respondents reported making medical inquiries prior to conditional offers of employment at a fairly high rate (medical exams = 12.3%, pathology based psychological tests = 17.4%). These are somewhat alarming numbers considering that a plaintiff may have grounds to file a lawsuit if he or she discovered that not being hired was due to a medical condition or disability. It is not clear why these agencies neglect to adhere to these regulations and suggestions. Many agencies may not be aware of the guidelines and just simply continue old practices that have worked in the past. Others may be aware of guidelines but are willing to take the risk of using certain procedures (e.g., medical inquiries prior to conditional offers), believing they are exempt from such policies due to the nature of the job of police officer. In many ways, departments may be justified in this position, given that certain criteria are unique to that of a police officer and are job-related. For example, individuals with severe emotional or psychological problems should be excluded from consideration for a police officer position, given the nature of the job. One would think this could be justified in a court of law if necessary, but it is still a risk departments may not wish to take.

Departments appear to consider the psychological assessment component of the selection process as a procedure that has an all-or-none value. In other words, the majority of agencies use a pass-fail approach to psychological assessment results, keeping candidates who pass and rejecting those who fail. This is consistent with Ho's (1999) study on the effects of test results and demographic factors on 420 police candidates in a North Carolina police department. Ho found the decision-making process in selection of officers was primarily testing oriented, whereby candidates who failed to achieve a satisfactory rating on any of the tests were less likely to be recruited.

These results indicate police agencies may be underutilizing the usefulness of a psychological evaluation. Many authors have argued that psychological assessment has incremental validity beyond simply screening out candidates with psychopathology. For example, certain personality instruments (e.g., IPI) have shown strong predictive power in determining those candidates who will likely have problems with absenteeism or poor supervisor ratings. The departments that use a pass-fail approach may be the same departments that only request assessments to rule out psychopathology. Conversely, agencies that weight the assessment results may be those that request a greater degree of input from the psychological assessment referral. Each approach could be justified based on the information they were seeking to obtain. However, it seems many departments may not consider the psychological results very useful beyond informing them of obvious problem candidates.

Limitations and Recommendations

Results from this survey need to be considered in light of the fact that only 155 municipal police departments participated in the study.

Although this size is not small, generalizability may be of concern because more than 12,000 municipal agencies exist in this country. Also, as previously mentioned, the survey was completed by police department personnel managers, not psychologists or other persons directly assessing the candidates.

One area that deserves greater attention is the validation of various selection methods and procedures within particular departments.

Although every procedure utilized by departments cannot be validated, many tests and procedures can be appropriately validated, particularly psychological tests. Given the predictive validity demonstrated with the MMPI-2, IPI, and CPI, departments may want to specifically request that these tests be used in the assessment process.

And until norms are developed for a department with these tests, results can be interpreted with the aid of broader normative data that are available through various testing companies (e.g., Caldwell Reports).

Examining whether a multiple-hurdle selection strategy is superior to a global evaluation process (where all candidates receive all measures) may be of great interest to police departments, as well. Economically speaking, departments would likely save considerable money if they employed a multiple-hurdle strategy. Each candidate could be rated at each stage or hurdle, and those not meeting a minimum standard could be disqualified. Those candidates who completed all the hurdles could then be given a total rating, allowing comparisons and selections to be made based on the number of available positions. And in terms of psychological evaluation, departments may wish to request that the psychological evaluators rate or rank candidates.

Ratings could include broad categories (e.g., highly acceptable, acceptable, marginally acceptable, unacceptable) that could then be incorporated into the overall selection rating process. This would broaden the usefulness of the psychological evaluation beyond simply ruling out obviously poor or problematic candidates.

Lastly, although various psychological tests have shown predictive validity, studies are lacking in the value of other selection procedures (e.g., Civil Service Examination). It would be prudent for police departments to solicit and promote greater research into other procedures and tests that are both cost effective and predictive of important outcome criteria. This will likely occur with the assistance and expertise of diligent psychologists in the field.

4

INVESTIGATIVE INTERVIEWS OF CHILDREN

A Review of Psychological Research and Implications for Police Practices

KAMALA LONDON

In the 1970s, there was a shift in societal and legal views toward family issues. Whereas events that occurred among family members were once considered private affairs, the 1974 Federal Child Abuse Prevention and Treatment Act mandated that professionals such as physicians, teachers, police, and social workers report suspected cases of child maltreatment. As reporting and public awareness of child abuse increased, child welfare agencies and police were flooded with suspected cases of abuse.

As a response to children's increasing presence in the legal system, researchers began to empirically study children's ability to give accurate testimony. The purpose of this article is to review the psychological research pertaining to interviewing child victims-witnesses. Interview guidelines based on psychological research are reviewed. Furthermore, implications for police practices are discussed in light of the psychological empirical work.

Until the 1980s, children were generally required to pass extended *voir dires,* or tests of their competency, before being allowed to give courtroom testimony (Ceci & Bruck, 1993). For instance, children were once required to demonstrate an understanding of "truth versus lie." Children under certain ages were sometimes forbidden from giving testimony, because their autobiographic memories were considered questionable (Ceci & Bruck, 1993). The courts no longer require that children undergo competency hearings but rather let the jury decide how much weight to give children's testimony. Also, in the 1980s, all states dropped former requirements that children's allegations of sexual assault be corroborated by either physical evidence or by adult witnesses (Ceci & Bruck, 1993). In sum, many legal barriers that once discouraged or prevented children from being the sole complainant to a crime were largely removed.

***

Editors' Note: This article was originally published in *Police Quarterly,* Vol. 4, No. 1, March 2001, pp. 123–144.

INVESTIGATIVE INTERVIEW TECHNIQUES AND FALSE ALLEGATIONS OF ABUSE

In the past 20 years, there has been a flood of research that has examined children's competency to act as court witnesses. Research suggests that children can often give accurate accounts of past events (e.g., Geiselman & Padilla, 1988; Poole & Lamb, 1998). However, research has also revealed that children may give inaccurate or blatantly false accounts when interviewed with certain techniques (for reviews, see Ceci & Bruck, 1993; Poole & Lamb, 1998). Children's competency to give accurate testimony is dependent on the quality of the investigative interview techniques.

Although memory skills certainly improve with age, young children have demonstrated accurate recall of past events, particularly with regard to action-related salient events (Davis, Tarrant, & Flin, 1989). For instance, Poole and Lindsay (1995) found that 3- to 4-year-olds and 5- to 7-year-olds accurately recalled a recent event. Children in their study interacted with "Mr. Science," who did various demonstrations. For instance, "Mr. Science" showed the children how to lift newspaper print with silly putty. Children were interviewed with nonsuggestive techniques immediately following their interactions. Even 3- and 4-year-olds were highly accurate in their recall of the events.

Goodman and Reed (1986) provided further support of children's competency to accurately report on past events. They staged an event and questioned adults and 6-year-olds about the event after a 4- to 5-day delay. They found few age differences in testimony when children were asked objective questions. Although the 6-year-olds were more likely than the adults to be misled about periphery events, they generally were not misled regarding central events.

Although research suggests that children can give accurate accounts of past events, a sizable literature also reveals that children sometimes give inaccurate or blatantly false accounts when interviewed (for review, see Ceci, Bruck, & Battin, 2000). For instance, Poole and Lindsay (1995) conducted a follow-up interview with some of the children who participated in the "Mr. Science" project. The second interview was conducted after a 3-month delay. For 3 consecutive days prior to the second interview, children's parents read them stories about experienced and non-experienced events pertaining to the "Mr. Science" project. The researchers then interviewed children with leading and non-leading questions. In the second interview, 41% of 3- to 4-year-olds reported having experienced fictitious events.

The now well-known case of Kelly Michaels raised researchers' attention to false allegations that may arise from suggestive interview techniques. Michaels, a 26-year-old nursery care worker at the Wee Care Nursery School in New Jersey, was charged with 115 counts of child sexual assault (CSA). Over a 7-month period of interviews, twenty 3- to 5-year-old children accused Michaels of sexual assault. Their accusations included bizarre claims that certainly would have produced physical evidence. For instance, children accused Michaels of putting peanut butter on their genitals and of sodomizing them with knives, forks, and Lego blocks. Despite the lack of physical evidence to corroborate these claims, Michaels was convicted and sentenced to 47 years in prison. After serving 5 years in prison, the case was overturned by appeals, in part based on an amicus brief that was filed by numerous child witness researchers on Michaels's behalf.

Examinations of interview records clearly show that investigators in the Michaels case used highly suggestive questions, combined with bribery and intimidation of the children (Ceci & Bruck, 1993). Children were repeatedly interviewed until they were "good boys or girls" and provided the interviewer with abuse information. For instance, during one interview, a child was told, "You told us everything once before. Do you want to undress my dolly? Let's get done with this real quick so we could go to Kings to get Popsicles," (*State v. Michaels,* 1993). Following high-profile cases such as the Michaels case, researchers turned their focus to examining how different questioning techniques affect children's accounts. The results from these studies reveal a variety of ways that interviewers can taint children's testimony.

Suggestive Questions

The Kelly Michaels case and the "Mr. Science" project conducted by Poole and Lindsay (1995) suggest that children sometimes make false allegations. The true proportion of criminal allegations that are false is difficult to establish in actual abuse cases, particularly cases such as sexual assault in which physical evidence may be lacking. A frequently cited rate of false reports in the psychological literature is 5% to 8% of CSA cases. Moreover, false allegations of sexual abuse are estimated to be as high as 50% when the alleged victim is from a family currently undergoing a divorce and custody battle (Raskin & Yuille, 1989). Considering that around 200,000 new abuse allegations arise each year (Finkelhor, 1984), if 8% of abuse allegations are false, then an astounding 16,000 people would be falsely charged with CSA each year.

Sometimes false allegations may unintentionally result from conversations with well-intentioned adults. Parents, teachers, and child-care workers seem to hold certain assumptions about behaviors that are indicative of abuse. For instance, if a teacher witnessed a preschool-aged child masturbating, such behavior might be brought to the attention of authorities (remember, teachers are mandated to report suspected cases of child abuse). Indeed, researchers have found that sexual acting out is more common in sexually abused than non-abused children (Koocher et al., 1995). However, non-abused children may also display sexual behavior. Non-abused children may learn about sexual activity through a variety of modes, including peers, siblings, parents, or television. Sexual play is rather common among children, with around half of 2- to 5-year-olds estimated to engage in genital manipulation (Chess & Hassibi, 1986). Despite the long history of investigators, therapists, and parents assuming that abuse occurred based on behavior such as phallic drawings, there is not adequate validity in such behavior to be diagnostic of abuse (Buros, 1989). In sum, sexual knowledge may originate from a variety of sources, and sexual activity is relatively common among children.

Parents or teachers may become alarmed at a child's behavior and report their suspicions to social welfare agencies or police. However, some children may simply be displaying normal childhood behavior. Even in cases in which the child seems to clearly make an abuse allegation (e.g., "My bottom was licked at daddy's"), alternative explanations are possible (e.g., the family dog licked the child). However, investigators have traditionally assumed a priori that children who came to their attention were abused. Traditionally, investigators saw their role as collecting information to confirm the abuse (Ceci & Bruck, 1993).

Some investigators have used suggestive, leading questions to satisfy their perhaps well-meaning intentions of corroborating abuse (Ceci & Bruck, 1993; Warren, Woodall, Hunt, & Perry, 1996). Unfortunately, this hypothesis-confirming approach to conducting abuse investigations may elicit false statements from the child. Suggestive, leading questions may cause some nonabused children to assent to abuse. Numerous studies have found that children may succumb to suggestive questions (for a review, see Bruck & Ceci, 1999). Once false statements emerge, it is difficult to reliably distinguish between true and false reports, as false statements are often rich in detail (Bruck, Hembrooke, & Ceci, 1997).

***

Interestingly, children [tend] not to succumb to misleading questions when interviewed by a 7-year-old child (Ceci, Ross, & Toglia, 1987, Experiment 2). Ceci et al. (1987) suggest that children see adults as authority figures and attempt to please the adult by agreeing with their questions. Therefore, children may be particularly susceptible to leading questions from authority figures such as police officers (Walker-Perry & Wrightsman, 1991).

On the other hand, Goodman and colleagues (e.g., Goodman, Aman, & Hirschman, 1987; Goodman, Hirschman, Hepps, & Rudy, 1991) have conducted numerous studies that suggest children may sometimes be resistant to suggestive questions. For instance, Goodman, Rudy, Bottoms, and Aman (1990) conducted a project in which 4- to 7-year-olds played with a clown and were interviewed about the event 10 to 12 days later. They found that children generally were resistant to misleading questions about the event. However, in this study, children were only questioned once by a non-intimidating adult. Even so, some children in the study did agree to suggestive questions that might be construed as indicative of abuse.

***

Once children agree to suggestive events, Ceci and colleagues (Ceci & Bruck, 1995; Ceci, Huffman, Smith, & Loftus, 1994) suggest that they may actually come to believe that the suggested events occurred. Young children sometimes have difficulties with memory-source monitoring (Ceci & Bruck, 1995; Taylor, Esbensen, & Bennett, 1994). Therefore, children may continue to report such non-experienced events as having actually occurred when subsequently questioned.

In sum, using suggestive, leading questions during investigative interviews heightens the risk of eliciting inaccurate or erroneous reports from children—reports that may persist during subsequent interviews. Leading questions seem to emerge when the investigators seek to confirm rather than test the hypothesis that a child was abused. Leading questions are also quite likely to be challenged in court, potentially ruining the child's credibility.

The main implication for interviewing child witnesses that emerges from the suggestibility literature is that interviewers should take a hypothesis testing rather than a hypothesis-confirming approach. With the hypothesis testing approach, interviewers should consider whether factors other than abuse might explain some of the child's behavior. Interviewers should consider who first came forward with the abuse charges and any potential motivation that parents might have to encourage a child to make false allegations. Investigators should also consider base rate behavior of sexual play rather than viewing sexual play as a confirmation of abuse. Clearly, leading questions should be avoided.

Repeated Questions

Repeated questioning may also lead children to report false allegations of abuse. The effect of repeated interviews on children's statements depends on factors such as the timing of the repetition and the types of repeated questions (Poole & Lamb, 1998). If repeated interviews are conducted, then interviewers must be particularly careful to avoid leading questions.

Ceci and colleagues (Ceci & Bruck, 1995; Ceci et al., 1994) found that preschool children are especially prone to agree with repeated leading questions. In their study, preschoolers selected cards with statements such as "Got finger caught in mousetrap and had to go to the hospital." The cards were read to children who were then asked if the event ever occurred. Initially, most children disagreed with the statements. However, after 12 weeks of being interviewed once a week, more than half of the children gave false narratives of at least one event. [Twenty-five percent gave] false narratives to a majority of the non-experienced events. Children's reports tended to be rich in detail. Furthermore, following debriefing, 27% of children refused to believe that the suggested event did not actually occur.

On the other hand, repeated interviews may sometimes help children provide new details of a past event (Howe, Kelland, Bryant-Brown, & Clark, 1992). Multiple interviews may help a confused but cooperative witness by helping him or her learn to talk about the event. Bradley and Wood (1996) examined 234 cases of corroborated CSA and found that 6% originally denied abuse. Thus, repeated interviews may sometimes be necessary for children to disclose abuse information.

However, investigators must use caution during repeated interviews. If asked repeated specific questions, children may change their responses, thinking the adult is repeating the question because the child provided the wrong answer.

***

In the actual legal setting, children are interviewed an average of 11 times before reaching court (McGough, 1994). Police administrators may help lessen the number of times children are interviewed by coordinating with other agencies (e.g., protective services) involved. By coordinating in advance with other social service agencies, interviews could be conducted by a team of professionals. If children are repeatedly interviewed by different professionals (e.g., a social worker and then a police officer), the interviewers should be careful to explain that they are not aware of the information that the children have already told others and would like to learn about it. Children are less likely to be misled if they are told in advance that the interviewer has no prior knowledge of the events in question (Toglia, Ross, Ceci, & Hembrooke, 1992).

Language Development

False allegations of abuse may also arise from linguistic confusion. Research suggests that it is necessary for investigative interviewers to have a rather sophisticated understanding of language development. Adults, including interviewers, often ask questions that are confusing to children (Brennan & Brennan, 1988; Warren et al., 1996). To complicate matters further, children who have experienced abuse may display delayed language development (Beeghly & Cicchetti, 1994).

Typical conversations with adults and children are quite different from proper interview conversations. Adults typically converse with children in a highly structured manner. Gleason (1977) suggests that adults are directive during their conversations with children to promote language development. Adults often make leading and reinforcing statements during normal conversations.

Understanding children's language development is a complex task for interviewers. Interviewers must learn and practice a proactive linguistic style with young children. There is little evidence to suggest that interviewers automatically conduct interviews with these linguistic principles in mind. Rather, investigative interviews with children appear to be conducted in a linguistic manner similar to typical adult-child conversations. Hence, police administrators should encourage specialized training in interviewing child witnesses.

Subtle variations in interviewers' talk with children can have a tremendous impact on their reports. Both children and interviewers may be confused at the other's communicative intent. Research indicates that children often misunderstand seemingly simple words and concepts. For instance, children are often confused by words related to "touch" (Warren, 1992). Children may state that "He put his fingers inside me," but say no to the question "Did he touch you?" A.G. Walker (1994) notes that children may have a different understanding of commonly used words than adults. For instance, children may think that to remember something, it must first be forgotten. Thus, if asked whether they remember a particular event, children may say no simply because they have remembered it all along.

Investigators should also avoid questions about emotional concepts (e.g., "How did that make you feel?") Aldridge and Wood (1997) found that until around age 8, children easily become confused by words such as fear, anxiety, and anger. Even until age 14, children's understanding of the concept of emotion may differ from that of adults (Aldridge & Wood, 1997).

Children may also not fully understand or be able to report concepts of time (Friedman, 1991). Instead of trying to get a specific date and time of an alleged abusive event, investigators should ask more general questions. For instance, investigators could inquire as to whether the alleged victim was on break from school, whether the abuse allegation occurred following a school day, and so forth. Asking children about specific times and dates may only serve to discredit the child in the courtroom.

Investigators must also pay attention to syntactical development. Research suggests that investigators should avoid using passive tenses during questioning. Passive tense questions have been shown to confuse children until around ages 10 to 13 (A.G. Walker, 1994). Furthermore, investigators should avoid multiple and negatively phrased questions, as these may also confuse children (A.G. Walker, 1994).

Children may also display confusion toward adult language pragmatics. For instance, children sometimes fail to realize or indicate topic transitions (Fivush & Shukat, 1995; Poole & Lindsay, 1995). Poole and Lindsay (1995) found that when children were asked final open-ended questions about the "Mr. Science" project, the requests often led to off-topic responses. They found that even 8- to 10-year-olds would stray from the relevant topic when asked such questions. If children make frequent topic shifts, then interviewers must be sure to clarify the information.

In sum, it is important for interviewers to work toward minimizing and recognizing linguistic confusion. Children may not tell adults that they are confused but rather attempt to answer the questions. Hughes and Grieve (1980) found that 5- to 7-year-olds often gave answers of yes or no to bizarre questions such as "Is milk bigger than water?" Warren and McCloskey (1997) found that when children were confused about a topic, they often either agreed with or paraphrased interviewers' prior statements. Such statements could lead investigators to superfluous conclusions.

The main implication for investigative interviews based on the child witness-language literature is that investigators must have a general understanding of language development. Investigators should be sensitive to the children's developmental level, allowing them to set the language level of the interview (Poole & Lamb, 1998). Awareness and sensitivity to language development can minimize interviewer-child miscommunication.

***

INTERVIEWING THE CHILD WITNESS: GENERAL RECOMMENDATIONS

There is no single structured interview that can be used to question all children. Interviewers must remain flexible to accommodate the varying characteristics of criminal cases. The interviewer should "consider life circumstances of individual children and adapt their methods accordingly" (Poole & Lamb, 1998, p. 8). The general interview techniques recommended below are flexible in that they focus on how to gather information rather than on what specific information to gather.

Pre-Interview Preparation

Research is lacking to address whether the quality of the interview is affected according to the amount of information collected prior to the interview. Prominent child investigation researchers Poole and Lamb (1998) suggest gathering some information about the allegations and learning some personal information about children to use in rapport building. Having some prior knowledge regarding the allegations or the children's family may help interviewers clarify details of the children's report. For instance, knowing whether children recently took sex education or whether the family is undergoing a divorce may be useful in considering alternative hypotheses to the abuse allegations.

Rapport Building

First, interviewers should introduce themselves to children. They should allow the children to become familiar with the interview environment and ask any questions. Interviewers should begin building rapport with children by asking open-ended questions about non-abuse-related topics such as school. Research suggests that building rapport may increase the accuracy of the children's statements. For instance, Saywitz, Geiselman, and Bornstein (1992) had detectives from a sheriff's department interview third and sixth graders about staged events. They found that children who participated in interviews that began with open-ended rapport building made the fewest mistakes in their accounts. Furthermore, Sternberg et al. (1997) found that interviews that began with open-ended rapport building produced twice as many details and words than did brief rapport building with closed questions. See Sternberg et al. (1997) for an example of an open-ended rapport-building protocol.

Interviewers should explain to children the goals and the general rules of the interview, including that they have the right to say, "no," "I don't remember," and "I don't understand" (Poole & Lamb, 1998). Children often think that they must answer every question adults ask, regardless of whether they know the answer (Moston, 1990). Interviewers should explain to children that they have the right to express confusion and to correct any false interpretations. In Warren, Hulse-Trotter, and Tubbs (1991), the researchers warned 7-year-olds, 12-year-olds, and adults that they may be asked some tricky, confusing questions during an interview. They found that all age groups were more resistant to suggestion when given such a warning.

Rapport building also allows children practice in being informative (Sternberg et al., 1997). Not only does this allow children to become relaxed and familiar with the interviewers, but it also establishes the tone of the interviews. Interviewers should be encouraging and supportive to children (Goodman et al., 1990). However, interviewers should avoid comments such as "good boy" to specific disclosure responses, as such encouragement could be leading. Children should be encouraged to be active participants in the interviews (Goodman et al., 1991; Poole & Lamb, 1998). As children begin to communicate, interviewers can partially assess the children's language abilities.

To foster rapport, it is best for one person to interview the child (Poole & Lamb, 1998). Although a team approach of police–socialworker interviews is highly recommended (Poole & Lamb, 1998), a single person should do the interviews. One-way mirrors and microphones ideally would be available to allow others to add questions to the interview. If this is not feasible, then a second investigator can sit in the room and take notes. Additional questions could be written and passed to the primary interviewer.

Interview Environment

Interviews should take place in environments that contain minimal distractions to children. Investigators should avoid wearing a police uniform or a gun, inasmuch as this likely will be distracting (Poole & Lamb, 1998). To maximize children's concentration, the room should be simple, cheerful, uncluttered, and non-threatening (Poole & Lamb, 1998).

The investigative environment should allow audio and video recordings of children's statements. Recorded interviews seem useful for several reasons. First, recordings allow investigators to counter claims of poor investigation techniques. In turn, recordings may also encourage proper interview techniques. Second, videotapes allow investigators to look back through children's accounts to review and clarify their communicative intent. Third, videotaped testimony may reduce the number of times that children are interviewed.

On the other hand, investigators must be prepared to have their interview methods challenged by the defense. Furthermore, inconsistencies between the videotaped interviews and the children's courtroom testimony may cast doubt on their reliability. Regardless, a general consensus appears to be emerging among researchers that the potential advantages of recording the interview outweigh the potential disadvantages. Interviews should be audiotaped and videotaped (e.g., Ceci & Bruck, 1995; Lamb, 1994; McGough, 1994, 1995; Poole & Lamb, 1998; Raskin & Yuille, 1989; Walker-Perry & Wrightsman, 1991).

Truth Versus Lie Ceremony

Investigators should avoid asking children to provide a narrative description of "truth versus lie." Such a question is abstract and confusing even to school-aged children (Pipe & Wilson, 1994; A.G. Walker, 1994). Furthermore, researchers have found that children's ability to explain "truth versus lie" does not predict the accuracy of their statements (Goodman et al., 1987; Pipe & Wilson, 1994). Researchers have only recently begun to examine the efficacy of different types of truth-lie discussions in increasing the veracity of children's reports (e.g., Huffman, Warren, & Larson, 1999; London & Nunez, 2001). Currently, there is inadequate evidence to direct the practice of truth-lie discussions with children. However, if a truth-lie ceremony is conducted, then interviewers should use concrete questions (Poole & Lamb, 1998).

Open-Ended Questions

Open-ended questions should be used as much as possible during investigative interviews. Open-ended questions allow children to respond to questions in a variety of ways. Children tend to be more accurate on their free recall than in response to forced-choice questions. Poole and Lamb (1998) emphatically state, "*Regardless of the experimental procedures, the ages studied, the cognitive capacity of the subject, or the length of the delay between events and the interview, open-ended questions are more likely to elicit accurate accounts*" (p. 53, emphasis in original).

Although open-ended questions produce more accurate recall, children tend not to report events in great detail during narrative reports (Poole & Lamb, 1998). For instance, in a study in which children were told secrets and later asked about the secrets from a second interviewer, children were much more likely to reveal their secrets when directly asked (Wilson & Pipe, 1995). Open-ended questions generally did not lead to commensurate disclosure.

Although specific questions may be necessary to gather more information, such questions increase the risk of inaccuracy (Poole & Lamb, 1998). Dent and Stephenson (1979) found that 19% of children's reports were inaccurate when asked specific questions compared with 9% when asked open-ended questions.

***

In sum, specific questions may be necessary to allow interviewers to gather more information and to clarify the information that children have already reported. Hence, interviewers should begin the interview with open-ended questions to be followed by a series of specific questions. When specific questions are used, care should be taken to phrase questions differently to explore whether children are simply agreeing to all questions. Yes-no questions should be avoided whenever possible. When using specific questions, children should be allowed to further describe their account.

Interview Aids

Anatomically detailed or anatomically correct dolls (AD dolls) became widely popular in the 1980s, despite the lack of standardized procedures or empirical support (Poole & Lamb, 1998). Even in the early 1990s, Conte, Sorenson, Fogarty, and Rosa (1991) found in a U.S. survey of more than 200 professionals that 92% reported using AD dolls in child abuse investigations. Kendall-Tackett and Watson (1992) found in a Boston survey that 62% of police officers and 80% of mental health workers reported using AD dolls.

AD dolls were assumed to help children describe abuse for a variety of reasons. Interview aids such as dolls were speculated to act as memory aids and to lessen children's embarrassment caused by verbally describing sexually explicit information. Dolls were thought especially to help younger children overcome language deficits. Some investigators even tried to infer abuse based on children's play with AD dolls (assuming abused children would display more sexual play than non-abused children).

The efficacy of interview aids such as AD dolls was based solely on intuition. Empirical studies now cast serious doubt on the utility of AD dolls. First, abuse cannot be reliably inferred based on children's play because non-abused children may also display sexual play (Realmuto, Jensen, & Wescoe, 1990). Second,

studies show that the use of AD dolls does not lead children to recall more information than interviews with no aids (Bruck, Ceci, & Francoeur, 2000; DeLoache & Marzolf, 1995). Third, the dolls likely do not help younger children overcome language deficits because younger children probably do not understand the purpose of the dolls. That is, younger children have difficulties understanding the symbol-referent nature of AD dolls (DeLoache, 1995). Finally, if dolls are used to encourage children to first disclose abuse, then the dolls can be leading (Bruck & Ceci, 1996).

In general, police administrators should discourage the use of investigation aids such as AD dolls and drawings for interviewing children (Yuille et al., 1993). Dolls should not be used as a diagnostic tool (Everson & Boat, 1990). If dolls or drawings are used, then it should only be in helping children clarify information that they have already disclosed (e.g., names of body parts).

Closing the Interview

Investigators should close the interview by asking children if they have anything further they would like to add about the events that were discussed. Children should be allowed to ask any final questions. Children or their parents should be given contact information in case they want to further discuss something (Poole & Lamb, 1998).

***

THE NECESSITY OF TRAINING INVESTIGATING OFFICERS IN INTERVIEWING CHILD WITNESSES

It is difficult to assess whether and to what extent psychologically based interview techniques are applied in actual interviews. Ethical considerations in police interviews often prevent controlled police studies. Police interviews can obviously have serious consequences, so experimental studies with actual victims of crime may not be conducted. Furthermore, resource limitations (e.g., time and money) may prevent well-intentioned police departments from utilizing new investigative procedures.

Thus, for police departments, economy and efficiency are also practical concerns regarding investigative procedures.

Police have traditionally seen their role as one of simply gathering the facts from cooperative witnesses (Ainsworth, 1995). That is, traditionally, police officers have lists of the information that they should gather but are left untrained regarding how to gather it. Fisher, Geiselman, Raymond, Jurkevich, and Warhaftig (1987, p. 178) cited one police officer as stating, "Basically, you just ask them who, what, when, where, why, and how."

Even with proper training and policies, officers may not apply proper interview techniques (Geiselman et al., 1987). Questioning children is very complex; it may be difficult for officers to change their communication styles. Aldridge and Cameron (1999) administered a one-week intensive training course to police and social workers on interviewing children. An examination of subsequent videotaped interviews revealed that there were no differences in performance between trained and untrained interviewers.

Role-playing and feedback may be important for officers first learning the psychologically based interview methods (Geiselman et al., 1987). New recruits should be trained in the methods before they learn maladaptive interview habits.

***

Conclusion

The role of police officers traditionally has been to serve and protect the community. This role is inherently ambiguous, as officers encounter a variety of tasks on a daily basis. Police are expected to be experts in a wide variety of domains, including interrogating suspects, interviewing victims and witnesses, gathering physical evidence, and operating equipment such as police vehicles and firearms. Considering the tremendous range of duties for which the police officers are responsible, it seems questionable to expect them to also gain the expertise necessary to interview child witnesses. A better alternative may be to train selected officers who will be responsible for taking the initial reports and subsequently investigating the case.

Interviewing children is a complicated endeavor. Recent psychological research has found that the quality of children's reports is dependent on the quality of the investigative interview. This article reviewed some of the steps that investigating officers can take to increase the reliability of children's reports. In addition, police administrators can help investigators reach this goal by endorsing specialized training and by ensuring that the appropriate interview environment is provided.

The nature of investigative interviews does not allow for a simple recipe that can be applied when questioning all children. Interviewers need special skills and training. A variety of interview protocols that maximize children's accuracy and minimize distortion are now available. However, research is unclear as to whether or to what extent these interview protocols are being applied in actual forensic settings. Future research should work toward further improving investigative techniques. Researchers also must consider the feasibility of law enforcement officers or child welfare workers applying these techniques.

5

PSYCHOLOGICAL ASPECTS OF CRIME SCENE PROFILING

ROBERT J. HOMANT
DANIEL B. KENNEDY

Through movies such as *Silence of the Lambs* and television series such as *Millennium* and *Profiler,* crime scene profiling has come to the attention of the general public. According to Douglas, Ressler, Burgess, and Hartman (1986), profiling may be defined as "a technique for identifying the major personality and behavioral characteristics of an individual based upon an analysis of the crimes he or she has committed" (p. 405). Numerous books and articles have described the origins of the FBI's efforts to develop and implement a formal process for crime scene profiling, which began systematically in 1978 (Annon, 1995; . . . Douglas & Olshaker, 1995, 1997; Hickey, 1997; . . . Ressler & Schachtman, 1992).

These accounts, together with the following literature that we will cite, represent a mixture of journalistic, autobiographical, and more empirically based information on profiling. Furthermore, much of the empirical literature directly relating to profiling has been published without being subjected to peer review. For the most part, these sources give a highly positive impression of the effectiveness of crime scene profiling.

Although a few critics have raised cautioning voices (Hickey, 1997; Keppel, 1995), not only does the utility of such profiling seem to be generally accepted, but it is being extended into areas far beyond its original design. . . .

The purpose of this article is to review the theoretical underpinning of profiling; to examine the existing studies of its reliability and validity, especially as practiced by the FBI and FBI-trained profilers; and to comment on the application of profiling to various problem areas. We will begin with a general description of the profiling process and distinguish it from certain related attempts at prediction.

DISTINGUISHING CRIME SCENE PROFILING

The Process of Crime Scene Profiling

Profiling is referred to by various terms in the literature: psychological profiling, criminal

Editors' Note: This article was originally published in *Criminal Justice and Behavior*, Vol. 25, No. 3, September 1998, pp. 319-343. We have deleted much of the validity research discussed in the article but have retained summary statements about that research.

personality profiling or assessment, criminal behavior profiling, offender profiling, criminal profiling, and investigative profiling (Annon, 1995). Currently, the official FBI term is *criminal investigative analysis*. The authors believe that, for better or worse, the term *profiling* has become too well established to change. In this article, therefore, we will use the term *crime scene profiling* to help focus on exactly what is being attempted and to help distinguish the area from related efforts that are also referred to as profiling.

Crime scene profiling is specifically based on the techniques developed by the FBI's Behavioral Science Unit, which bas evolved into the Profiling and Behavioral Assessment Unit. The process was developed particularly to deal with cases of serial homicide and/or serial rape. Because of the typically chance connection between perpetrator and victim in these kinds of crime, and because a perpetrator frequently commits crimes across various jurisdictions, such cases are especially troublesome to local law enforcement.

The how-to of profiling is set out especially well by Dietz (1985), Douglas et al. (1986), and Geberth (1990). The profiler typically begins with complete photographs and descriptions of the crime scene. This includes information about the general character of the location, including traffic patterns and ease of access for various types of individuals. If the crime is a homicide, an autopsy of the victim is required to assist in reconstructing the sequence of the crime. [If it is] a rape, it is hoped that the victim can reconstruct all interactions with the rapist, especially including all the verbal and nonverbal techniques used by the offender to gain control. The profiler also requires a complete victim profile, including general lifestyle and a detailed account of behaviors prior to the victimization. All physical evidence is expected to be at the disposal of the profiler. This includes such classic clues as footprints, blood spatters, and tools or paraphernalia used. Such evidence is typically given even more weight than psychological speculation. In addition, any knowledge of the perpetrator's pre- and post-offense behavior is sought, as well as all information from other crimes that may be linked to the same perpetrator by physical or behavioral evidence.

The profiler then attempts to give as complete a description of the perpetrator as possible. This might include gender, age, race or ethnicity, level of intelligence or schooling, military service status, job status, living circumstances, nature of interpersonal relationships, and even the make and color of the perpetrator's car. The numerous descriptive statements are seen as hypotheses, and it is not expected that all will prove correct.

***

Goals of Profiling

Profiling was originally intended to help law enforcement discover who the criminal is—either by narrowing an overwhelming list of suspects to a small subgroup or by providing new avenues of inquiry. Other uses were quickly found, however. Thus, case histories (e.g., Douglas & Olshaker. 1995) document the use of profiles to give police advice on how best to interrogate a suspect and to tell prosecutors the approach to cross examination most likely to break down a defendant. Profiling has been used to help set traps to flush out the offender, for example, by planting information in the media. It has been used to predict dangerousness as a factor in sentencing or at a parole hearing or to determine whether a threatening note should be taken seriously.

Proponents of profiling are normally cautious in their claims. For example, they stress that profiling is more an art than a science. They suggest that it should be limited to cases that show severe psychopathology (Geberth, 1990; McCann, 1992; Pinizzotto, 1984) and for which there is a sufficient database of known offenders from previous similar cases. This caution would seem to limit profiling mostly to serial rapes and serial murders; at other times, however, profiling seems to be extended to cases of single rape or murder, as well as to arson, bombing, and threats of various types. Profilers have also applied their efforts to distinguishing accidental, autoerotic asphyxiation from suicide or homicide to hostage negotiations, stalking, and even bank robbery—not all of which necessarily involve significant psychopathology.

The Validity Issue

The issue of the validity of crime scene profiling takes different forms depending on the context. From a law enforcement point of view, there is no need to wait for assurances that profiling in general is a valid process, as long as there are not any more promising alternatives and as long as the process is used cautiously. For example, a promising lead should not be abandoned just because it does not fit a profile, and no lead should be focused on too narrowly. From a forensic point of view, when profiling becomes courtroom evidence . . . it is important that such evidence is seen as probabilistic, and even though conclusions are based on an "art," it is still important that the profiler be able to articulate the basis for various inferences. Finally, from a social scientific point of view, there is a need to validate profiling not just for each of the individual purposes for which it is used (e.g., identifying suspects, predicting dangerousness) but also for each type of crime (e.g., homicide, rape, arson). As a research strategy, of course, one might begin by trying to establish the validity of the process for its principal use and then focus later on its extended uses.

As far as we can determine, no one has attempted to assess the validity of crime scene profiling in real-life situations. Such a study would present some unique problems. The main problem is the lack of an objective criterion against which to test a sample of actual profiles. Holmes (1989) reported that less than half of profiled cases had been solved. Even when the identity of the offender is unambiguously determined, there is still a large subjective element in deciding how well the person fits the profile. Ideally, the profile should also be compared to any cleared suspects in the case to guard against taking advantage of general statements that might fit most potential offenders. It may also be that if a profile is reasonably accurate, it is more likely to lead to an arrest, creating a spuriously positive impression of profiling accuracy for those profiles that can be evaluated.

***

Other Types of Profiling

To evaluate crime scene profiling, it is important to distinguish it from two related processes: psychological profiling and offender profiling. Although the literature on profiling uses all three

terms more or less interchangeably, we believe that more precise terminology is critical if we are to fully appreciate the validity issues involved. Two other procedures, geographic profiling and equivocal death analysis, are blends of the three basic types and also need to be distinguished.

Psychological profiling. By psychological profiling, we mean the interviewing and testing of an individual to determine whether his personality matches the established personality characteristics of a certain class of offenders. This procedure has been most developed in the area of child sexual abusers, where such profiles are sometimes called on to lend supporting evidence that a particular offender was more or less likely to be guilty of such a crime.

***

Crime scene profiling and psychological profiling have in common the attempt to understand and make predictable the behavior of psychologically deviant individuals. In contrast to psychological profiling, however, crime scene profiling starts with known behavior (the crime, as witnessed or reconstructed from the scene) and infers characteristics of the offender. In psychological profiling, the profiler starts with a known individual (who can be tested and interviewed in depth) and tries to project to behavior.

Offender profiling. What we term offender profiling is strictly an empirical procedure, in which no assumptions about the motivation or personality of the offender are necessary. Simply by gathering a large amount of data, either systematically or by more loosely collected anecdotal information, law enforcement agents construct a description of the type of person most commonly involved in a certain type of offense. For example, someone driving at a certain speed, at a certain time of day, in a certain type of car, and of a certain general appearance may fit the profile of a drug courier and be stopped for a search. This type of profiling has been credited with reducing some types of criminal behavior, but it raises legal and ethical problems when ethnicity, gender, and age are part of the profile (DeOeneste & Sullivan, 1994; Easteal & Wilson, 1991).

Crime scene profiling shares with offender profiling the use of empirical data from previous similar offenses. But although offender profiling stops with generalizations about a class of offenders, crime scene profiling is only useful insofar as it can distinguish a particular offender from a general type. Also, rather than being limited to a participant's reasonably observable features, crime scene profiling attempts to extrapolate to the entire lifestyle of the offender.

Equivocal death analysis. Equivocal death analysis drew professional attention when the FBI was asked by the Navy to investigate the cause of an explosion aboard the *USS Iowa* that killed 47 sailors in 1989. Briefly put, the FBI concluded that the explosion was the result of a murder-suicide, committed by a spurned homosexual gunnery officer. Discontent with this conclusion led to a congressional investigation, which commissioned a panel of 14 prominent psychologists and psychiatrists to review the FBI procedures (Jeffers, 1991; Poythress, Otto, Darkes, & Starr, 1993). A clear majority of the panel was critical of the FBI procedures and conclusions, mainly on the grounds that there was no scientific basis for them.

The FBI agents involved in the process (and testifying before Congress) viewed equivocal death analysis as an extension of crime scene profiling. Poythress et al. (1993) specifically noted the lack of concern on the part of one of these agents for the issue of validity and also noted the total absence of any meaningful studies of the validity of equivocal death analysis. . . . Poythress et al. view equivocal death analysis as much more closely related to psychological autopsy (which attempts to clarify the motivation of a known individual who engaged in a particular act-suicide or accidental death) than to crime scene profiling. . . .

***

Geographic profiling. Developed as part of his doctoral dissertation at Simon Fraser University by Detective Inspector Kim Rossmo of the Vancouver Police Department (1995a, 1995b), geographic profiling blends the insights of modem geography with the contributions of environmental criminology (Brantingham & Brantingham, 1981; see also Kennedy, 1990). It is clearly allied to crime scene profiling, in that it attempts to generalize from linked crime scene locations to the probable residence or base of operations of an unknown offender. Although primarily empirical (taking into account such variables as bus routes and travel time), geographic profiling does employ the concept of a mental map and tries to reconstruct a psychological representation of the crime-relevant areas in which the offender feels comfortable. A related approach used by Godwin and Canter (1997) also attempts to construct a social psychological portrait of the offender.

***

To summarize, the five types of profiling that we have differentiated all have in common the goal of making some sort of inference about an individual's personality or behavior. All are, to some extent, dependent on a model that portrays human behavior as having a good deal of consistency. The inferential burden seems to us to be by far the greatest in crime scene profiling: Not only must the personality of an unknown individual be assembled from behavioral clues, but that hypothesized personality must then be used to generate further attributions about the individual. Because trait theory and the concept of offender types is central to this process, we will briefly review some of the key studies in these areas before turning our attention to studies directly involved with the validity of crime scene profiling.

THE THEORETICAL BASIS FOR PROFILING

Trait Theory and Profiling

Crime scene profiling rests on the assumption that at least certain offenders have consistent behavioral traits. This consistency is thought to persist from crime to crime and also to affect various non-criminal aspects of their personality and lifestyle, thus making them, to some extent, identifiable.

In the field of psychology, trait theory has had a somewhat checkered past, with many researchers finding little consistency of particular traits across time and situations, let alone any pattern of personality across different traits (Kendrick & Funder, 1988). Trait theorists have responded by shifting to measures that combine data from a large number of observations across situations. Hartup and van Lieshout (1995) also suggest that antisocial behavior might be an especially stable behavior trait for aggressive persons— whether because their personalities do not change much, the genetic contribution remains constant, or they tend to remain in aggression-fostering environments.

Caspi and Moffitt (1995) cite a number of studies that, taken together, support the theory that a relatively small group of adolescents engage in life-course persistent antisocial behavior. This form of antisocial behavior has been found to correlate with various genetic, environmental, and personality variables that help account for its persistence. Presumably, individuals who display life-course persistent antisocial behavior make up the bulk of the adult incarcerated offender population. A much smaller subset of this group, in turn, would be representative of the type of offender for whom profiling is thought to be appropriate. Various research studies have attempted to identify these offender subtypes.

Offender Types

Crime scene profiling is based on the assumption that a portrait of an individual offender can be drawn that will distinguish that person from what is known about a class of offenders in general. A particular serial rapist, for example, needs to be distinguishable from the generalized picture that could be obtained by simply using modal values of known serial rapists. Although not absolutely necessary in a logical sense, the existence of reliably identifiable subtypes within any class of offenders at least supports the claim that such narrowing of the field is possible. Furthermore, much of the research work on profiling has involved the attempt to identify such subtypes of offenders.

One of the most frequent areas for developing offender typologies concerns sex offenders, particularly rapists. This research has been reviewed by Prentky and Knight (1991; see also

Knight & Prentky, 1990) in the context of developing their own nine-category typology of rapists for the Massachusetts Treatment Center. Prentky and Knight identified several variables that reliably distinguished certain aspects of rapists' behavior. Perhaps most relevant to the area of crime scene profiling is the finding that lifestyle impulsivity and the presence of sexual fantasies are important predictors of recidivism (and therefore are relevant to serial rape). Other variables, such as irrational attitudes, dominance, sadism, history of child sexual abuse, social competence, aggression, and alcohol use have also been found to be of varying usefulness in distinguishing among rapists. Whether these separate variables can be combined into an empirically valid, practically useful typology, such as that proposed by Knight and Prentky, remains to be demonstrated.

Groth, Burgess, and Holmstrom (1977) proposed a simple typology of rapists that was based on two main types, each divided into two subtypes. According to Groth et al., power, anger, and sexual motives are present in all rapes, with either power or anger predominating. Rape is seen as a pseudosexual act, meaning that the sexuality involved is merely instrumental to gratifying the dominant motives of power or anger. . . .

The theorizing of Groth et al. (1977), modified somewhat by Hazelwood and Burgess (1987), became central to the FBI's efforts to profile serial rapists. In-depth interviews were conducted with 41 incarcerated serial rapists (Hazelwood & Warren, 1989a, 1989b, 1990). In one study of these rapists, Hazelwood, Reboussin, and Warren (1989) identified a subgroup of serial rapists whom they termed "increasers." Unlike the majority ($n = 31$) of the serial rapists, the increasers ($n = 10$) escalated their use of force with succeeding rapes. They also differed in that they raped more frequently and engaged in more sadistic acts. However, no developmental differences were found between the two subgroups, so it is not clear how a profiler might use the information that a particular series of linked rapes was probably committed by an increaser. Furthermore, in this particular study, all coding disagreements between interviewers were resolved "through an assessment of all available information" (p. 69). Thus, we do not know how reliable any attempt would be to classify someone as an increaser, even based on direct interviews with the individual.

***

To summarize this section on offender types, several studies of extreme groups of rapists and murderers have found that some personality and behavioral distinctions can be made within these groups and that there is some reliability in making these distinctions. There is also some evidence linking these distinctions to differences in how offenders carry out their crimes. In many respects, however, these studies are closer to psychological rather than crime scene profiling, in that they typically begin with a sample of known offenders. In the next section, we will look at those studies that bear even more directly on the reliability and validity of crime scene profiling.

DIRECT STUDIES OF CRIME SCENE PROFILING

Crime Scene Classification Variables

Before looking at specific studies of the profiling process, it will be necessary to clarify the distinction between organized and disorganized crime scenes and offenders. This distinction is fairly well described in the profiling literature. Ressler and Burgess (1985) list some 25 variables that distinguish the personality, socioeconomic background, and crime scene behavior involved in the two types of offender. Compared to disorganized offenders, organized offenders are described as more intelligent, more socially competent, more likely to be responding to some precipitating situational stressor, and more likely to show care, planning, and control in the criminal act. Because of these factors, organized offenders are viewed as more difficult to catch.

The classification is complicated somewhat by the use of a mixed type. Exactly how much overlap of elements is needed before a crime scene should be called mixed is not clear; probably most crime scenes could be classified as mixed. Also, because the FBI profiler is more likely to be called in on the tougher cases,

profiling is more likely to be attempted on relatively organized crime scenes, so that any statement about the distribution of the crime scene classification variable would be misleading. Some points that are not clear in the literature include whether the mixed category should be applied only to the crime scene or also to the offender, and whether and how offenders might change or evolve during their career from organized to disorganized and vice versa.

The difference between organized and disorganized offenders is further complicated by three distinctions that profilers make about the crime scene: the MO (modus operandi), the signature, and (possible) staging (Douglas & Munn, 1992; Geberth, 1995). The MO refers to the method used by the offender to accomplish the crime; it is essentially learned and changeable behavior. The signature refers to behaviors that are related to the offender's personality—specifically, the unique fantasies—and that go beyond what is needed to accomplish the crime. Although it is described as "never changing" (Douglas & Munn, 1992, p. 3), it is also possible for the signature to "evolve" from crime to crime. Profilers typically argue that the signature is more important than the MO, both for linking crimes and for deriving an offender profile. Finally, staging refers to deliberate efforts by the offender (or others) to alter the crime scene so as to mislead investigators. The presence of staging may be detected by "inconsistencies in the forensic findings and in the overall 'big picture' of the crime scene" (Douglas & Munn, 1992, p. 7). Douglas and Olshaker (1995) see staging as an aspect of MO in that it is part of the criminal's basic plan for getting away with the crime. Sometimes, however, the alteration in the crime scene can represent posing—for example, using the victim as a sort of prop to communicate a symbolic message—and thus can be a part of the signature (Douglas & Olshaker, 1995). Exactly how the profiler can determine whether some aspect of a particular crime scene represents posing as opposed to staging is not clear.

It would seem from these definitions that the categories organized/disorganized apply partly to the signature aspect and partly to the MO. On one hand the degree of organization is seen as reflective of the criminal's personality (Ressler,

Burgess, Douglas, Hartman, & D' Agostino, 1986) and therefore related to signature. On the other hand, the fact that some offenders may learn from their early crimes and become more careful offenders seems more characteristic of the MO aspect of the crime. In any event, the interrelationships of these concepts need more clarification.

***

Reliability of Crime Scene Classification

The extent to which crime scenes could be reliably classified as organized/disorganized was the subject of a study by Ressler and Burgess (1985). Sixty-four cases were taken from FBI files. An agent familiar with the case presented all relevant crime scene information to five other agents of varying experience. The measure of reliability was the percentage of agreement by the five listeners with the classification of the presenting agent. The bulk of the classifications were into the categories organized or disorganized, although the categories mixed and unknown were also used (making agreement by chance somewhat less likely). The obtained agreement was 74.1 %—that is, about three fourths of the time, the agents listening to the presenter's details agreed with the presenter's classification of the crime scene. Between any two agents, across all 64 crime scenes, the agreements ranged from 45% to 89%, with experienced agents achieving at least 62% agreement.

***

The Process of Profiling

Although many methodological weaknesses need to be addressed, the studies reviewed to this point offer some support for the claim that experienced profilers can classify crime scenes with some reliability and that this classification can be related to identifiable features of the offender. What remains to be determined is whether profilers do anything more than would experienced investigators applying old-fashioned deduction. . . .

To test the effectiveness of trained crime scene profilers as opposed to other criminal investigators, Pinizzotto and Finkel (1990) compared five groups of participants on two profiling tasks. The five groups consisted of four FBI profiling experts, six police detectives specially trained in profiling by the FBI, six experienced but not trained police detectives, six clinical psychologists, and six inexperienced undergraduate students. Each group received extensive case materials from two actual closed cases: a homicide and a rape. Participants were instructed to write detailed profiles about the probable offender based on the case materials and were asked a series of objective questions about the offender (with the correct answers based on the actual convicted offenders). Results are complicated both by the number of variables on which the groups were compared and by the fact that the FBI experts did not participate in all phases of the study.

Six findings seem especially relevant here. (a) The FBI-trained detectives wrote much longer, more detailed profiles (the FBI experts were not included in this comparison). (b) Five police detectives (not part of the five participating groups) rated the FBI-expert or FBI-trained profiles as the most helpful. (c) FBI-trained detectives scored more objectively correct responses on the sex offender case than other groups (FBI experts not given). However, the FBI-trained group had the poorest score on the homicide case. Group differences were generally small—one or two points on a five-point scale. (d) Subjects were asked to identify the correct offender from a lineup consisting of five written descriptions of possible suspects. In the sex offense case, all six FBI experts and five of six FBI-trained detectives were correct, trailed by experienced detectives (four of six) and psychologists (three of six). Only one of six students was correct. Results are not given for the homicide case, except to report that the two profiler groups were no longer superior, and all groups did poorer than with the rape case (which must have been difficult for the student group). (e) The FBI-trained detectives recalled more details of the homicide case but were edged out by the experienced detectives on the sex offense case (FBI experts not given). (f) FBI-trained detectives cited more details as important for both cases. Groups did not differ in how they processed the case details (i.e., in whether they used specific vs. global details to make attributions).

***

Summary of Relevant Findings

In summary, there is enough research to suggest that crime scene profiling may have sufficient reliability and validity to be useful for some purposes. The literature suggests that the concept of behavioral traits and consistency across situations is respectable, if measured in broad contexts. Some antisocial behavior, especially if based on underlying psychopathology, may have a high degree of consistency. Within the narrow category of sexual offenders and murderers, some theoretically reasonable and reliable distinctions can be made. Crime scenes can be categorized with some degree of reliability and have been found to correlate with some offender characteristics. Those trained in profiling have been found to produce longer, more detailed reports, possibly with increased accuracy, and field agencies have been generally positive in their feedback.

At the same time, all of the supporting data seem somewhat tentative, and much of the research is in-house and done on the same common core of offenders. Inaccurate profiles often seem to be ignored or forgotten (Jenkins, 1994; Porter, 1983; Rosenbaum, 1993). Although all profilers caution that profiling is an art and that mistakes can be made, the occasional dramatic success tends to encourage pushing the envelope to new applications. Keppel (1995) has observed that many FBI profiles are generalizations about what is known of serial killers and are not helpful for narrowing suspect lists.

IMPLICATIONS FOR THE USE OF PROFILING

Our take on the evidence at this point is that it is important to expect that a significant number of mistakes will occur with profiling. Where these mistakes can be guarded against, there is no reason not to use it. For example, in the area of criminal investigation, certainly no significant

leads should be overlooked simply because someone does not fit a profile, and no particular suspect should be focused on without other supporting evidence.

In other situations, advice is harder to give. An interviewer may only get one chance to break a suspect in an interrogation or, even more so, during a courtroom cross-examination. In such situations, if a particular profiler has developed a track record of credibility and has specific advice as to how to proceed, one would need to have strong reasons to ignore the advice. Or, in dealing with a hostage taker where lives are at stake and one or another strategy must be followed, again the experienced profiler's advice, backed by soundly articulated reasoning, should be given some weight.

Suggested Research

Research on the validity of crime scene profiling suffers especially from two limitations. One is the lack of access for neutral researchers to a representative sample of actual profiles. The second problem concerns the criterion: The accuracy of a profile can only be determined in cases where the criminal has been clearly identified. This second problem is compounded by the possibility that accurate profiles may be more likely to result in solved cases; thus, inaccurate profiles may be less likely to come to light.

The practical issue with profiling is whether it leads to an increase in successful police investigations. In this sense, even an inaccurate profile may be useful, for example, by stimulating a line of inquiry. Probably the only way that this practical validity (or utility) could be determined would be by a truly randomized experiment in which profiling was withheld from some otherwise suitable cases. We do not seriously propose that such a study be done, of course, on the grounds that no method that has promise should be withheld from the types of cases with which profilers typically deal.

A more limited study that might be possible would be to make available all profiles from solved cases. This would at least permit researchers to make more or less objective judgments about the accuracy of the various elements of the profile. One limitation that we foresee in such a study is that profilers often do not clarify the basis for their predictions. Thus, a piece of physical evidence that leads to a straightforward conclusion may make the profile sound much more intuitive than it really is. There may also be legitimate policy reasons to deny neutral researchers access to FBI files. One obvious concern has to do with the privacy needs of victims and their families. A less obvious problem might be the publication of too much information that could be useful to offenders who stage crime scenes. Nevertheless, until neutral researchers have some way of determining the accuracy of the various elements of a representative sample of profiles, compared against some meaningful baseline data, the validity of the entire process has to remain in a great deal of doubt.

In the meantime, we recommend that more attention be paid to the specific concepts used by profilers. For example, objective scales for categorizing crime scenes could be developed. MO, signature, staging, and posing need to be more carefully operationalized and distinguished. Relationships between crime scenes and offender characteristics, when known, should be cross-validated on new samples of offenders.

On a larger scale, more objectively gathered qualitative data on experiences with profiles should be obtained. This would involve a more careful tracking of profiles that are generated and a comparison with actual offenders when outcomes are known. How exactly did the profile lead or not lead to the offender? How many of the elements of the profile fit the offender? Although some of this information is available anecdotally in biographical material (Douglas & Olshaker, 1995, 1997; Ressler & Schachtman, 1992), it does not seem to have been gathered systematically (e.g., to permit failures to be more carefully scrutinized).

Finally, more attention should be paid to the various uses to which profiling is being put—from various types of crimes, to interrogation advice, to predictions in negligent security cases (Kennedy & Homant, 1997). It is important that a halo effect not be created, whereby a finding of profiling success in one area might be taken as indicative of all possible uses.

6

CRIMINAL PROFILING

Real Science or Just Wishful Thinking?

DAMON A. MULLER

The subject of criminal profiling has caught the public's imagination in recent times, with references to it appearing in all forms of media. The most well-known example of criminal profiling in the popular media is in the film *Silence of the Lambs,* based on the Thomas Harris novel of the same name. Several television shows have also recently been based around the premise of criminal profiling, including *Millennium, Profiler,* and even *The X-Files.* It is interesting to note that all of these popular portrayals of profiling are somewhat inaccurate because they suggest that profiling is a magical skill somewhat analogous to a precognitive psychic ability.

Those who practice criminal profiling have claimed that it is alternatively a science or an art, depending on whom you listen to. Even those who confess that it is more an art than a science (e.g., Ressler & Shachtman, 1992) still point to supposedly scientific studies to support their claims that it is in fact worth using. Yet, one of the biggest hurdles standing in the way of acceptance of criminal profiling is that there is

very little authoritative material on it, and almost nothing in the way of scientific studies to support the claims of the profilers.

Many of the law enforcement agencies around the world are still quite skeptical of the work of criminal profilers. Holmes and Holmes (1996) observe that an offender profile is usually only called in when the police have exhausted all other leads, sometimes including psychics and astrologers. Techniques such as forensic DNA analysis have become essential to modern criminal investigation, possibly because one can point to the strong scientific basis on which they are founded. Yet most people have no idea how effective profiling is, let alone how it works, apart from what they have picked up from the media.

The aim of this article is to look beyond the ubiquitous media hype that surrounds profiling and critically examine the reality. Initially the two main approaches to profiling will be examined in some detail, highlighting the differences and similarities of the approaches. Profiling is usually conducted on serial offenders, which

Editors' Note: This article was originally published in *Homicide Studies*, Vol. 4, No. 3, August 2000, pp. 234-264. Here, it has been shortened considerably, with sections on defining science and some of the conclusions removed. The emphasis here is on describing profiling and highlighting available research.

will also be examined, along with some of the research findings and controversies surrounding serial offenders. The approaches to criminal profiling will then be examined in light of two criteria for a science: the need for a paradigm and the requirement of falsifiability. The empirical support and problems with each of the approaches will be discussed, as will the studies that have empirically examined profiling. It is concluded that the current approaches to profiling do not yet have any substantial empirical support, but that they do have the potential to be scientific if they are worked on.

WHAT IS CRIMINAL PROFILING?

Definitions

Criminal profiling is the process of using available information about a crime and crime scene to compose a psychological portrait of the unknown perpetrator of the crime. The information that the criminal profiler uses is often taken from the scene of the crime, and takes into account factors such as the state of the crime scene, what weapons (if any) were used in the crime, and what was done and said to the victim. Other information used in criminal profiling can include the geographic pattern of the crimes, how the offender got to and from the crime scene, and where the offender lives. The actual process of profiling differs from one profiler to another (depending on the training of the profiler), but the aim remains the same: to deduce enough about the behavioral, personality, and physical characteristics of the perpetrator to catch him.

According to Holmes and Holmes (1996), psychological profiling has three major goals to provide the criminal justice system with the following information: a social and psychological assessment of the offender(s), a psychological evaluation of relevant possessions found with suspected offenders, and consultation with law enforcement officials on the strategies that should be used when interviewing offenders. Not all profiles involve all of these three aspects, with the role of the profiler usually being dictated largely by the needs of the law enforcement officials for whom they are consulting.

Also, not all crimes are suitable for profiling. Holmes and Holmes state that profiling is only appropriate in cases in which the unknown offender shows signs of psychopathology or the crime is particularly violent or ritualistic. Rape and arson are also considered by Holmes and Holmes to be good candidates for profiling.

A profile will rarely by itself solve a crime or catch a criminal, but is designed to be an aid to the investigating police (Wilson & Soothill, 1996). The profile will rarely be so accurate as to suggest a certain individual as being responsible for the crime, but should point the police in the right direction and help reduce the possible number of subjects. When the police have no leads, a profile might suggest some potentially helpful area that the police might have overlooked. Despite what the movies might suggest, profilers do not go running around the countryside solving crimes for hapless local police or rescuing hostages from dangerous psychopaths.

It is important to note that criminal profiling is not just one technique and that there are several distinct approaches to profiling. Wilson, Lincon, and Kocsis (1997) list three main paradigms of offender profiling: diagnostic evaluation (DE), crime scene analysis (CSA), and investigative psychology (IP). Other approaches to profiling exist, such as geographic profiling (Holmes & Holmes, 1996), but these will not be discussed in this article. The two latter approaches, both of which have been adapted and modified somewhat by various practitioners depending on their needs, will be discussed in the current report. The first method, DE, is not so much a discipline as the adaptation of psychotherapeutic (largely Freudian psychoanalytic) theory to crime by individual practitioners. As the DE approach relies mainly on clinical judgment, and as it is approached by each practitioner in a different way, there is no one body of work that can be examined to determine whether it is scientific, and as such will not be discussed here. . . . The more widely known of the remaining two approaches, CSA, was developed by the Behavioral Science Unit (BSU) of the American Federal Bureau of Investigation (FBI). It is the FBI approach to profiling that has been popularized by films such as *Silence of the Lambs* and television shows such as *Profiler*. The other, less publicly well-known, approach was developed by Professor David Canter, a British academic psychologist. Canter's theories are IP and owe more to environmental psychology than to traditional criminal investigation. Although these methods have similarities, they are different enough to warrant separate treatment.

CSA

As mentioned above, the FBI approach is the more popular approach to criminal profiling. Although it is true that many people will have heard of criminal profiling and will associate it with the FBI, until recently there has been very little publicly available information as to what it actually is and how it works. Within the past few years, however, those who developed profiling with the FBI have written several popular books. Former BSU agents Ressler (Ressler & Shachtman, 1992) and Douglas (Douglas & Olshaker, 1995, 1997) have written books with journalists describing their experiences as profilers. Yet despite these books, which are more biographical than anything else, there is little authoritative information on the actual mechanics of the FBI profiling process.

Holmes and Holmes (1996) provide what is probably the best description of the underlying rationale that the FBI uses to profile offenders. The CSA approach, which is primarily applicable to serial murderers, places offenders into two broad categories on the basis of their crime and the crime scene. The two types of offenders are the disorganized asocial offender and the organized nonsocial offender, although in recent times the FBI tends to refer to these as simply disorganized and organized offenders, respectively (e.g., Ressler, Burgess, & Douglas, 1988). Ressler states that the simplistic dichotomy was to enable police who had little or no knowledge of psychological jargon to understand what the BSU thought was a basic differentiation between two distinct groups of offenders (Ressler & Shachtman, 1992). Holmes and Holmes (1996) note that this categorization is particularly applicable to crimes such as rape, sexual assault, mutilation, and necrophilia.

The disorganized offender will usually be of low intelligence, often demonstrating some sort of severe psychiatric disturbance, and will have probably had contact with the mental health system. He will often be socially inept with few interpersonal relationships outside his immediate family, and will be sexually incompetent if he has any sexual experience at all. The crime scene of the disorganized offender will often show little or no premeditation, with whatever is at hand used for a weapon and usually left at the crime scene. The victim (selected more or less at random) will have been quickly overpowered and killed, with the killing often showing extreme overkill and brutality (what the FBI refer to as a "blitz" attack; see Douglas & Olshaker, 1995). The victim's face will often be severely beaten in an attempt to dehumanize her, or she will be forced to wear a mask or blindfold. If the victim is sexually assaulted, it will often be postmortem, with mutilation to the face, genitals, and breasts not uncommon. The body will often be left at the murder scene, but if it is removed, it is more likely that the offender wants to keep it as a souvenir than to hide evidence (Holmes & Holmes, 1996; Ressler, Burgess, & Douglas, 1988; Ressler & Shachtman, 1992).

The types of offenders who make up the organized and disorganized dichotomies are relatively straightforward and are, as the names suggest, organized and disorganized personalities. The organized offender is usually reasonably intelligent but an underachiever with a sporadic education and employment history. He is often married and socially adept, at least at face value, but usually has an antisocial or psychopathic personality. The crime scene left behind by an organized offender will show signs of planning and control. The offender will often bring his own weapons and restraints, which he will then take with him after the crime. The victim will be a targeted stranger, very often female, with the offender searching for either a particular sort of victim or merely a victim of convenience. The victim will often be raped, and the offender will control the victim by using threats and restraints. The offender will usually torture the victim, killing in a slow, painful manner, which the killer will have fantasized about extensively beforehand. The body will also usually be hidden, often transported from the place where the killing occurred, and may be dismembered by more forensically aware killers to delay identification.

From the analysis of the crime scene, the investigator should then be able to determine some characteristics of the perpetrator, which will be of use to the investigating police.

According to Ressler et al. (1988), criminal profiling is a six-stage process. The first stage is referred to as Profiling Inputs, and concerns the collection of all of the information that might be pertinent to solving the crime. This includes photos of the crime scene, the preliminary police report, information about the victim, and all of the collected forensic information. The second stage is the Decision Process Model, in which the information is organized and a preliminary analysis is conducted. In this stage, the homicide type and style are determined (e.g., whether it is a single, mass, spree, or serial murder). Several other important factors are determined in this stage, such as the intent of the offender (e.g., whether homicide was the primary objective or whether it was secondary to another crime), the risk status of the victim (a prostitute would be an example of a high-risk victim, whereas a married woman who lived in a middle-class area would probably be a fairly low-risk victim), and the risk the offender would have been putting himself in to commit the crime. The length of time that was taken to commit the offense is determined and information about the locations (such as where the offender was abducted and where the killing was actually performed) is also investigated.

The third stage of the profiling process, Crime Assessment, is presumably the inspiration for the title of Douglas's book, *Journey Into Darkness* (Douglas & Olshaker, 1997), as it is where the profiler attempts to reconstruct the crime in his or her head. This is where the profiler attempts to "walk in the shoes" of both the victim and the offender, or what the media likes to refer to as "getting into the mind of the killer." It is at this stage that the crime is categorized as organized or disorganized, as the profiler tries to determine how things happened, how people behaved, and how the offender planned and executed the crime. Also considered is the offender's motivation for the crime, such as what the offender hoped to achieve with the crime. The selection of a victim is considered, as is whether the offender staged the scene (modified the crime scene to confuse police). Common

elements of the crime scene that are thought to have significance for identifying certain types of offenders, such as types and locations of wounds and the positioning of the body, are also examined.

It is not until the fourth stage, the Criminal Profile, that the profiler ties all of the above information together and the profile is actually constructed. The profiler attempts to describe the person who committed the crime and proposes strategies that might be most effective in apprehending that particular offender. The profiler constructs the profile by examining all of the information pertinent to the crime in the light of his or her experiences with other similar crimes. The finished profile will contain anywhere between a few paragraphs and several pages of information about the unknown offender, depending on how much material about the crime was forwarded to the profiler. The following elements are commonly found in a profile: the age, race, gender, and general appearance of the offender; the offender's relationship status and any notable points about his relationship history; his likely occupation; and any notable features of his employment, education, or military record. The profiler also includes whether the offender lived in or was familiar with the area, the behavior of the offender both before and after the crime, some basic features about the offender's personality (including whether he has an organized or disorganized personality), and significant belongings that the offender may own, such as pornography. It also contains suggested strategies for interrogating, identifying, and apprehending the victim.

The *fifth stage,* the *Investigation,* is where the profiler submits a written report to the agency investigating the crime, which is added to their investigative efforts. If a suspect is identified and a confession is obtained, then the profile is judged to have been successful. If any additional information becomes available (e.g., new evidence or another connected murder), the new information is given to the profilers so that the profile can be re-evaluated. . . . The *sixth stage* is the *Apprehension,* and assumes that the correct offender has been caught. The profile and the profiling process are evaluated in terms of the actual offender so that future profiles might be even more accurate.

IP

Unlike CSA, IP is more a collection of related theories and hypotheses than a comprehensive methodology. As mentioned previously, IP originated in Britain, mainly due to the work of David Canter, an environmental psychologist who was then the head of the psychology department at the University of Surrey (Canter, 1989). Canter (1994) reports that he was first approached in 1985 by British police who were interested in determining whether psychology had anything to offer police to help them apprehend criminals. Although he observes that police are often very resistant to anything new or to any outsiders telling them how they should do their jobs, Canter's advice proved very helpful to the police in catching John Duffy. Duffy, who was dubbed the "Railway Rapist" by the media, committed approximately 25 rapes and three murders in London between 1982 and 1986 (Nowikowski, 1995). Since that case, Canter has worked on over 60 murder and rape cases in the United Kingdom (Casey, 1993).

Canter (1989) claims that psychology is directly applicable to crime, as crime can be seen as an interpersonal transaction in which criminals are performing actions in a social context (often just between themselves and their victims). He argues that our methods of psychological interaction are ingrained into our personalities, and reasons that the actions the criminal performs while engaging in a crime are direct reflections of the way they will act in other, more normal, circumstances. He postulated five broad approaches with which psychology can be used to profile offenders.

The first is interpersonal coherence, which proposes that actions performed by criminals make sense within the criminals' own psychology. For instance, the offender will select victims that are consistent with the important characteristics of people who are important to the offender. For example, there is some anecdotal evidence that serial killers only attack those of the same ethnicity as themselves in the United States (Canter, 1989). Therefore, the psychologist should be able to determine something about the offender from the victim and the way the offender interacted with the victim (where this can be determined, such as with rape). The second approach is the significance of place and time. The locations the offender chooses in which to commit the offenses will usually have some sort of significance to the offender. People are unlikely to murder or rape in locations that are unfamiliar to them, as these are crimes of control, and the offender will not be able to feel completely in control in a strange environment. Therefore, if all of the crimes are committed in a certain geographic location, there is a high chance that the offender lives or works around the area. The third approach, criminal characteristics, involves looking at crimes and offenders and seeing if differences can lead to classifications of offenders into categories and subcategories. Canter does not actually provide an example of such as classification, but one attempt to do this has been the FBI Crimes Classification Manual (Douglas, Burgess, Burgess, & Ressler, 1992). Douglas and Olshaker (1995) state that "we set about to organize and classify serious crimes by their behavioral characteristics and explain them in a way that a strictly psychological approach such as DSM [Diagnostic and Statistical Manual of Mental Disorders] has never been able to do" (p. 346). Canter (1994), however, is quite critical of the FBI approach—especially the organized-disorganized dichotomy used by the FBI—arguing that there is too much overlap between the two categories for it to be helpful and that they have no theoretical backing. It will be interesting to see an attempt to derive a system like this by the proponents of IP and see what similarities and differences to the CSA system they come up with.

The fourth approach, criminal career, seeks to take advantage of the observation that criminals do not change the way they commit crimes throughout their criminal career, although they may escalate the crimes. Even escalation, though, may be a result of what has happened to the offender while committing earlier crimes, and it may be possible to negatively extrapolate back to earlier crimes committed by the offender where more evidence might be available. The fifth and final approach is forensic awareness. When a serial offender takes steps to cover his tracks, such as forcing his rape victim to take a bath or combing her pubic hair to remove any of his own hair, it is a clear sign that he has had some previous contact with police. The particular type of forensic awareness displayed by the offender should be a direct indication of the offender's previous police contact, and should help narrow the range of offenders to those with records for particular prior offenses.

Although this has been a fairly brief overview of some of Canter's suggestions, one particular area, that of space and time, has received a reasonable amount of attention and has been empirically tested. Wilson et al. (1997) report that the "circle hypothesis" (as it is referred to in Canter, 1994) is one of the more prominent of the IP theories. This approach is built on the hypothesis that serial offenders will tend to operate within an area where they feel comfortable (e.g., close to their own homes) and has many similarities to the independently developed field of geographic profiling (Holmes & Holmes, 1996). In a recent paper, Godwin and Canter (1997) investigated the spatial behavior of 54 U.S. serial killers, each of whom had killed at least 10 times. They investigated the relationship of the offender's home to the locations at which he encountered and then dumped the bodies of his victims and the changes over time. Godwin and Canter found that the serial killers in the sample were likely to encounter and abduct nearly all of their victims close to their own home. The offender would then travel some distance, usually in a different direction for each offense, to dump the body. They also found, however, as the number of offenses progressed, the offender was more likely to dump the bodies close to home, reflecting perhaps a growing confidence with his ability to remain undetected.

The study by Godwin and Canter (1997) clearly demonstrates that experimental psychology, and IP in particular, does have something to offer police investigating serial crimes. Although psychological profiling alone will not catch an offender, the aim is to supplement police investigative efforts and give the police additional information that might focus their investigation.

Serial Murderers

One of the concepts most frequently associated with criminal profiling is that of the serial offender. This is partly due to some of the conditions under which profiling is most useful, but more to do with the fact that whenever profiling is mentioned in the popular media it is usually in the context of profiling a serial killer. As discussed later, serial offenders have had considerable input into the development of profiling, and any discussion of profiling would be amiss if it were not to discuss serial offenders.

In addition to making good newspaper headlines, serial killers are excellent candidates for criminal profiling. Unlike most offenders, serial killers often spend a great deal of time fantasizing about and executing their crime. The fact that they kill multiple times, generally mutilating their victims, and often demonstrate some sort of psychopathology means that there is frequently a lot of material for profilers to work with (Wilson et al., 1997). These killers generally have no obvious motive for the killing, are the hardest offenders to apprehend, and their crimes are the ones that profiles are most often sought for (Holmes & Holmes, 1996).

Although serial murder has recently captured public attention, it is by no means a new phenomenon. The most well-known serial killer, who has been extensively profiled in recent times, was probably Jack the Ripper, who killed at least five women in the Whitechapel area of London in 1888 (Jenkins, 1994). Yet the term serial killer, popularized by Ressler (Ressler & Shachtman, 1992), is a relatively recent one and the definition is still the subject of some debate. We might think of a serial murderer as an individual who commits a series of homicides over an extended period of time, with at least a few days in between at least some of the killings. This distinction of time between the killings is important to distinguish serial killing from mass murder, in which one person kills many people in a spree, such as the recent Port Arthur massacre in Tasmania.

One of the initial hurdles in defining serial murder is how many people need to be killed before an individual is classified as a serial murderer. This has important implications for research and for the development of profiling. Some believe that two murders are enough to justify the label of serial murder (Holmes & Holmes, 1996), whereas others would argue that up to four murders are necessary (Jenkins, 1994). Whatever cutoff point is chosen, the important question should be whether serial murder (and by extension, serial murderers) is qualitatively and quantitatively different from other murders. Is it simply the number of people that are killed that defines an offender as a serial killer, or is there some fundamental difference between serial killers and all other murderers?

The motive of the serial killer is a subject that is still open to some debate. As mentioned above, many serial killings appear to lack a clear motive, with the victims often not known to the offender and seemingly chosen at random. Ressler et al. (1988) suggest that almost all serial murders are sexual in nature, although their use of the term sexual in this case seems to be inspired by the Freudian notion of psychosexual development. A more current view of both serial murder and serial rape is that it is not about sexual gratification per se, but rather about the exercise of power and control over the victim (Canter, 1994; Egger, 1997). In fact, it seems that there is little difference between serial rape and serial murder, with Egger (1997) observing that it does not take much to turn a violent rape into a murder. Thus, the term sexual might be interpreted in the context of the killer's attempt to sexually control and dominate his victim.

It is important to know the extent of the problem that serial killers pose because they generally require a great deal of effort to apprehend. If serial killers are really a rare phenomenon, then it may not be worth focusing all these resources into profiling them. The problem is, it is not even known with any confidence how many serial killers there are or how many people are the victims of serial killers. In Australia, for example, it seems that serial murderers are reasonably rare, but then there are not that many murders in Australia of any sort. For example, in Australia from 1991–1992 there were 312 murders, with 309 identified suspects/offenders and 42 incidents for which an offender was not identified (Strang, 1993). This is relatively low when we consider that Washington, D.C., a single North American city, has over 500 reported homicides each year (Chappell, 1995). To confuse matters, when serial killers are suspected, they attract much more attention than any other murder. One of the more infamous of the Australian serial killers was John Wayne Glover, the "Granny Killer" who killed six elderly women in 1989 and 1990 in Sydney's North Shore district. According to Hagan (1992), these killings prompted one of the most extensive police investigations in Australia's history.

Serial murder usually involves the killing of a stranger and is therefore hidden somewhere in the crime statistics under the category of stranger homicide. The question is, What proportion of the stranger homicides can be attributed to serial murder? Egger (1990) notes that it is very difficult to tell, but the FBI often tends to take the pessimistic view that most of the stranger homicides are due to serial killers (Ressler et al., 1988). The FBI is probably not a very impartial judge in these matters, because as Jenkins (1996) notes, they have a vested interest in making serial offending seem to be much worse than it is. A more reasonable explanation might be to use the suggestion of Polk (1994) that the majority of these stranger homicides are so-called "honor contests" in which fights between mainly young men, often over a trivial incident, lead to death. Kapardis (1992) also notes that there are at least five separate categories of stranger homicide, and that serial and mass murder only makes up an extremely small proportion of stranger killings in Victoria, Australia.

***

Is Profiling Scientific?

CSA

CSA relies heavily on the experience and intuition of the profiler, both of which are difficult to empirically test. One of the main problems with a scientific analysis of CSA is that its proponents have never felt the need to have it scientifically verified. Yet . . . there are various aspects of this technique that may be amenable to investigation.

***

CSA does have the potential to be scientific (with some work), but the main problem seems to be that it does not want to be scientific. Douglas, the FBI agent who was responsible for hiring profilers for the BSU, states that in a profiler "degrees and academic knowledge [are not] nearly as important as experience and certain subjective qualities" (Douglas & Olshaker, 1997, p. 30). Jenkins (1996) states that criminal profiling is the FBI's special area of expertise, something that they believe that they do better than anyone else in the world. In essence, in the United States at least, the FBI has a monopoly on criminal profiling and it does not look like they are about to endanger that by telling anyone else how it works—or even if it works.

Although there might be some validity to the argument that revealing too much about how profiling is done might reveal to offenders ways in which they can avoid being apprehended (assuming, of course, that serial offenders read psychology or criminology journals), the dangers of not having the techniques open to investigation are even more serious. Canter (1994) states quite succinctly that "a doctor is not expected to operate on hunch and intuition, to learn his trade merely from hearing how others have treated patients in the past, to have no firmly established principles to operate on" (p. 275). Although the experience of police officers is certainly valuable and should not be overlooked, if we have no way of measuring the effectiveness of this approach we may be missing something important.

IP

Unlike CSA, IP was designed from the beginning with science in mind, but this does not mean that it is a science in itself. Canter and his colleagues have attempted to use established psychological principles and research methodology to create a discipline that is empirically sound and open to peer review. IP has a great deal of potential to become a science, but it still has a long way to go before it will be recognized as a discipline in itself.

***

Wilson et al. (1997) claim that one of the main problems with the IP approach to profiling is that it does not actually tell us anything new,

except to propose new avenues to explore. This is probably a somewhat extreme view, as applying the application of psychological knowledge to criminal investigation potentially has great value. Canter has shown that the application of psychological principles and methodologies can, for example, help identify where the offender might live and what his job might be (e.g., Godwin & Canter, 1997). It is very easy for those in academia to remain aloof and remote from the real world, yet this is an attempt to make some practical use of psychology by applying it to genuine social problems.

Even within Great Britain, Canter is not without his critics. Copson et al. (1997) state that "it seems to have been assumed by some observers that Canter's is the only systematic approach to profiling in use in Britain, not least because he says so" (p. 13). Copson and his colleagues, proponents of the DE model of profiling, claim that statistical approaches to profiling (such as those used in IP) are only reliable so long as the data set that they are based on is reliable. As has been mentioned previously, it is extremely difficult to determine even how many serial killers there are, let alone get reliable statistics on their activities and characteristics. They argue that until a more reliable database is built up, the clinical judgment of practitioners is a more reliable way to construct a criminal profile. Although it is true that there is lack of reliable data on serial offenders, criminologists have spent years collecting data on "normal" (i.e., non-serial) rapes and murders, which may be able to contribute to profiling. What is not known, however, is how applicable these data are to serial offenders.

STUDIES CONDUCTED ON PROFILING

CSA

If profiling is to be thought of as a science and a science is defined by the studies that examine its theories, then the defining study for the FBI approach would be that published under the title of *Sexual Homicide: Patterns and Motives* (Ressler et al., 1988). This study is basically the foundation on which the scientific basis of the FBI approach to profiling rests. The fact that there have been so few published studies on the FBI approach means that the scientific credibility of the FBI approach rests solely on this study. The study, which attempts to determine the antecedents of serial murder, presents both qualitative and quantitative data. In the sample examined the researchers find a large amount of support for their hypothesis that the serial offender is the result of a developmental process, with most of the subjects reporting that they had troubled childhoods. For example, 69% of the respondents reported a history of alcohol abuse in their families while growing up, and 74% reported that they were psychologically abused (Ressler et al., 1988). The authors also provide quotes from the offenders that seem to support their hypothesis that most serial homicides are sexual in nature. Unfortunately, this study does have some fundamental flaws, which call into question the legitimacy of the approach.

One of the first things that any social science researcher learns is the danger of using retrospective self-report studies. . . . This research methodology is open to considerable abuse and can be very inaccurate. For example, using the present topic, if you are talking to a person who was a neighbor of a serial killer when he was young, then the subject will be quite likely to selectively recall information that they think will be of interest to the researcher. There is also a very real danger of subjects' lying (e.g., to impress the researcher) and there is often no way to verify the veracity of the data.

The study conducted by Ressler et al. (1988) consisted mainly of interviews with 36 convicted serial killers who were in prison. Most, if not all, serial killers would be classified under DSM-IV (American Psychiatric Association, 1994) as suffering from antisocial personality disorder (Egger, 1997). In the mass media, this usually translates into their being referred to as psychopaths or sociopaths. According to Davison and Neale (1994),

> the adult antisocial personality shows irresponsible and antisocial behaviour by not working consistently, breaking laws, being irritable and physically aggressive, defaulting on debts and being reckless. He or she is impulsive and fails to plan ahead. In addition, he or she shows *no regard for truth* [italics added] nor remorse for misdeeds. (p. 271)

Surely the psychopathic serial killer is the least suitable person on whom to conduct retrospective self-report research. Furthermore, the study included only convicted and imprisoned serial offenders who were willing to participate in the study, which most criminologists would consider to be an unacceptably biased sampling procedure (Wilson et al., 1997). For example, there may be some fundamental difference between those serial offenders who get caught and those who are able to evade capture. Thus, the profiling based on the imprisoned serial offender may not be appropriate for catching all serial offenders.

One of the most important factors of the CSA model of criminal profiling is the dichotomous categorization of offenders as organized or disorganized offenders, but how useful is this distinction? Holmes and Holmes (1996), for example, state that these categories are more useful in "lust killings" than in other sorts of serial murder that do not show evidence of sexual motives. Although the concepts of the organized and disorganized offenders are discussed at length in Ressler et al. (1988), they do not attempt to use the data from the offenders in their sample to support or explain this typology. Ressler and Shachtman (1992) hypothesize that about one third of all serial killers are disorganized offenders and the remaining two thirds are organized offenders, but offer no data to support the claims. Wilson et al. (1997) claim that it is actually more of a continuum between organized and disorganized than two distinct types, with many offenders falling into the mixed category that displays features of both the organized and disorganized offenders.

The real truth is that we simply do not know. As far as the author knows, there have never been any published empirical studies on the differences between various subtypes of serial offenders. The organized/disorganized typology is the brainchild of the BSU, and although they have published information about it, they have never actually articulated any theoretical basis for the typology on which a study might be based.

Ressler et al. (1988) provide an excellent example of how politics and ideology may influence one's objectivity. The FBI, as North America's premier law enforcement organization, is a bastion of White, middle-class, conservative views, a fact admitted by many of the agents themselves (e.g., Douglas & Olshaker, 1995; Ressler & Shachtman, 1992). Is it then surprising that the FBI experts believe that serial killers often come from broken homes (where they are often raised by a single mother) and report daydreaming, masturbation, confusion about sexual preference, and an interest in pornography as features of their childhood?

It is also important to remember that the only thing that has been determined so far is a correlation between factors such as abuse or neglect in childhood and serial killers. This does not imply that serial offending is causally related to an individual's having a difficult childhood or an obsession with pornography. Egger (1997) describes one serial killer, Arthur Shawcross, who did not show any evidence of coming from a dysfunctional or violent family. Rather than the antecedents of Shawcross's offending being environmental, as CSA might argue, they appeared more to be biological with Shawcross being involved in a number of serious accidents, some of which involved cerebral concussion. Examples such as this tend to cast doubt on the validity of the CSA paradigm of the development of serial offending.

IP

The most obvious of the studies conducted on IP, in which Godwin and Canter (1997) investigated the spatial patterns of serial murderers in the United States, has been described in some detail previously. Professor Canter and many of his colleagues have a history in experimental psychology, and several other studies have been published in the psychological and criminological literature. As yet there has not been a great deal of experimental work on the core features of IP, that of the narrative of the offender and how it is reflected in the crimes. Some of the other research that the IP department at the University of Liverpool are working on includes the decision-making process of detectives, psychological autopsies (investigating the course of actions that leads to an assault) and investigative interviewing ("What Is Investigative Psychology?" 1997).

Although the overall paradigm itself has not been experimentally tested, some of the theories that contribute to IP have. In one example, Canter and Kirby (1995) look at the conviction history of child molesters. This study investigated the validity of the common assumption that child molesters will have a history of sexually deviant behavior and assaults on children, and that these men will escalate their offending from minor to more serious sexual offenses. Interestingly, they found that these assumptions, which are often held by police officers, had no empirical basis. They found that these offenders were more likely to have had a history of convictions for theft, burglary, and violent offenses than for prior minor sexual offenses. They also found that there was little evidence to suggest escalation from less serious offenses. For example, very few of the men who were child molesters had any history of indecent exposure.

The Canter and Kirby (1995) study has very obvious implications for profiling sexual offenders, as it suggests strategies for narrowing the range of potential suspects by suggesting the offenses that the offender is more likely to have been convicted of in his past. A less obvious implication of this study is for CSA, where the assumptions and preconceptions that the profilers have about certain offenders greatly influence the profile. This study suggests that in the case of child molesters these assumptions are likely to lead the profile astray.

An interesting point to note about the Canter and Kirby (1995) study is that it does not seem to fit within the paradigm of the criminal narrative. This could be taken as evidence that IP is not scientific, as the paradigm is not broad or thorough enough to cover all of the work in the area. Another way to look at it, however, is as providing a less direct support for the paradigm. Canter (1994) does not just believe that criminals have narratives but that all people do, and that these narratives are developed by the individual's experiences of interacting with the world. Canter (1994) notes that police officers also tend to have rather limited narratives, with their explanations of how criminals operate formed mainly from their experience of police work and by what they observe in the courts. What Canter and Kirby (1995) have demonstrated is that, at least in regard to sex offenders, the narratives that the police have to explain the behavior of sex offenders may be too limited and are in some cases misleading. Although this does not directly support the idea of criminal narratives, it does provide some support for the narrative per se, and thus does fit within the paradigm of IP.

Other Related Studies

***

In probably the most comprehensive experimental study on profiling conducted to date, Pinizzotto and Finkel (1990) examined profiles conducted by professional profilers, detectives, psychologists, and students for a series of cases. The study was looking at whether the accuracy of the profiles differed between the groups and whether there was a qualitative difference between the profilers and the non-profilers in the process in which the profile was constructed. The accuracy of the profilers varied depending on the case, with the profilers more accurate than all of the other groups combined in the sex offender case, but these same profilers not especially accurate for the homicide. With regard to the sex offender case, the profilers were significantly more accurate for items such as the gender, age, and education of the offender. In the homicide case, however, the detectives were significantly more accurate than the profilers in regard to the offender's employment and the relationship of the offender's residence to the crime scene. It was also found that the profilers wrote richer, more detailed reports than the non-profilers and that the profilers recalled more details that were necessary to generate the profile. There are, of course, some problems with the study. The psychologists and students used, for instance, had no special interest in policing or profiling, so it would be expected that those who have to construct profiles for a living were both better prepared and more invested in the process, and thus tried harder than the non-profilers (Pinizzotto & Finkel, 1990).

Does It Actually Work?

In asking profiling to be scientific, we are trying to establish with some reliability whether profiling is of any use to us. Many police officers have shown a great deal of skepticism about profiling, partly due to the fact that they see apprehending offenders as their particular area of expertise, but also because it is still such a poorly developed field (e.g., Davies, 1994). As has been discussed above, the experimental evidence is still not overwhelming, but studies such as those conducted by Pinizzotto and Finkel (1990) suggest that profiling might have some validity. Experimental verification is not what will win the police over, however. Police still persist in using psychics to help them solve difficult cases, although Wiseman and West (1997) have shown experimentally that there is absolutely no validity to the claims made by psychics in regard to criminal investigations.

The real test of profiling is not experimental studies in the laboratory, but evaluations on how well profiling actually performs in practice. Wilson et al. (1997) suggest, somewhat naively, that after looking at the track record of profiling so far the suggestion is that it works. They base this claim on a case study of selected high profile crimes, but do not give any references or source for the data. The main problem with this claim is that it is purely anecdotal. Related to that is the problem of reporting bias, as we are only likely to hear about cases in which profiling has been used if the case was successfully resolved and the profile was accurate.

Organizations such as the FBI are, understandably, reluctant to release figures on the successes and failures of the profiles that they provide. Although figures such as an 80% success rate have been circulated (e.g., Ressler & Shachtman, 1992), there has yet to be any data put forward to substantiate this claim. According to Ressler et al. (1988), the accuracy of each profile is looked at after an offender has been apprehended so that the profilers may learn from their errors. The evaluation is not performed in public, and most people have no knowledge of how accurate profiles actually are. This is becoming increasingly important, as more private individuals are commissioning profiles themselves (or requesting that the investigating police do) for cases in which they have an interest. We would not tolerate other participants in criminal investigations (such as forensic DNA analysts) withholding data on the effectiveness of their techniques, so why do we tolerate it with psychological profiling?

There is also the question as to how accurate a profile actually has to be to be of help to the investigating authorities. Obviously an incorrect profile has the potential to mislead the investigation, but this may only be a problem if the police place a greater amount of faith in the profile than they do in their own investigative skills. Pinizzotto (cited in Wilson et al., 1997), for example, found that from 192 requests for profiles, only 17% actually were used to help identify the suspect. More positively, 77% of the respondents reported that the profile had helped them to focus their investigation. Overall, however, if profiles are consistently found to be incorrect in at least some aspects, police will quickly lose faith in their worth.

CONCLUSIONS

Offender profiling, in all its various guises, is still very much a discipline that is yet to be proved. Unlike much of psychology or criminology, the accuracy of an offender profile may have profound implications. If a profile of an offender is wrong or even slightly inadequate police may be misled, allowing the offender to escape detection for a little while longer—and innocent people may be dead as a result. This is not to say that we should ignore profiles or that police should not use them, but that we should approach profiling with caution. We should not blindly accept or rely on something that may not have any relationship to the truth. This article has demonstrated that, of the two main approaches to offender profiling, IP is easily more scientific than CSA. Whereas IP has produced testable hypotheses and has several empirical studies to back up its claims, CSA is based mainly on experience and intuition of police officers and is not particularly amenable to testing. We cannot say which approach is more successful (defining successful as providing information that results in more arrests) as there is no reliable published information on the effectiveness of the various approaches. There is a great deal of anecdotal evidence supporting CSA and it is more widely depicted in the press than IP; yet this is not enough to indicate that it is significantly more successful than IP. Clearly, the effectiveness of the approaches is a subject in which more investigation is needed.

7

POLICE INTERROGATIONS AND FALSE CONFESSIONS

JAIME S. HENDERSON

Many people believe they know when someone is lying, and in most cases, they will assert this knowledge with a great level of certainty. However, research has consistently demonstrated that the general public, as well as law enforcement officers, is generally overconfident in its assessments as to whether a person is being honest. Granhag and Stromwall (2001b) report that higher rates of accuracy are shown in detecting truthful statements than deceptive statements and that there is a very weak correlation between accuracy and confidence.

What makes people so confident they can detect deception, and why are they unable to do so? Many researchers have examined these questions and have concluded that a combination of social, cognitive, and situational factors plays a significant role in the decision-making process. In addition, individual stereotypes about liars may impede unbiased thought processes (Granhag & Stromwall, 2001b). For example, many people believe that a liar will not look you in the eye or will display other incriminating nonverbal behavior, such as foot tapping.

Deception detection is an integral part of the interrogation process in law enforcement. Police officers must determine whether the suspect is being truthful or dishonest. This decision can be monumental, especially in cases lacking forensic or corroborating evidence. Are we confident enough in human observation and decision-making processes to allow officers to assume guilt or innocence based only on interrogation? In a study of deception-detection abilities among police, Mann, Vrij, and Bull (2004) discovered accuracy rates only above the level of chance. Officers often focused on body language to determine truth and relied upon information provided in police manuals (e.g., Inbau, Reid, Buckley, & Jayne, 2001). As will be noted in this article, it is difficult to discern truth from lies based solely on determinants such as eye movements, squirming, sweating, and one's intuition.

Police officers often employ some form of interrogation tactic(s) based on their initial assessment of the suspect. Although these psychological approaches in the interrogation room may serve a purpose and play a hand in eliciting a confession, the interrogative method also has adverse effects. Given the right circumstances, which can be a combination of factors that will be later addressed in detail, the suspect may divulge incriminating—but false—information. False confessions do occur during the investigation process, though it is difficult to document an actual false confession rate. As

Kassin (1997, p. 224) points out, "a confession may be true even if it is coerced and even if the accused retracts the statement and proceeds to trial, and a confession may be false even if the defendant is convicted, imprisoned, and never heard from again."

Social science research in this arena has fallen into several categories, including direct observation of actual police interrogations, exploration into psychological vulnerabilities of individuals claiming to have made a false confession at some point in their life, and study of the characteristics of interrogators. This chapter begins with a brief legal history, an overview of the forms of false confessions, and the importance of confession evidence. It then discusses in more detail the research in the above categories.

LEGAL HISTORY

The Fifth Amendment of the U.S. Constitution specifies several citizens' rights, including the right not to incriminate oneself in criminal matters. Even before the landmark ruling in *Miranda v. Arizona* (1966), the U.S. Supreme Court had heard a number of cases relating to Fifth Amendment rights during police interrogations (i.e., *Ashcraft v. Tennessee,* 1944; *Bram v. United States,* 1897; *Brown v. Mississippi,* 1936; *Escobedo v. Illinois,* 1964). In the *Miranda* case, the Supreme Court ruled police must inform suspects, prior to custodial interrogation, of their constitutional rights to silence and appointed counsel. The dynamic involved in interrogations is unavoidably daunting, thereby weakening an individual's resistance against self-incrimination. Because of the inherent, intimidating nature of the interrogation process, statements must clearly be made by the free will of the suspect. The Court was aware of coercive interrogation tactics being used on suspects and sought to protect suspects as well as deter police officials from engaging in questionable techniques.

The legal history of Supreme Court cases surrounding interrogations and confession evidence has established rules of engagement for police and their suspects, rules that are often bent or ignored. In the years since *Miranda,* the Supreme Court has issued a number of rulings both clarifying its decision and narrowing its scope (see, generally, Thomas & Leo (2002). Although these decisions are not reviewed here, it is important to note that a recent challenge to the *Miranda* warnings has been overcome. In *Dickerson v. U.S.* (2000), the Court reaffirmed that Miranda rights were established law, and all suspects should be made fully aware of these rights prior to custodial interrogation.

FALSE CONFESSIONS

Numerous factors contribute to the elicitation of a false confession. These factors include various aspects concerning the suspect, the interrogator(s), and the crime in question. Researchers have discovered that confessions, in general, are most likely when the evidence against suspects is strong (Gudjonsson, 1999; Moston, Stephenson, & Williamson, 1992; Softley, 1980). Therefore, police may suggest or even pretend that they have evidence in an effort to get a suspect to confess. "Typically, false confessions arise from a combination of factors which have to do with decision-making processes, psychological vulnerabilities, and interpersonal and custodial influences" (Gudjonsson, 1999, p. 417).

Types and Definitions

False confessions exist in several forms and have different components. Kassin and Wrightsman (1985) differentiated three types of false confessions: voluntary, coerced-compliant, and coerced-internalized. A *voluntary* confession involves "spontaneous incriminating statements made without external pressure" (Horselenberg, Merckelbach, & Josephs, 2003, p. 1). In other words, the suspect knows he or she is innocent, yet deliberately misleads police. This might occur to protect another person or, more likely, to achieve some notoriety. By contrast, suspects may firmly believe in their innocence, yet offer a *coerced-compliant* confession to avoid being subjected to an uncomfortable interrogation, elude harm possibly threatened by interrogators, or ensure the receipt of a promised deal or benefit (Kassin & Kiechel, 1996). The third type—*coerced-internalized* confessions—are delivered by suspects who come to believe they actually committed the crime and thus disclose their "guilt."

Although the last seems implausible, research (Kassin & Kiechel, 1996; Horselenberg et al., 2003) has shown that people will sign a false confession, actually believing they committed a wrong, particularly in the presence of false incriminating evidence. Surprisingly, participants in one research project were manipulated to sign a false confession even when there were negative consequences for the actions to which they were admitting (Horselenberg et al., 2003). With respect to police interrogations, Kassin and Kiechel (1996) suggest that internalized confessions may be induced by the presentation of false incriminating evidence. For example, a suspect may be told that an eyewitness saw him entering the premises of a store at the time it was robbed. The suspect may begin to believe there is a real possibility of guilt simply because the evidence points in his direction.

Research has also suggested that it is possible for someone to deliver a coerced-compliant confession without demonstrating any glaring psychological impairments (Santilla, Alkiora, Magnus, Ekholm, & Niemi, 1999). One need not be suffering from psychosis or a neurotic disorder to fall victim to individual and situational factors, as well as to pressure as a result of tactics used by the interrogator(s). However, there is evidence that persons with personality disorders may be susceptible to making false confessions to police (Gudjonsson, 1999, 2003).

Gudjonsson and Clark (1986) identified two types of false confessors. The first consists of individuals who confessed because, at the time of interrogation, they believed they probably had committed the crime, but later came to the realization that this may not have been so. Such might occur in the case of a substance abuser whose memory of events was impaired. The second group, which research indicates is the larger of the two, is comprised of suspects who knew they were innocent the entire time, but confessed to alleviate the pressure of interrogation. This second group is found to be more compliant, while the first group tends to be more suggestible.

Although it is impossible to determine the rate of false confessions, some researchers have studied confessions that were later proved to be false. Leo and Ofshe (1998, p. 449) identify four subtypes of these confessions: "the suspect confessed to a crime that never happened, evidence clearly demonstrates that the defendant could not possibly have committed the crime, the true perpetrator was identified and his guilt established, or the defendant was exonerated by scientific evidence." While these may seem obvious, courts in some of these cases were unaware of the circumstances or failed to acknowledge them and upheld the confession over all other evidence.

Confession Evidence

Confessions are more persuasive than other forms of incriminating evidence (Kassin, Goldstein, & Savistsky, 2003; Trowbridge, 2003). Mock jurors were more likely to convict based on a confession, even when they believed the confession was coerced, suggesting that confessions increased conviction rates (Kassin et al., 2003, Leo & Ofshe, 1998). However, recent case law suggests judges should exclude confessions obtained by promises or threats (Kassin, 1997). Some trickery, though, is permitted. Kassin (1997) identifies the specific problems or dangers associated with confession evidence.

> Police routinely use deception, trickery, and psychologically coercive methods of interrogation; . . . these methods may, at times, cause innocent people to confess to crimes they didn't commit; and . . . when coerced self-incriminating statements are presented in the courtroom, juries do not sufficiently discount the evidence in reaching a verdict. (p. 221)

There are three factors of reliability when interpreting confessions. If at least one of the three criteria are met, there is high likelihood that the confession is genuine and should serve as evidence. The three criteria are as follows: unknown evidence is discovered as a direct result of the confession, very specific and unusual crime facts are revealed that were unknown to the public, or crime details not easily guessed or known to the public are revealed during the confession (Leo & Ofshe, 1998).

However, detectives operate under a "visibility cover" that shields decision-making processes from colleagues or the public, and they do not necessarily consider the reliability of a confession. The assessments they make must be taken at face value (Williams, 2000, p. 228). One may simply suggest audio or videotaping all confessions to remedy this issue—in fact, the trend today is to tape confessions. Nevertheless, Granhag and Stromwall (2001a, p. 87) caution against relying too heavily on videotapes, because interrogators "pay more attention to different cues when interacting with a suspect than do observers watching the same suspect on video."

Interrogators have the advantage of experiencing the dynamic face to face. Video or audiotapes are just one segment of the entire process and may not be representative of the entire history and context of interactions between police and the suspect (Williams, 2000). "Taping neglects the prevalence of interviewing and questioning outside the police station and prior to the official interrogation itself, and the video mitigates any appreciation for the ideologies, working rules and techniques which influence and condition officer-suspect interactions" (Williams, 2000, p. 231).

Expert testimony on coercive police interrogation tactics and coerced confessions may assist individuals who have succumbed to police pressure. This testimony may also clarify relevant research to the jury. It is not guaranteed that the courts will allow expert testimony, however. In cases where experts are allowed to testify, the outcome may be beneficial for the confessor. In *United States v. Hall* (1997), the defendant's kidnapping conviction was overturned by the Seventh Circuit Court of Appeals because expert testimony concerning police coercion was erroneously excluded in the trial court proceedings. The court ruled that an expert witness should have been allowed to testify about the susceptibility of the suspect to falsely confess.

There are varying interpretations of what defines coercion, threatening behavior, deceit, and trickery in the interrogation room (Baldwin, 1993). Tapes of interrogations may present a biased perspective, and police officers, courts, lawyers, and judges believe it easier to detect lies in person (Granhag & Stromwall, 2001a). Therefore, it is not surprising to learn that "few confessions are ever challenged in court, and

fewer still are challenged successfully" (Baldwin, 1993, p. 326).

INTERROGATIONS

Police interrogations are essentially custodial in nature, which is to say that the individual being questioned is not free to leave. Prior to interrogations, police may interview individuals of interest, including individuals who are not suspected of a crime. These interviews are "designed to obtain clarification and elaboration of the relevant facts from witnesses, potential witnesses, victims or informants" (Bartol & Bartol, 2004b, p. 265). During the interview, officers may make the pivotal decision that there is cause to consider someone a suspect and move to the interrogation phase. "The primary purpose of criminal interrogation is to obtain a confession from a suspect or to gain information that will lead to a conviction" (Bartol & Bartol, 2004b, p. 262).

Kassin et al. (2003) acknowledge two problems with the transition from interview to interrogation. First, no empirical evidence suggests that police officers are adept at determining truth from dishonesty at high levels of accuracy. Second, proceeding to the interrogation stage leads police to have a somewhat biased approach if they operate under the assumption that the suspect is guilty (Granhag & Stromwall, 2001b; Gudjonsson, 2003; Kassin et al., 2003, Mann et al., 2004).

Interrogation Techniques

Kassin and McNall (1991) identify two general interrogation approaches, minimization and maximization. Minimization is a technique "in which the detective lulls the suspect into a false sense of security by providing face-saving excuses, citing mitigating circumstances, blaming the victim, and underplaying the charges" (Kassin & Kiechel, 1996, p. 125). Conversely, maximization involves "scare tactics designed to intimidate a suspect believed to be guilty" (Kassin, 1997, p. 223). Interrogators employ various methods within these two approaches in the quest for a confession. They may present false evidence, tag-team the suspect with good-cop/bad-cop acts, use information obtained from prison informants, fake friendship, and at times play the religion card (Kassin & Kiechel, 1996).

Approaches taken by police may differ in the absence of evidence or when the evidence is circumstantial or weak. The strategies they use may become more persuasive, and the line of questioning becomes even more dependent on feedback from interrogators. Moston and Stephenson (1993) identify five questioning tactics that are independent of evidence in the interrogation. The first is simple *repetition,* commonly referred to as probing. This involves repeating a question, suggesting to the suspect that his or her answer was either wrong or unacceptable. As a second tactic, the interrogator may pause after the suspect has delivered a response; this *silence approach* is used to encourage the suspect to elaborate on an answer.

The most common form of feedback provided when evidence is lacking is the outright *accusatorial method* that involves insults or straightforward statements implying the suspect is lying. The fourth tactic entails *comments on body language.* An interrogator may claim the suspect's body language indicates he or she is being untruthful. Individuals who believe interrogators possess these diagnostic skills may become extremely unnerved at such comments (Moston & Stephenson, 1993). The final approach commonly used when officials lack evidence is *attempting to elicit sympathy for the victim* from the suspect. Interrogators attempt to induce in the suspect feelings of guilt or entitlement to the victim or the victim's family. They may also suggest that if a confession is delivered, the subject might not have to testify in court.

The most widely used technique for police interrogations is the Reid technique, outlined in Inbau et al.'s *Criminal Interrogations and Confession* (2001). The Reid technique consists of nine steps that "are designed to overcome resistance by confronting the suspect with their guilt, followed by the offering of sympathy, understanding and an alternative theme that minimizes the moral seriousness of the act" (Kassin et al., 2003, p. 188). Bartol (1983) posits that police manuals generally recommend a persistent line of questioning geared at obtaining specific information. Unfortunately, asking

closed, leading questions may increase the suggestibility of the suspect and decrease the accuracy of responses.

Many techniques recommend that the interrogator enhance the method with underlying psychological principles. Bartol and Bartol (2004b) identify three psychological principles commonly employed by interrogators: psychological control, tension induction, and interrogator confidence. Basically, the interrogator must confidently exert and maintain control over the entire proceeding, while creating tension for the suspect in hopes of inducing a confession.

Varying techniques also include different forms of questions. The inquiries may be accusatorial in nature such as, "You disposed of the weapon, didn't you?" Conversely, the questions may be an information-gathering strategy that utilizes open-ended questions such as, "Tell me what happened after you left the bar." Accusatorial questions tend to be used when the evidence against the suspect is very strong (Stephenson & Moston, 1994). The timing and the context in which the interrogator chooses to use the differing strategies are crucial.

Empirical Research on Interrogations

Leo (1996) spent nine months observing the interrogation process within an urban police department. Based on these experiences, he likened the interrogation to a "confidence game based on the manipulation and betrayal of trust" (Leo, 1996, p. 259). He outlines four distinct stages in the interrogation/confidence game (Leo, 1996, p. 262). The first stage, *qualifying the suspect,* involves an assessment of the suspect and the facts of the case. The case file must be read in its entirety, and the interrogator decides which interrogative tactic to employ based on his or her impression of the suspect and the case facts.

Next, the interrogator must *cultivate the suspect.* "The interrogator must encourage the suspect to respond to his overtures, and induce a submissive mood in the suspect" (Leo, 1996, p. 263). Casual banter may be exchanged, or the interrogator may choose intimidation as a tool. Either way, the *Miranda* waiver must be negotiated in full detail before the interrogation can proceed (Leo, 1996). That is, the suspect must agree to answer questions, preferably without the assistance of an attorney.

The interrogator must then focus on *conning the suspect* into confessing. This can be the pivotal point in the interrogation, as the interrogator is essentially seeking the suspect's trust and asking the suspect to do the right thing and confess (Leo, 1996). It is during this stage that false confessions may potentially occur. The suspect must trust the investigator, who is the major source of information the suspect has during that process.

The final step outlined by Leo is *cooling off the suspect*. This is important for many reasons. The officer knows that once counsel enters the picture, the legality of the confession may be challenged. The interrogator wants the suspect to take responsibility for his or her actions and to believe confessing was the right decision (Leo, 1996). Interestingly, Leo discovered that most suspects did not see through the confidence game employed by officers and believed the tactics they used.

In another research project, Baldwin (1993) paints a much tamer picture of the interrogation process. This was, though, a study of interrogations in Great Britain and may not be representative of those conducted in the United States. Baldwin's study included 600 video and audiotapes of interrogations. Based on numerous observations, he concluded that there is considerable mythology surrounding interrogations. Baldwin observed that—contrary to popular belief—most interrogations involved amenable suspects and uncomplicated exchanges between the interrogator and suspect. Baldwin did not detect much resistance or belligerence on behalf of the suspect or the interrogator in his sample. In a majority of cases, the interrogator simply asked what happened and listened as the suspect disclosed information.

Moston and Stephenson (1993) conducted a study including more than 1,000 interrogations, also in Great Britain. Within this sample, the evidence suggested that suspects were not generally coerced to confess against their will, and those who claimed innocence at the beginning of the interrogation process maintained their innocence through the entire interrogation. Moston et al. (1992) found three characteristics that appeared influential in the outcome of interrogations: strength of evidence, offense severity, and legal advice. The most powerful factor was strength of evidence; that is, when the evidence against the suspect is overwhelming it is highly likely the suspect will confess. Surprisingly, the type of offense and the suspect's criminal history were not associated with the outcome of interrogations in this study (Moston et al., 1992).

SUSPECTS

As previously established, no single factor can explain a false confession. A multitude of circumstances and factors contribute to the phenomenon. Most interesting, perhaps, are characteristics involving the suspect. Which individual characteristics, along with personal cognitions, take an active role in the suspect's decision to confess to a crime he or she did not commit? To answer this question, many researchers use the Gudjonsson Suggestibility Scales (GSS; Gudjonsson, 1997). These scales are used to determine the extent to which people will give in to leading questions and to what degree stories may be altered in the presence of negative feedback from the interrogator. The GSS were developed primarily for use in forensic settings, such as criminal interrogation. (However, they are primarily a research tool and are not routinely administered by police as part of the interrogation process. Alternately, an expert witness testifying to the possibility that a confession was not made voluntarily could allude to a suspect's score on the GSS.)

Gudjonsson and Clark (1986, p. 84) define interrogative suggestibility as "the extent to which, within a closed social interaction, people come to accept messages communicated during formal questioning, as the result of which their subsequent behavioral response is affected." People are active recipients of suggestive influences from individuals with whom they are interacting, as well as the social and physical environments that serve as the source of suggestibility for suspects subjected to interrogation (Gudjonsson & Clark, 1986). Gudjonsson (1991) also asserts that interrogative suggestibility is different than other traditionally defined types of suggestibility, which can be reliably measured using the Gudjonsson Suggestibility Scales.

Coping strategies that suspects develop and employ when dealing with the uncertainty and expectations during interrogations are important components of interrogative suggestibility (Gudjonsson, 1991). Suspects may be hesitant to admit uncertainty and feel as if they are expected to generate quality answers that may or may not be true. Interrogators need to be very aware of the expectations suspects may perceive.

Gudjonsson (1999) discovered that low scores on the Gough Socialization Scale, higher scores on the EPQ Neurotic Scale, and elevated scores on the Gudjonsson Compliance Scales distinguished the false confessors from the other offenders. In addition, as noted previously, persons diagnosed with personality disorder have been shown to be susceptible to making false confessions to the police (Gudjonsson, 1999, 2003). In a sample of college students, self-reported delinquency, impulsivity, and antisocial personality characteristics were significant predictors of past false confessions to authority figures such as teachers and parents (Gudjonsson, Sigurdsson, & Einarsson, 2004).

Other individual factors found to be positively associated with interrogative suggestibility are acquiescence, anxiety, situational stress, and the tendency to confabulate (Gudjonsson, 2003; Santtila et al., 1999). Based on research conducted by Gudjonsson (1991, 1999, 2003) interrogative suggestibility and compliance appear to be the psychological characteristics most relevant to cases of false confessions. Santilla et al. (1999) administered a self-report questionnaire to prisoners; results revealed that false confessors claimed to be more compliant than other prisoners. Researchers also suggest that guilt and shame may create an emotional state conducive to delivering a false confession.

Inevitably, there are occasions in which interrogations proceed for very long periods of time. There have been documented cases where suspects who were sleep deprived and not using all of their mental faculties confessed simply out of exhaustion (Blagrove, 1996). Similar circumstances with drug addicts are likely to elicit a confession as the suspect is suffering from withdrawal, coupled by extreme emotional reactions (Santilla et al., 1999). However, such confessions are susceptible to being suppressed by courts, if it is demonstrated that they were not given after a knowing, intelligent waiver of the right to remain silent.

Moston et al. (1992) note that along with interrogation techniques, a suspect's background, offense characteristics, and contextual factors may determine the suspect's initial response to an allegation. However, Moston and Stephenson (1993) discovered that suspects with a criminal record were not more likely to confess than were suspects without a criminal record. Baldwin (1993) reported suspects usually stuck with their initial claim of innocence, guilt, or somewhere in between. Of the 600 cases in his study, only 20 were persuaded to change their story. Irving and Hilgendorf (1980) state that in situations where suspects lack information about the effect of decisions, or about the long-term consequences at stake, their decision making will be impaired due to lack of information available to them. All they know is the information provided by the interrogator.

INTERROGATORS

False confessions induced by police officers may be one of the most crucial official errors (Leo & Ofshe, 1998). As gatekeepers to the criminal justice system, police officers make the initial decisions and gather the evidence that determines whether individuals will be prosecuted. A confession is, of course, a key piece of evidence. Therefore, it is not surprising that a large majority of research on police interrogations focuses on the interrogators themselves, their techniques, how they interpret the information provided by the suspect, and the accuracy of that interpretation. As previously noted, the interrogation may be a means of legitimizing a police theory concerning a crime. Therefore, the motives as well as the integrity of the interrogator are subject to scrutiny.

Law enforcement agencies are constantly under pressure to solve cases, especially those alarming the community. This pressure can create a police attitude prime for eliciting false confessions. "Interrogators sometimes become so committed to closing a case that they improperly use psychological interrogation techniques to coerce or persuade a suspect into giving a statement that allows an arrest" (Leo & Ofshe, 1998, p. 440).

It is common belief among law enforcement officials that they are able to discern whether a suspect is being truthful or deceptive, particularly when the suspect is questioned in a nonconfrontational manner (Inbau et al., 2001; Mann et al., 2004; Meissner & Kassin, 2002). Unfortunately, experience and training lead officers to believe they can make these judgments with high accuracy by observing verbal and nonverbal cues (Inbau et al., 2001; Mann et al., 2004; Meissner & Kassin, 2002). Rarely are police instructed in how to avoid eliciting false confessions or to be cognizant of what may serve as the impetus for a false confession. Additionally, law enforcement officers are unaware of the forms false confessions may take and their distinguishing characteristics. Manuals insist that the techniques provided therein will not produce false confessions (Inbau et al., 2001; Leo, 1996).

During his observational study of police interrogations, many police officers told Leo (1996) that they rely on a sixth sense to assist in determining the suspect's guilt or innocence. This is distressing considering the fact that research has shown humans are not always accurate judges of truth and deception. Police officers also admit to believing no innocent person can be coerced into a false confession, even when police employ the most intimidating tactics (Inbau et al., 2001; Leo, 1996). Apparently, this misconception has influenced court decisions as well. In 1983, the North Carolina Supreme Court allowed questionable interrogation tactics in *State v. Jackson.* A police officer had fabricated evidence against the suspect by photographing a knife covered in blood with fingerprints and informing the suspect positive fingerprint identification had been made. Although the officer clearly fabricated evidence to elicit a confession, the Court felt the tactics were constitutional, because they would not make an innocent person confess.

Often, interrogations begin under a presumption of guilt made by the interrogator. This presumption has been shown to bias the interrogator's interpretations of verbal and nonverbal cues during the interrogation (Kassin et al., 2003). When interrogators assume guilt in this way, they may develop tunnel vision. Williams (2000) explains that police are susceptible to tunnel vision and that it heavily influences the techniques they choose to apply. Therefore, this may lead to self-fulfilling prophecy, in which all information divulged by the suspect is concordant with the interrogator's beliefs. Meissner and Kassin (2002) assert that while training and experience may increase an individual's ability to detect deception, it may also increase bias.

Research has demonstrated a probing effect. Suspects who are probed, or asked the same questions repeatedly, are viewed as more believable when their answers are consistent (Granhag & Stromwall, 2001a, 2001b). There is also thought to be a primacy effect, in which information processed early in a sequence of questions may carry more weight than information introduced later (Granhag & Stromwall, 2001b). These researchers also found that consistency among details of the confession was the most common cue used to determine truthfulness.

Past studies indicate that the social status of the interrogator potentially influences the suspect as well (Gudjonsson & Clark, 1986). Interrogators who appear to be well informed and articulate and who exude confidence and authority may create more demand characteristics during the encounter than perhaps a new officer fumbling through the case file while questioning the suspect erratically. Expression of demand characteristics may be implicit or explicit, providing cues for the suspect as to how he or she should respond (Gudjonsson & Clark, 1986). It is imperative that individuals interrogating suspects are mindful of the demand characteristics and observer bias that exist within this unique interaction. Interestingly, though, a study conducted by Kassin and Norwick (2004) demonstrated that regardless of the detective's disposition (neutral, sympathetic, or hostile) participants believed their own innocence was enough to ensure freedom. As a result of this confidence in innocence, over half of the respondents waived their *Miranda* rights.

In general, it is believed that feedback provided by interrogators can guide the suspect's responses. Gudjonsson and Clark (1986) assert that negative feedback has a more profound effect on the suspect than positive feedback. Depending on the intensity of the feedback, it is suggested that negative feedback has a direct effect on an individual's mood, altering the suspect's confidence level as well. If the mood change is detected by interrogators, it may be misinterpreted as a sign of guilt, further complicating the situation. Feedback provided by interrogators may shift the suspect's focus from his or her own mental faculties to responding to cues from the interrogator. Law enforcement agencies must be thorough and attempt to restrain any personal biases. Officers should routinely compare information elicited in confessions with facts of the case.

CONCLUSION

The reluctance to believe that innocent people would confess to a crime they did not commit is not merely a feature within the criminal justice system, but reflects cultural beliefs as well (Gudjonsson, 1999). Yet, 22 hours of intense interrogation involving psychological games coupled with sleep deprivation and false incriminating evidence may have anyone questioning his or her innocence.

It is imperative that interrogators increase their awareness of false confessions and modify techniques where necessary to further legitimize the interrogation process. Law enforcement agencies must be thorough and attempt to restrain any personal biases. Officers should routinely compare information elicited in confessions with facts of the case. Nevertheless, as Williams (2000, p. 228) states, officers depart from the law when they feel it is justified. They may act on a noble cause in which they see themselves as acting in the best interest of the public or they may genuinely believe that the suspect in custody is guilty.

It is clear that there are problems with the police interrogation process, and there have been some efforts at reform. These reforms have taken two approaches, court decisions and legislative changes geared at protecting the suspect's rights and the use of audio and videotapes to increase the accountability of police decisions and reports (Williams, 2000).

Countries other than the United States have taken measures to address concerns of false confessions. In England, for example, all interrogations are videotaped, and all law enforcement officers in England and Wales receive training in the cognitive interview (Trowbridge, 2003), which avoids using suggestive or leading questions. Research has indicated that cognitive interviewing techniques improve witness recall (Trowbridge, 2003). Though there may be a trend in the direction of videotaping confessions in the United States, this does not always extend to the entire interrogation.

Past efforts to stimulate change in interrogation tactics have failed for many reasons. Williams (2000, p. 225) explains that suspects do not always completely comprehend their rights and may not be able to adequately communicate this. Further, working rules within police departments create loopholes or maneuvers that allow officers to effectively avoid legally mandated changes.

Legislative reforms have been unsuccessful for similar reasons. According to Williams (2000), the inadequacy of legislation is due to the ambiguity and inconsistency of our legal system in regard to procedures and guidelines. Police officers work under a low visibility and have a position of high autonomy, thus making it difficult to monitor their actions. Finally, the legislation cannot effectively deal with the resistance of police working rules. New and innovative tactics will continually circumvent the legal system wherever officers feel it necessary to do the job as they see fit.

Stephenson and Moston (1994, p. 157) point out that "there is a conflict of interest between interviewer [interrogator] and suspects, which makes it inappropriate, at least in England, to abandon entirely their confession-oriented approach." Clearly, this is the case for law enforcement officials in the United States as well. Blaming law enforcement officers for eliciting false confessions is not the answer. It has been established that factors pertaining to the suspect—for example, suggestibility or desire for notoriety—contribute to the false confession as well. Moreover, police officers only know what they are taught. If interrogation manuals claim that these tactics, when employed properly, will not result in a false confession, officers cannot be expected to be cognizant of the serious ramifications. Furthermore, officers may simply be modeling interrogation behaviors of their mentors or predecessors. Undoubtedly, a more objective approach is necessary. It would be beneficial to include the topic of false confessions in interrogation training.

Finally, although considerable research has been generated concerning interrogation tactics and false confessions, there is need for more. Additional research should be geared toward those who are intricately involved in the interrogation process. In addition, prominent researchers in the area must continue to communicate the results of their studies to the police community and other professionals within the criminal justice system (e.g., judges and lawyers). It may not be too optimistic to hope that some of this research may find its way into the hands of police academy educators and law enforcement training manuals.

UNIT 3

CRIMINAL AND DELINQUENT BEHAVIOR

Introduction and Commentary

Among criminologists, explanations (or theories) of juvenile delinquency and criminal behavior range from those that are individually based to those that indict the broad society in which the individual is embedded. At one pole are biologically based explanations—such as those related to psychopathy. At the midpoint of the continuum we find those theories that consider multiple individual and social influences on a person's behavior, such as the theories focusing on resilience. At the other pole are theories that reject individual differences and place the blame for crime on society at large, such as those that suggest that a capitalist society encourages those who hold power to commit crimes (e.g., political crimes or corporate crimes).

Most of the readings in this section were selected to represent psychologically based theories or crimes that have received considerable attention in the psychological research. The **Curt Bartol** selection, written specifically for this book of readings, summarizes literature on resilience, a concept that began to appear in the delinquency literature in the 1980s. Resilience helps us understand why some children and adolescents, even if embedded in a neighborhood with high rates of antisocial behavior, are able to take a different path. Bartol first summarizes the risk factors that have traditionally occupied theorists and researchers (e.g., poverty, low

intelligence, deviant peer groups) and then moves on to the protective factors that allow the child to overcome adversity. He ends by addressing promising approaches to developing resilience in children often considered at risk of committing serious antisocial behavior.

At-risk children and adolescents as well as those not typically considered at risk may be susceptible to illegal drug use. Furthermore, some adolescents and young adults, in particular, have taken advantage of drugs to facilitate sexual assault. In the next selection, **Elena Pope and Michelle Shouldice** discuss substance use and abuse in the context of acquaintance rape. The authors, both physicians, have written an up-to-date, informative review of the properties and effects of these date-rape drugs, which not only decrease resistance but also impair the victim's memory of the event. Moreover, their presence in the victim is difficult to detect, and specific tests must be requested. The authors thus provide helpful information, not only for potential victims but also for investigators.

Like acquaintance rape, a crime that has received considerable recent attention is stalking. Defining this illegal behavior presents unique challenges, however. In addition, the perceptions of the stalking target are crucial. The selection by **Lorraine Phillips, Ryan Quirk, Barry Rosenfeld, and Maureen O'Connor** focuses on this important aspect. The researchers conducted two experiments that examined how college students, male and female, perceived behavior described in a variety of vignettes. They wondered whether the perception of stalking was affected by such variables as the gender of the perpetrator and the target, past experiences with stalking, and the relationship between the stalker and the target. Some gender effects were found, with women in one study being somewhat more likely than men to perceive behavior as stalking. However, there were several unanticipated findings as well.

In the next selection, we move from discussion of specific crimes to characteristics of some perpetrators, specifically criminal psychopaths. **Robert Hare**, arguably the foremost contemporary researcher and expert on psychopathy, reviews what psychology has learned about this rare phenomenon. Psychopaths—who are believed to comprise between 11 and 25% of the prison population, depending upon the study—are extremely resistant to treatment, but they often play the treatment game quite well. Hare's article is part literature review and part personal recollection of a struggle to have psychopathy recognized, accepted, accurately diagnosed, and understood.

Those who offend against children are the topic of the next article by **Robert Prentky, Raymond Knight, and Austin Lee**. Prentky et al. summarize research findings on child sexual molestation, including its frequency and characteristics of the offenders, such as their social competence and the developmental influences on their adult behavior. For example, research has found that caregiver inconstancy—frequent changes in a child's primary caregiver—is a powerful predictor of sexual violence as well as attachment disorder in adulthood.

Not all sex offenders are alike, a finding made very clear in this reading. Even within a category of these offenders, there are important differences. Thus, the article outlines systems for the classification of child molesters, including the *Diagnostic and Statistical Manual of Mental Disorders* (DSM-IV) classification and the heavily researched model developed by the Massachusetts Treatment Center, the MTC:CM3. There is also discussion of the various approaches to sex offender treatment and the methods of assessing risk of future offending.

As a group, the above readings represent either cutting-edge theory in criminal psychology (e.g., resilience, psychopathy, classification of sex offenders) or crimes that are serious, widespread, and often resistant to efforts at prevention and prosecution (e.g., acquaintance rape, stalking, child sexual assault). They will likely continue to capture the research attention and theory building efforts of criminal psychologists.

8

RESILIENCE AND ANTISOCIAL BEHAVIOR

CURT R. BARTOL

Over the past quarter century the literature of juvenile delinquency has experienced an interesting paradigm shift. Until that time, references to *children at risk* or to *risk factors* for delinquency or serious antisocial behavior predominated. Depending on the writer's theoretical orientation, children were considered at risk if they were poor, lacked good cognitive skills, were undernourished, had attention deficits, came from one-parent families, associated with delinquent peers, were physically or sexually abused, or experienced a multiple of other individual, family-based, or educational problems.

It has now become apparent, though, that a significant number of children who are considered at risk do not engage in serious, persistent, antisocial behavior but rather develop into prosocial and productive adults (Doll & Lyon, 1998). That is, despite experiencing a stressful, disadvantaged, or abusive childhood, many children do not engage in serious delinquency and, indeed, mature successfully. Researchers began to refer to this as resilience and to search for factors that might account for it (Garmezy, 1991; Werner, 1987). Thus, while risk factors remain a major concern, their conceptual opposites—protective factors—are now considered equally important. Knowledge about

the personal attributes of resilient children and the environmental influences they experience will help greatly in the prevention and treatment of delinquent and antisocial behavior among at-risk populations.

We should note at the outset that the term *juvenile delinquent* is troublesome in several aspects. It is a legal classification assigned by the juvenile or family court after it has been determined that a juvenile has committed a criminal act. Accordingly, delinquency is behavior against the criminal code committed by an individual who has not reached adulthood, as defined by state or federal law. However, many juveniles commit crimes but are never formally declared delinquents. Others are informally called delinquents by adults without being arrested by police or processed by the courts. Still others—who meet the age criterion for delinquency—are tried in criminal courts rather than juvenile courts and consequently never adjudicated delinquent.

Psychologists prefer the term *antisocial behavior* to refer to the more serious habitual actions that violate personal rights, laws, or widely held social norms. Included in this definition is a wide assortment of behaviors ranging from homicide and sexual assault to verbal assault and vandalism. Though self-destructive behaviors such as substance abuse or suicide are also often called antisocial behaviors, we restrict our definition here to "recurrent problem behaviors that lead to injury to others or arrest" (Dodge & Pettit, 2003, p. 350). Arrest and subsequent court processing cannot be the only indicators of antisocial behavior because, as indicated above, many of these actions go undetected or escape the attention of law enforcement. They are, of course, still problematic. Consequently, the concepts in this chapter are relevant to both juvenile delinquency, as legally defined, and more generally to antisocial behavior. Although the terms will be used interchangeably, the focus will be on antisocial behavior. We will begin the chapter with a brief discussion of the risk factors that have long been identified in the research before moving on to discuss the concept of resilience and summarize its accompanying protective factors.

RISK FACTORS

Risks can be defined "as processes that predispose individuals to specific negative or unwanted outcomes" (McKnight & Loper, 2002, p. 188). Risk factors refer to individual attributes and developmental experiences that are believed to increase the probability that a person will engage in persistent antisocial or delinquent behavior. Researchers have identified a host of risk factors, often dividing them into four somewhat overlapping categories: (1) individual attributes, (2) family characteristics, (3) extrafamilial influences, and (4) psychobiological and health factors.

Individual risk factors include inadequate cognitive and language ability, a troublesome temperament (Bates, Pettit, Dodge, & Ridge, 1998; Dodge, 2002; Kochanska, 1998), poor self-regulation skills and impulsivity (Patterson, DeGarmo, & Knutson, 2000; Stoolmiller, 2001), low motivation, inadequate interpersonal and social skills, low self-esteem, and a negative self-concept. Family risk factors include faulty or inept parenting, parental psychopathology (especially depression), antisocial siblings, and various kinds of maltreatment and abuse. Examples of extrafamilial risk factors are antisocial peers, inadequate schools, inadequate social networks

and support systems, and the stress of living in dangerous and violent neighborhoods. Extrafamilial developmental factors may also include poverty and its concomitants of malnutrition, lead poisoning, low birth weight, living under conditions of chronic violence, and the many other effects of socioeconomic disadvantage. Examples of psychobiological and health factors include risk factors that involve hereditary influences, prenatal influences, postnatal diseases, and inadequate nutrition and medical care.

Most risk factors by themselves probably do not directly engender serious antisocial or delinquent behavior. Even parental psychopathology or a poor self-concept does not necessarily produce it. Rather, the research evidence suggests that it takes some combination of risks over a period of time to encourage criminal or delinquent behavior (Lösel & Bender, 2003).

Although a considerable amount of research on the relationship between risk factors and juvenile delinquency has been conducted over the years, until recently very little attention has been directed at those dispositions and influences that enable children to cope, adjust, and overcome adverse circumstances. These attributes and events—which are collectively called protective factors—are now believed to play significant roles in encouraging many children to avoid participation in serious antisocial or delinquent behavior. For many psychologists, studying the influence of protective factors on the developmental trajectories of nondelinquent children is a much more positive approach. It is clear that many children have a variety of protective factors and that it is easier to create such factors than to focus exclusively on overcoming the negative effects of risk factors. By emphasizing strengths rather than limitations, this approach offers more hope for dealing effectively with children and adolescents who otherwise might follow the path of serious antisocial behavior. The study of resilience also helps us formulate effective strategies and policies for the prevention and treatment of antisocial behavior.

PROTECTIVE FACTORS

As we have seen, risk factors place an individual at elevated risk for involvement in antisocial behavior. Protective factors insulate or shield the individual from the adverse effects of risk factors (Walters, 2002). Children who are exposed to many risk factors but are able to overcome their effects because of the presence of protective factors are called *resilient*. Put another way, protective factors help build resilience in children and adolescents.

Resilience is generally defined as "successful coping with or overcoming risk and adversity, the development of competence in the face of severe stress and hardship, and success in developmental tasks or meeting societal expectations" (McKnight & Loper, 2002, p. 188). Resilience, then, is the ability to bounce back quickly and adaptively from negative emotional experiences (Tugade & Fredickson, 2004). In an effort to emphasize the ongoing and changing developmental aspects of resilience, a few researchers define the concept as "a dynamic process encompassing positive adaptation within the context of significant adversity" (Luthar, Cicchetti, & Becker, 2000, p. 543). Some researchers also distinguish between the terms *resilience* and *resiliency*. For them, resilience refers to a dynamic developmental process, whereas resiliency refers to a personality trait or attribute that is relatively stable over the course of a lifetime (Masten, 1994). However, there is increasing evidence that, although resilience may be subjected to developmental fluctuations, at-risk children who show resilience at one stage of their lives tend to show resilience across their entire life span (Luthar et al., 2000). Consequently, it becomes difficult to make the fine distinction between resilience and resiliency with any kind of precision. Therefore, to avoid confusion, the term resilience will be used broadly here to encompass both the process and the personality trait.

At a minimum, two critical conditions must be met before a child can be called resilient. First, the child must have been exposed to significant threats or severe adversity, ranging from a single stressful event such as war to an accumulation of ongoing negative experiences, such as abuse. Second, the child must demonstrate the achievement of positive adaptation despite major assaults on the developmental process (Luthar et al., 2000). It should also be noted that resilience has been conceptualized as

an outcome or process that does not eradicate risk, but allows an individual to compensate for it successfully. Resilient children do not simply evade the negative outcomes associated with risk, but are able to take risk head-on and adapt in the face of such adversity.

Research on resilience also underscores the perspective that children have different vulnerabilities and protective systems at different ages and points during their development (Masten & Coatsworth, 1998). For example, infants, because of their total dependence on parents or caregivers, are highly vulnerable to the consequences of mistreatment by these adult figures. Adolescents, on the other hand, tend to be more vulnerable to the experiences they have with friends and school, which would be well beyond the understanding of young children (Masten & Coatsworth, 1998).

The study of resilience arose from the study of risk as pioneering investigators realized that there were many children who flourish in the midst of extreme adversity (Masten & Coatsworth, 1998). Prior to the current resilience research, the conventional wisdom was that growing up in oppressive and adverse conditions inevitably damages children and thwarts normal development (Waller, 2001). It was assumed, also, that children who survived and emerged psychologically healthy from severe adversity were very unusual or special. However, systematic research on resilience in children soon revealed that the original assumptions about the dire and irrevocable effects of growing up under adverse conditions were wrong or misleading (Masten, 2001) and that resilience in children is far more common than originally supposed (Bonanno, 2004). In essence, most children are far more adaptive and resilient than we might expect. According to Masten (2001), "Resilience does not come from rare and special qualities, but from the everyday magic of ordinary, normative human resources in the minds, brains, and bodies of children" (p. 235).

In recent years, developmental research has been able to identify some common characteristics of resilient children and adolescents. In general, the accumulating evidence reveals that resilient children exhibit positive social, interpersonal, and cognitive competencies that help them survive and succeed while living under high stress and adverse environments. They are often described as having an optimistic, zestful, and energetic approach to life, are curious and open to new experiences, and demonstrate a strong tendency for laughter and positive emotionality (Tugade & Fredickson, 2004). Another repetitive theme that emerges from the research literature is that resilience is developed from close relations with supportive and loving caregivers, effective schools, and connections with competent, caring adults in the wider community (Luthar et al., 2000). Children and adolescents who participate in serious, violent behaviors or chronic delinquency rarely display these qualities or these experiences. In fact, research suggests that resilient youth not only do not engage in serious or violent delinquency, they usually do not participate in delinquent gangs or use illegal drugs either (Tit & Huizinga, 2002).

Research on Resilience

The study of resilience in children at risk began in earnest during the 1970s (Masten, 2001). Having originated in the disciplines of psychiatry and developmental psychology, it has tended to focus on the individual, often to the exclusion of the psychosocial environment (Waller, 2001). Thus, resilience was initially conceptualized as the result of personality traits or coping styles that allowed some children to progress along a developmental trajectory even when confronted with considerable adversity.

One of the earliest studies on resilience was Werner's (1987) longitudinal research in what is known as the Kauai study. Werner and her collaborators (Werner, Bierman, & French, 1971; Werner & Smith, 1977, 1982; Werner, 1987, 1993) followed a cohort of 698 children, living on the Hawaiian island of Kauai, from birth to adulthood. This longitudinal study spanned the years 1954–1986 and included data from pediatricians, psychologists, public health personnel, and social workers. The project identified a number of personality, constitutional, and environmental variables that presumably distinguished children who became delinquent from those who did not.

We should note that Werner's measure of delinquency raises problems, although it is not unusual in delinquency research. Of the 698 children, 102 were labeled delinquent based solely on official records or police and family court files. A vast majority of these 102 juvenile offenders (both males and females) committed relatively minor offense violations, such as traffic violations or running away. This word of caution should be kept in mind as we review the findings of the study.

Nevertheless, Werner (1987) stated that a combination of about a dozen variables provided the best prediction for eventual delinquency. For example, children with a history of a difficult temperament, hyperactivity, substandard living conditions, low IQ, and unstable conflictful home life were more likely to be delinquent than children without these background variables. However, a significant number of these children (total of 72) with four or more of these features in their background did not become delinquent, indicating that predicting delinquency on the basis of background variables is unwarranted.

Werner divided those children with four or more high-risk variables into a resilient group (those who did not become delinquent) and a vulnerable group (those who became delinquent). She reports that one of the strongest differences between the two groups was the mother's perception concerning the child's temperament. Mothers of the resilient children perceived them as affectionate, cuddly, good-natured, and easy to handle. Resilient children also demonstrated a positive social orientation toward others. They were more skilled at engaging others and recruiting care, help, and support from siblings, peers, grandparents, neighborhood adults, and teachers. As the children got older, they were described as active, sociable, easy tempered, independent, and self-confident. They did better in school, communicated well, and had considerable curiosity about things in their world. As young adults, many continued their education beyond high school, were achievement oriented, and had a stable employment history. The families of the resilient children also had fairly extensive social support systems. That is, they had many supportive adults and caretakers available to them when problems arose.

Children in the vulnerable group were far different. Mothers of these vulnerable children perceived them as being difficult to handle.

They believed their children exhibited more temper tantrums, eating, and sleeping problems. The children's orientation toward others was negative and aggressive. Overall, the families of vulnerable children seemed to have meager support systems.

Following the Kauai study, research has continually discovered that resilient and adaptive children and adolescents do not usually engage in serious, chronic delinquency or antisocial behavior (Coie, 2004; Conduct Problems Prevention Research Group, 2004: Lösel & Bender, 2003; Masten & Coatsworth, 1998). Resilient children and adolescents, in spite of heavy exposure to risk factors, are accepted by peers; have excellent interpersonal and social skills; do well in school; are usually good-natured, active, independent, and self-confident; and have a very positive self-concept. They develop and sustain strong connections to competent and caring adults in the family and community. And they demonstrate strong cognitive abilities and self-regulation skills that help them control their impulses, frustrations, and anger.

Some research has focused on youth resilience after being away from institutional rearing characterized by extreme deprivation. Studies of Romanian adoptees provide dramatic documentation of developmental catch-up in many of the children, both physically and cognitively (Masten, 2001). The degree of catch-up by the age of four was spectacular (Rutter & ERA Study Team, 1998). "As observed in many other situations of extraordinary adversity, the capacity for developmental recovery when normative rearing conditions are restored is amazing" (Masten, 2001, p. 233). However, this does not mean that all children exposed to deprivation recover well. Some develop serious and chronic problems, including antisocial behavior, partly as a result of their earlier experiences with adversity. Systematic investigations of why some children respond adaptively while others do not should offer a promising framework for intervention and treatment.

Clearly, then, it is in society's interest to encourage and provide conditions that promote the development of resilience in children and adolescents at risk. It is also clear that many children—even if immersed in numerous risk factors—can overcome their effects. As articulated by Masten (2001), "Attention to human capabilities and adaptive systems that promote healthy development and functioning have the potential to inform policy and programs that foster competence and human capital and aim to improve the health of communities and nations while also preventing problems" (p. 235). The following sections will review those protective factors most conducive to the development of resilience in youth exposed to high risk.

ENVIRONMENTAL FACTORS

Although much of the theoretical and research work has tended to view resilience as a quality of the individual, a strong argument can be made that it also reflects the quality of the social context in which the child develops. Many developmental theorists have argued that resilience to aversive childhood contexts results from a cumulative and interactive mix of genetic (e.g., temperament), personal (e.g., cognitive ability), and environmental (e.g., family, community support systems) risk and protective factors (Rutter, 1999; Werner, 1995). Therefore, resilience is not only a quality of individuals but is also reflective of the social contexts in which they are embedded.

Family Influences

A majority of experts would agree that the family is the single most important social environment in any child's development. Protective factors within the family include such characteristics as warmth, cohesion, enlightened discipline, and cultural and ethnic identification (Barbarin, 1993). For many decades, research has shown that good parental functioning in at least one parent or at least one adequate and stable caregiver is crucial to the development of resilience and healthy functioning (G. Smith, 1999; Waaktaar, Christie, Borge, & Torgerson, 2004). Research has also consistently shown that effective parenting generally prevents serious antisocial behavior or delinquency (Dubrow, Edwards, & Ippolito, 1997; Masten, 2001). Emotionally attentive, supportive, and interested parents promote nondelinquency and prevent serious, persistent antisocial behavior from developing in their children (Lösel & Bender, 2003; Stouthamer-Loeber et al., 1993).

Parental attributions about child misbehavior and the discipline styles parents use to reduce such behavior also powerfully influence the development and persistence of antisocial behavior in children (Snyder, Cramer, Afrank, & Patterson, 2005). For example, researchers have found that when parents make negative or hostile attributions about their children prior to school entry, the children are likely to be disruptive and exhibit other antisocial behavior at school (Nix et al., 1999; Snyder et al., 2005). Parental hostile attributions refer to descriptions of a child's behavior as careless, selfish, defiant, inconsiderate, bad, or hostile. Moreover, many of these parents tend to blame the misconduct on the basic traits of the child. Interestingly, negative parental attribution also has a strong link to harsh punishment and disciplinary tactics by parents (Snyder et al., 2005).

Peer Influences

Recent studies have discovered that supportive, prosocial peers are among the most important network factors contributing to resilience in children and adolescents and to the prevention of antisocial behavior (Waaktaar et al. 2004). Children seek out other children who are fun to be with and who share common interests. In addition, resilient children appear to be skillful at sustaining peer relations that are mutually beneficial. That is, resilient children have interpersonal and social skills that facilitate and enhance, rather than undermine, the goals and interests of their peers. Recent research indicates that sibling support is also a strong protective factor in the development of resilience (Ozer, 2005).

One of the strongest predictors of later involvement in antisocial behavior is early rejection by peers (Dodge, 2003; Laird, Jordan, Dodge, Pettit, & Bates, 2001; Parker & Asher, 1987). More specifically, those children who were rejected for at least two or three years by second grade had a 50% chance of displaying significant antisocial behavior later in adolescence, in contrast with just a 9% chance for those children who managed to avoid early peer rejection (Dodge & Pettit, 2003). Aggressive behavior appears to be a key factor that

promotes peer rejection. Children tend to reject those children who frequently use forms of physical aggression as their preferred way of dealing with others. Moreover, children who are both physically aggressive and socially rejected by their peers have a high probability of becoming serious delinquents during adolescence. Researchers Coie and Miller-Johnson (2001), for example, conclude from their review of the literature that "those aggressive children who are rejected by peers are at significantly greater risk for chronic antisocial behavior than those who are not rejected" (p. 201).

Positive peer relations have been thought to contribute to the development of empathy and also reinforce and model self-regulation and prosocial behavior (Eisenberg, 1998; Waaktaar et al., 2004). Studies find that peer-rejected and aggressive children are deficient in being able to emotionally and cognitively put themselves in the place of others (Pepler, Byrd, & King, 1991). They are deficient in role-taking skills and they lack the ability to empathize. As a result, these youths, with increasing age, become less concerned about the consequences of violence, including the suffering of the victim or the amount of peer rejection they receive.

Positive peer relations are also believed to reduce significantly the tendency to display hostile attribution bias. According to Nigg and Huang-Pollock (2003), the term *hostile attribution bias* was first used by Nasby, Hayden, and Depaulo (1979) to describe the tendency of some aggressive children to routinely attribute hostile intent to other children, even if the other children have no such intentions. Hostile attribution bias begins to develop during the preschool years in most children who display it. Highly aggressive children, for instance, repeatedly fail to respond adaptively to minor provocations from others. In ambiguous situations they are inclined to perceive even slight transgressions of others as threatening. Therefore, unclear intentions from peers are often met with aggressive overreactions. If a classmate accidentally spills a drink near his belongings, the highly aggressive boy believes this was a deliberate attempt to damage his possessions and he responds with physical aggression. Peer-rejected and aggressive children appear to be less equipped cognitively for dealing with ambiguous or conflict situations.

Resilient youth also appear to place themselves in healthier contexts, generating opportunities for success or raising the odds of connecting with prosocial mentors in a manner consistent with the concept of niche seeking. In other words, resilient children have a knack for selecting and creating social environments that enable them to grow and thrive. Even infants have considerable power to elicit assistance from parents and caregivers, especially from adults that are sensitive to their needs. The quality of this relationship has predictive significance for success in later developmental tasks, such as better problem solving in toddlers and better peer relations in middle childhood. Youngsters who are persistently antisocial either have abandoned this strategy or do not have the necessary judgment for negotiating socially acceptable ways of getting their needs met.

Community and Neighborhood Social Support

The research associating resilience with neighborhood factors is sparse, but it does indicate that neighborhoods supplement the other environmental and individual-level factors associated with resilience by providing a context in which children can be exposed to positive influences (Wandersman & Nation, 1998). Several studies have demonstrated the positive effects of social network factors such as dense adult friendship networks and the adult monitoring and supervision of youth in reducing serious delinquency. These data support the position that youth are mentally and physically healthier in neighborhoods where adults talk to each other and get along (Wandersman & Nation, 1998). A strong social network in which adults are connected to each other produces healthy outcomes. Several studies (e.g., Garbarino & Kostelny, 1992; Garbarino, Kostelny, & Dubrow, 1991) support this hypothesis and clearly demonstrate the importance of good social networks in preventing child abuse, child antisocial behavior, and violence, even in areas of concentrated poverty (Wandersman & Nation, 1998).

Supportive extrafamilial relationships can be found in church affiliations, neighborhood organizations, and schools that effectively promote competence in social and cognitive domains (Barbarin, 1993). These social interactions play an important role in the development of resilience. Based on their extensive review of the relevant literature, Lösel and Bender (2003) conclude, "The availability and use of social support from family members, relatives, teachers, educators, ministers of religion, and friends . . . contribute to resilience" (p. 164).

INDIVIDUAL FACTORS

Cognitive Skills

According to Nigg and Huang-Pollock (2003), "cognitive problems in the child usually contribute to difficult interactions with caretaker, interfere with socialization, and leave the child unprepared to adapt to the greater diversity he or she faces within a high-risk environment" (p. 237). Good cognitive functioning, however, provides protection from the many negative influences of risk factors. The specific cognitive skills and abilities that contribute to resilience are intelligence, language skills, and other cognitive perceptions of self, such as self-efficacy and talent (Olsson, Bond, Burns, Vella-Broderick, & Sawyer, 2003).

It is clear that intelligence exists in multiple forms and relates to a wide assortment of abilities. Gardner (1983), for example, describes seven different types of intelligences or cognitive styles. They are linguistic (or language intelligence), logical-mathematical, spatial (used in getting from one place to another), musical, body kinesthetic (such as what good athletes and dancers have), insight into oneself, and understanding of others. There are probably many more types, such as wisdom, spirituality, synthesizing ability, intuition, metaphoric capacities, humor, and good judgment (Gardner, 1986, 1993, 1998). Gardner considered the last two of the primary seven—insight into oneself and the understanding of others—features of emotional intelligence. A deficiency in this form of intelligence may play a prominent role in human violence. Individuals who continually engage in violence may lack significant insight into their own behavior and possess little sensitivity or empathy toward others.

For our purposes, intelligence will be defined as the ability to adapt, learn, and engage in abstract thought (Nigg & Huang-Pollock, 2003). It is usually measured by various intelligence tests or scales. A nearly universal finding in the research literature is that children with a higher level of measured intelligence are more likely to be more resilient (Aldwin, 1994: Lösel & Bender, 2003). Although a large amount of research links cognitive deficits to antisocial behavior in children and adolescents (Nigg & Huang-Pollock, 2003, p. 227), considerable research has also shown that youth with high or above average intelligence are far less likely to participate in serious or chronic delinquency (Lösel & Bender, 2003). "Intelligent children may be more capable of planning their behaviour, anticipating negative outcomes, settling conflicts verbally, developing alternatives to aggressive reactions, and making better decisions" (Lösel & Bender, 2003, p. 155). Intelligent children are more likely to develop better and more realistic coping strategies and because of their cognitive skills are more likely to learn nonaggressive problem-solving capabilities at an early age. Furthermore, intelligent children usually perform well at school, a behavioral pattern that provides them with a powerful source of achievement and self-esteem that can buffer other stressors. More broadly, intelligent children receive greater levels of social reinforcement from the general social environment (e.g., teachers and other significant adults) than less intelligent children (Born, Chevalier, & Humblet, 1997). Inversely, "children with worse than average intellectual skills may find it difficult to negotiate threatening situations, disengage from school because of feelings of failure, or fail to learn as much from their experiences" (Masten & Coatsworth, 1998, p. 213).

Good intelligence may also reflect the central importance of cognition and language to adaptation during early development, and it appears to have specific and very important protective functions (Masten & Coatsworth, 1998). Interestingly, the verbal and language aspects of intelligence seem to be one of the more important components of the relationship between intelligence and delinquency. Nigg and Huang-Pollock (2003) affirm:

> Early specific weakness in verbal-learning and verbal-reasoning modestly but reliably predicts later persistent offending, conduct disorder, and antisocial outcomes, whereas nonverbal intelligence does not do so. . . . Weakness in verbal intelligence is associated with the subgroup of delinquent youth with early onset and chronic patterns of antisocial behavior . . . even though not all of those youth [with poor verbal skills] have antisocial outcomes. (Nigg & Huang-Pollock, 2003, p. 231)

Perhaps more importantly, good verbal intelligence contributes substantially to language development.

Language Development

Language is a powerful tool for parents and other socializing adults to use in transmitting and expressing social expectations and values. It is also the primary means by which children can communicate their needs, frustrations, and concerns. Therefore, language serves both as a form of external communication and as the basic internal ingredient for thinking and self-regulation. In essence, language plays a major constructive role in the growth of all cognitive processes. According to Keenan and Shaw (2003), language is the "primary means by which children learn to solve problems nonaggressively and effectively decrease negative emotions such as anger, fear, and sadness" (p. 163). Toddlers with better communication skills are easier to socialize. This is because they comprehend parental instructions better, are more able to develop internal controls of their emotions and behaviors, and can communicate their wishes better (Lahey & Waldman, 2003). Hence, these children are less likely to become highly frustrated during interactions with their parents.

On average, children utter their first word between 8 and 14 months of age (Ganger & Brent, 2004). During this time, they add words to their repertoire at a relatively slow rate. By age 24 months, children have an average vocabulary level of 300 words (Ganger & Brent, 2004). For the average child, there is a substantial amount of growth in language during the second year of life (Keenan & Shaw, 2003). In addition, it is widely held that children's rate of vocabulary acquisition does not simply increase but undergoes a discrete transition at approximately 50 words. During this stage, children presumably switch from an initial stage of slow vocabulary growth to a subsequent stage of faster growth (Ganger & Brent, 2004). Although the reasons for this transition remain debatable, it is often called the *vocabulary spurt*, the *vocabulary burst*, or the *naming explosion* in the developmental research literature.

By the end of the preschool period, the average child has internalized—primarily through the use of language—rules that are linked to the ability to inhibit behavior, follow rules, and manage negative emotions (Keenan & Shaw, 2003; Kochanska, Murray, & Coy, 1997). In addition, the child demonstrates more empathy and prosocial behavior toward others as a result of language development (Keenan & Shaw, 2003).

Delayed language development is believed to increase stress and frustration for many children and impede normal socialization (Keenan & Shaw, 2003). Toddler language development at ages 6 months, 18 months, and 24 months predicts later delinquency and antisocial behavior for boys, even when socioeconomic status (SES) and test motivation is controlled (Nigg & Huang-Pollock, 2003; Stattin & Klackenberg-Larson, 1993). A higher incidence of expressive language delay also has been observed among male children who display disruptive behaviors during the preschool years and antisocial behavior during the school years (Dionne, Tremblay, Boivin, Laplante, & Pérusse, 2003). A similar finding was reported by Stowe, Arnold, and Ortiz (2000), who found that delayed language functioning was associated with observed disruptive behaviors in male preschoolers. Interestingly, although early delays in language attainment may be a powerful predictor of highly antisocial behavior in boys, the current research pertaining to girls is sparse and inconclusive.

What might explain this association between language and delinquency or antisocial behavior? Researchers theorize that, when language deficits limit general communication, the child may use disruptive behavior to compensate for limited communication skills (Dionne et al., 2003). Basically, early language delay and limited communication skills may predispose a child to employ more physically aggressive tactics for dealing with the social environment. Frustrated about not getting their needs met through normal communication and social strategies, the children are drawn to more physical, demonstrative behavior to get their way. There is a circular effect, however, since aggressive and disruptive behaviors interfere with creating a conducive social or academic learning environment. Therefore, antisocial behavioral patterns may, in turn, curtail language development. In contrast to children with language deficits, verbally advantaged children may benefit from their verbal skills by developing prosocial behaviors and may thus steer away from the antisocial trajectories (Dionne et al., 2003).

Executive Functions

Closely related to intelligence and language development is the concept of executive functions. The concept is largely based on complex neuropsychological functions and includes such technical terms as set shifting, interference control, inhibition planning, and working memory (Nigg & Huang-Pollock, 2003). Executive functions more simply refer to deliberate problem solving and the regulation of one's thoughts and actions (Tremblay, 2003; Zelazo, Carter, Reznick, & Frye, 1997). For example, given the problem of being unable to open a container, what might a typical 6-year-old boy do? Several tactics are available. Keep trying, ask the teacher for help, or have a temper tantrum. The child with poor self-regulation is likely to have a tantrum.

Several studies of school-age children and adolescents have demonstrated a strong relationship between different aspects of executive functions and aggressive and antisocial behavior (Morgan & Lilienfeld, 2000; Nigg, Quamma, Greenberg, & Kusche, 1999; Séguin, Tremblay, Boulerice, Pihl, & Harden, 1999; Tremblay, 2003). Deficits in executive function have also been shown for disruptive and problem preschoolers (Hughes, Dunn, & White, 1998; Hughes, White, Sharpen, & Dunn, 2000; Speltz, DeKlyen, Calderon, Greenberg, & Fisher, 1999; Tremblay, 2003). According to Nigg and Huang-Pollock (2003), youngsters with executive function deficiencies, in addition to having self-regulation problems, probably have difficulty in foreseeing consequences of behavior and in the development of empathy.

Self-Regulations Skills

In their relationships with adults, children begin to acquire tools that enable them to control their behavior in numerous ways. They gain increasing control over their attention, emotions, and behavior. Together, this set of skills is known as self-regulation. Difficulty regulating negative emotions is strongly related to aggression and violence. For the average child, self-control begins to emerge in the second year, as does the concern and empathetic feelings for others. Children are expected to become reasonably compliant with parent requests and to internalize the family and cultural standards for behavior. This aspect of self-control begins to emerge in the third year of life, or between two and three years of age.

Self-regulation also involves children being able to direct their attention, "enabling them to shift or focus their attention more readily or to persist in attending, skills that will help them function in classroom or a play activity with peers" (Masten & Coatsworth, 1998, p. 208). As the child gets older, good attention regulation is associated with prosocial behavior and peer popularity. Conversely, poor self-regulation and noncompliance to the wishes of caretakers and teachers set the stage for aggressive, disruptive behavior in the classroom, academic problems, and peer rejection.

The research on self-regulation as a whole strongly suggests that these skills are extremely important for the development of resilience. They begin to emerge in early childhood and are shaped in part by a child's experiences. Thus, sensitive and consistent caregiving and warm but firm parenting styles all have been associated with the development of self-control and compliance with social rules. However, research also suggests that a child's own disposition or temperament may have an effect.

Temperament refers specifically to persistent individual differences in social and emotional responding that are believed to constitute the foundation for many personality traits later in life. As it is currently used in the research, *temperament* is assumed to (1) have a constitutional or biological basis, (2) appear in infancy and continue throughout life, and (3) be influenced by the social environment. Researchers also often refer to three broad types of child temperaments: the easy child, the slow-to-warm up child, and the difficult child (e.g., Thomas & Chess, 1977). As noted earlier, resilient children are often described as having sunny temperaments or are perceived by their parents as being easy babies, even under the most trying conditions (Aldwin, 1994). However, many chronically antisocial children tend to demonstrate difficult temperaments (e.g., emotional lability, restlessness, short attention span, negativism, roughness) as young children (Lösel & Bender, 2003; Moffitt, Caspi, Dickson, Silva, & Stanton, 1996). "An easy temperament makes interaction with caregivers smooth, and is also reinforced. In contrast, children with a difficult temperament are more frequently targets of parental criticism, irritability, and hostility" (Lösel & Bender, 2003, p. 152). A difficult temperament becomes particularly problematic when parents lack financial and social resources, are under stress or pressure, and lack the knowledge or skill for dealing with the difficult child.

Although temperament is present at birth, it must be emphasized that its manifestations can be quickly modified by the social environment, especially by parents and significant caregivers. Difficult temperaments can be challenging, but a nurturing and warm caregiver environment in which rules are firmly laid out can prevent, change, or eliminate antisocial behavior in children.

Positive Emotions

Emotions influence how children perceive and respond to others and events. Emotions can inspire or discourage the child from taking action, and they contribute to or disrupt our interpersonal relationships (Lagattuta & Wellman, 2002). Positive emotions—which include joy, interest, contentment, pride, and love—all share the ability to build a child's enduring personal resources (Frederickson, 2001). Negative emotions include hostility, anger, anxiety, sadness, and despair. Positive emotions and positive beliefs are important ingredients for building psychological resilience. Even though highly resilient children and adolescents may experience high levels of anxiety and frustration under stressful or pressure situations, their reliance on positive emotions to adapt to these conditions is very effective in their long-term coping (Tugade & Frederickson, 2004).

One way children and adolescents may experience positive emotions in the face of adversity is by finding positive meaning in ordinary events and within the adversity itself (Folkman & Moskowitz, 2000; Frederickson, 2001). The belief and the emotion are reciprocal. Not only does finding positive meaning trigger positive emotion, but also positive emotions, because they broaden thinking, should increase the likelihood of finding positive meaning in subsequent events, even highly negative ones (Frederickson, 2001). Youths who experience more positive emotions than others become more resilient to adversity over time.

Motivational Factors

Psychologists have long distinguished between intrinsic and extrinsic motivation. Intrinsic motivation refers to behavior provoked by pleasure and enjoyment, whereas extrinsic motivation is behavior encouraged by external pressures or constraints (Henderlong & Lepper, 2002). Intrinsic motivation is doing something because it is enjoyed for its own sake, such as doing a puzzle or a painting. Extrinsic motivation is doing something to receive rewards from others, such as hopes to receive a gift or money. Resilient children tend to demonstrate significant amounts of intrinsic motivation. Although it is well known that praise encourages intrinsic motivation, the kind and quality of the praise is very important (Henderlong & Lepper, 2002). Specifically, intrinsic motivation is most effectively encouraged and developed through praise that encourages competence and self-efficacy. In other words, the child is praised for attempts at mastery over something, such as puzzle-solving ability, language development, or reading activity. On the other hand, praise that is based primarily on social comparisons—ranking the child or making comparisons to the performance or abilities of others—is problematic. Not surprisingly, schools and what transpires within them are often targeted by resilience researchers. For example, an emphasis on social comparison in the classroom necessitates that some children receive positive feedback while others receive negative feedback (Henderlong & Lepper, 2002). "After all, not everyone can be at the top of the class" (Henderlong & Lepper, 2002, p. 785). Thus, praise based solely on social comparison may, in the long run, not be helpful. It may leave children unprepared for the eventual and inevitable negative feedback they are bound to experience as they progress through school.

PREVENTION AND INTERVENTION

With increasing awareness of the protective factors that promote resilience in children and adolescence, theorists, researchers, and policymakers are now attempting to apply this knowledge toward the prevention and intervention of antisocial behavior. Prevention programs that promote cognitive and social competencies in the child or adolescent, improve childrearing practices in the family, and enrich the development and maintenance of effective social support systems are most likely to be effective in the long run. As Masten (2001, p. 235) writes, "The great threats to human development are those that jeopardize the systems underlying these adaptive processes, including brain development and cognition, caregiver-child relationships, regulation of emotion and behavior, and the motivation for learning and engaging in the environment."

Strategies include the enhancement of a child's strengths and interests, as well as the reduction of risk or stressors and the facilitation of protective processes. Overall, the rallying cry for many programs focusing on enhancing resilience has become, "Every child has talents, strengths, and interests that offer the child potential for a bright future" (Damon, 2004, p. 13). These attitudes reflect a major transformation in the conceptualization of prevention of antisocial behavior and other childhood problems over the past several decades.

There is little doubt that living conditions in the poorest inner city neighborhoods are extremely harsh and the daily onslaught of violence, substance abuse, racism, child abuse, and hopelessness are highly disruptive to a child's normal development. For many children who are exposed to an adverse family life and inadequate living arrangements with little opportunity to develop even the rudiments of social and interpersonal skills for dealing effectively with others, the damage may be irreparable. Clearly, the longer a child is exposed to this adverse environment, the more difficult it may be to modify his or her life course away from crime and delinquency. Hence, successive intervention programs must not only begin as early as possible, but must also be intensively directed at as many causes and negative influences as possible. Guerra and her colleagues (Guerra, Huesmann, Tolan, Van Acker, & Eron, 1995) recommend that interventions begin no later in life than the first grade (before age 8). In addition, there is evidence to suggest that the earlier the signs of antisocial behavior, the more serious or violent the antisocial behavior or delinquency will be later (Tolan & Thomas, 1995).

As we have seen, for any program to be truly effective it must go beyond merely affecting the child but must affect the whole social context within which he or she is developing. Research has continually shown that the most successful interventions concentrate on the family—including all members (e.g., siblings, grandparents, uncles and aunts) if possible. As discussed earlier, certain family relationships and parenting practices are strongly related to serious antisocial behavior. More important, these family characteristics seem to be linked to delinquency regardless of ethnic or socioeconomic status (Gorman-Smith, Tolan, Zelli, & Huesmann, 1996). The family characteristics most closely associated with serious delinquency are poor parental monitoring of the child's activities, poor and inconsistent discipline, and a lack of family closeness or cohesion. Research indicates that emotional closeness and family cohesion, where the child receives emotional support, adequate communication, and love, are essential in the prevention of antisocial behavior and serious delinquency (Gorman-Smith et al., 1996).

There is no single means of maintaining equilibrium following highly aversive events, but rather there are multiple pathways to resilience (Bonanno, 2004). For example, McKnight and Loper (2002) found that the most prominent resilience factors in adolescent girls at risk for delinquency were an academic motivation and a desire to go to college, an absence of substance abuse, feeling loved and wanted, a belief that teachers treat students fairly, parents trusting adolescent children, and religiosity.

Waaktaar et al. (2004) conducted a study to explore how resilience or protective factors could be used to help at-risk youths. The youth averaged 12.3 years of age, and a little over a third were girls. They represented a medley of cultural and ethnic backgrounds, including the West Indies, the Far East, Central Asia, the Arab world, and northeast Africa. All the participants had experienced serious or multiple life stresses, and, at the time of the study, were not receiving "satisfactory help" through "psychiatric" intervention.

The researchers targeted four resilience factors for therapeutic intervention: positive peer relations, self-efficacy, creativity, and coherence. Positive peer relations were defined as prosocial interactions, peer acceptance, and support. Self-efficacy is the belief that one can achieve desired goals through one's own actions (Bandura, 1989, 1997). Creativity in this context refers to individual talent to create an artistic or other communicative product, such as a song, dance, film, play, poem, or short story. This approach requires that children be encouraged to express themselves and their experiences symbolically. Coherence refers to the ways in which people cognitively and emotionally appraise themselves and their circumstances. It involves "helping young people to find a coherent meaning to their past, present, and future life through positive thinking, accepting the reality of their bad experiences, avoiding self-blame for uncontrollable circumstances and finding adaptive paths forward" (Waaktaar et al., 2004, p. 173). The researchers discovered that child therapy that focuses on these four concepts has the potential to enhance resilience significantly.

A deeper understanding of resilience can be greatly facilitated by consideration of cultural and ethnic factors (Barbarin, 1993). Ethnic group identity, within both the family and the neighborhood, is an essential component of any explanatory model or prevention program. Factors and characteristics delineated with one population of children cannot be attributed directly to another culturally and ethnically different population of children (Hampson, Rahman, Brown, Taylor, & Donaldson, 1998). Programs that have shown long-term success have utilized multipronged approaches concentrating on treating children through their broad social environment and with particular sensitivity to the family's cultural background and heritage. Intervention programs that neglect the gender, ethnicity, socioeconomic status, and other demographic markers that affect the development of antisocial behavior are destined to fail. Even poverty may affect individuals differently on the basis of their ethnicity and the meaning of poverty within a given cultural context (Guerra et al., 1995).

An excellent illustration of a culturally sensitive program developed for resilience development is Project SELF, a school curriculum designed to promote self-esteem, self-efficacy, and improved problem-solving skills in inner-city fourth-grade black children through a culturally based curriculum (Hampson et al., 1998). The researchers write,

> Using a pre/post evaluation design with a control group, we demonstrated that students who received the program exhibited greater improved knowledge of the curriculum, elevated self-esteem, a greater sense of self-efficacy, and improved long-term consequential thinking skills as compared to controls. (Hampson et al., 1998, p. 24)

What really made the difference, the researchers concluded, was the program's focus on "the students' own ancestral history, biology, beliefs and values, choices and potential" throughout the curriculum (Hampson et al., 1998, p. 27). In order to improve resilience, the researchers reasoned, a minority child must touch base with his or her cultural or ethnic identity.

Notably lacking in existing research on resilience is the role played by biology and genetic factors (Luthar et al., 2000). It is clear that biological factors affect psychological processes, and psychological processes in turn affect biological factors. It may be that resilience is strongly affected by genetic or biological predispositions, whereas resilience may be more strongly affected by the social environment. Therefore, effective intervention programs should also include prenatal and perinatal medical care, and intensive health education for pregnant women and mothers with young children. These services reduce the delinquency risk factors of head and neurological injuries, exposure to toxins, maternal substance abuse, nutritional deficiencies, and perinatal difficulties.

UNANSWERED QUESTIONS

Over the past few years, research has shifted away from simply identifying protective factors and has focused more on trying to understand the underlying protective processes (Luthar et al., 2000). Consequently, rather than studying which child, family, or environmental factors are involved in resilience, the recent emphasis has been attempts to understand how such factors may contribute to it. As researchers have identified the characteristics of resilience and determined the forces of the social environment that contribute to resilience, there has also been a discernible shift to build and strengthen programs that enhance and foster the development of protective mechanisms. However, although resilience studies have been able to indicate clear risk and protective factors in human development, the knowledge of exactly how these factors work is still lacking (Waaktaar et al., 2004). Perhaps even more challenging is how these systems can be most effectively implemented in working with at-risk children.

One of the many questions that need to be answered revolves around the multidimensional nature of resilience. Can we expect, for instance, at-risk children who demonstrate resilience in one area to show a comparable resilience in other areas? If an at-risk child does well in school, can we expect that child to demonstrate positive outcomes in his or her social or emotional lives to the same degree? So far, the research suggests a tentative "yes" to both questions. A very promising feature of effective intervention, for example, seems to be that improvement in one resilience characteristic of a child is likely to also affect other resilience factors in that child, creating what are called *positive chain reactions* by clinicians (Waaktaar et al., 2004).

A sobering problem, however, is reflected in a recent report summing up several decades of resource-enhancing preventive interventions, such as the Head Start project. Intervention effects tend to persist only as long as the intervention continues, "and only 'magic' will help if the intervention does not address the basic problems of poverty, illness, parental dysfunction, high-risk neighborhoods and unemployment" (Waaktaar et al., 2004, p. 179).

Summary and Conclusions

This overview examined why some children and adolescents do not engage in serious, violent antisocial behavior—despite being exposed to a multitude of risk factors—while other youths begin their persistent criminal careers after being exposed to similar risk conditions. The chapter focused on the numerous protective factors that may shield at-risk youngsters from the onset of antisocial behavior and how these factors can contribute to prevention and intervention programs. This review also suggested ways to enhance these protective factors through the development of resilience in children and adolescents.

The number of intervention, prevention, and treatment programs that have been tried on children at risk for delinquency and antisocial behavior is overwhelming. For many years, very few were shown to be effective in long-term lasting effects. Part of the problem is that so many of them concentrated on reducing risk factors, to the exclusion of building on protective factors and resilience. Risk factors (e.g., poverty, poor health services, violent neighborhoods) are often societal problems that cannot be easily rectified without considerable political clout, influence, and enormous financial resources.

However, there is mounting evidence that prevention programs that are carefully designed and implemented can be effective in preventing antisocial behavior in children and adolescents (Nation et al., 2003). The research indicates that most effective programs for dealing with at-risk children and preadolescents should focus on the development of resilience (Lösel & Bender, 2003).

Programs that are most successful for dealing with at-risk children are appropriately timed, socioculturally relevant, comprehensive, and use varied teaching methods (Nation et al., 2003). Programs that are appropriately timed provide interventions that occur in a child's life when they will have maximal impact. In most cases, interventions should begin early, usually before preschool or at school entry. Successful problems are also not based on one-size-fits-all but are sensitive to cultural, ethnic, and geographical differences and needs (Castro, 2005). Each child has his or her unique way of viewing the world through the lens of cultural and linguistic experiences. For any intervention program to be successful it must build on these differences (Bartol & Bartol, 2004a). Programs that are comprehensive target the development of cognitive, language, and social skills. Varied teaching methods involve interactive instruction designed to provide active, hands-on experiences that increase the child's skills and self-confidence. Providing opportunities for children to develop strong, positive relationships is consistently associated with positive outcomes and resilience building.

We have much knowledge about what needs to be done, but often this knowledge is not implemented into programs across the country. One of the more prominent problems in implementation is that there is a gap between the science-based prevention programs and what is provided by practitioners to families and children (Gendreau, 1996a; Nation et al., 2003; Morrisey et al., 1997). Practitioners cannot afford to implement research-based programs that were developed on well-funded, university-based research grants (Nation et al., 2003). Some innovative way to bridge this gap is necessary if we are to move forward on prevention and intervention for those children at risk to become delinquent.

The resilience factors and the intervention programs that were reviewed in this chapter indicate that focusing exclusively on risk factors alone is not enough, nor is it realistic. Enhancing protective factors and developing resilience in at-risk children while reducing risk factors is far more likely to produce long-lasting, positive results. More important, this is a far more optimistic and hopeful approach. As noted by Lösel and Bender (2003, p. 180) "being aware of protective processes and resilience may help practitioners or policymakers to counter the pessimism and resignation associated with a 'nothing-works' ideology." This awareness also helps policymakers decide how the limited resources should be allocated.

9

DRUGS AND SEXUAL ASSAULT

A Review

ELENA POPE
MICHELLE SHOULDICE

Recent statistical figures illustrate an alarming trend in sexual assault. According to a U.S. study, 25% of women have been sexually assaulted during their lifetime (Schwartz, 1991). In 75% of the cases, the assailant was known to the victim (National Victim Center and CrimeVictims Research and Treatment, 1992). The incidence is even higher in adolescents and young women. One study estimated the lifetime prevalence of date rape among adolescents to be between 20% and 68% (Rickert & Wiemann, 1998). Apart from younger age, there are other demographic characteristics that have been reported to increase vulnerability to date rape, including early sexual activity, earlier age of menarche, past history of sexual abuse or prior victimization, and higher acceptance of rape myths and violence toward women. An independent risk factor seems to be the use of alcohol and drugs (Rickert & Wiemann, 1998). According to the American Academy of Forensic Sciences, one third of cases of sexual assault occurred in the context of alcohol use (Li, 1999).

Other studies quote that more than 75% of the perpetrators and more than 50% of the victims had been consuming alcohol before the assault (Koss, 1984; Koss & Dincro, 1989; LeBeau et al., 1999). The effects of alcohol may contribute to misinterpretation of friendly cues as sexual invitation, decreased coping mechanisms, and inability to defend against an attack (Rickert & Wiemann, 1998).

But alcohol is not the only substance associated with sexual assault. Various drugs have recently been reported to be used in association with sexual assault by an acquaintance (LeBeau et al., 1999). All of these drugs have a similar clinical profile: rapid onset of action and ability to induce sedation and anterograde amnesia (inability to recall events after ingestion). Moreover, their formulation is such that they can be added to drinks without the victim's knowledge (Smith, 1999). When used in combination with alcohol, potential for central nervous system (CNS) depression (sedation) increases and so does the risk of sexual assault (Le Beau et al., 1999).

Editors' Note: This article was originally published in *Trauma, Violence, and Abuse,* Vol. 2, No. 1, January 2001, pp. 51-55.

Flunitrazepam (Rohypnol)

Rohypnol is a fast acting benzodiazepine, 10 times more potent than diazepam (Valium) (Matilla & Larni, 1980). Its effects consist of rapid induction of sleep (hypnotic effect), sedation, and muscle relaxation (Simmons & Cupp, 1998). These effects, coupled with anterograde amnesia and relatively low cost, make Rohypnol very attractive for a potential perpetrator (Calhoun, Wesson, Galloway, & Smith, 1996). The drug is not legal in Canada or the United States but is marketed in South America, Asia, and Australia by Hoffman LaRoche Pharmaceuticals. It is supplied as 0.5 mg, 1 mg, and 2mg tablets in bubble packaging, which gives the appearance of a prescribed medication. Rohypnol is tasteless, odorless, and soluble in alcohol. Because of reports of its use as a date rape drug, a new formulation has been produced that dissolves more slowly, changes clear drinks into a bright blue color, and clouds dark beverages.

Once absorbed, Rohypnol quickly distributes into body tissues from plasma, then is metabolized and excreted mainly by the kidneys (Simmons & Cupp, 1998). Its half-life (time at which 50% of the drug is eliminated from the body) is about 20 hours. However, because it is readily distributed into various tissues, its clinical effects are much shorter than its half-life. Typically, Rohypnol's effects begin approximately 20 to 30 minutes post-ingestion and peak at 2 hours. Psychomotor impairment, such as delayed reaction time, muscle relaxation, and amnesia, can last up to 12 hours (Simmons & Cupp, 1998). The severity and duration of sedative effects may be accentuated by use of alcohol, carbonated beverages, and coffee (Calhoun et al., 1996).

The detection of Rohypnol is difficult. Urinary metabolites are present in very low concentration, and detection can be accomplished only within 72 hours of ingestion (Smith, 1999). Various laboratory methods have been tried to enhance the ability of detection. Recently, a sensitive assay using gas chromatography/mass spectrometry (GC-MS) technique was developed with a limit of detection of 2 ng/mL (LeBeau et al., 1999; Simmons & Cupp, 1998). When submitting a victim's urine sample, one has to be familiar with the capabilities of the laboratory used or, ideally, submit specimens to specialized laboratories.

GHB

GHB is also known as gamma-hydroxybutyrateor sodium oxylate. It is currently available legally only as an investigational drug for the treatment of narcolepsy (Smith, 1999). Between 1996 and 1999, the Drug Enforcement Administration (DEA) received 22 reports of sexual assaults committed under influence of GHB (Smith, 1999).

GHB causes CNS depression (sedation) secondary to direct action at the brain receptor level (GABAb). The initial symptoms, occurring 15 to 30 minutes after ingestion, consist of drowsiness, confusion, and dizziness. Rapid decrease in level of consciousness (even coma), vomiting, and respiratory depression may follow (Smith, 1999). Occasionally, patients experience terrifying hallucinations and paranoia. As with Rohypnol, anterograde amnesia is common, which may limit the victim's ability to provide detailed recall of the assault. The spectrum of clinical symptoms is dose dependent. Doses of 10 mg/kg induce amnesia and somnolence, whereas doses exceeding 50 mg/kg can lead to coma and severe respiratory depression ("Gamma-Hydroxy Butyrate Use," 1997). The sedative effects may be enhanced by the use of alcohol or other drugs.

The usual formulation of GHB is a white powder that can be added to any liquid. The resultant solution is colorless and odorless with a mild, salty or soapy taste. The onset of action is short (15 to 30 minutes). Sedation may last a few hours, with full recovery approximately 8 hours after ingestion. Occasionally, dizziness may last up to 2 weeks (Smith, 1999).

Given the short half-life (20 minutes to 1 hour) of GHB, detection is very difficult. Urine assays using GC-MS can detect GHB in certain laboratories if done within 12 hours of ingestion of the drug (LeBeau et al., 1999; Smith, 1999).

Ketamine

Ketamine is a general anesthetic used widely in medicine. Its illicit use has been reported, and DEA received at least one case report in which

Ketamine was used to facilitate sexual assault (Smith, 1999).

The major effects of Ketamine consist of analgesia (decreased pain) and amnesia, with an onset approximately 20 minutes after ingestion. Higher doses may lead to a feeling of detachment from the surroundings and floating. Hallucinations and rapid eye movements (nystagmus) have also been reported (Smith, 1999). Intravenous as well as oral preparations are available. The standard anesthetic dose is 2mg/kg intravenously or 5 to 10 mg/kg intramuscularly. The dosage used for illicit purposes is unknown. Ketamine undergoes extensive hepatic (liver) metabolism and elimination by the kidneys.

Currently, there is no available detection test.

MDMA (Ecstasy)

Ecstasy is a synthetic chemical derived from an essential oil of the sassafrass tree. Merck first synthesized this chemical in 1912. Given the psychotherapeutic effects and its growing popularity, Ecstasy became illegal in the United States in 1985. Currently, it is a very popular drug, particularly at rave parties. Because of the big demand, anything can be sold as Ecstasy, with potentially serious results.

Ecstasy's effects consist of euphoria, disinhibition, and dizziness. Other symptoms described in association with Ecstasy are nystagmus (involuntary eye movements) and hallucinations (Morland, 2000). Dangerous effects associated with it derive from hyperthermia (increased body temperature) leading to dehydration, hyponatremia (decreased body salt), seizures, and irregular cardiac rhythm (Ajaelo, Koenig,& Snoey, 1998).

MDMA (Ecstasy) is readily absorbed and starts acting approximately 30 to 60 minutes after its ingestion. The peak effects tend to occur at around 1 to 5 hours, with symptoms lasting up to 8 hours depending on the ingested amount. It is metabolized in the liver and eliminated by the kidneys as an active metabolite usually within 24 hours after intake. The hallucinogenic effects are typically seen in doses ranging from 50 to 150 mg.

The presence of the drug can qualitatively be detected in blood and urine by using methods such as thin layer chromatography and gas or gas-liquid chromatography (Jurado, Gimenez, Soriano, Menendez, & Repetto, 2000). However, because various labs have different detectable concentration limits, consultation with laboratory staff should occur.

CONCLUSION

Date rape is a common occurrence, especially among young women and adolescents. Drugs and/or alcohol may be used with the intention of decreasing resistance to the assault by causing sedation as well as by decreasing detailed recollection of the events by the victim because of induced amnesia.

The most common substances reported in association with sexual assault are alcohol, cocaine, and marijuana. This is not surprising because they make up a great majority of street drugs. However, other drugs such as Rohypnol, GHB, Ketamine, and Ecstasy have recently been associated with sexual assault, probably because of their amnesic potential. All of these drugs share several features: CNS depression (sedation), impaired judgment, impaired memory, decreased motor control, and decreased inhibition. Depending on the dose of the drug and/or use of other substances (especially alcohol), clinical effects can be significant enough to lead to respiratory depression, irregular heart rhythm, and coma.

The possession, sale, or use of most of these drugs is a criminal offense in most of the United States and in Canada. Hence, the detection of these drugs is of paramount importance, particularly given the victim's frequent difficulty recollecting the events surrounding the assault or the details about the perpetrator. Detection of these drugs may be problematic because of limitations in laboratory testing methods. The short half-life of these drugs in combination with a victim who may not seek medical attention immediately due to an inability to recall events may make detection of these drugs even more problematic. A recent review suggested a standard protocol for specimen collection in rape victims (LeBeau et al., 1999). This includes a specimen collection as soon as possible after the event. Urine specimens should be obtained within 72 to 96 hours after ingestion and kept refrigerated. Blood specimens are less useful. It is important to know that, with the exception of Ecstasy, standard toxicology screening rarely detects substances potentially used in sexual assault, and specific testing must be requested. A high index of suspicion is therefore recommended, particularly in sexual assault cases when the victim reports sedation or an inability to recall events clearly. Blood analysis is possible if collection is obtained within 24 hours of the assault and the specimen is collected in a tube with sodium fluoride or potassium oxalate preservative. The testing request should specify what substance is suspected. Knowledge about a laboratory's ability to detect these substances is very important.

10

Is It Stalking?

Perceptions of Stalking Among College Undergraduates

Lorraine Phillips
Ryan Quirk
Barry Rosenfeld
Maureen O'Connor

As public interest in stalking crimes grew during the past decade, critics have increasingly pointed to the ambiguity ("vagueness") present in most legal definitions of stalking (e.g., Jordan, Quinn, Jordan, & Daileader, 2000; Mullen, Pathé, & Purcell, 2000). For example, California's anti-stalking law specifies that the behavior must "be such as would cause a reasonable person to suffer substantial emotional consequence" (California Penal Code, Section § 646.9, 1990). Even New York's recent anti-stalking law, developed long after concerns regarding definitional ambiguity had been raised and litigated, requires that the victim must experience a "reasonable fear of material harm" from the stalker for the behaviors to qualify as "stalking" (New York Criminal Procedure Law, Section § 120.45,

1999; Pappas, 2000). But despite attempts to define the contours of stalking, these laws offer little, if any, guidance as to what behaviors would qualify as inducing a "reasonable fear" or engendering "substantial emotional harm." Indeed, the same behaviors could be interpreted as frightening by one individual yet seem flattering or absurd to another (Jordan et al., 2000). How then does one determine whether a stalker's actions meet the legal requirement for criminal prosecution or even constitute stalking in lay terms?

Despite the importance of understanding individual differences in perceptions of stalking, research has rarely focused on understanding the factors that influence these perceptions. At one extreme of this continuum are the occasional reports, although largely anecdotal, of

Editors' Note: This article was originally published in *Criminal Justice and Behavior*, Vol. 31, No. 1, February 2004, pp. 73-96. We have omitted portions of the literature review and the results sections of both studies discussed herein.

false accusations of stalking (often termed "false victimization syndrome" (Mohandie, Hatcher, & Raymond, 1996; Pathé, Mullen, & Purcell, 1999; Sheridan & Blaauw, 2004). On the other hand, many stalking victims fail to recognize or interpret the harassment they are subjected to as "stalking," and therefore, they neglect to seek appropriate help or take protective measures that might be necessary. More critically, third-party observers, such as police officers or coworkers, may find it particularly difficult to perceive the behavior as sufficiently threatening to the target to constitute stalking. Even when stalking or harassment is accurately recognized, individual reactions vary tremendously, with some stalking victims moving to another state and changing their identity and others continuing their lives seemingly without significant interference. Clearly, perceptions of the risk posed by a stalker play a central role in determining how an individual should react. These same perceptions will also determine the efficacy of stalking laws as law enforcement officials, prosecutors, judges, and, ultimately, jurors must also evaluate whether particular behaviors rise to the level of unlawful stalking.

Although early attention to stalking focused largely on celebrity victims and gradually expanded to the general public, stalking has only recently been identified as a significant problem plaguing college students. Several studies have observed high rates of stalking among college students that far exceed the prevalence rates found in the general population (e.g., Bjerregaard, 2000; Fremouw, Westrup, & Pennypacker, 1997; Haugaard & Seri, 2000). For example, Fremouw and his colleagues (1997) reported that 27% of the women and 15% of men in their sample of West Virginia University students had been stalked. Bjerregaard found a comparable rate of stalking among college students; 25% of the women in her sample and 11% of the men reported this experience. Not surprisingly, female victims in Bjerregaard's sample were more likely than males to be threatened by their stalker and were also more likely to express fear for their physical safety. In fact, female stalking victims reported twice the level of fear compared to male victims, even when they had received similar threatening communications.

Despite the importance of victim perceptions in both defining and reacting to stalking, very little research has attempted to identify factors that influence these perceptions. Hills and Taplin (1998) studied the perceptions of Australian adults in response to a stalking vignette that varied across two dimensions, the nature of the perpetrator/target relationship . . . and the presence or absence of an implicit threat. . . . Interestingly, despite a growing body of research demonstrating that stalkers who were previously involved in an intimate relationship with the target of their harassment (i.e., "former intimates") are more likely to be violent than are offenders who target strangers (e.g., Rosenfeld, 2003), both categories of targets reported fear, but the likelihood of calling the police was significantly greater in response to the "stranger" vignette. The presence of a threat, on the other hand, had no impact on perceived fear, but it did correspond to an increased likelihood of calling the police. . . .

Dennison and Thomson (2000) also studied a large sample of Australian adults ($N = 540$) in their investigation of the influence of situational variables on determinations of stalking and perceptions of the perpetrator's intentions. They, too, studied perpetrator/target relationship (strangers, acquaintances, or former intimates), the intent of the perpetrator (whether there was explicit evidence of actions that would instill fear or cause emotional harm), and the impact this behavior had on the victim (extreme fear, moderate fear, or no fear). . . .

In a subsequent study, Dennison and Thomson (2002) expanded this methodology in a study of 1,080 Australian adults by adding an additional variable—that is, perpetrator persistence. Because their previous study utilized a vignette in which perpetrators were highly persistent, they added two additional conditions describing perpetrators whose actions reflected either moderate or low levels of persistence. As in their previous study, the vast majority of respondents (83%) characterized the behavior described in the vignette as stalking, but they found a significant difference across gender, with 86% of women labeling the vignette as stalking compared to 78% of men. Not surprisingly, degree of persistence and the presence of specific intent were significantly associated with the determination that stalking had occurred. They also found that women were more likely than men to perceive the perpetrator as intending to inflict fear and cause physical or mental harm to the target. Although they also observed a number of effects for perpetrator/target relationship, these associations were more complex (often taking the form of interaction effects). However, because their vignettes only depicted a male perpetrator and a female victim, the extent to which these gender effects reflect a greater concern or awareness of stalking on the part of women in general versus a greater concern for the potential violence inflicted by males is unknown. Moreover, in many analyses, the magnitude of the gender effects they observed was relatively modest. Nevertheless, the authors concluded that the factors that influence perceptions of stalking might be more complex than had been previously thought.

Interestingly, analogous research literature focusing on sexual harassment perceptions has evolved over the past decade that has examined the influence of individual- and situational-level variables on determinations of whether behaviors were perceived as sexual harassment. Fairly consistently, gender of the participant plays a small but significant role in explaining sexual harassment judgments (e.g., Gutek et al., 1999; Rotundo, Nguyen, & Sackett, 2001 . . .). But this gender effect may also be explained by sexist attitudes and perceptions of the target's credibility (see Wiener & Hurt, 1999). Interestingly, a target's prior personal experience with sexual harassment does not appear to influence sexual harassment perceptions (Stockdale, O'Connor, Gutek, & Geer, 2002).

The sexual harassment literature shares many similarities to the emerging research on perceptions of stalking and provides a context for understanding the gender effects found in both literatures. In an effort to supplement this small but growing body of research, the current investigations focused on whether behaviors would be more or less likely to be considered stalking depending on situational factors . . . and participant characteristics. . . . In the first of these studies, the behavior of the perpetrator was described in a relatively ambiguous manner to increase the variability of subjective perceptions as to whether the vignette described

stalking and whether a risk of harm existed, whereas the second study systematically manipulated the seriousness of the behavior.

Specifically, it was hypothesized that female participants and those who report having previously been the target of stalking would be more likely to label the vignettes as "stalking" and would associate greater risks to the perpetrators' behavior. In addition, the impact of terminology (i.e., use of the term stalking versus a description of repetitive harassment behaviors) on reports of whether one has been stalked was explored. In the second study, similar effects regarding participant gender were hypothesized (i.e., female participants would be more likely than men to label the vignettes as stalking), although it was anticipated that the proportion of participants labeling the vignettes as stalking would increase as the severity of the behaviors increased. Both studies also hypothesized that vignettes describing a male perpetrator and a female target would be readily classified as stalking and would generate higher levels of safety concerns.

EXPERIMENT 1

Method

Participants were students in introductory psychology classes at a large private university in the northeast United States; the students volunteered for this study as a method of fulfilling the course research requirement. Participants were informed that they would be participating in a study of perceptions of behavior in which they would read a series of vignettes and answer several questions that pertained to each. Each participant received a questionnaire packet that contained one of six stalking vignettes, all of which described interactions between a male and a female using a 2 × 3 design to vary gender of the perpetrator and target (male perpetrator pursuing a female target and female perpetrator pursuing a male target) and the relationship between these individuals (stranger, acquaintance, and a previous romantic relationship or former intimate). Figure 10.1 presents examples of these vignettes. Participants also completed a brief demographic questionnaire, and they read and responded to two additional vignettes with

Figure 10.1   Sample Stalking Vignettes: Experiment 1

Prior intimate relationship. Jane and Joe, both of whom are doctors, had been dating for several months. Joe realized that things were not working out in the relationship and decided that it would be best to break up with Jane. Jane, however, wanted to continue the relationship. Since the breakup, Jane has called Joe several times, but he no longer answers her phone calls. Jane has also sent flowers and other gifts to Joe's house along with personal letters. Lately, Joe thinks that he has seen Jane outside his house.

Acquaintance. Jane is a doctor in a large hospital where Joe, another doctor, was recently hired. Shortly after meeting Jane, Joe became interested in pursuing a relationship with her. Joe called Jane on the telephone, but she indicated that she was not interested in a relationship. Since then, Joe has called Jane several times, but she no longer answers his phone calls. Joe has also sent flowers and other gifts to Jane's house along with personal letters. Lately, Jane thinks that she has seen Joe outside her house.

Stranger (no prior relationship). Joe, a doctor, was interviewed by the local news after his hospital announced that it would be laying off employees. Jane, a doctor too, saw Joe on television being interviewed. Jane found Joe to be very attractive and was interested in pursuing a relationship with him. Jane called Joe on the telephone, but he indicated that he was not interested in a relationship. Since then, Jane has called Joe several times, but he no longer answers her phone calls. Jane has also sent flowers and other gifts to Joe's house along with personal letters. Lately, Joe thinks that he has seen a woman outside his house.

---

accompanying questions that served as a filler to distract attention from the stalking vignette.

After reading the vignette, participants indicated their reactions to a series of questions using a Likert-type scale from 1 (*definitely*) to 5 (*definitely not*). These questions included whether the behavior described in the vignette constituted stalking . . . , whether the target should be worried about his or her safety, whether the target should meet with the perpetrator, whether the perpetrator would become violent, whether the target should seek help from the police or security, and whether the perpetrator needs psychiatric treatment. To ease interpretation of the data, responses to several of these questions were reversed so that a higher score on all variables reflected a greater degree of concern over the perpetrator's behavior.

Participants were also asked several questions that pertained to their personal experiences with stalking. The wording in the primary question used to assess prior stalking victimization was also varied to ascertain whether the term *stalking* influenced perceptions of one's own experiences. Toward this end, half of the participants were asked whether they had "ever been stalked," and the remainder were asked whether they had "ever been repeatedly followed (i.e., more than once) and/or harassed by another person." Participants who responded affirmatively to this question were asked to provide details regarding the stalking experience, including

the number of times they have been stalked . . . , the length of time this behavior continued, and the occurrence of several specific stalking behaviors (e.g., receiving unwanted gifts, waiting outside of work or school, etc.).

***

DISCUSSION

The results of this study contradicted our hypothesis that female participants would be more likely to label the vignettes as stalking compared to male participants. Moreover, there was no difference in perceptions of whether the behavior described constituted stalking between vignettes describing a male perpetrator and female target versus a female perpetrator and male target (although the three-way interaction effect suggests that some complex relationships between character gender and perpetrator/target relationship may exist). This interaction clearly requires further analysis before any conclusions can be drawn. Finally, there was no relationship between prior experience as a target of stalking and perceptions of stalking, again contradicting commonsense assumptions regarding the influence of past experience on perceptions of behavior. This null finding, however, is consistent with the emerging literature on perceptions of sexual harassment, which demonstrate that prior sexual harassment victimization does not influence perceptions of whether behaviors constitute sexual harassment (Stockdale et al., 2002).

Despite the compelling findings observed in this study, a number of questions arose, such as whether young, predominantly Caucasian undergraduates are an appropriate reference group against which to base conclusions regarding stalking perceptions. In addition, because the behaviors described in these vignettes were deliberately vague, it is unclear whether similar findings would emerge if the behaviors described were more strongly suggestive of stalking. These limitations were addressed in the subsequent study in which vignettes varied according to the severity of the stalking behaviors described (rather than the relationship between perpetrator and target). This study also included a substantially larger sample with considerably greater diversity in terms of ethnicity, age, and socioeconomic levels.

EXPERIMENT 2

Method

Participants in the second study consisted of 376 undergraduate and graduate students in an urban, public college that has the primary mission to provide undergraduate and graduate training in criminal justice and related fields. Participants were recruited through undergraduate and graduate classes. Each participant was given one of six possible vignettes that described an interaction between a man and a woman (Tom and Mary) who met at a party. Based on the New York State anti-stalking law, three scenarios depicting potential stalking behavior were developed. One scenario depicted behaviors that did not meet the definition of stalking under New York State law, while a second scenario depicted behaviors that were consistent with stalking in the fourth degree (misdemeanor stalking), and the third scenario depicted behaviors that were consistent with stalking in the third degree (felony stalking). Each of these scenarios was built on the previous one such that the length of each scenario became slightly longer as the criminality of the perpetrator's behaviors increased (Figure 10.2). Finally, two versions of each of these three

scenarios were created—one describing a male perpetrator and a female victim and a second describing the reverse scenario, thus resulting in a total of six conditions.

After reading the vignette, participants indicated their reactions to a series of questions using a 5-point, Likert-type scale where 1 = *definitely* and 5 = *definitely not*. These questions included whether the behavior described in the vignette constituted stalking . . . , whether the behavior would be considered a crime (specifically, stalking under New York law), whether the perpetrator has a legitimate purpose for contacting the target, whether the target should be worried about his or her safety, whether the perpetrator would become violent, and whether the perpetrator suffered from mental illness. Participants were also asked about their own familiarity level with New York anti-stalking law along with a series of demographic questions.

DISCUSSION

This study further supported the earlier findings regarding the lack of any influence of either participant or perpetrator/target gender on perceptions of whether stalking has occurred. On the other hand, these data supported the previous finding that vignettes describing a male perpetrator and female target elicited greater concerns regarding safety than vignettes describing a female perpetrator and a male target. Contrary to the expectations, female participants were no more likely than male participants to label the vignettes as stalking. However, these results support the distinctions made by New York State's anti-stalking law, as participants were more likely to correctly identify both of the vignettes describing fourth-degree stalking and third degree stalking as stalking as compared to the no-stalking condition (but no significant differences existed between the two stalking vignettes). Interestingly, although few differences in perceptions were observed across ethnic groups, there was no identifiable pattern to these findings, and the relatively small number of participants in some categories limits the ability to interpret these findings.

***

Figure 10.2   Study Two: Sample Vignettes With Conditions Embedded—Tom pursuing Mary

---

(Paragraph 1) *All conditions.* Tom met Mary at a party that a mutual friend hosted. They talked for a while at the party before going their separate ways. Mary worked at the local bank as a teller. Mary noticed that Tom began coming into the bank to make transactions.

(Paragraph 2) *No stalking condition.* Usually he would wave at Mary if he saw her, and a few times, he waited specifically for Mary to help him with his transaction. After a few weeks of the same pattern, Mary was beginning to question Tom's intentions. She didn't think that anyone could possibly have as much banking to do as Tom seemed to have.

(Added to Paragraph 2) *Third- and fourth-degree stalking conditions.* Within a few weeks, Tom started calling the bank to make sure Mary was working before he came in. Mary took a week off from work and went out of town. When she came back to work her manager was very angry with her. "Some guy named Tom keeps calling at least 6 or 7 times a day to see where you are at. I told him not to call here anymore." The bank manager warned Mary that if this continued he would have to fire Mary.

(Paragraph 3) *No stalking condition.* Mary, not sure of how to reach Tom, called their mutual friend. Mary was informed that Tom is very shy but found her very easy to talk to and would like to take her out on a date. Mary called Tom and thanked him for his interest in her. She then explained that she was not interested in dating anyone but would like to remain friends with Tom. Tom agreed and told Mary that if she changed her mind to just call him.

(Added to Paragraph 3) *Third- and fourth-degree stalking conditions.* Mary also told Tom that the bank that she works for does not like its employees to receive too many personal phone calls. Mary told Tom that if it is an emergency, he is welcome to call her at the bank, but she does not want to lose her job. Tom agreed.

(Paragraph 4) *No stalking condition.* Mary still saw Tom at the bank, but now she was seeing him when she went to the market, and he was on the same bus that Mary takes to and from work. When Tom would see Mary, he would wave or smile. Mary decided to tell Tom to stop following her. When she did, Tom told her that she was nuts. "This is a small town. What market would you like me to shop in? Where do you think I should do my banking?" Mary just shrugged her shoulders and told Tom that she didn't care where he shopped or banked as long as she wasn't around. Despite confronting Tom, Mary would still see Tom when she was working or running errands, but he would not acknowledge Mary.

(Added to Paragraph 4) *Fourth-degree stalking condition.* The next day Mary came to work to find a teddy bear holding a red rose with a card signed "your special friend Tom." Later that morning, Tom called her to see if she received the gift. Mary thanked him and reiterated that she could not receive phone calls. Later that day Tom called just to say "Hi" and then called to find out if she would like to go to dinner. Mary turned Tom down and asked him to stop calling her. The next day Tom called Mary at the bank to apologize for his behavior and promised never to call again.

(Added to Paragraph 4) *Third-degree stalking condition.* The following week when Mary was leaving work, Tom was waiting in the bank parking lot. Mary ignored Tom when he said hello to her and just walked [away]. Tom became very angry and began to yell at Mary. "I don't understand you, Mary. . . . I am a really nice guy and would make you happy if you only let me. I only came here to apologize to you. Why won't you go out with me? Do you really think that you are so much better than me?. . . . Just wait. . . . It is only going to be a matter of time before you go out with me." Tom then walked away. The next day Tom called Mary at the bank to apologize for his behavior.

GENERAL DISCUSSION

With a growing number of anti-stalking laws defining stalking in terms of whether the individual had a "reasonable fear" of harm, the need to understand how individuals perceive stalking behaviors has become increasingly evident. These studies addressed several important aspects related to perceptions of stalking in complementary ways. In particular, these studies represent some of the first attempts to systematically analyze the extent to which stalking behaviors, victim perpetrator relationships, and gender (of both the parties and the respondents) influence determinations of whether stalking has occurred and the potential risk posed to victims.

The first study utilized a vignette in which the determination of whether stalking had actually occurred was ambiguous. In this context, the relationship between target and perpetrator (i.e., strangers, coworker acquaintances, or former dating partners) and the gender of these actors (i.e., male perpetrator/female target vs. female perpetrator/male target) significantly influenced responses to the stalking vignettes. Specifically, participants were significantly less likely to characterize the vignette as stalking when the actors were described as having previously been involved in an intimate relationship compared to the vignette describing the two characters as having been merely acquaintances or having had no prior relationship (strangers). Interestingly, this apparent reluctance to characterize harassing behaviors as stalking when a prior relationship exists stands in contrast to the growing body of epidemiological data demonstrating that stalking is far more common among prior intimates compared to acquaintances or strangers (e.g., Budd & Mattinson, 2000; Tjaden & Thoennes, 1998).

On the other hand, although gender of the vignette characters did not influence determinations of whether stalking had occurred, it did influence perceptions of safety for the target of the behaviors. Several indicators of concern for safety differed significantly depending on the perpetrator/target gender, including whether the target should be concerned for his or her safety, should seek help from the police or hospital security, and should meet with the perpetrator. Interestingly, a question directly targeting the risk of violence (i.e., "How likely is it that Joe/Jane will be violent toward Jane/Joe?") did not differ by perpetrator/target gender, suggesting that the influence of gender on perceived risk may be somewhat subtle. Alternatively, participants may be more sensitive to fear-inducing behaviors when the target is a woman, even though they do not fear explicit assault or violence per se.

The perception of male stalkers as more dangerous than female stalkers, although clearly logical, is not consistent with the existing empirical data. Rates of violence among female stalkers have been comparable to those for males in several studies (Purcell, Pathé, & Mullen, 2001; Rosenfeld, [2003]; Rosenfeld & Harmon, 2002), and there is no evidence that the severity of violence inflicted by women stalkers is substantially less than males. Yet the finding that male stalkers engender more concern than female stalkers echoes the data presented by Sinclair and Frieze

(2000), who observed that men generate more fear in those individuals whom they pursue than women do, even when they do not display overt indications of aggression.

The second study utilized a similar methodology, but instead of comparing responses to an ambiguous vignette, vignettes were systematically varied in terms of the severity of stalking behavior (i.e., vignettes that did not fulfill the New York State definition of stalking vs. vignettes characterizing misdemeanor and felonious stalking). In these analyses, in which gender of the perpetrator and target were varied in a similar manner to the first study (male perpetrator/female target vs. female perpetrator/male target), severity of stalking clearly influenced determinations of whether stalking had occurred (supporting the validity of the experimental manipulation). Participants were significantly more likely to consider the behaviors described to be criminal (i.e., reflecting stalking) in the vignettes describing third and fourth-degree stalking (felony and misdemeanor, respectively) compared to the no-stalking vignette. There were no differences between the third- and fourth-degree stalking vignettes regarding criminality. As in the first study, perpetrator/target gender did not influence determinations of stalking but did influence safety concerns, as participants considered the stalker to be significantly more likely to harm the target when the perpetrator was male and the target was female versus the reverse scenario (female perpetrator/male target).

Gender of the participant, however, appears to have a more complex effect on stalking perceptions. In the second study, women participants were somewhat more likely to perceive the vignettes as indicative of stalking than were men, regardless of the perpetrator/target gender. This finding is similar to the gender effect found by Dennison and Thompson (2002). Yet, in the first study, no such main effect emerged. Instead, a significant three-way interaction effect between participant gender, gender of the vignette characters, and relationship of the vignette characters was found. Both men and women appeared more likely to identify the behavior described in the stranger vignette as stalking when the perpetrator was of the same gender as the participant, whereas they rated the acquaintances vignettes as more indicative of stalking when the target was of their same gender. This pattern may reflect a tendency to identify with the behavior of the perpetrator in the stranger vignettes and the target in the acquaintance vignettes, decreasing the likelihood that participants would identify the behavior described in the vignette as inappropriate (i.e., stalking). Because perpetrator/target relationship was not varied in the second study, it is unclear whether these effects would have remained consistent in cases where the stalking behaviors were more clear-cut. Thus, although there may be some differences in how men and women perceive certain aspects of stalking, these differences are quite modest and inconsistent. Also observed in the second study was an unexpected influence of ethnicity on safety concerns and attributions for the stalking behavior. Because there was no consistent pattern to these findings, their implications are unclear. Furthermore, the first study was almost entirely composed of Caucasian participants, precluding the analysis of any ethnicity effects. Clearly, these findings, which have not emerged in any of the published research to date, require further exploration.

[In the first study,] contrary to the expectations, participants who reported personal prior experience of having been stalked did not differ from those who reported no such experience in relation to perceptions of stalking or risk of harm. (These data were not available in the second study). Although it was anticipated that participants who had been previously stalked would be more attuned to this behavior—and therefore be more likely to identify harassing behaviors as stalking—this pattern did not emerge. This null finding might reflect sample limitations, as stalking victimization among college students may be different in nature, intensity, and impact from stalking victimization among the general population (hence, the substantially higher rates of stalking victimization reported by college students compared to the general population). Individuals who have experienced more severe types of stalking than that of typical college students might have more readily identified the vignettes as indicative of stalking, whereas the college students studied in this investigation did not reveal this pattern.

Alternatively, this null finding may reflect a limitation of the study methodology, as more striking differences might emerge with different vignette characteristics (e.g., more overt or potentially dangerous stalking behaviors). Yet, similar null findings regarding the lack of influence of past experience on harassment perceptions have been reported in the context of sexual harassment (Stockdale et al., 2002). Thus, although commonsense assumptions often foster the belief that past experience with harassment may sensitize targets to future harassment, these null findings call such assumptions into question.

Despite the consistency across these two studies with regard to many aspects of stalking perceptions, several methodological limitations are noteworthy. First, although there is no doubt that stalking occurs among college undergraduates, the nature of these experiences may be quite different than among the general population. However, this criticism is substantially less valid for the data reported in the second study, in which participants ranged in age from 18 to 60 and reflected a broad diversity of ethnic and socioeconomic backgrounds. Moreover, many of these findings supported and extended those of previous researchers who used samples drawn from the general public (i.e., Dennison & Thompson, 2000, 2002; Hills & Taplin, 1998), suggesting that sample differences may not have dramatically influenced the study results.

Also, although ecological validity concerns may apply to the analysis of ambiguous vignettes in the first study (i.e., the behaviors described were not indisputably reflective of stalking), this criticism does not apply to the second study, and yet similar results regarding gender effects emerged. The second study, however, utilized vignettes of varying lengths, as each vignette built on the previous one by adding additional stalking behaviors (to be consistent with the legal standards for stalking offenses in New York). Thus, the finding that increasing levels of stalking severity were associated with increased likelihood of labeling the behaviors as stalking is confounded by the amount of information presented in the vignettes. Future research should evaluate the possibility that vignette length influences perceptions of stalking.

The analysis of the perpetrator/target relationship is also necessarily limited. First, this variable was included only in the first study, and in this vignette, the actors were described as physicians. The characterization of the actors as credible authority figures may have decreased the likelihood that some respondents would identify the behaviors as indicative of stalking, particularly among a college student sample in which respect for authority figures may be heightened. Because this variable was not included in the second study, it is unclear whether similar relationship influences would occur in a scenario in which stalking was less ambiguous, although the results of previous research (e.g., Dennison & Thompson, 2002) suggest that the influence of situational variables may be less pronounced as the ambiguity of the behaviors decreases. Nevertheless, by varying the perceived credibility and/or prestige of the vignette characters, this potentially important determinant of participant stalking perceptions may emerge as a significant factor, either in isolation (i.e., a main effect) or in conjunction with other variables (i.e., interaction effects).

Despite these limitations, the present investigations represent one of the few attempts to analyze the interrelationships between characteristics of the harassment and characteristics of the respondents in terms of perceived stalking and risk of harm. These findings demonstrate that both participant gender and the characteristics of the perpetrator and target influence perceptions of stalking and the risks associated with this behavior. The implications of these findings for the legal system are multiple, including the possibility that jurors' perceptions may differ in a systematic manner whether a stalking victim's claims of reasonable fear are justified. Also, the relatively lesser concern paid to female stalkers in these studies suggests an important avenue for clinical intervention, as male stalking victims may underestimate the risk of harm posed by a female stalker. Clearly, further attention is needed to better understand the perceptions and stereotypes that influence behavior in response to stalking.

11

PSYCHOPATHY

A Clinical Construct Whose Time Has Come

ROBERT D. HARE

Psychopathy is a socially devastating disorder defined by a constellation of affective, interpersonal, and behavioral characteristics, including egocentricity; impulsivity; irresponsibility; shallow emotions; lack of empathy, guilt, or remorse; pathological lying; manipulativeness; and the persistent violation of social norms and expectations. This article is a personal, selective view of some major changes and trends in the empirical research on psychopathy from 1974 to 1994. The focus is on the assessment and diagnosis of psychopathy and its implications for the mental health and criminal justice systems, with brief reference made to several recent trends in the application of cognitive neuroscience to the study of the disorder.

Let me begin with a framework that helps me to make sense of what often appears to be senseless behavior (Hare, 1993, 1995). Psychopaths can be described as intra-species predators who use charm, manipulation, intimidation, and violence to control others and to satisfy their own selfish needs. Lacking in conscience and in feelings for others, they cold-bloodedly take what they want and do as they please, violating social norms and expectations without the slightest sense of guilt or regret. Viewed in this way, it is not surprising that in spite of their small numbers—perhaps 1% of the general population—they make up from 15% to 25 % of our prison population and are responsible for a markedly disproportionate amount of the serious crime, violence, and social distress in every society. Furthermore, their depredations affect virtually everyone at one time or another, because they form a significant proportion of persistent criminals, drug dealers, spouse and child abusers, swindlers and con men, mercenaries, corrupt politicians, unethical lawyers, terrorists, cult leaders, black marketeers, gang members, and radical political activists. They are well represented in the business and corporate world, particularly during chaotic restructuring, where the rules and their enforcement are lax and accountability is difficult to determine (Babiak, 1995). It is not uncommon for psychopaths to emerge as "patriots" and

Editors' Note: This article was originally published in *Criminal Justice and Behavior,* Vol. 23, No. 1, March 1996, pp. 25–54. Some background information about the DSM and some recidivism research have been omitted.

"saviors" in societies experiencing social, economic, and political upheaval (e.g., Rwanda, the former Yugoslavia, and the former Soviet Union). Wrapped in the flag, they enrich themselves by callously exploiting ethnic, cultural, or racial tensions and grievances.

***

THE CONSTRUCT OF PSYCHOPATHY

Psychopathy began to emerge as a formal clinical construct in the last century, but references to individuals we now readily recognize as having been psychopathic can be found in biblical, classical, medieval, and other historical sources (Cleckley, 1976; Rotenberg & Diamond, 1971). Like most clinical constructs, psychopathy has been, and continues to be, the subject of considerable debate, scientific and otherwise. Some commentators, no doubt influenced by the inconsistent, fuzzy, and legalistic ways in which the term has been used, have suggested that the disorder is mythological, a view that appeals to those who feel uncomfortable about psychiatric labels or the role of individual differences in abnormal and antisocial behavior. Clinical and empirical evidence, however, clearly indicates that the construct, whatever we label it— psychopathy, sociopathy, antisocial personality disorder, dyssocial personality disorder— is anything but mythological. It is true that the etiology, dynamics, and conceptual boundaries of the disorder are the subject of much speculation, but at the same time, there is a reasonably consistent clinical tradition concerning its core affective, interpersonal, and behavioral attributes. Interestingly, this traditional view of psychopathy cuts across a broad spectrum of groups, including psychiatrists, psychologists, criminal justice personnel, and experimental psychopathologists, as well as the lay public (. . . Cleckley, 1976; Davies & Feldman, 1981; . . . Livesley, Jackson, & Schroeder, 1992; . . .).

Of course, agreement on the descriptive features of a disorder means little unless it can be shown that the features define a valid clinical construct capable of reliable identification. That they do, in my opinion, is beyond question. Descriptively, the clinicians "got it right," and my own research efforts are firmly grounded in their work. However, translating their keen insights into solid empirical research has long been hampered by inadequate measurement of the construct.

THE ASSESSMENT OF PSYCHOPATHY

Progress in any discipline is difficult without psychometrically sound procedures for measuring key constructs. Psychopathy is no exception, and the lack of such procedures has hindered not only the development of a body of replicable, theoretically meaningful research findings but also society's acceptance of psychopathy as an important clinical construct with practical implications.

DSM-II

The second edition of the American Psychiatric Association's *Diagnostic and Statistical Manual of Mental Disorders* (DSM-II) appeared in 1968. In line with clinical tradition, it described psychopaths (referred to as people exhibiting an antisocial personality) as unsocialized, impulsive, guiltless, selfish, and callous individuals who rationalize their behavior and fail to learn from experience (American Psychiatric Association, 1968). However, DSM-II did not provide explicit diagnostic criteria for the disorder, and in the 1970s, many researchers attempted to operationalize the disorder in other ways (see review by Hare & Cox, 1978). For example, my colleagues and I made global ratings of psychopathy based on clinical accounts of the disorder (especially those by Cleckley, 1976). Other researchers used scales derived from self-report inventories, such as the Minnesota Multiphasic Personality Inventory (Dahlstrom & Welsh, 1960) and the California Psychological Inventory (Gough, 1969). The psychometric properties of most of these procedures, as indicants of psychopathy, were unclear, and the tenuous relationships they bore to one another made it difficult or impossible to generate a solid body of replicable research findings (Hare, 1985). I might add that although self-report and other personality tests play an important role in clinical assessment, their use as reliable indicants of psychopathy for clinical or research purposes cannot be recommended.

DSM-III

With the publication of DSM-Ill (American Psychiatric Association, 1980), the diagnostic situation improved in one respect but worsened in another. The improvement was the introduction of a list of explicit criteria for psychopathy, now referred to as antisocial personality disorder (APD). Unfortunately, these criteria consisted almost entirely of persistent violations of social norms, including lying, stealing, truancy, inconsistent work behavior, and traffic arrests. Among the main reasons given for this dramatic shift away from the use of clinical inferences were that personality traits are difficult to measure reliably and that it is easier to agree on the behaviors that typify a disorder than on the reasons why they occur. The result was a diagnostic category with good reliability but dubious validity, a category that lacked congruence with traditional conceptions of psychopathy. . . .

THE PSYCHOPATHY CHECKLIST AND ITS REVISION

In 1980, I first described a research tool for operationalizing the construct of psychopathy (Hare, 1980). Later referred to as the Psychopathy Checklist (PCL), it was revised in 1985 and formally published several years later (Hare, 1991; see also Hart, Hare, & Harpur, 1992). Recently described as "state of the art" (Fulero, 1995, p. 454), the PCL-R is a 20-item clinical rating scale completed on the basis of a semi-structured interview and detailed collateral or file information. Each item is scored on a 3-point scale according to specific criteria. The total score, which can range from 0 to 40, provides an estimate of the extent to which a given individual matches the prototypical psychopath, as exemplified, for example, in the work of Cleckley (1976). The PCL-R's psychometric properties are well established with male offenders and forensic patients and, to an increasing extent, with female (Strachan, 1994) and adolescent (Forth, Hart, & Hare, 1990) offenders. Indices of internal consistency (alpha coefficient, mean inter-item correlation) and inter-rater reliability are high, and evidence for all aspects of validity is substantial. Mean PCL- R scores in male and female offender populations typically range from about 22 to 24, with a standard deviation of from 6 to 8. Mean scores in forensic psychiatric populations are somewhat lower, about 20, with about the same standard deviation. For research purposes, a score of 30 generally is considered indicative of psychopathy, although some investigators have obtained good results with cutoff scores as low as 25.

The high internal consistency of the PCL and PCL-R indicates that they measure a unitary construct, yet factor analyses of each version consistently reveal a stable two-factor structure (Hare et al., 1990; Harpur, Hakstian, & Hare, 1988). Factor 1 consists of items having to do with the affective/interpersonal features of psychopathy, such as egocentricity, manipulativeness, callousness, and lack of remorse, characteristics that many clinicians consider central to psychopathy. Factor 2 reflects those features of psychopathy associated with an impulsive, antisocial, and unstable lifestyle, or social deviance. The two factors are correlated about .5 but have different patterns of correlations with external variables. These patterns make theoretical and clinical sense. For example, Factor 1 is correlated positively with prototypicality ratings of narcissistic and histrionic personality disorder, self-report measures of narcissism and Machiavellianism, risk for recidivism and violence, and unusual processing of affective material (see below). It is correlated negatively with self-report measures of empathy and anxiety. Factor 2 is most strongly correlated with diagnoses of APD, criminal and antisocial behaviors, substance abuse, and various self-report measures of psychopathy. It is also correlated negatively with socioeconomic level, education, and IQ. The PCL-R factors appear to measure two facets of a higher-order construct, namely, psychopathy.

Comparisons between the PCL-R and the DSM-III-R category of APD are illuminating. . . . Although PCL-R scores are significantly correlated with diagnoses of APD in forensic populations, the association is an asymmetric one. This is because in these populations, the base rate for PCL-R-defined psychopathy is much lower (15% to 25%) than the base rate for APD

(50% to 75%). Most of the psychopaths also meet the criteria for APD, but most of those with APD are not psychopaths. That is because APD is defined largely by antisocial behaviors and consequently taps the social deviance components of psychopathy (Factor 2) much better than it does the affective/interpersonal components of the disorder (Factor 1). APD more or less leaves out the personality traits necessary to differentiate between psychopathic and other criminals.

Although my colleagues and I have taken great pains to differentiate between psychopathy and APD, some clinicians and investigators use the labels as if the constructs they measure were interchangeable. They are not, and the failure to recognize this simple fact results in confusion and misleading conclusions (see Hare, in press; Mealey, 1995).

The Psychopathy Checklist: Screening Version

The PCL-R takes several hours to complete, too long for the average clinician working in acute psychiatric and mental health facilities. Several years ago John Monahan asked if it would be possible to develop a brief version of the PCL-R for use in the John D. and Catherine T. MacArthur Foundation project on the prediction of violence in the mentally disordered. With generous support from the foundation, we began development of the 12-item Psychopathy Checklist: Screening Version (PCL:SV; Hart, Cox, & Hare, 1995; Hart, Hare, & Forth, 1993). The PCL:SV is conceptually and empirically related to the PCL-R and can be used as a screen for psychopathy in forensic populations or as a stand-alone instrument for research with non-criminals, including civil psychiatric patients (as in the MacArthur Foundation project). It has the same factor structure as the PCL-R, with the affective/interpersonal and socially deviant components of psychopathy each being measured by six items.

Psychopathy in Children

Most clinicians and researchers are reluctant to speak of psychopathic children, yet it is likely that the personality traits and behaviors that define adult psychopathy begin to manifest themselves in childhood (Lahey & Kazdin, 1990; Robins, 1966; Robins & Rutter, 1990). If so, early intervention is essential if we are ever to have any hope of influencing the development and behavioral expression of the disorder. The problem, however, is complicated by general failure to differentiate the budding psychopath from other children who exhibit serious emotional and behavioral problems, particularly those children diagnosed with conduct disorder, attention-deficit hyperactivity disorder, or oppositional defiant disorder.

Recently, Frick, O'Brien, Wootton, and McBurnett (1994) modified the PCL-R items so that they were suitable for children and could be rated by parents and teachers. In a sample of clinic-referred children between the ages of 6 and 13 years, the items identified much the same two-factor structure (although in reverse order) as that found with adults (Harpur, Hare, & Hakstian, 1989). One dimension was associated with impulsivity and conduct problems (similar to PCL-R Factor 2) and the other with the interpersonal and motivational aspects of psychopathy, such as lack of guilt, lack of empathy, and superficial charm (similar to PCL-R Factor 1). These two dimensions had different patterns of associations with a variety of external variables, including conduct disorder. An important implication of their findings is that children with conduct disorder constitute a small subset with, and a larger subset without, psychopathic features. Presumably, each subset has a different developmental history and requires different treatment strategies.

DSM-IV

In preparation for DSM-IV (American Psychiatric Association, 1994), the American Psychiatric Association carried out a multi-site APD Field Trial (Hare, Hart. & Harpur, 1991; Widiger & Corbitt, 1993). Stated goals of the Field Trial were to shorten the criteria set and to improve coverage of the traditional symptoms of psychopathy. These symptoms were represented by a 10-item psychopathic personality disorder (PPD) criteria set derived from the PCL:SV and by the ICD-10 criteria for dyssocial personality disorder (World Health Organization, 1990). The PPD items were as follows: lacks remorse, lacks empathy, deceitful and manipulative, glib and superficial, inflated and arrogant self-appraisal, early behavior problems, adult antisocial problems, poor behavioral controls, impulsive, and irresponsible. The results of the Field Trial were described in detail by Widiger et al. (in press).

Many researchers and clinicians hoped that the Field Trial would bring the diagnosis of APD back on track, but it did so only in a limited sense, and certainly not explicitly or formally. The DSM-IV criteria for APD remain problematical (see Hare & Hart, 1995). . . .

***

DSM-IV presents clinicians working in the criminal justice system with an additional problem. The term *psychopathy* was absent in DSM-Ill-R. The DSM-IV text (American Psychiatric Association, 1994) now says that antisocial personality disorder "has also been referred to as psychopathy, sociopathy, or dyssocial personality disorder" (p. 645), thereby making it easier for forensic clinicians to use the construct of psychopathy in their reports or court testimony. Indeed, the text makes many references to the personality traits traditionally associated with psychopathy. However, the listed diagnostic criteria for APD actually identify individuals who are persistently antisocial, most of whom are not psychopaths. . . .

It seems that DSM-IV—perhaps inadvertently—has established two different sets of diagnostic criteria for APD, one for the general public and one for forensic settings. Individuals diagnosed as APD outside of forensic settings might not be so diagnosed once they find themselves in prisons or forensic hospitals, unless they also exhibit personality traits indicative of psychopathy. The inclusion of such traits in the forensic diagnosis of APD apparently is a matter of judgment for the individual clinician; as a result, a given offender or defendant might be diagnosed as APD by a clinician who chooses to use only the listed criteria and as *not* APD by one who chooses to include psychopathic personality traits in the diagnosis. In each case, the diagnostic strategy would be consistent with DSM-IV guidelines, a situation that should provide some interesting courtroom debates.

***

. . . [A]n unfortunate consequence of the approach adopted in DSM-IV is that, now more than ever, researchers and clinicians will be confused about the relationship between APD and psychopathy, sometimes using them interchangeably and other times treating them as separate clinical constructs. Perhaps most serious will be situations in which a clinician diagnoses an offender or forensic patient as APD according to the formal DSM-IV criteria, and then uses the research literature on psychopathy to make statements about treatability, likelihood of re-offending, and risk for violence. As I indicate below, the predictive validity of psychopathy, as measured by the PCL-R, is impressive but has little direct relevance to APD.

Psychopathy: Continuum or Discrete Category?

One of the questions often raised by clinicians, researchers, and the public is this: Do psychopaths differ from the rest of us in degree or in kind? Many researchers (e.g., Blackburn, 1993; Livesley & Schroeder, 1991) prefer dimensional conceptualizations of personality disorders, whereas formal diagnostic systems, such as DSM-IV, make it difficult to adopt anything other than a categorical view (i.e., that an individual is either APD or not APD).

Recently, Harris, Rice, and Quinsey (1994) used extensive file information to obtain PCL-R scores for 653 male forensic patients, in order to determine if the dimensional PCL-R reflected a dimensional or a categorical construct. Using four different taxonometric methods, they obtained results consistent with the hypothesis that psychopathy is a discrete category, or taxon. Their procedures allowed for the emergence of only two groups or classes of patients, those in the psychopathy taxon and those not in the taxon. They concluded that the optimal PCL-R score for inclusion in the psychopathy taxon was about 25, somewhat lower than the cutoff score of 30 recommended for research purposes (Hare, 1991). More recently, David Cooke (personal communication, November 21, 1994) analyzed two large sets of PCL-R scores, one from male offenders who had taken part in research conducted by my laboratory and the other from his own stratified random sample of the Scottish prison population. Cooke's analyses differed from those of Harris et al. (1994) in two important ways: His PCL-R scores were based on both semi-structured interviews and file information, and his taxonometric procedures allowed for the emergence of more than two classes of offenders. Each of his two samples yielded three classes, one clearly being a psychopathy taxon. The optimal PCL-R score for inclusion in this taxon was between 28 and 32, in line with the recommended cutoffs for the diagnosis of psychopathy.

The results of these studies are certainly suggestive, but more research is needed, in part because of problems with taxonometric methods, but also to determine the generalizability of the findings, not only in different samples and cultures but with different procedures for the assessment of psychopathy.

PSYCHOPATHY AND THE CRIMINAL JUSTICE SYSTEM

Over the past two decades, one of the more dramatic changes in our view of psychopathy has been in its significance to the criminal justice system, particularly with respect to the assessment of risk for recidivism and violence. Guze (1976), for example, noted that once a person had been convicted of a felony, psychiatric diagnoses, including sociopathy, were not very helpful in predicting criminal activities. This view, however, was compromised by the use of diagnostic criteria at that time that permitted almost 80% of felons to receive a diagnosis of sociopathy. By way of contrast, there is now an extensive literature indicating that current assessments of psychopathy, either by themselves or as part of risk equations, are highly predictive of treatability, recidivism, and violence. This literature is based almost entirely on research involving the use of the PCL-R. For this reason, each of the studies referred to in the rest of this article used the PCL-R for the assessment of psychopathy, unless otherwise indicated.

Psychopathy and Crime

Although some psychopaths manage to ply their trade with few formal contacts with the criminal justice system, their personality clearly is compatible with a propensity to violate many of society's rules and expectations. The crimes of those who do break the law run the gamut from petty theft and fraud to cold-blooded violence (Hare & McPherson, 1984; Kosson, Smith, & Newman, 1990; Wong, 1984). However, it is primarily the violence of psychopaths that captures the headlines, particularly when it ends in an apparently senseless death.

The ease with which psychopaths engage in instrumental and dispassionate violence (Cornell et al., 1993; Serin, 1991; Williamson, Hare, & Wong, 1987) has very real significance for society in general and for law enforcement personnel in particular. For example, a recent study by the Federal Bureau of Investigation (1992) found that almost half of the law enforcement officers who died in the line of duty were killed by individuals who closely matched the personality profile of the psychopath.

Although the typical criminal career is relatively short, there are individuals who devote most of their adolescent and adult life to delinquent and criminal enterprises (Blumstein, Cohen, Roth, & Visher, 1986). Many of these career criminals become less grossly antisocial in middle age (Blumstein et al., 1986; Robins, 1966). About half of the criminal psychopaths we study show a relatively sharp reduction in criminality around age 35 or 40, primarily with respect to nonviolent offenses (Hare, McPherson, & Forth, 1988). Their propensity for violence and aggression appears to be rather persistent across much of the life span, a finding also reported by Harris, Rice, and Cormier (1991). I should note that age-related reductions in overt criminality do not necessarily mean that the individual has become a warm, loving, and moral citizen. Robins (1966) observed that many psychopaths become less grossly antisocial with age but remain thoroughly disagreeable individuals. My own experience with several "reformed" or "resocialized" psychopaths can certainly attest to the folk validity of her observation (Hare, 1993).

The question I would ask is this: Are age-related reductions in the criminality of psychopaths paralleled by changes in core personality traits, or have these individuals simply learned new ways of staying out of prison?

Although I share the view of many clinicians that the personality structure of psychopaths is too stable to account for the behavioral changes that sometimes occur in middle age, empirical, longitudinal evidence is needed to resolve the issue. Meanwhile, a recent cross-sectional study of 889 male offenders provides a clue to what we might expect (Harpur & Hare, 1994). The offenders ranged in age from 16 to 70 at the time they were assessed with the PCL or the PCL-R. Scores on Factor 2 (socially deviant features) decreased sharply with age, whereas scores on Factor I (affective/interpersonal features) remained stable with age. These results are consistent with the view that age-related changes in the psychopath's antisocial behavior are not necessarily paralleled by changes in the egocentric, manipulative, and callous traits fundamental to psychopathy. . . .

Recidivism and Risk for Violence

Perhaps the most dramatic change over the past 20 years in the perceived- and actual-importance of psychopathy to the criminal justice system has been in its predictive validity. Various actuarial systems generally did a fairly good job in predicting criminal behavior, and the use of personality traits resulted in little or no incremental validity. As a psychopathy researcher, I always found this situation perplexing. I could never understand, for example, why two individuals with much the same scores on some actuarial device based on similar criminal and demographic characteristics—but one egocentric, cold-blooded, and remorseless and the other not, could possibly present the same risk. That they do not is clearly indicated by the results of a score of recent studies. . . .

***

Recidivism Following Treatment

In my home city of Vancouver, it is not uncommon for a trial judge to accept expert testimony that a defendant convicted of a serious crime is a psychopath and then to sentence him to a prison where "he can receive treatment." Much the same scenario probably is played out in many other jurisdictions. The uninformed

views of the judge and the protestations and anecdotes of those who run prison programs notwithstanding, there is no known treatment for psychopathy. This does not necessarily mean that the egocentric and callous attitudes and behaviors of psychopaths are immutable, only that there are no methodologically sound treatments or "resocialization" programs that have been shown to work with psychopaths. Unfortunately, both the criminal justice system and the public routinely are fooled into believing otherwise. As a result, many psychopaths take part in all sorts of prison treatment programs, put on a good show, make "remarkable progress," convince the therapists and parole board of their reformed character, are released, and pick up where they left off when they entered prison.

Several . . . studies illustrate the point. For example, Ogloff, Wong, and Greenwood (1990) reported that psychopaths, defined by a PCL-R score of at least 30, derived little benefit from a therapeutic community program designed to treat personality-disordered offenders. The psychopaths stayed in the program for a shorter time, were less motivated, and showed less clinical improvement than did other offenders. It might be argued that even though the psychopaths did not do well in this program, some residual benefits could conceivably show up following their release from prison. However, in a survival analysis, Hemphill (1991) found that the estimated reconviction rate in the first year following release was twice as high for the psychopaths (83%) as for the other offenders (42%).

Some of the most popular prison treatment and resocialization programs may actually make psychopaths worse than they were before. Rice, Harris, and Cormier (1992) retrospectively scored the PCL-R from the institutional files of patients of a maximum-security psychiatric facility. They defined psychopaths by a PCL-R score of 25 or more, and non-psychopaths by a score below 25. They then compared the violent recidivism rate of 166 patients who had been treated in an intensive and lengthy therapeutic community program with 119 patients who had not taken part in the program. For non-psychopaths, the violent recidivism rate was 22% for treated patients and 39% for untreated patients. However, the violent recidivism rate for treated psychopaths was *higher* (77%) than was that for untreated psychopaths (55%). How could therapy make someone worse? The answer may be that group therapy and insight-oriented programs help psychopaths to develop better ways of manipulating, deceiving, and using people but do little to help them understand themselves.

***

Sex Offenders

The past few years have seen a sharp increase in public and professional attention paid to sex offenders, particularly those who commit a new offense following release from a treatment program or prison. It has long been recognized that psychopathic sex offenders present special problems for therapists and the criminal justice system. Indeed, some jurisdictions make provision for designating convicted sex offenders as psychopaths and for sentencing them to indefinite terms of detention. . . .

The prevalence of psychopathy—defined by a PCL-R score of at least 30—appears to be relatively high among convicted rapists. Forth and Kroner (1994) reported that in a federal prison, 26.1 % of 211 rapists, 18.3% of 163 mixed sex offenders (including child molesters), and 5.4% of 82 incest offenders were psychopaths. Forth and Kroner's (1994) sample of sex offenders included 60 who were either serial rapists or rapists who killed their victims; 35% of these offenders were psychopaths. The prevalence of the disorder seems to be particularly high among offenders adjudicated by the courts as "sexually dangerous." For example, Prentky and Knight (1991) found that 45.3% of 95 rapists and 30.5% of 59 child molesters in the Massachusetts Treatment Center for Sexually Dangerous Persons at Bridgewater met the PCL criteria for psychopathy.

Sex offenders generally are resistant to treatment (Quinsey, Harris, Rice, & Lalumiere, 1993), but it is the psychopaths among them who are most likely to recidivate early and often. For example, Quinsey, Rice, and Harris (1995), in a follow-up of 178 treated rapists and child molesters, concluded that psychopathy functions as a general predictor of sexual and violent recidivism. In a survival analysis, they found that within 6 years of release from prison, more than 80% of the psychopaths, but only about 20% of the non-psychopaths, had violently recidivated. Many, but not all, of their offenses were sexual in nature. Most dangerous of all were psychopaths sexually "turned on" by violence (Rice, Harris, & Quinsey, 1990).

The implications of psychopathy are just as serious among adolescent sex offenders as among their adult counterparts. Preliminary results from a longitudinal study of adolescent sex offenders (ages 13 to 18) released after treatment at a forensic facility in Vancouver revealed that the mean PCL-R score for 193 male sex offenders was 21.4 (*SD* = 7.0), with about 18% meeting our criteria for psychopathy (O'Shaughnessy, Hare, Gretton, & McBride, 1994). Survival analyses indicated that the reconviction rate for sexual offenses in the first 36 months following release was low (i.e., less than 10%) and unrelated to psychopathy. However, the pattern for other types of offenses was quite different. Thus, within 36 months of release, about 70% of the psychopaths and 40% of all other offenders had been convicted of a non-sexual offense. The results were most striking within the first 12 months of release; the reconviction rate for non-sexual crimes was about 55% for psychopaths, but only about 15% for all other offenders. About 31 % of the psychopaths and only 14% of the other offenders had been convicted for a non-sexual violent offense within 12 months of release. One conclusion is that, following release, many of our adolescent sex offenders, and most of the psychopathic ones, were more likely to be convicted of a non-sexual than a sexual offense. Many of these individuals were not so much specialized sex offenders as they were offenders, and their misbehavior—sexual and otherwise—presumably was a reflection of a generalized propensity to violate social and legal expectations. If so, it may be as important to target antisocial tendencies and behaviors as it is to treat sexual deviancy.

COGNITIVE NEUROSCIENCE AND THE CRIMINAL JUSTICE SYSTEM

Twenty years ago, much of the theory and research on psychopathy was influenced by prevailing theories of learning, emotion, and motivation (Hare, 1978; Hare & Schalling, 1978). We learned much about the biological (especially the autonomic) correlates of psychopathy and about the role of rewards and punishments in establishing and maintaining psychopathic behavior. Although scientifically valuable, much of this work had little practical impact on the general public or on forensic and mental health workers. The situation is beginning to change dramatically, primarily because of the increasing use of procedures and paradigms from cognitive psychology and neuroscience (see Newman & Wallace, 1993). Research on cognition and emotion is particularly interesting because of its potential implications for the issue of criminal responsibility.

Clinicians have long maintained that the cognitions, language, and life experiences of psychopaths lack depth and affect. Recent laboratory research provides neurophysiological support for this view. Space prevents anything more than brief reference to some of this work. Perhaps the most interesting findings are that psychopaths seem unable or unwilling to process or use the deep semantic meanings of language; their linguistic processes appear to be relatively superficial, and the subtle, more abstract meanings and nuances of language escape them (Gillstrom, 1994; Intratoretal., 1995; Williamson, Harpur, & Hare, 1991). Furthermore, behavioral, electrocortical, and brain imaging research adds weight to the clinical belief that psychopaths fail to appreciate the emotional significance of an event or experience (Intrator et al., 1995; Larbig, Veit, Rau, Schlottke, & Birbaumer, 1992; Patrick, 1994; Williamson et al., 1991).

In short, psychopaths appear to be semantically and affectively shallow individuals. Presumably, the deep semantic and affective networks that tie cognitions together are not well developed in these individuals (Hare, 1993). Perhaps this is why psychopaths show, on close examination, signs of what seems to be a subtle form of thought disorder. For example, Williamson (1991) scored the audio taped narratives of male offenders for cohesion and coherence in discourse. She found that the narratives of the psychopaths contained more than a normal amount of logical inconsistencies, contradictions, and neologisms and showed a tendency to derail or "go off track." In some respects, it is as if psychopaths lack a central organizer to plan and keep track of what they think and say (Gillstrom & Hare, 1988).

Why do these cognitive and linguistic problems typically go undetected? For one thing, psychopaths use their own attributes to put on a good show. Intense eye contact, distracting body language, charm, and a knowledge of the listener's vulnerabilities are all part of the psychopath's armamentarium for dominating, controlling, and manipulating others. We pay less attention to what they say than to how they say it—style over substance. Because it is so easy to become sucked in by psychopaths, my research group routinely videotapes all of our interviews for later, more detached, analysis. We advise others to do likewise.

The cognitive, linguistic, and behavioral attributes of psychopaths (Hare, 1993; Newman & Wallace, 1993) may be related to cerebral dysfunction, particularly in the orbito/ventromedial frontal cortex (Gorenstein & Newman, 1980; Intrator et al., 1995; Lapierre, Braun, & Hodgins, 1995). This dysfunction need not actually involve organic damage (Hart, Forth, & Hare, 1990), but could reflect structural or functional anomalies in the brain mechanisms and circuitry—including the orbito/ventromedial frontal cortex, medial temporal cortex, and amygdala—responsible for the coordination of cognitive and affective processes (Intrator et al., 1995). Behavioral and neuroimaging studies indicate that damage to these regions can produce a dissociation of the logical/cognitive and affective components of thought (Damasio, Grabowski, Frank, Galaburda, & Damasio, 1994), or even what Damasio, Tranel, and Damasio (1987) refer to as *acquired sociopathy*.

The relevance of this to the criminal justice system is that very little of what we do is based solely on logical appraisals of situations and their potential ramifications for us and others.

In most cases, our cognitions and behaviors are heavily laden with emotional elements. As Damasio (1994) recently put it, "emotion is integral to the process of reasoning" (p. 144). I would argue that it is also an essential part of "conscience." However, it is this very element that is missing or seriously impaired in psychopaths; their conscience is only half formed, consisting merely of an intellectual awareness of the rules of the game. The powerful motivating, guiding, and inhibiting effects of emotion play little role in their lives, presumably not so much by choice as because of what they are. In effect, their internalized rule-books are pale, abridged versions of those that direct the conduct of other individuals.

In most jurisdictions, psychopathy is considered to be an aggravating rather than a mitigating factor in determining criminal responsibility. However, I've been asked if research evidence of the sort presented above—affective deficit, thought disorder, brain dysfunction—might lead some to view psychopathy as a mitigating factor in a criminal case. As one psychiatrist put it, perhaps psychopathy will become "the kiss of life rather than the kiss of death" in first-degree murder cases. This would be appalling, because psychopaths are calculating predators whose behavior must be judged by the rules of the society in which they live. However, the issue is really one for the judicial system to settle. If psychopathy is used as a defense for a criminal act, the flip side of the coin is that the disorder currently is untreatable, and any civil commitment likely would be permanent.

BAD, MAD, OR BOTH?

There is a related issue that complicates matters even further. Psychopaths typically are judged legally and psychiatrically sane. Many clinicians and investigators believe that psychopathy is incompatible with psychoticism, and there is some evidence to support their position (Hart & Hare. 1989). Not everyone agrees with this view, though. Some argue that psychopathy and schizophrenia are part of a common spectrum of disorders. Cleckley (1976) himself considered psychopathy to be closer to psychosis than to normality; after all, he titled his book *The Mask of Sanity* for a reason. Also, some forensic psychiatrists say that they occasionally see a mentally disordered offender who is both a psychopath and a schizophrenic. A recent study by Rasmussen and Levander (1994) suggests that diagnostic co-morbidity of this sort is not uncommon in maximum security psychiatric units housing severely violent or dangerous patients. They evaluated 94 consecutive admissions to such a unit in Norway and found that 22 patients met the PCL-R criteria for psychopathy. Of these, 12 (55%) also satisfied the DSM-III-R criteria for schizophrenia. They suggested that in such patients, schizophrenia may be superimposed on an underlying syndrome of psychopathy and, conversely, that psychopathy may be a vulnerability factor for schizophrenia. In any case, the combination would seem to be a particularly dangerous one, assuming that diagnoses are valid.

I suspect that genuine cases of psychosis-psychopathy co-morbidity are rare. More common are psychopaths who malinger, that is, fake psychotic symptoms in order to avoid prison. They present a particularly difficult problem for the mental health and criminal justice systems, typically bouncing back and forth between prisons and forensic psychiatric facilities (Gacono, Meloy, Sheppard, Speth, & Roske, 1995). Criminal psychopaths are more likely to be bad than mad.

THE FUTURE

Psychopathy has long been a poor relative of experimental psychopathology, even though it has no equal in terms of the amount and degree of social, economic, physical, and emotional distress generated. The number of dedicated researchers is small and the research funding miniscule in comparison with the manpower and funding devoted to schizophrenia, the affective disorders, and even antisocial personality disorder. The nature of psychopathy, however, provides just as much of a challenge as does any other clinical disorder. Of course, it is easier and more convenient to study psychiatric patients than psychopaths. The former manifestly are impaired and either seek or are sent for treatment, where they provide a steady pool of readily available research subjects for well-funded programs designed to understand and help them. Psychopaths, on the other hand, suffer little personal distress, seek treatment only when it is in their best interests to do so, such as when seeking probation or parole, and elicit little sympathy from those who study them. Furthermore, studying them in a prison environment is fraught with so many institutional and political problems, inmate boycotts, staff roadblocks, and red tape that most researchers simply give up after a few projects. In addition, and unfortunately in my view, resources have been targeted primarily at programs and projects that eschew the politically incorrect idea that individual differences in personality are as important as determinants of crime as are social forces.

As the title of this article implies, the situation is changing rapidly. Even those opposed to the very idea of psychopathy cannot ignore its potent explanatory and predictive power, if not as a formal construct then as a static risk factor. In the next few years, indices of psychopathy almost certainly will become a routine part of the assessment batteries used to make decisions about competency, sentencing, diversion, placement, suitability for treatment, and risk for recidivism and violence. Because psychopaths with a history of violence are a poor risk for early release, more and more will be kept in prison for their full sentence, whereas many other offenders will be released early with little risk to society. However, unless we are content simply to warehouse high-risk offenders, we must develop innovative programs aimed at making their attitudes and behaviors less self-serving and more acceptable to the society in which most eventually must function.

Following publication of a book written for the general public (Hare, 1993), scores of people called or wrote to ask why I devoted so much space to psychopathic criminals and so little to the psychopaths with whom they daily lived and worked and who somehow always managed to stay out of prison. Many of these correspondents seemed caught up in emotionally damaging and dangerous situations from which there apparently was no escape (see Meloy, 1992). Their plight raises an issue that urgently needs to be addressed and researched: the prevalence of psychopathy in the general population and its expression in ways that are personally, socially, or economically damaging but that are not necessarily illegal or that do not result in criminal prosecution. We study incarcerated offenders for two reasons: the base rate for psychopathy is high, and we have access to enough solid information to make reliable assessments. However, we must find ways of studying psychopaths in the community if we are ever to provide some relief for their victims, which is to say, all of us.

Prognostications are always risky, but the next decade will certainly see dramatic advances in our understanding of psychopathy, in large part because of increasing cross-cultural and interdisciplinary collaborations. Family and twin studies will combine with developmental investigations to provide the first solid data on the interactive roles of heredity and environment. Neuroimaging and neurophysiological protocols will lead to new insights into brain structure and function and may set the stage for effective intervention programs. Finally, there will be a continuation of the recent trend toward integration of pure research and practical application, for example, the conceptual linkage between the neurophysiological evidence of abnormal affective processes in psychopaths and their penchant for callous, cold-blooded behavior.

12

CHILD SEXUAL MOLESTATION

Research Issues

ROBERT A. PRENTKY

RAYMOND A. KNIGHT

AUSTIN F.S. LEE

INTRODUCTION

Few criminal offenses are more despised than the sexual abuse of children, and few are so little understood in terms of incidence (the number of offenses committed), prevalence (the proportion of the population who commit offenses), and re-offense risk. Despite longstanding public concern over the medical, emotional, and monetary costs associated with child sexual victimization, rigorous programs to enhance the accuracy of predictive decisions involving sexual offenders are of fairly recent origin. Because of inadequate methodologies, studies on the psychology, behavior, treatment, and recidivism rates of child molesters have often yielded inconsistent findings. The uncertainty of information about sexual offenders raises questions about the effectiveness of special commitment statutes and ad hoc discretionary and dispositional decisions directed toward this group.

Before it can combat child molestation effectively, the criminal justice community must first understand it. Empirical knowledge of the factors that lead individuals to sexually abuse children can support and inform the sentencing, probationary, clinical, and supervisory decisions that must be made with regard to child molesters. This report is divided into four main sections. Section 1 discusses the frequency of child sexual molestation and factors leading to sexual deviancy in individual offenders. Section 2 includes classification models for typing and diagnosing child molesters and describes treatment approaches and strategies for community-based maintenance and control. Section 3 talks about re-offense risk as it relates to criminal justice decisions and discusses predictors of sexual recidivism. To illustrate the variability of recidivism among child molesters, section 4 presents the findings of a 25-year follow-up study of 115 released offenders. [Editor's note: Section 4 is omitted here.] Finally, some of the

Editors' Note: This is a research report published by the U.S. Department of Justice, National Institute of Justice, June 1997, NCJ 163390. The Executive Summary has been omitted.

shortcomings of current approaches to reduce child molester re-offense risk are touched on in the report's conclusion, and an argument is made for post-release treatment and aftercare programs.

The information included in this Research Report has been distilled from several inter-related reports and studies sponsored by the National Institute of Justice (NIJ) to strengthen the efficacy of intervention and prevention strategies and ultimately reduce child sexual victimization rates.

SECTION 1. OCCURRENCE AND ETIOLOGY

Frequency of Child Sexual Abuse

The assumption that sexual crimes against children and teenagers are underreported is now commonly accepted. Sexual offenses apparently are more likely than other types of criminal conduct to elude the criminal justice system. This inference is supported by the reports of both sex offenders and sexually abused children. Offenders report vastly more victim-involved incidents than those for which they were convicted (Abel, Becker, Mittelman, et al., 1987). It is impossible to determine how representative these anonymous self-reporting offenders are, compared to all of the non-incarcerated and unidentified sex offenders in the population.

A telephone survey of a national probability sample of 2,000 children between the ages of 10 and 16 revealed that 3.2 percent of girls and 0.6 percent of boys had suffered, at some point in their lives, sexual abuse involving physical contact. If one infers that those statistics can be generalized to the rest of the country, children have experienced (but not reported) levels of victimization that far exceed those reported for adults (Finkelhor & Dziuba-Leatherman, 1994). This finding is consistent with a recent report indicating that teenagers are at greater risk than adults for rape (BJS, 1996).

In addition to underreporting, incidence estimates are also affected by a number of methodological problems. Although research on criminal conduct of any type may be hampered by these difficulties, sexual crimes seem to be especially susceptible. For instance, sexual offenses involve behavior that is not as clear-cut

as that occurring in nonsexual crimes (such as robbery, burglary, or auto theft) because they often include nonsexual offenses (e.g., kidnapping, breaking and entering, or simple assault) as well as a variety of different sexual violations. The criminal charges springing from such a litany differ from one jurisdiction to another, and the resulting conviction may be for a "lesser," that is, nonsexual, offense (e.g., pleading out to simple assault). Given this unevenness in legal system dispositions, it is not surprising to find wide variations among—and wide ranges within—incidence/prevalence estimates.

Characteristics of the Offender

The sexual abusers of children are highly dissimilar in terms of personal characteristics, life experiences, and criminal histories. No single "molester profile" exists. Child molesters arrive at deviancy via multiple pathways and engage in many different sexual and nonsexual "acting-out" behaviors.

Sexual focus. Evidence shows that sexual focus in child molesters comprises two separate components. The first is intensity of pedophilic interest, i.e., the degree to which offenders are focused or "fixated" on children as sexual objects. The second component involves the exclusivity of their preference for children as sexual objects. The second component is inversely related to social competence, as measured by the extent and depth of adult social and sexual relationships, and it is independent of the intensity of pedophilic interest.

Physiological arousal. Logic suggests that a behavioral dimension of sexual interest in children would be accompanied by varying degrees of physiological arousal to them. Plethysmographic assessment (i.e., measurement of penile volume changes [phallometry] in response to sexual stimuli) has demonstrated an ability to discriminate between child molesters and comparison groups of non-molesters (Barbaree & Marshall, 1988; Freund & Blanchard, 1989 . . .) as well as among subgroups of child molesters defined by victim gender preference (same sex vs. opposite sex) and by relationship to victim (incest vs. non-incest). For example, exclusive incest offenders demonstrate far less sexual arousal in response to children than do extrafamilial child molesters. Offenders with strong pedophilic interest show more sexual arousal to depictions of children than their low-fixated counterparts.

Victimization of offenders as children. Some support exists for the notion that child molestation may be related to an offender's restaging or recapitulation of his own sexual victimization. Tests of the recapitulation theory on a sample of 131 rapists and child molesters revealed that child molesters who committed their first assault when they were 14 or younger were sexually victimized at a younger age than were offenders who committed their first assault in adulthood. They also experienced more severe sexual abuse than offenders with adult onset of sexual aggression (Prentky & Knight, 1993). No evidence of recapitulation of sexual abuse among rapists was found in this study. It should be pointed out, however, that regardless of whether or not they were sexually abused (and, if so, by whom and at what age), *all* offenders in the sample went on to commit sexual offenses.

By itself, sexual victimization is too narrow a factor to explain child molestation. No inexorable link exists between experiencing sexual abuse as a child and growing up to be a child molester; the "outcome" of child molestation is a much more complex phenomenon. Most victims of childhood sexual abuse do not go on to become perpetrators. As is true for other kinds of maltreatment, childhood sexual victimization becomes a critical element in the presence or absence of a variety of other factors (e.g., co-occurrence of other types of abuse, availability of supportive caregivers, ego strength of child-victim at the time of abuse, and treatment), all of which moderate the likelihood of becoming a child molester. In addition, the severity of the long-term effects of childhood sexual abuse is influenced by clear morbidity factors (e.g., age at onset of abuse, duration of abuse, the child's relationship to the perpetrator, and invasiveness and/or violence of the abuse). The weight and significance of having been sexually abused are specific to the individual child molester.

Social competence. A variety of studies have documented the inadequate social and interpersonal skills, under-assertiveness, and poor self-esteem that, in varying degrees, characterize individual offenders (Araji & Finkelhor, 1985; Marshall, Barbaree, & Fernandez, 1995 . . .). Social competence deficits are pervasive among child molesters and must be considered clinically significant. As is true for sexual abuse suffered by offenders during childhood, however, social competence deficits constitute but one important factor in the complex etiology of child molestation.

Impulsive, antisocial personality. Research shows that child molesters who committed their first sexual offense in adolescence had histories of being disruptive in school (verbally or physically assaulting peers and teachers), showed high levels of juvenile antisocial behavior, and, as adults, manifested a greater degree of non-sexual aggression. For some types of child molesters, sexual offenses are part of a longer criminal history, reflecting an antisocial lifestyle and impulsive behavioral traits that probably had been present from childhood (Prentky & Knight, 1993; Prentky, Knight, & Lee, 1997; Quinsey, Rice, & Harris, 1995). A history of impulsive, antisocial behavior is a well-documented risk factor associated with some child molesters.

Developmental influences. Recognition of the multiple factors that determine child molestation has led clinicians and investigators to examine the antecedent and concurrent experiences that place sexual abuse in a developmental context. One variable, "caregiver inconstancy," measures the frequency of changes in primary caregivers and the longest time spent with any single caregiver; it reflects the permanence and consistency of the child's interpersonal relationships with significant adults. Caregiver inconstancy, a powerful predictor of the degree of sexual violence expressed in adulthood (Prentky, Knight, & Lee, 1997) interferes with the development of long-term supportive relationships, increasing the likelihood of an attachment disorder. Attachment disorders may be characterized by intense anxiety, distrust of others, insecurity, dysfunctional anger, and failure to develop normal age-appropriate social skills. Thus, specifiable early childhood experiences may lead to interpersonal deficits and low self-esteem that severely undermine development of secure adult relationships. Individuals having these interpersonal and social shortcomings are more likely than others to turn to children to meet their psychosexual needs.

SECTION 2. TYPOLOGY AND TREATMENT

Classification of Child Molesters

Diagnosis and assessment. Just as the childhood and developmental experiences, adult competencies, and criminal histories of child molesters differ considerably, so do the motives that underlie the behavior patterns that characterize their sexual abuse of children. Thus, informed decisions about these offenders require some understanding of the dimensions believed to be important in discriminating among them. Diagnosis aims to reduce this diversity by assigning the offender to a class or group of individuals with similar relevant characteristics. Identifying and measuring these relevant characteristics is the task of assessment.

A reliable, valid classification system can improve the accuracy of decisions (1) in the criminal justice system (where dangerousness and re-offense risk are assessed and resources are allocated), (2) in the clinical setting (where a more informed understanding of particular classes of offenders can be used to optimize treatment plans), and (3) in the design of more effective primary prevention strategies. A classification model may also help in deciphering critical antecedent factors that contribute to different outcomes (i.e., different "types" of child molesters).

DSM-IV classification. The 1994 edition of the *Diagnostic and Statistics Manual of Mental Disorders* (*DSM-IV*) places pedophilia under the heading, "Sexuality and Gender Identity Disorders" (American Psychiatric Association, 1994). According to *DSM-IV*, the onset of pedophilia "usually begins in adolescence," and its course is "usually chronic." Specific behavioral criteria for diagnosing pedophilia are listed, as follows:

- The subject has experienced, for at least 6 months, recurrent intense sexual urges or fantasies involving sexual activity with a prepubescent child (age 13 or younger).
- The subject has acted on these urges or is markedly distressed by them.
- The subject is at least 16 years old and at least 5 years older than the victim. (Late adolescent subjects who are involved in ongoing relationships with 12- or 13-year-old youngsters are excluded.)

Three other specifications figure in this classification system: (1) whether the client is sexually attracted to males, females, or both; (2) whether the offenses are limited to incest; and (3) whether the client is an "exclusive" (attracted only to children) or "nonexclusive" type.

Although the *DSM-IV* classification system may succeed in isolating the "pedophilic" child molester, it fails to capture those incest and extrafamilial offenders without known 6-month histories of sexualized interest in children. Requiring evidence that an individual has met the first (and critical) diagnostic criterion dealing with "recurrent intense sexual urges or fantasies" involving children will inevitably screen out a large number of child molesters.

Sex-of-victim model. Classification of child molesters on the basis of their victims' sex—same-sex, opposite-sex, or mixed-group offenders—has shown stability over time (Fitch, 1962; Langevin, Hucker, Handy, et al., 1985). In addition, it has demonstrated predictive validity as well as some concurrent validity (e.g., it corresponds as expected with penile plethysmographic responsiveness to stimuli depicting specific ages and sexes) (Freund, 1965, 1967a; Frisbie, 1990 . . .). Many reports have suggested that, among extrafamilial offenders, same-sex child molesters are at highest risk to re-offend, and opposite-sex child molesters are at lowest risk. However, the sex-of-victim distinction has not received consistent support. In contrast to the typical finding, at least four recent studies found either no differences in recidivism rates among groups or differences that were opposite to prediction (Abel, Becker, Murphy, & Flanagan, 1981; Prentky & Quinsey, 1988; . . .).

The reasons for discrepant findings based on the sex-of-victim distinction are unclear, although several possibilities come immediately to mind:

- The large number of unreported sexual assaults on children.
- Possible biases against reporting homosexual encounters.
- Situational factors that might lead to assaults on the less-preferred sex.
- Incarceration after a single assault.

Further, some studies do not distinguish between incest offenders, who are almost exclusively heterosexual in their choice of victims, and non-incest offenders. Assuming that "true" incest offenders (that is, those whose offenses are exclusively intra-familial) constitute a clinically and theoretically meaningful group of child molesters, the proportion of such cases in any particular sample might affect the differences found between same- and opposite-sex offenders.

Clinically derived multidimensional systems. In the earliest taxonomic systems for child molesters, which were based exclusively on clinical experience, three subtypes consistently appeared:

- Offender with an exclusive and longstanding sexual and social preference for children (Common Type 1).
- Offender whose offenses are seen as a shift or regression from a higher, adult level of psychosexual adaptation, typically in response to stress (Common Type 2).
- Offender who is a psychopath or sociopath with very poor social skills and who turns to children largely because they are easy to exploit—not because they are preferred or even desired partners (Common Type 3).

The most historically important of these hypothetical subtypes are the "fixated" and the "regressed" (Common Types 1 and 2, respectively). Implicit or explicit in the various systems that attempted to define fixated and regressed types was an assessment of achieved level of social competence. In addition to being described as having more intense pedophilic interest, fixated offenders were also typically differentiated from regressed offenders by marital status, number and quality of age-appropriate heterosexual relationships, and achieved educational and occupational levels. The fixated child molester was hypothesized to have a negligible history of dating or peer interaction in adolescence and adulthood, and, if married, the quality of his relationship was considered to be poor.

Regressed offenders, in contrast, were described as more likely to have been married and to have developed appropriate heterosexual relationships prior to their "regressive" sexual offenses. Thus, the construct of social competence was clearly involved in the distinction between fixated and regressed types, but, when empirically tested (Conte, 1985) this distinction was found to be flawed. Results showed that the two groups were not homogeneous. Indeed, social and interpersonal competence were found to be independent of fixation (Finkelhor & Araji, 1986).

The MTC: CM3 model. To meet the need for a clearly operationalized, reliable, valid taxonomic system for child molesters, researchers at the Massachusetts Treatment Center (MTC) for Sexually Dangerous Persons developed MTC:CM3, a two-axis typology [see Figure 12.1]. On Axis 1, fixation and social competence are completely independent dimensions, and each has distinct developmental antecedents and adult adaptations (Knight, Carter, & Prentky, 1989) The concept of regression was dropped in developing MTC:CM3, and a newly defined fixation dimension (i.e., "intensity of pedophilic interest") was crossed with a dimension of social competence, yielding four independent types:

- High fixation, low social competence (Type 0).
- High fixation, high social competence (Type 1).
- Low fixation, low social competence (Type 2).
- Low fixation, high social competence (Type 3).

A new behavioral dimension ("amount of contact with children") was added on a separate coordinate (Axis II) and became a powerful discriminator with respect to re-offense risk. In addiion, the degree of violence employed by an offender was differentiated into dimensions of physical injury (high/low) and sadism

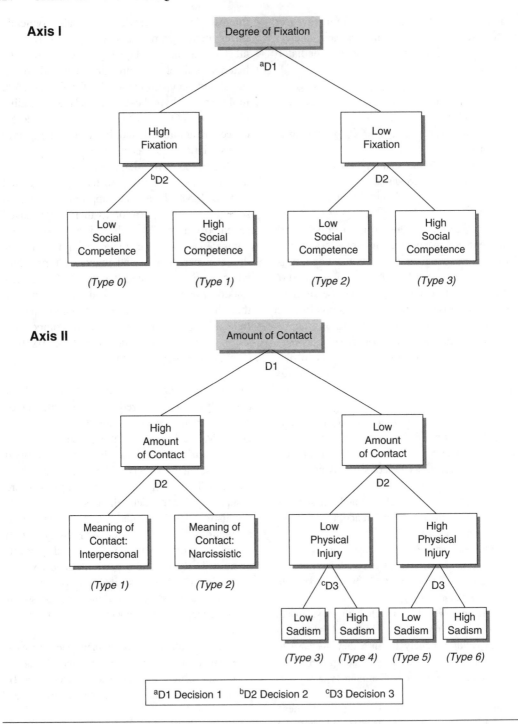

Axis I

Axis II

^aD1 Decision 1   ^bD2 Decision 2   ^cD3 Decision 3

Figure 12.1   Flow Design of the Decision Process for Classifying Child Molesters on Axis I and Axis II of MTC: CM3

Table 12.1   Hypothetical Profiles of MTC: CM3 Axis II Types

	Interpersonal (Type 1)	Narcissistic (Type 2)	Exploitative (Type 3)	Muted Sadistic (Type 4)	Nonsadistic Aggressive (Type 5)	Sadistic (Type 6)
Amount of Contact With Children	High	High	Low	Low	Low	Low
Sexual Acts	Fondling, Caressing, Frottage, (Non-phallic sex)	Phallic Non-sadistic sex	Phallic Non-sadistic sex	Sodomy "Sham" sadism[a]	Phallic Non-sadistic sex	Sadism
Relationship of Offender to Victim	Known	Known or Stranger	Stranger	Stranger	Stranger	Stranger
Amount of Physical Injury to Victim	Low	Low	Instrumental[b]	Instrumental[b]	High	High
Amount of Planning in Offenses	High[c]	Moderate	Low	Moderate	Low	High

a. "Sham" sadism implies behaviors or reported fantasies that reflect sadism without the high victim injury present in Type 6.

b. Instrumental aggression implies only enough force to gain victim compliance.

c. Interpersonal types know their victims and may spend a considerable amount of time "grooming" them (setting them up), but the offenses often appear to be unplanned or spontaneous.

(present/absent), yielding six distinct Axis II subtypes whose hypothetical characteristics are shown in exhibit 2. Exclusive incest offenders were omitted in the design of MTC:CM3; including such offenders in this system would require considerable reconceptualization and revision. Although further revision of MTC:CM3, including integration of Axis I (fixation and social competence) and Axis II (amount of contact with children, degree of injury to victim, and sadism), is necessary, validity studies conducted thus far clearly support the primary structural changes in this model (Knight, 1989, 1992; Prentky, Knight, & Lee, 1997).

Course and prognosis among child molesters. Among child molesters, both the course (progression of symptoms associated with the condition) and the prognosis (forecast of the probable course and likelihood of recovery) vary considerably. For example, onset ranges from early adolescence to middle adulthood (as in the case of some exclusive incest offenders). The prognosis ranges from cases of lifelong, intractable pedophilic interest that is resistant to treatment to isolated instances of incest in adults with a sexual preference for peers, ample remorse and victim empathy, and a high likelihood of "recovery."

Clinical Management of Offenders

Treatment. Over the past decade, the provision of therapeutic services for sex offenders has increased significantly. A 1994 survey reported 710 adult and 684 juvenile treatment programs (Longo, Bird, Stevenson, & Fiske, 1994) up from 1985 survey results that showed 297 adult and 346 juvenile treatment programs (Knopp, Rosenberg, & Stevenson, 1985). Broadly speaking, sex offender treatment programs employ four approaches:

- Evocative therapy, which focuses on (1) helping offenders to understand the causes and motivations leading to sexually deviant and coercive behavior and (2) increasing their empathy for the victims of sexual assault. This approach may include individual, group, couples/ marital, and family therapy. Group therapy may be eclectic or issue focused (i.e., specialty groups may target substance abuse, adult children of alcoholics, victim empathy, victim survivors, social skills/assertiveness training, black awareness, gay identity, or Vietnam veterans).

- Cognitive behavior therapy, which focuses on sexual assault cycles and techniques that interrupt those cycles; altering the beliefs, fantasies, and rationalizations that justify and perpetuate sexually aggressive behavior; and controlling and managing anger. Studies of relapse prevention, the most commonly employed cognitive behavioral model, report that, for child molesters, the most frequently identified experiences prior to committing an offense were planning the offense (73 percent of sample) and low victim empathy (71 percent of sample) (Pithers, 1990; Pithers, Martin, & Cumming, 1989).

- Psychoeducation groups or classes, which use a more didactic approach to remedy deficits in social and interpersonal skills; they teach anger management techniques, principles of relapse prevention, and a range of topics that includes human sexuality, dating and communication skills, and myths about sexuality and relationships.

- Pharmacological treatment, which focuses on reducing sexual arousability and the frequency of deviant sexual fantasies through the use of anti-androgen and antidepressant medication.

These approaches are not mutually exclusive, and the ideal treatment program (yet to be identified) would employ combinations of them. State-of-the-art intervention at this point (cognitive behavior therapy and, when appropriate, medication) can effectively reduce re-offense rates. For example, recidivism rates for new sexual offenses by child molesters treated under the cognitive behavior therapy model, with a focus on relapse prevention, were 4.6 percent in a 3-year follow-up study (Marques et al., 1993) and 3 percent in a 6-year follow-up study (Pithers & Cumming, 1989). The non-volunteer control group in the 3-year follow-up had a sexual recidivism rate of 8.2 percent, yielding an apparent treatment effect of 3.6 percent.

When these failure rates are compared to those for Years 3 and 5 in the MTC study . . . of sex offenders who did not receive cognitive-behavior therapy, the presumptive effectiveness of treatment in reducing the probability of sexual re-offense is between 7 and 15 percent. A recent meta-analysis of 12 sex offender treatment studies ($N = 1,313$) found that the overall recidivism rate for untreated sex offenders was 27 percent, while for treated offenders it was 19 percent—an apparent treatment effect of 8 percent (Hall, 1995). These statistics suggest that treatment can reduce child molester recidivism. The wide variability in study findings on re-offense rates of both treated and untreated offenders, however, makes efforts to find optimal treatment interventions as problematic as efforts to assess and predict recidivism.

Community-based maintenance and control. The vast majority of sex offenders are released eventually. Thus, community-based clinical management and control of child molesters are indispensable parts of any rehabilitation program if public safety is to be ensured. An effective community-based maintenance program for child molesters should include the following components:

- Coordination by highly trained and well-supervised parole agents and probation officers who carry small caseloads (15 to 20 offenders) to ensure intensive surveillance/supervision.
- Mandatory treatment by therapists trained and supervised in cognitive behavioral theory with sex offenders; this is especially critical for adjustment and maintenance.
- Evaluation for medication.
- Proper monitoring and supervision of vocational, social, recreational, and leisure activities.
- Confidential notification of local police departments and/or the district attorney's office.

Registration with the criminal justice system is a widely practiced, reasonable procedure that should be considered a part of an offender's aftercare plan. Community notification, however, is an untested management technique—that has at least as many potential problems as benefits—and must be empirically evaluated. Indeed, the general notification of laypersons outside the criminal justice system may increase, rather than decrease, the risk of recidivism by placing extreme pressure on the offender; examples of stressors include threats of bodily harm, termination of employment, on-the-job harassment, and forced instability of residence.

Continuity of treatment is considered a critical factor in managing sex offenders. Maintenance is forever, and relapse prevention never ends. Community-based clinical management must be supportive, vigilant, and informed by current wisdom about maximally effective maintenance strategies.

SECTION 3. REOFFENSE RISK

Dispositional Decisions

Recidivism rates are highly variable, making it impossible to draw any reliable conclusions about re-offense among child molesters as a group. Most recent studies have been conducted in order to evaluate treatment efficacy; consequently, little is known about recidivism independent of some treatment intervention. Moreover, variations in recidivism rates associated with different treatment programs are difficult to interpret. [Comparing] recidivism rates across studies is confounded by [a number of factors.] These include differences in the statutes and sentencing and parole guidelines among jurisdictions; duration of exposure (i.e., time in the community, where the child molester is at liberty to re-offend); offender characteristics; treatment-related variables (including differential attrition rates, program integrity, and amount of treatment); amount and quality of post-treatment supervision; and many other factors.

The criminal justice system is responsible for certain discretionary decisions concerning sex offenders, most of which rest on a presumption about an individual offender's dangerousness or re-offense risk. Examples of decisions driven by underlying assumptions about the probability of recidivism include:

- Whether to leave an offender in the community on probation.
- Whether to parole an offender and, if so, the level/duration of supervision needed.

- Whether to recommend compulsory treatment.
- Whether to require registration with the police.
- Whether to notify the community.

From a forensic standpoint, potential dangerousness is a question central to the disposition of sex offenders. Yet, there is no reliable body of empirically derived data that can inform and guide decision making about re-offense risk—primarily because of methodological differences in existing studies . . .

Predictors of Sexual Recidivism

Although ample evidence exists to demonstrate the predictive superiority of statistical (actuarial) risk assessment methods over clinical judgment, few concerted efforts have been made to develop and empirically test actuarial prediction devices for sexual offenders. The one obvious exception is the work of investigators in Canada, who have focused on psychopathy, measures of prior criminal history, and phallometric assessment to predict sexual recidivism (Quinsey, Rice, & Harris, 1995). A recent study on risk assessment among extrafamilial child molesters included three of the dimensions used in MTC:CM3 (fixation, social competence, and amount of contact with children). Study researchers argued that the MTC:CM3 assessment of fixation—a behavioral measure of the strength of an offender's pedophilic interest—may serve as a viable substitute for phallometry, which is intrusive and much more expensive (Prentky, Knight, & Lee, 1997).

Risk assessment study of extrafamilial offenders. The predictive value of a rationally derived composite of variables for assessing re-offense risk, based on archival data (prison and criminal records), was tested in a follow-up study of extrafamilial child molesters who had been discharged from the Massachusetts Treatment Center over a period of 25 years. The sample of 111 represents 96.5 percent (N=115) of all child molesters discharged between 1960 and 1984.

Data reveal differential predictive accuracy depending on the type of criminal behavior being examined. Three variables—degree of sexual preoccupation with children (fixation), paraphilias (fetishism, transvestism, and promiscuity), and number of prior sexual offenses predicted sexual recidivism, while those variables that reflect impulsive, antisocial behavior predicted recidivism for nonsexual crimes involving physical contact with a victim and violent (sexual and nonsexual) crimes.

Unlike other recent studies (e.g., Hanson, Steffy, & Gauthier, 1993), this study found no evidence for the utility of alcohol history, social competence, and sex of child-victim as predictors of re-offense. In the case of victim sex, one explanation for these inconsistencies may be due to sampling differences. The sample of child molesters examined in this study had an average of three known sexual offenses prior to release. This sample had a higher base rate probability of re-offense than would likely be observed in an unscreened sample of child molesters recruited from the general prison population. Among child molesters who are at higher risk to re-offend, the victim's sex may be less important to accurate prediction than such factors as degree of sexual preoccupation with children and impulsivity.

Predictive accuracy. The variables associated with re-offense risk among child molesters that were examined for discriminant validity had reasonable predictive accuracy with regard to both sexual and nonsexual re-offending; overall predictive accuracy was approximately 75 percent. The results of this study are sample-specific and may not be generalizable. The potential uniqueness of this sample is suggested by the study's failure to find any predictive efficacy for the victim-sex variable.

Although risk assessment procedures that rely exclusively on archival data may never achieve the efficiency of much more time-intensive procedures—such as the penile plethysmograph or a comprehensive interview that assesses psychopathy (e.g., The *Hare Psychopathy Checklist-Revised, PCL-R*) (Hare, 1991)—the distinct advantages of an archival scale include its ease of use (i.e., it does not require the compliance or even the presence of the offender), cost efficiency, and relatively high reliability. Despite these presumptive advantages, the ability of such an archivally based procedure to reasonably discriminate across samples remains to be demonstrated.

***

Conclusion

Sexual offenders constitute the one category of dangerous criminals most subject to either special commitment statutes or ad hoc discretionary and dispositional decisions. These laws and the decisions that they require are often based on assumptions about sex offenders that are, at best, misleading and, at worst, erroneous. Given the serious concerns about sex offenders within the criminal justice system and society at large, the need for valid diagnostic and assessment tools is urgent. Indeed, the most formidable task is to develop empirically corroborated estimates of sexual re-offense probabilities for different subgroups of sex offenders under standardized operational conditions.

Practitioners, researchers, and legislators should be guided by moderation, clear vision, and empirical evidence. Over the years, many laws governing sex offenders have been enacted and later repealed (Carter & Prentky, 1993; Grubin & Prentky, 1993). Two timely examples of presumably well intentioned but problematic legislation are the much-discussed community notification laws and the new California law requiring repeat sex offenders to choose between "chemical castration" (i.e., treatment with anti-androgenic medication) or surgical castration. The California statute poses difficulties on several counts:

• From an ethical standpoint, mandating either an intrusive, irreversible surgical procedure or treatment with a drug that the U.S. Food and Drug Administration has not approved for use with sex offenders is highly questionable.

• From a practical standpoint, sex offenders cannot be relied on to comply with a drug regimen to which they have not consented and from which they cannot withdraw. Moreover, the apparently compliant offender can easily circumvent the effects of the drugs or the surgery by buying testosterone (steroids) on the street.

• From an empirical standpoint, the law makes the invalid assumption that all sex offenders are motivated by uncontrollable sexual urges. Chemical reduction of testosterone is appropriate for some, but not all, child molesters; when medication is used, it must be included as one component of a treatment plan that includes therapy. It is critical to keep in mind, however, that surgical or chemical reduction of testosterone will not, by itself, solve the problem of child molestation.

Reducing the risk of recidivism among sex offenders is a problem for which no easy answers or shortcuts exist. Treatment provided in prison must be continued after offenders are released into the community. Reintegration is especially problematic for child molesters. Detailed aftercare plans, orchestrated by well-trained and supervised parole agents and probation officers, are essential to reducing re-offense risk and should include consideration of the vocational, psychotherapeutic, pharmacological, social, and recreational needs of the offender.

Clearly, the most compelling motive for treating child molesters is the reduction in victimization rates that is presumed to result. Society resists treating sexual offenders, however, because to do so is perceived as a humane response to intolerable behavior. If treatment can be demonstrated to reduce the probability of re-offense, then working on the development and refinement of treatment methods and procedures is an essential secondary intervention.

The criminal justice community faces difficult, but not insuperable, challenges as it moves to balance the right of the community to be protected with the rights of offenders. If those professionals who deal with the victims and perpetrators of child molestation are willing to harness their collective energy, pull in a common direction, and speak with a single firm voice, properly informed laws can be enacted that will better control child molesters and make communities safer for children.

UNIT 4

VICTIMOLOGY AND VICTIM SERVICES

Introduction and Commentary

Services to victims and research focusing on victims of crime have only recently been recognized as important components of forensic psychology. Yet, many psychologists are more likely to come into contact with victims than with offenders. As we noted in Chapter 1, forensic psychologists evaluate and treat crime victims, testify about the effects of their experience in both criminal and civil courts, and train law enforcement officers on effective approaches to interviewing them. Death notification, informing individuals of the sudden death of a loved one, is another example of their many tasks. The articles in this section help us better understand the psychological effects of victimization.

The first two articles deal with covictims of homicide—individuals who are deeply affected by homicide but have been largely ignored by both researchers and the criminal justice system. **Marilyn Peterson Armour** focuses on the covictims who are family members or close friends of a homicide victim. She observes that treatment providers do not have sufficient information on the needs of covictims. Grief and trauma are the two main psychological states they experience. However, as Armour notes, the often-cited steps of the grief process, including the literature on finding meaning in the deaths of loved ones, do not apply to this particular group of individuals.

We rarely think of police officers as covictims of homicide, but **Isaac Van Patten and Tod Burke** suggest that, in at least one form of homicide, they may well be. Specifically, an officer who investigates child homicides may experience a unique form of critical incident stress (CIS) and be considered "a secondary or vicarious victim" of the homicide. Testing a causal model of stress, Van Patten and Burke learned that the most significant predictor of stress for these investigators was the presence of traumatic stimuli at the crime scene. The article includes recommendations for lending therapeutic support to those who investigate child homicides.

The reading by **Bonnie Fisher, Leah Daigle, Francis Cullen, and Michael Turner** reports on findings from a national random sample of female college students regarding the extent to which they have been sexually victimized and information on whether they reported their victimization. Whereas the great majority did not report the crime to police or college officials, three fourths of the respondents indicated they had told someone, usually a friend rather than a family member or mental health worker. Although this is not a surprising finding, it leads the authors to discuss implications for college and university officials as well as treatment providers. The article also includes an interesting discussion on the differences between feminist and conservative interpretations of the results of this study.

A different form of self-reported victimization—antigay violence—is highlighted in the article written by **Kristen Kuehnle and Anne Sullivan**. Bias or hatred of an individual or group because of sexual orientation is the second most frequent form of hate or bias crimes, following those motivated by racial hatred. In this descriptive study, the authors report on the characteristics of 241 incidents of violence against gays, lesbians, or transgendered individuals. In contrast to past research on victimization, the typical victim of antigay violence was not a young African American male, but rather an older male or transgendered individual, Latino or White. The authors also report where the victimizations occurred, relationships between victims and offenders, and whether the victims reported the incidents to police and sought medical attention.

As a group, these readings sensitize us to the psychological effects of victimization and possible relationships between and among various forms of victimization. Although the selections focus on violent victimization, readers should be aware that researchers are beginning to pay more attention to the psychological effects of nonviolent victimization, such as fraud or burglary. Although the harm resulting from these offenses does not tend to be physical in nature, victims of these offenses often feel vulnerable, helpless, and cynical about persons and institutions in which they had trust.

13

EXPERIENCES OF
COVICTIMS OF HOMICIDE

Implications for Research and Practice

MARILYN PETERSON ARMOUR

F amilies of homicide victims are a hidden but sizable population whose numbers are not included in crime statistics (Amick-McMullan, Kilpatrick, Veronen, & Smith, 1989; Peach & Klass, 1987; Sprang, McNeil, & Wright, 1989). In 1999, 15,530 persons were killed in the United States (Federal Bureau of Investigation, 1999a). The number of victims, when covictims of homicide are included, rises exponentially depending on how many family members and close friends are affected. Indeed, a national prevalence telephone survey conducted by Amick-McMullan, Kilpatrick, and Resnick (1991) showed that 9.3% of the 12,500 adults contacted were survivors of homicide victims. The special needs of this population have been given less attention than other forms of victimization (Amick-McMullan et al., 1991; Freeman, Shaffer, & Smith, 1996; Thompson, Norris, & Ruback, 1998). As a consequence, mental health professionals who treat clients from this population have not been exposed to some of the unique aspects of their emotional devastation and are

accordingly limited in their knowledge of how to help them. The purpose of this article is to discuss the relevance of theories on bereavement, trauma, and meaning-making to covictims of homicide; synthesize the studies on covictims; identify intervention strategies; and provide implications for practice, policy, and research.

COVICTIMS OF HOMICIDE

Death by murder creates a vastly different experience for many covictims than deaths caused by acute causes or lengthy terminal illness, suicide, or accidental death (Rando, 1996). First, they are left to struggle with the fact that the death of their loved one was caused by the willful, unanticipated, and violent act of another person. Second, they may be stripped of their rights to privacy and how they are publicly portrayed (Doka, 1988; Peterson, 2000; Redmond, 1996; Spungen, 1998). Third, because murder is a crime against the state, they often become

Editors' Note: This article was published in *Trauma, Violence, & Abuse*, Vol. 3, No. 2, April 2002, pp. 109-124. We have deleted large portions of the literature review but have included representative studies from each area.

bystanders whose needs are secondary to the state's concern for fairness and justice in apprehending, trying, and convicting the murderer. For many covictims, bereavement is not a private and personal matter marked by sadness but rather a process that is heavily controlled by the social milieu. Moreover, Stuckless (1996) found that those mourners (inclusive of covictims of homicide) who attributed culpability to a particular perpetrator for the death of their loved ones tended to feel angrier, have stronger vengeful feelings, and find life less comprehensible, manageable, and meaningful than mourners whose loved ones died of illness or accidents and did not attribute culpability to a particular perpetrator.

These conditions create a variety of consequences. Many covictims of homicide suffer from traumatic grief that is a unique blend of trauma and grief in which the bereaved person's need to defend against intrusive stimuli related to the violent death may block their ability to mourn (Rynearson & McCreery, 1993; Spungen, 1998). Although Spungen (1998) indicated that the traumatic grief paradigm is still evolving, she described it as characterized by shock that induces a wide array of both physical and emotional responses that stimulate the sympathetic nervous system and the shattering of basic assumptions about the world. In addition, traumatic grief may evoke rage, fear, horror, guilt, and shame.

In addition, covictims of homicide can feel socially stigmatized by having had a loved one murdered (Doka, 1988). They may be shunned by friends and family or blamed or slandered for the way the victim died or even for the way the victim lived. The lack of social validation uproots survivors from their communities and changes the basis for their belonging. Covictims can experience lengthy investigations, protracted court trials, and the withholding of information deemed crucial to the state's case (Peterson, 2000; Spungen, 1998). In many instances, they live with the threat of the murderer's possible parole. Any and all of these experiences can strip away the illusion of being protected and in control (Bard & Sangrey, 1986; Janoff-Bulman, 1992; Masters, Friedman, & Getzel, 1988; Rinear, 1988; Spungen, 1998; Ulman, 1988). These experiences can shatter the trust and faith in the world as it was believed to be (Janoff-Bulman, 1992).

No one scenario is common to the lives of covictims of homicide. Murder remains unsolved in 31% of cases (Federal Bureau of Investigation, 1999b). Hence, the tragedy may remain unbuffered by solution, punishment, retribution, or redemption. Murder occurs between family members in 12% of cases (Spungen, 1998). Hence, the tragedy may remain locked in estranged relationships, legal standoffs, and emotional impasses. Although every covictim of homicide faces, to varying degrees, emotional firestorms, changes in social networks, involvement in social institutions, and disruptions in meaning systems, the circumstantial features of each homicide further compound the complexities that make homicide bereavement different.

RELEVANCE OF LITERATURE TO THE EXPERIENCES OF COVICTIMS OF HOMICIDE

The experience of covictims of homicide has been included as part of the general literature on trauma, bereavement, and meaning-making. The trauma literature is relevant to comprehending their encounters with traumatic death, criminal victimization, and the shattering of assumptions about order, meaning, and self-worth. The bereavement literature is pertinent to appreciating the complexity of their grief reactions. The literature on meaning-making is germane to understanding how they cope in the aftermath of the tragedy.

Trauma Literature. Covictims of homicide are often regarded as more traumatized than bereaved (Masters et al., 1988; Redmond, 1996; Rinear, 1988; Rynearson, 1984, 1988; Rynearson & McCreery, 1993). On a cognitive level, covictims may report the existence of intrusive, repetitive thoughts, and/or nightmares (Rando, 1993). On an affective level, covictims may describe intense emotions including rage, terror, and guilt as well as numbness and dissociation. On a physiological level, covictims may identify disturbances in sleep and appetite, headaches, gastrointestinal upset, and increased startle responses. On a behavioral level, covictims may note their avoidance of homicide-related stimuli, hypervigilant awareness of their surroundings, efforts to track down the murderer, and relationship disruptions. These reactions may be short lived or evolve into full-blown posttraumatic stress disorder (PTSD) (Amick-McMullan et al., 1991). They may also be accompanied by anxiety due to feeling endangered and apprehensive, helplessness and powerlessness caused by the realization that one cannot undo or recover what has been lost, survivor guilt, and personality disturbances related to efforts to ward off anxiety and aggression (Rando, 1993).

Trauma reactions are a common response to being confronted with murder. Indeed, some studies (Parkes, 1993a; Rando, 1993; Rynearson & McCreery, 1993; Spungen, 1998) have shown that the bereavement of homicide survivors is trumped by trauma in that trauma reactions interrupt and impede mourning. For example, although emotional numbing may be an adaptive response to ward off intrusive thoughts and feelings, it may also seal off the ability to access sadness related to the loss of the loved one. Rando (1993), Horowitz (1986), and Courtois (1988) have developed strategies for addressing the numbing symptoms, managing the undercontrol inherent in intrusive-repetitive states, and ameliorating the anxiety associated with posttraumatic stress reactions. Although many of these interventions were developed with other traumatized populations such as Vietnam veterans or incest victims, they are transferable to covictims of homicide.

In addition to grieving the loss of a loved one, covictims contend with the sense of having been victimized by a deviant or atypical social act. Accordingly, they may come to see themselves and be treated by others as deviant or atypical and tend to internalize the stigma attached to the crime of murder (Doka, 1988). . . .

***

In addition to the trauma caused by murder and the trauma from having been criminally victimized, covictims of homicide also experience the trauma from the abrupt disintegration of their inner world (Getzel & Masters, 1984; Janoff-Bulman, 1992; Masters et al., 1988; Rinear, 1988). Systems of meaning that previously helped them to survive an unpredictable world are suddenly obsolete and invalid for many. . . .

The trauma of covictims of homicide is multidetermined. In addition to the trauma being triggered by the murder, crime victimization, and the shattering of meaning systems, trauma can also be induced by insensitive reactions from the media and the criminal justice system as well as from a naive and curious public (Redmond, 1989). The interface between covictims of homicide and the larger community, however, has not been studied in depth.

Bereavement Literature. Homicidal grief has been described as prolonged and extreme (Rando, 1993; Spungen, 1998). The depth of rage, horror, and vengefulness creates extreme reactions. Prolonged grief is caused by lengthy involvements with the criminal justice system, posttraumatic stress reactions, and the difficulty adjusting to unnatural dying. Although these characteristics may be normal for covictims of homicide, they become atypical or abnormal when compared to the reactions associated with natural or "uncomplicated" death (Middleton, Raphael, Martinek, & Misson, 1993). Rando (1993) maintained that homicidal grief falls within the syndrome of complicated mourning because the mode of death prevents mourners from moving through the processes or stages that are critical for resolving grief and mourning. . . .

Unfortunately, the experience of covictims of homicide does not support core assumptions inherent in grief work. First, grief work presumes that continuing the attachment with the deceased is symptomatic of pathology because it does not allow for the reinvestment of energy in current life tasks (Stroebe & Gergen, 1996; Stroebe & Schut, 1999). For covictims, continuing the attachment is a strong indicator of their love for and commitment to correcting the injustice of their loved one's death (Peterson, 2000). . . .

Second, grief work presumes that grieving is time limited, follows a uniform set of stages, and has an end point (Stroebe & Gergen, 1996; Stroebe & Schut, 1999). Covictims of homicide, however, do not expect closure (Peterson, 2000; Spungen, 1998). Instead of seeing their experience as transitory, they discover that their grieving is ongoing and takes different directions based on time and circumstances. The daily process of covictims, for example, is heavily controlled by the state's agenda for bringing the murderer to justice and other external events. . . .

Third, grief work presumes that adapting to the loss requires the bereaved to bring the reality of loss into their awareness and not suppress their emotions (Stroebe & Gergen, 1996; Stroebe & Schut, 1999). Covictims of homicide adapt to their loss by learning to live with the enormity of their ongoing pain (Peterson, 2000).They do not necessarily accept that the expression of emotions is a catalyst for wellness. Some find that the expression of anger and rage leaves them immobilized and feeling out of control. Others believe that keeping their emotions keeps them connected to their loved one. Still others decide to hold onto their emotions so they do not lose more than they already have. . . .

***

Literature on Meaning. Because homicide shatters meaning systems, covictims of homicide must find ways to rebuild their beliefs in personal invulnerability, a perception of the world as meaningful, and a perception of self as positive (Janoff-Bulman, 1992). Meaning-making provides a mechanism for coping with the stress and reducing the dissonance between the horrific reality of murder and the person's preexisting assumptions about safety, order, and meaning (Horowitz, 1976; Janoff-Bulman, 1992; Park & Folkman, 1997; Patterson & Garwick, 1994; Taylor & Bogdan, 1984; Thompson & Jangian, 1988). Finding meaning in or making sense of the murder are two ways to reconcile the discrepancies and achieve inner resolution (Frankl, 1969; Janoff- Bulman, 1992; Nadeau, 1998; Neimeyer, 2000). Finding meaning in the suffering restores a sense of purpose and agency and counters the meaninglessness of what has occurred. Making sense of the murder reconstructs what happened and reestablishes the perception of order in the world.

The literature on meaning-making rests on the supposition that it is possible for people to either find positive meaning in misfortune or make sense out of negative experiences. Wortman et al. (1993) studied the responses of family members of victims killed in automobile accidents and found that 72% of the participants were unable to make any sense out of or find

any meaning in their loss. Similarly, Silver, Boon, and Stones (1983) researched how incest victims made sense of the violation. More than 50% of participants were unable to make any sense of it, and 80% reported still searching for meaning after 20 years. Although homicide studies have not specifically addressed the attempts by covictims to make sense out of or find meaning in the tragedy, it is likely that most of this population would also have difficulty making sense out of a senseless act. Indeed, it is possible that their prolonged grieving reflects their inability to sufficiently answer the question "Why?" or find reason to move forward.

Theorists who question the suppositions in theories of meaning-making have also noted possible problems that may be pertinent to covictims of homicide. Van der Kolk et al. (1996) maintained that the goal of making sense may be an unrealistic expectation for traumatized persons. "To find reason or congruity in such horrors seems an impossible task" (p. 370). . . .

***

HOMICIDE STUDIES

Studies of covictims of homicide are sparse (Amick-McMullan et al., 1991; Freeman et al., 1996; Thompson et al., 1998). They focus on the trauma response to the exclusion of other dimensions of the post-homicide experience (e.g., stigmatized identity, death notification, family dynamics, criminal justice encounters). Moreover, the studies are fragmented and do not reflect a consistency in research direction. For purposes of this article, the literature has been divided into clinical and descriptive studies, empirically based studies, and intervention studies. Clinical and descriptive studies derive from client records, case studies, interviews, and participant observation. With some exceptions (i.e., Spungen, 1998, and Parkes, 1993b), the descriptive and clinical studies were done in the 1980s and were informed primarily by practice. Empirically based studies use assessment instruments and surveys to report results related to prevalence and incidence, establish associations between significant variables, and show differences between experimental and control groups. Intervention studies report on the effectiveness of particular treatments applied to covictims of homicide. . . .

***

Descriptive and Clinical Studies. The first accounts of the difficulties encountered by family members appeared during the 1970s and 1980s (Bard & Sangrey, 1986; Burgess, 1975; . . . Sprang et al., 1989). They were descriptive and drawn from clinical studies. They validated the unique problems of being covictims of homicide by describing their trauma reactions, dissatisfaction with the criminal justice system, and struggle for meaning.

Burgess (1975) recognized the uniqueness of homicidal grief that included (a) an acute grief reaction to the double impact of an untimely death and homicide of a loved one and (b) a protracted reorganization process due to the sociolegal processes. Drawing on their experience of providing services to covictims, Getzel and Masters (1984) noted the difficulties their clients experienced in their efforts to reorganize their lives. They warned that unless family members could reconceptualize the now negative and tainted belief system about the stability and goodness of human contact and interaction, their grief would remain unresolved and disabling. In a later study, Masters et al. (1988) observed that the grief reaction for these clients was not a sequential process but consisted of a series of crises, each of which required a new process of working through. Collectively and over time, these crises gave death by murder an unrelenting chronic quality that could never be integrated and put behind. Masters et al. again noted the extent of the violation to their client families' assumptive world but commented that instead of renewing their previous faith, these families needed a new vision of society and a new community of believers to replace what they had lost.

***

Spungen (1998) is included in this review of descriptive studies because she has written the only extensive guide for professionals based on 16 years of working with covictims of homicide. This guide details, among other topics, the significance of the death notification, the impact of homicide on the family system, and suggestions for handling demands from social institutions such as the media and criminal justice system. Spungen insisted that current approaches to bereavement do not incorporate the diverse psychological and emotional repercussions of homicide. She advocated for a new model that is an amalgam of interventions from both the fields of trauma and grief. Spungen further maintained that traumatic grief is normal for covictims of homicide and called for criteria to distinguish normal homicide bereavement from complicated homicide bereavement.

Empirical Studies. Empirically based studies emerged in the late 1980s and 1990s. Their findings validated the descriptive studies and delineated some of the risk factors that may exacerbate or relieve trauma and distress symptoms. Generally, the studies do not build on the results of each other. Collectively, however, they demonstrated that trauma reactions are considered the major criterion of severity of victimization consequences (Thompson et al., 1998).

Rinear conducted the first (1988) survey with covictims of homicide. Her work, based on 237 members of Parents of Murdered Children support groups, showed the impact of psychosocial stressors on the destruction of personal beliefs, which she suggested gave rise to traumatic stress symptomatology. Using the framework provided by Janoff-Bulman (Janoff-Bulman, 1985; Janoff-Bulman & Freize, 1983), Rinear examined how the stressors on covictims threatened their beliefs in personal invulnerability, a meaningful and comprehensible world, and their self-worth. Although Rinear's work has not been expanded, her survey thrust the concept of meaning and meaning-making to the forefront.

***

Although many studies have noted that covictims of homicide wrestle with both grief and trauma, few studies have specifically considered the interplay between the two psychological conditions. Rynearson and McCreery (1993) examined the intensity and relationship of trauma responses to bereavement in severely traumatized patients (N = 18). They found that the coexistence of trauma and loss created a synergism of delayed recovery. Specifically, "[t]he piercing and recurring reenactment imagery [reported by the covictims in their study] . . . created anticipatory dread and fear of its involuntary repetition" (p. 260). Efforts to block the imagery tended to impair the more introspective and reflective demands of acknowledging and adjusting to the loss.

***

Thompson and Vardaman (1997) investigated whether various types of religious coping reduced distress in a sample of covictims (N = 150) randomly drawn from public records in an urban community. They found that religious support from clergy and church members was the only coping activity out of six possible behaviors moderately related to decreased distress. Indeed, three of the other behaviors (pleading, discontent with God, and attempts at good deeds) were related to increased distress.

Thompson et al. (1998) used randomly selected control groups to compare the PTSD and distress reactions of female African American covictims of homicide (N = 150) with groups of comparable African American survivors of other trauma and African American women in an epidemiological data set. Thompson et al. found that the homicide sample was significantly higher on PTSD symptoms than the other trauma group. . . .

The empirical literature recognizes the severity of post-homicide reactions as a reliable indicator of the distress experienced by covictims of homicide. Indeed, nearly all the studies represent efforts to distinguish those factors that increase or relieve distress. The destruction of personal beliefs (Rinear, 1988), inhibition of mourning (Rynearson & McCreery, 1993), and negative relationships with the criminal justice system (Amick-McMullan et al., 1989) increase distress. The lack of social support also increases distress as shown by unmarried females who minimally use social supports (Sprang et al., 1993) and siblings of murder victims who are isolated as a consequence of difficulties with peers and lack of involvement with mental health services (Freeman et al.,

1996). In contrast, religious support may decrease distress somewhat (Thompson & Vardaman, 1997). For mothers of homicide victims, greater emotional involvement and physical proximity prior to the homicide increase distress. Distress is also exacerbated by the association between drugs and homicide as well as the impersonality of the death notification done outside the home. After the homicide, distress is increased by lessened economic resources and the loss of being a mother (Thompson et al., 1998).

Besides the focus on risk factors for increased distress, the empirical literature has shown that the covictim status from an emotional standpoint is not limited to immediate family members. Rather, many Americans are covictims by virtue of the fact that they have lost close friends and relatives to murder (Amick-McMullen et al., 1991). Indeed, the results of the prevalence study done by Amick-McMullen et al. lends credence to the argument that the sizable covictim population has been treated as invisible.

Intervention Studies. Several intervention strategies have been developed to address the unique needs of this population. Lyon, Moore, and Lexius (1992) described and compared the results from two kinds of groups for covictims of homicide— a structured time-limited educational group and a self-help/mutual support group. Eight structured time-limited (6 weeks) and professionally led groups gave homicide survivors (N = 41 families) information about the grieving process and the criminal justice system. These groups also used the interaction between group members to reduce their isolation, normalize their experiences, and help them gain control and mastery over their lives. . . . Both types of groups were deemed effective as well as complementary to and compatible with each other.

Umbreit, Bradshaw, and Coates (1999) and Umbreit and Voss (2000) described an emerging intervention between covictims of homicide and incarcerated offenders called Victim Offender Mediation and Dialogue (VOMD). This intervention is a restorative justice initiative that gives family members, in select situations, the opportunity to address the damage done to them through a face-to-face dialogue with the offender. VOMD accords covictims the recognition that they were previously denied by the state's need to bring the murderer to justice. Moreover, this program affirms their experience by letting covictims tell the offender how the crime affected them and ask questions about the details of the murder. Preliminary results show a positive response from both covictims (N = 11) and offenders (N = 9): 100% of covictims and 89% of offenders found the mediation very helpful. Of those surveyed, 91% of covictims and 78% of offenders said their overall outlook on life had changed since the meeting and they were definitely more positive and at peace with life circumstances.

Temple (1997) developed a treatment model for inner-city families of homicide victims that used principles of Contextual Therapy as described by Boszormenyi-Nagy and his associates (Boszormenyi-Nagy, 1986; Boszormenyi-Nagy & Spark, 1973) to restore family functioning, prevent retaliatory violence, and encourage the development of future plans based on honoring the memory of the murdered family member. Contextual Therapy recognizes the power of family ties and uses issues of fairness and justice to address the injuries in the family as well as existential bonds of indebtedness and connectedness. In addition to helping family members weave new forms of loyalty and attachment to both the dead and the living, following murder, Temple incorporated White and Epston's (1990) technique of "therapeutic certificates" with children to acknowledge their competence, worth, and the successful completion of a rite of passage relative to their achievements in therapy. Although no formal assessment was done, Temple incorporated his evaluation of client change into the "therapeutic certificates" given to the clients.

Intervention strategies focus programmatically and therapeutically on ways for covictims of homicide to regain a sense of control over their lives. Studies by Lyon et al. (1992), Umbreit et al. (1999), Umbreit and Voss (2000), and Temple (1997) show that giving them information about what lies ahead, providing them with communities that affirm their struggles, offering them opportunities for legislative action, assisting them to redress the damage with the offender, and evolving larger philosophical meaning systems enable survivors to take action on their own behalf.

***

CONCLUSION

Covictims of homicide are a hidden and substantial part of the United States population who are not accorded status in the criminal justice system or in society. Though they are crime victims, they are not part of the crime statistics kept by any government agency. Literature on trauma, bereavement, and meaning reflects different dimensions of the post-homicide experience. Because much of this literature was developed from populations other than covictims of homicide, it needs to be modified when applied to this group. The few studies on the consequences of homicide for surviving family members indicate that trauma is a significant factor in a covictim's response to murder. Some studies have begun to delineate risk factors that can exacerbate trauma and distress. Other studies have introduced intervention strategies to help relieve and empower covictims. Covictims of homicide need to be recognized as a distinct and vulnerable population. Future research should broaden the scope of inquiry beyond PTSD to include other important aspects of the post-homicide experience. The practice field has to develop innovative models to address the idiosyncratic, unique, and complex needs of family members. Finally, work with covictims calls for a blending of approaches that includes models of community practice, family therapy, restorative justice initiatives, support groups, school interventions, and advocacy with formal institutions such as the criminal justice system and the media.

14

CRITICAL INCIDENT STRESS AND THE CHILD HOMICIDE INVESTIGATOR

ISAAC T. VAN PATTEN
TOD W. BURKE

In the past 20 years, substantial advancements have been made in the recognition of the deleterious effects of critical incident stress (CIS) among law enforcement personnel (Kureczka, 1996; Reese, Horn, & Dunning, 1991). Typically, the study of CIS in law enforcement has emphasized such areas as the response to mass casualty incidents such as airplane crashes, line-of-duty fatalities, or officer-involved shooting incidents (Foreman, 1991; McMains, 1991; Shaw, 1991; Solomon & Horn, 1986). CIS is not limited to these events or to patrol officers who often respond to such disasters. Homicide investigators are often called on to investigate horrific crimes, including crimes where the victims are children. It has been the experience of the authors that investigators report that crimes involving children are the most difficult for them to work and maintain their emotional and psychological equilibrium. Therefore, it is the purpose of this pilot study to examine the effects of CIS on the homicide investigator who has been exposed to child fatalities.

The definition of CIS varies. Gentz (1991) stated, "A critical incident may be defined as an event requiring an extraordinary degree of adaptation by the individual who experiences it" (p. 119). Melick, Logue, and Frederick (1982) noted that a critical incident is not limited to a single event but is a series of events (before and after the incident) that cumulatively affects the way a person reacts. The most widely recognized definition of CIS (and the one used for this research) suggests that a critical incident is one that causes a person to have "unusually strong emotional reactions that have the potential to interfere with his or her ability to function either at the scene or later" (Mitchell in Garrison, 1991).

HISTORY OF CRITICAL INCIDENT STRESS

CIS has its origins in trauma research on acute crisis response (burnout), posttraumatic stress syndrome, and post-traumatic stress disorder

Editors' Note: This article was first published in *Homicide Studies*, Vol. 5, No. 2, May 2001, pp. 131-152. In addition to tables, an appendix and portions of the discussion and conclusions sections have been omitted.

(PTSD). The word stress, meaning hardships, straits, adversity, or affliction, is derived from Latin and was used in the English language as early as the 17th century (Hinkle, 1977). Research on stress began in earnest in 1936 with the pioneering work of Canadian physician Hans Selye (Barrett, 1985). Selye (1982) defined stress as the nonspecific response of the body to any demand made on the person. Selye contends that the body responds to stress in three stages: alarm, resistance, and exhaustion. Selye calls this three-stage response to stress the general adaptation syndrome (GAS). During the alarm stage, the individual is alerted to potential threats. The resistance stage is characterized by fatigue, anxiety, tension, and irritability. If the individual is unable to adapt during the resistance stage, the symptoms may advance to the exhaustion stage in which physical and emotional illness is likely (Selye, 1974). Stress is the initial stage of the burnout syndrome (D. E. Payne, 1984).

Burnout is a psychophysiological phenomenon characterized by emotional exhaustion, depression, and cynicism that occurs among individuals who have frequent emotional pressure associated with intense involvement with people over a period of time (Maslach & Jackson, 1984; Pines, Aronson, & Kafry, 1981). Freudenberger (1977) noted that sufferers of burnout often do not recognize the traits commonly associated with stress; rather, they find fault with everything and everyone around them, complaining about their work organization, contributing less, and reacting cynically toward others. If traumatic events characteristic of stress and burnout are not addressed effectively, a debilitating chronic condition known as posttraumatic stress syndrome, leading to PTSD, may develop (Foreman, 1991).

Posttraumatic stress syndrome is not a new concept. In fact, "PTSD symptoms have long been associated with disaster and war trauma" (Foreman, 1991, p. 86), particularly with Vietnam era veterans (Blak, 1991). The *Diagnostic and Statistical Manual of Mental Disorders (DSM-IV)* (American Psychological Association, 1994) defines two variant forms of diagnoses related to exposure to critical incident stress: acute stress disorder (ASD) and PTSD. PTSD may manifest itself as an acute response,

a chronic response, or a delayed response to the stressor event. In both instances, exposure to human death is clearly identified as meeting the criteria for a precipitant stressor event. The substantive difference between the two disorders is related to the chronicity of the symptoms, with ASD representing the more acute reaction and briefer symptom duration. A number of studies have identified the prevalence of PTSD in police officers that have been exposed to death (Gersons, 1989; Kuch & Travis, 1995; Martin, McKean, & Veltkamp, 1986).

Additional symptoms of PTSD may include nightmares, reenactments, guilt, denial, emotional numbing, shock, feelings of loss, disorganized thought, memory impairment, detachment, panic, anxiety, inability to concentrate, poor judgment, and lack of trust (Horowitz, 1976; Liebert, 1991; Titchener, 1986). Symptoms commonly observed in PTSD may also be noticed among those experiencing CIS, including flashbacks, time distortion, loss of control, heightened sense of danger, sorrow, survivor guilt, psychosomatic disorders, anniversary reaction, nausea, headaches, hyperventilation, withdrawal, intrusive thoughts, increased alcohol/ drug consumption, and/or relationship difficulties (Gentz, 1991; Horn, 1991; Klein, 1991). The relationship between PTSD and CIS appears to be semantic.

Another distinguishing characteristic of posttraumatic stress syndrome has recently been proposed by Lenore Terr (1991) and serves to break the syndrome into Type I and Type II variants. Type I trauma refers to the effects on the human psyche of a single traumatic incident. Alternatively, the traumatic effects of prolonged, repeated exposure to CIS results in the Type II variant. Subsequently, this concept has been further developed by Judith Herman (1992). Herman suggested that the Type II syndrome be called complex PTSD to reflect the relatively greater exposure to ongoing stressors and the development of a distinct symptom cluster. Her proposal was considered for inclusion in the *DSM-IV* under the designation "disorders of extreme stress not otherwise specified" (DESNOS).

Although not included in the *DSM-IV* as a separate diagnostic category, research into complex PTSD has continued (Pelcovitz et al., 1997). As currently conceptualized, symptoms are clustered into five main categories: alterations in regulating affective arousal, alterations in attention and consciousness, somatization, chronic characterological changes, and alterations in systems of meaning. Of particular importance is the realization that an individual may be suffering from the symptoms of PTSD as well as DESNOS at the same time (van der Kolk, 1996).

Many occupational settings are potentially stressful (Burke, 1991; French, Rogers, & Cobb, 1974; Kahn, 1970; Revicki & May, 1985). However, law enforcement possesses unique stressors . . . , such as role ambiguity, lack of administrative support, responsibility for others, unpredictability, fear and danger, inadequate reward system, shift work, community aversion, the judicial system, and exposure to traumatic experiences and human suffering (Carter, 1994; Kroes, Margolis, & Hurrell, 1974; . . . Violanti & Aron, 1995). Criminal investigators may experience stressors based on their role and responsibility within the criminal justice arena.

According to Osterburg and Ward (1997), the responsibility of the investigator includes the determination of a crime, jurisdiction of the crime, gathering and preserving relevant evidence, recovering property, identifying potential suspects and witnesses, apprehension of perpetrators, and testifying in court. Although criminal investigators experience similar stressors of any patrol officer, they may encounter stressors unique to their role. For example, Stratton (1984) identified six stressors commonly reported by investigators: caseload, time, lack of cooperation from citizens, fishbowl experience, role conflict, and assignment.

Many investigators are required to handle a number of cases simultaneously within a short period of time. They are overwhelmed in paperwork and find that there is not enough time to effectively complete investigative details.

Investigators are often hampered by citizens who fail to report crimes or who are hesitant to get involved in the investigative process. Highly publicized cases also create stress among investigators who perceive that they are constantly being watched by not only their supervisors, but also by the media.

Investigation, by nature, is a tedious process requiring extensive report writing and reading, follow-up questioning, and surveillance (which often proves uneventful or productive). This may cause role conflict in those officers who believe that criminal investigation is an exciting adventure as portrayed in movies, books, and television.

Whereas some investigators are assigned to property crimes, others investigate crimes against persons. Those officers who are repeatedly exposed to interpersonal, manmade violence and trauma, particularly those who investigate child fatalities, are at risk for CIS and anxiety-based illness such as PTSD and DESNOS.

DEATH AND THE POLICE SUBCULTURE

Although it is endemic to the police culture that dealing with death will be a necessary aspect of the job, very little is actually known about police officers and death encounters (Henry, 1995). It is worth noting that law enforcement is the only contemporary occupational field where there is frequent, intense, and intimate contact with people who have been killed by intentional violence. Although other occupational groups—for example, firefighters and emergency medical personnel—have frequent death encounters, it is almost always in a different context.

Henry (1995) suggests that this unique exposure by the police officer to death contributes directly to the coping style employed. Law enforcement is a closed society that trusts only slowly, if at all. One aspect of entry into this restricted domain is how the individual officer handles his or her confrontation with death in the field. As a primary coping strategy, police officers learn to distance themselves from death and to trivialize the significance of a dead body. According to Henry, this psychic closing off leads to a disconnect between the emotional and cognitive aspects of dealing with death.

Dealing with a dead body evokes both profound affective and cognitive responses in human beings (Went, 1979). This confrontation necessitates an encounter with one's own mortality, which is emotionally evocative in its own right. Typically, the police officer experiences guilt, shame, and embarrassment as a part of the affective response to death (Gersons, 1989; Henry, 1995; Went, 1979). This intense emotional response stands in stark contrast to the demands of the job. The primary coping strategies employed by the homicide investigator are denial and dissociation, cutting off the emotional response in favor of the necessary cognitive requirements of the task at hand. Went reported that repeated exposure to death had the effect of reducing the level of experienced anxiety by police officers, with homicide investigators and crime scene technicians becoming the most inured to death (Henry, 1995).

The degree to which an investigator is able to effect this emotional dissociation is directly related to the degree to which he or she identifies with the victim (Gersons, 1989; Jones, 1985; Ursano & McCarroll, 1990). A child victim represents a unique case in that it is considerably more difficult for investigators to create the emotional distance necessary to protect themselves. Confronting the body of a murdered child is made more difficult because of the perceptions of innocence, premature death, and the totality of the child's victimization (Ursano & McCarroll, 1990). When forced to confront death in the form of a child homicide victim, the identification with the victim is typically much greater than when dealing with adult victims (Jones, 1985; Ursano & McCarroll, 1990). With this increased identification, the experience of stress is intensified in a situation where the investigator is constrained by the professional role to suppress the natural emotional expression of that stress (Henry, 1995).

The murder of a child is also a direct expression of society's failure to protect its most innocent citizens (Maney & Kedem, 1982). It is ironic that the first year of life represents the single largest exposure to death by homicide (Alder & Polk, 1996; Kunz & Bahr, 1996; Wilson, Daly, & Daniele, 1995). The most likely perpetrators of this murder are the parents of the slain child. Kunz and Bahr (1996) report that in the first week of life, the perpetrator is almost always the mother. In the period from 1 week to 13 years of age, it is equally likely to be the mother or the father. In the teen years, the most likely perpetrator is the father. The very demographics of the phenomenon force the investigator to identify with the child victim. Given that the police mission is to protect and serve, for many investigators, a child murder

is a double insult. When investigating a child homicide, the officer is confronted with a professional failure (to protect) and a personal failure in his or her tendency to identify with the victim as a member of a family.

In considering the factors that contribute to the stress experienced by homicide investigators, Sewell (1993) identified several areas unique to law enforcement. First, he notes the stress generated by administrative pressures to rapidly solve the crime as well as the pressure to carry on "business as usual." In many investigations, the work environment contributes to the stress of the investigation. Specifically, this contribution to the stress load is in the form of being forced to work in an ad hoc environment, constantly associating with witnesses and bystanders, as well as the constant strain of media attention. Sewell also pointed out that a homicide investigation puts considerable role strain and conflict on the investigators. This can range from the necessity to maintain a professional demeanor for colleagues and the public to conflicts in the investigator's own family responsibilities.

Sewell (1993) noted that a significant stressor is the traumatic stimuli and the response to the crime scene itself. Although most investigators cope with this in the short term through emotional distancing, dark humor, and professional focus, the chronic effects of this stress are largely an unknown. Gersons (1989) noted that the effects of exposure to traumatic stimuli were related to the degree of identification with the victim and the violence evident at the crime scene. The symptoms of this traumatic exposure are thought to have a gradual onset and to be chronic in nature.

CAUSAL MODEL OF STRESS

It is the intention of this research to explore a causal model of stress in death investigators who have been exposed to child homicide. Of particular interest is an examination of the above factors identified by Sewell (1993) as contributors to the experienced stress of homicide investigations. On the basis of anecdotal reports and the review of the literature (Henry, 1995; . . . Ursano & McCarroll, 1990), it is expected that exposure to the violence of a child murder will be a significant contributor to the manifest stress in homicide investigators. If this proves to be the case, then the death investigator can be considered as a secondary or vicarious victim of the child homicide.

INVESTIGATIVE HYPOTHESES

There are two hypotheses that were tested in the current research. The first is that homicide investigators would exhibit more stress-related symptoms than a normative sample of adult non-patients. The second hypothesis is that a significant portion of the stress experienced by homicide investigators could be attributed to the traumatic stimuli at the scene of a child homicide.

METHOD

Participants

The initial 41 participants for this study were recruited from the attendees at an in-service seminar held at the FBI Academy for the Virginia Homicide Investigators Association (VHIA). The VHIA is a professional association of law enforcement personnel actively charged with the responsibility of death investigation. Fourteen participants were members of a multi-disciplinary, multi-jurisdictional homicide investigation team based in Portland, Oregon. This team included both sworn law enforcement personnel and investigators from the medical examiner's system. A final group of 12 participants came from the General Investigations Division of the Bureau of Criminal Investigations, Virginia State Police (VSP). All 12 special agents for the VSP were actively involved in the investigation of violent crimes, including homicide. The total number of participants available for this study was 67.

PROCEDURE

The procedure used in this study was a survey . . . in which each of the participants completed two instruments designed to assess their experiences in death investigations involving child victims and relative number of stress-related symptoms. The first survey instrument, Experiences of Child Homicide Investigators, was designed specifically for this research and was used to capture demographic information, stress-related experiences, and their participation in critical incident stress management (CISM). Although the instrument has face and content validity, the criterion validity of the instrument is not known. The survey had an alpha coefficient of 0.91, indicating that the scale was internally consistent in its measurement of the stress experience.

The 12 core questions, designed to assess the different source areas of stress for the death investigator, used a 5-point Likert scale. The CISM questions included both yes-no format and Likert-scale questions. . . .

The second instrument, used to evaluate the dependent variable of stress-related symptoms, was the Symptom Checklist- 90–Revised (SCL-90-R) (Derogatis, 1983). The SCL-90-R has been frequently used as an instrument to evaluate the effects of psychological stress associated with such events as death, disaster, rape, pain, and other related phenomena (R. W. Payne, 1985). This 90-item self-report measure generates scores for nine different classes of symptoms (somatization, obsessive-compulsive, interpersonal sensitivity, depression, anxiety, hostility, phobic anxiety, paranoid ideation, and psychoticism) and three global measures of distress (Global Severity Index [GSI], Positive Symptom Distress Index, and Positive Symptom Total). For the purposes of this study, the GSI was used as a measure of the overall stress symptoms reported by the investigators.

Results

The typical respondent to the survey was a middle-aged (M = 40.33) male (90% male, 10% female) with 16 years in law enforcement (M = 16.19) and 6 ½ years in homicide investigations (M = 6.58). The majority listed their job as "investigator" (86.2%), whereas "criminalist" and "medical examiner's investigator" made up the balance (13.8%). The majority were married (75.4%), with 9.8% never married and 14.8% separated or divorced. The majority reported having some college education (57.6%), whereas another 19.7% reported having earned a bachelor's degree, and 18.2% reported having a graduate degree. This collection of homicide investigators was a well-educated group. Most of the participants were White (90.8%), with the balance from minority groups (African American = 6.2%, Hispanic = 1.5%, other =1.5%). The majority of the investigators reported being from a jurisdiction of more than 200,000 people (52.2%), which might well be a function of the participation by investigators with either a statewide or a multi-jurisdictional responsibility.

STRESS LEVELS

Each investigator completed the self-report SCL-90-R to provide an estimate of the level of stress-related symptoms that the individual was reporting at the time of the study. To determine the relative level of stress-related symptoms reported by this sample of homicide investigators, scores on the SCL-90-R were compared with the non-patient (normal adults) norm group used in the development of the SCL-90-R by using an independent t test for uncorrelated means.

The non-patient norm group was almost evenly split between males ($n = 493$) and females ($n = 480$). This group was generated using a stratified random sample from a large county in the eastern United States. Unfortunately, Derogatis (1983) was unable to further describe this group.

A t statistic was computed for each of the nine scales and for the GSI. In each instance, it was found that the scores for the homicide investigators were significantly greater ($p < .05$) than the norm group. Although these reported stress levels are nowhere near those reported by psychiatric outpatients, the level of stress-related symptoms reported by the investigators is significantly greater than one would expect to find in the general population.

EVALUATION OF THE CAUSAL MODEL

Sewell (1993) has proposed a causal model for the traumatic stress experienced by homicide investigators. He identified a number of categories of stressor experiences that he proposes

constitute the significant sources of the traumatic stress experienced by the investigator assigned to multiple homicide cases. Sewell's model has been adapted for purposes of this study of stress in child murder investigators. It was hypothesized that the most significant contributor to overall stress would be the traumatic stimuli (seeing the dead child, graphic remains) present at the crime scene.

For purposes of this study, stressors were evaluated using a stepwise multiple regression analysis to ascertain the contribution of the stressor variables to the level of stress reported by the investigators. These stress-related variables include the level of administrative pressure placed on the investigator to quickly solve the case and administrative pressure to carry on with the normal business of the agency (while continuing the active investigation of the child homicide). The actual work environment in which the investigators must operate is another stressor, and this includes the presence of witnesses and bystanders as well as the intrusive presence of the media. Also included in the variable work environment is the need to operate in an ad hoc environment away from the familiarity and comforts of the investigators' own office. Conflicting roles and responsibilities is another identified stressor for investigators. This includes conflicts generated in multi-jurisdictional task forces, the need to maintain a professional image for the public, the need to maintain a professional image within the department, and the stress generated by conflicts between professional and family responsibilities.

As noted above, one of the most difficult stressors is exposure to graphic stimuli at the crime scene itself. The nature of the job forces the homicide investigator to suppress normal emotional reactions to the viewing of a murdered child in order to continue to function in their professional capacity. Another group of stressors identified by Sewell (1993) is those involving a failure of mission. These include the inability to identify a suspect and the inability to establish sufficient evidence to arrest a known suspect. Finally, there is the stress caused by the time it takes from the charging of the suspect to the completion of the trial.

***

DISCUSSION

Henry (1995) has proposed the "psychology of survival" as an appropriate theoretical frame for understanding death encounters by police officers. He notes the frequent and intense encounters with violent death by police officers leaves an enduring mark on the human psyche. These psychological sequelae have been studied in such diverse populations as Holocaust survivors and combat veterans, all with a common theme of exposure to non-accidental death imposed by another human being. Henry suggests that, with the dearth of empirical research of the death encounter in police society, the psychology of survival is a useful framework for understanding the common themes and psychology of these experiences.

Several characteristics of the psychology of survival are indeed relevant. First, there is a tendency to form an insular culture that maintains psychological and emotional distance from civilians. Admission to this culture is not automatic by virtue of becoming a sworn police officer but rather is a gradual process. One mechanism through which the rookie police officer gains admission to this closed society is the death encounter. Tradition dictates that police officers shall remain emotionally aloof and even casual in their encounters with death (Henry, 1995; Went, 1979). This leads to a situation in which denial and dissociation become essential to the psychological survival of the officer.

This emotional dissociation also represents a necessary professional survival tactic for the homicide investigator. The necessary tasks of a crime scene evaluation, interviews with family and friends of the victim, and the ongoing pursuit of leads make it difficult for the investigator (unlike the patrol officer) to move on and forget the death encounter. In fact, quite the opposite is true. The homicide investigator is required, by virtue of the job, to remain immersed in a multitude of reminders of the death encounter. To complete the daunting tasks of bringing a case to successful resolution, it is essential that the investigator maintain emotional control throughout the investigation so as not to be misdirected in his or her pursuit of the suspect.

One circumstance that complicates this psychological survival strategy is when the homicide investigator is forced to deal with the murder of a child. A factor making it more difficult for the death investigator to invoke his or her normal coping mechanisms is the situation in which there is an emotional identification with the crime victim. In the case of the child homicide victim, the avoidance of this emotional identification is virtually impossible (Gersons, 1989; Jones, 1985; Ursano & McCarroll, 1990).

Prior research by Violanti and Aron (1995) has emphasized the administrative stressors experienced by law enforcement. However, Sewell (1993) suggested that there are stressors unique to the job of the homicide investigator. It was the purpose of this study to evaluate several of the variables identified by Sewell as a source of stress for death investigators. In particular, consideration of the effects of the traumatic stimuli encountered at the crime scene of a child murder was a central concern. Although it is an abiding characteristic of the homicide investigator's coping strategies to maintain as much emotional distance from the horrors of a crime scene as possible, this task is singularly difficult to accomplish. This is especially so when investigating the death of a child by homicide. If this is true, then it is to be expected that this exposure to the emotionally intense and psychologically toxic crime scene of a child homicide will exact a toll on those charged with the responsibility of investigating that murder.

This is, in fact, what was discovered in this pilot study of the effects of this type of CIS on the homicide investigator. First, it was discovered that the investigators participating in this study exhibited more stress-related symptoms than a comparison group of non-patient (normal) adults. Significantly, this general level of stress-related symptoms was less than that reported by a standardization group of adult psychiatric outpatients. In effect, the homicide investigators were reporting more stress than the average citizen, but not so much as to become significantly impaired. This is consistent with the dynamic proposed by Henry (1995) in his discussion of the psychology of survival. Although the stress is clearly having an impact on the lives of these investigators, they are continuing to operate in their assigned jobs. This is even more profound when one considers the relatively low level of CIS intervention experienced by these officers.

Having established that these investigators are experiencing significantly higher stress levels than would be expected, the next issue we sought to address was the possible direct causes of this stress. Sewell (1993) proposed a tentative model for evaluating the causal basis of CIS in homicide investigations. He suggested a number of distinct categories of potential stressors, including administrative, work environment, role and responsibility conflicts, and exposure to traumatic stimuli. For this evaluation, the GSI of the SCL-90-R was regressed against measures of stress levels produced by these different areas. The exposure to traumatic stimuli at the crime scene of a child homicide was the single biggest contributor to the stress levels reported by these officers. Exposure to traumatic stimuli alone accounted for a significant amount of the variance in the stress levels for these investigators. When exposure to traumatic stimuli was combined with the working environment of the homicide investigator, this causal model accounted for a third of the variance. Included in Sewell's (1993) construct of the working environment were such things as continuing involvement with bystanders and witnesses, the ad hoc nature of the situation (limited logistical and administrative support at the scene), and the creative techniques employed by the media to get the story ahead of their competition. In summary, the results of this study suggest that the most significant contributors to the stress levels of homicide investigators are those factors related to the acute exposure to the stimuli at and associated with the crime scene and immediate investigation.

***

CONCLUSION

In considering the results of this study, the reader needs to be aware of several cautionary limitations. First, the sampling procedure used was a nonrandom convenience sample. It is unknown how representative of the universe of homicide investigators this particular sample is likely to be. For that reason, the generalizations made to this larger population should be made with some caution. In future research, it would be helpful to compare the stress experienced by homicide investigators to other law enforcement personnel, as opposed to a more general population (adult, non-patients). This would allow for a perhaps more meaningful comparison of the magnitude of stress symptoms experienced by the homicide investigators (by comparison to a more similar group). Finally, the assessment of the causal variables was accomplished by an ex post facto, self-report survey, which necessarily relies on the accuracy of the investigator's memory. To that end, more direct observation of the homicide investigator would be recommended.

15

REPORTING SEXUAL VICTIMIZATION TO THE POLICE AND OTHERS

Results From a National-Level Study of College Women

BONNIE S. FISHER
LEAH E. DAIGLE
FRANCIS T. CULLEN
MICHAEL G. TURNER

Figures have revealed that the majority of female rape and sexual assault victims are between the ages of 16 and 24 (Rennison, 1999). It is not surprising, then, that considerable attention has been given to the sexual victimization of college women. Existing research has shown that college women are at an elevated risk for victimization. Studies have estimated that between 8% and 35% of female students are victims of sexual offenses during their college years (DeKeseredy & Schwartz, 1998; Fisher, Sloan, Cullen, & Lu, 1998; Koss, Gidycz, & Wisniewski, 1987).

Despite the prevalence of sexual offenses, a large proportion of victims did not report their sexual victimization to the police or to other authorities (Tjaden & Thoennes, 2000). Results from the National Crime Victimization Survey (NCVS) have consistently shown that rape and sexual assault have been the most widely underreported violent crimes. In fact, the 1999 NCVS results revealed that only 28.3% of these crimes were reported to the police (Rennison, 1999). Notably, other research has provided even lower estimates of reporting (Bachman, 1998; ... Tjaden & Thoennes, 2000). ...

Because of the extent of non-reporting, research has attempted to uncover the factors that affect the likelihood that sexual victimization will be reported to officials. Studies have

Editors' Note: This article was originally published in *Criminal Justice and Behavior,* Vol. 30, No. 1, February 2003, pp. 6-38. In addition to several tables, we have omitted sections of the literature review and detailed reporting of the results.

discovered that demographic characteristics of victims are correlated with the likelihood of reporting victimization incidents (Bachman, 1998; Gartner & Macmillan, 1995; Lizotte, 1985; Pino & Meier, 1999). For example, older women were more likely to report their sexual victimization to the police than were younger victims (Gartner & Macmillan, 1995). Research has also revealed that reporting to police or law enforcement is shaped by incident-related characteristics and contexts (see, e.g., Bachman, 1998; . . . Resnick, Saunders, Kilpatrick, & Best, 1999 . . .). Analyses of these incident factors have suggested that crime seriousness, victim-offender relationship, location of the offense, and the consumption of alcohol account for some of the variation in reporting. That is, offenses that resulted in injury, that involved a weapon, that were perpetrated by unknown assailants, and that occurred in unfamiliar places were the most likely to be disclosed to the police.

**

REASONS FOR NOT REPORTING

An analysis of the literature on reporting revealed that crime victims most often reported when they felt reporting would result in a positive outcome (Dukes & Mattley, 1977; Laub, 1981). That is, victims' belief that reporting will enable the police to catch offenders was often cited as an important motivator for reporting crime (Laub, 1981). Victims of sexual victimization, on the other hand, most often failed to report based on both the circumstances of the crime and on the psychological beliefs and fears of the woman herself. Coupled with the fact that sexual victimization is especially likely to be unreported to police, particular attention has been paid to these factors in hopes of discovering why such serious crimes go undisclosed.

It is thought that most crime victims do not feel responsible for their victimization; however, research has shown that rape victims tend to blame themselves for being raped. This self-blame tended to occur when victims were under the influence of alcohol at the time of the incidents and when they perceived that their own actions led to them being sexually victimized.

Furthermore, when victims thought that these actions would be judged negatively by others, they were likely to internalize blame (see Finkelson & Oswalt, 1995). This self-blame due to victims' own actions is particularly salient when it is considered that alcohol consumption is often involved in sexual victimization (Koss et al., 1987) and has been reported as a method by which assailants obtain nonconsensual intercourse (Pitts & Schwartz, 1993).

In addition to incident-specific reasons, other research has uncovered psychological factors that influence reporting of sexual victimization. Some victims may have feared retaliation by offenders if they reported the incident to the police. If the victims knew the offenders, then it would have been possible they feared additional victimization resulting from reporting (Bachman, 1998; Greenfeld et al., 1998; Tjaden & Thoennes, 2000). . . .

**

FACTORS RELATED TO VICTIM REPORTING

Seriousness of the incidents. Although all victims of sexual victimization suffer some form of harm, some crimes are more serious in nature and cause more physical and/or psychological harm. Research has shown that those incidents that involved the highest degree of injury were more likely to come to the attention of the police (Bachman, 1998; Felson, Messner, & Hoskin, 1999 . . .). Other aspects of criminal events that have influenced the seriousness of the incidents are presence of weapons, threats or use of force, completion of rape, and monetary losses (Gartner & Macmillan, 1995; Orcutt & Faison, 1988). In a study of 897 women who reported experiencing victimization, Gartner and Macmillan (1995) found that harm, economic loss, and use of a weapon together explained approximately 15% of the variation in reporting to police. In light of this finding, it has been suggested that victims are most likely to report when they perceive their victimization to be serious in nature (Greenberg & Ruback, 1992).

Victim-offender relationships. One of the most widely researched areas of influence concerning reporting of sexual victimization involves the effect of the victim-offender relationship. In general, victims have been less likely to report incidents to the police when offenders were relatives, intimates, or acquaintances than when crimes were perpetrated by strangers (Gartner & Macmillan, 1995; Pino & Meier, 1999 . . .). Consistent with the general victimization-reporting research, reporting sexual assaults was seen as more appropriate when offenders were strangers than victims' boyfriends (Ruback, Menard, Outlaw, & Shaffer, 1999).

***

Victim characteristics. Research has revealed that demographic characteristics of victims were related to reporting sexual victimization to the police. Similar to the reporting of other crimes, older victims of sexual offenses were more likely than were younger victims to report to the police (Gartner &Macmillan, 1995). Income level, education level, and race of victims also appeared to affect the reporting of sexual victimization. Thus, an analysis of NCVS rape data from 1979 to 1987 has shown that income was negatively related to reporting (Pino &Meier, 1999). A similar relationship has been found for education level: The more educated a woman was, the less likely she was to report being raped to the police (Lizotte, 1985).

The effect of the interracial nature of incidents has also been found to predict reporting to the police. Lizotte (1985), for example, reported that when offenders were African American and victims were Caucasian, victims were less likely to report the assault or rape to the police. Contradictory evidence, however, exists regarding the relationship between race and reporting of sexual victimization. Although some research has found that Caucasian women are most likely to report (Feldman-Summers & Ashworth, 1981), other studies have concluded that reporting was more likely when victims were African American (Bachman, 1998). Other research, however, has suggested that minority women were less likely to report rape to the police, evidence that those groups that have been historically distrustful of the police were less likely to see reporting to them as a desirable alternative (Feldman-Summers & Ashworth, 1981).

***

REPORTING TO OTHERS

Although it is well documented that sexual victimization has been likely to go unreported to the police, these incidents of victimization may have been disclosed to persons outside of the criminal justice system. In fact, research suggests that both juveniles and adults were more likely to tell authorities other than the police following incidents of violent victimization when the incidents occurred at school (Finkelhor & Ormrod, 1999). This pattern of disclosure was similar for victims of sexual offenses (see Koss et al. 1987). Thus, Pitts and Schwartz (1993) found that more than three fourths of rape victims tell someone, typically a female friend, about their experience. Similarly, other research has found that the majority of persons who were sexually victimized confided in a friend; however, few told family members or health or social work professionals (Dunn, Vail-Smith, & Knight, 1999; Golding, Siegel, Sorenson, Burnam, & Stein, 1989). A separate study on the factors that influence potential rape victims to report incidents found that women were more likely to tell their husbands, boyfriends, or other intimates than the police about their experience (Feldman-Summers & Ashworth, 1981).

***

RESEARCH STRATEGY

This study attempted to build on the existing literature in several ways. First, this study analyzed national-level data with detailed measures to uncover sexual victimization–reporting practices by college women. Although research exists on college victimization, few studies have examined data from national samples in the United States. Perhaps the most notable national study of sexual victimization of college women was conducted during the mid 1980s by Koss et al. (1987). Despite substantively extending the literature, numerous changes in postsecondary education have occurred since Koss et al.'s 20-year-old study was done in the early 1980s. For example, enrollment of women in college and universities has significantly increased during the past decade (U.S. Department of Education,

1993). Moreover, the changing social context and legal requirements mandated at these institutions may have altered the likelihood of women reporting their victimization on self-report surveys and to campus authorities (see Fisher, Hartman, Cullen, & Turner, 1999). To address these issues, this study used current national-level data to investigate the reporting of sexual victimization incidents by female college students.

A second advance this study attempted to make was methodological. This study has built on the methodological work done by Koss et al. (1987) and advances made by Kilpatrick and his colleagues (1992) and Tjaden and Thoennes (2000). . . . [W]e have extended their work by employing a two-stage measurement strategy used by the NCVS.

Third, few studies have examined the likelihood of reporting across multiple forms of sexual victimization. Most research has focused on the reporting of attempted or completed rapes (Bachman, 1998; Williams, 1984). Research that has employed a wider conceptualization of sexual victimization is limited and has focused on all adult women rather than on college women (see Gartner & Macmillan, 1995; Kilpatrick et al., 1987). To effectively measure reporting of a broad range of sexual victimization, this study measured incidents ranging from rape to sexual harassment, including attempted, threatened, and completed acts.

Fourth, as noted, studies have identified how characteristics of offenders, victims, and incidents influence reporting of sexual victimization. Few studies, however, have focused simultaneously on more than one of these categories of predictors or have explored the impact of multiple factors within each category. For example, studies rarely have included, in a single analysis, detailed information concerning victimization incidents and individual measures of victim and offender characteristics. To fill this void, this study used specific incident level information for each victimization and measured incident characteristics and individual factors to assess the determinants of reporting.

Fifth, the majority of previous research examined the extent of and the factors that affect reporting of sexual victimization to the police. This study investigated reporting to police as well as reporting to campus officials and to third parties. In doing so, we were able to investigate the extent to which sexual victimization incidents are reported to people other than the police. Furthermore, we explored how determinants of reporting vary according to whether incidents are disclosed to the police, campus authorities, or other people known to victims.

Finally, the results of this study have implications for the ongoing debate between feminist and conservative scholars over the extent to which sexual victimization is a problem that warrants intervention. Accordingly, the closing sections of this article discuss the salience of the findings for these competing perspectives.

METHOD

Sampling Design

The results reported in this study are part of a larger project, the National College Women Sexual Victimization study. Using computer-aided telephone interviews, professionally trained female interviewers administered the survey to a national-level sample of 4,446 female college students enrolled at 233 selected postsecondary institutions during the spring of 1997. Institutions were selected using a probability proportionate to the size of the female enrollment to ensure there was an adequate number of female students from which to randomly select to meet the needed sample size. Of the total institutions selected, there were 194 four-year schools and 39 two-year schools. Female students were then randomly selected within each institution included in the project. The response rate was 85.6% (for a detailed description, see Fisher, Cullen, & Turner, 2000).

***

DEPENDENT VARIABLES

Three measures of reporting were used in the analysis to determine if respondents decided to disclose an incident. First, respondents were asked if they or someone else reported the incidents to any police agency. If the incident was reported to any police agency, they were then asked to which police agency they reported. Police agencies included on-campus police or security departments, off-campus local or city police, county sheriff, or state police. This variable was labeled *reporting to any police agency.*

In addition, reporting to others was measured by asking if they told anyone else other than or in addition to the police about the incident. If they did report the incident to a third party, respondents were then asked whom they told. The second measure, reporting to at least one campus authority, was created using this information. Campus authorities included campus law enforcement, residence hall advisors, deans, professors, other college authorities, and on-campus bosses, employers, or supervisors. The third measure employed was reporting to at least one person other than a police agency or a campus authority. . . . These categories were not mutually exclusive because respondents could have indicated they told more than one type of person. For example, respondents could have told their parents and a friend about their experience.

INDEPENDENT VARIABLES

Incidents, offenders, victims, and contextual characteristics were operationalized to measure their possible influences on victims' decisions to report their sexual victimization.

Incident characteristics. For our analysis, the following four types of sexual victimization were employed: (a) rape, (b) sexual coercion, (c) sexual contact, and (d) threats. Each of these types, with the exception of threats, includes completed and attempted acts. We recognize that not all of the incidents defined as sexual victimization would qualify as criminal acts. . . . The seriousness of incidents was measured with the following three variables: (a) if respondents suffered any injury, (b) the presence of a weapon, and (c) if victims considered the incident to be rape.

Offender characteristics. Research has consistently reported that characteristics of offenders

may affect decisions to report. To take these types of characteristics into account, we included the following two measures: (a) the victim-offender relationship and (b) whether victims' race/ethnicity was different or the same as offenders' race/ethnicity. The victim-offender relationship was measured using the following five categories: (a) current or ex-intimates, (b) fellow students, (c) known others, (d) strangers, and (e) friends.

Victim characteristics. A set of four independent variables measured the individual characteristics of victims. Consistent with previous victimization research, the demographic characteristics included age of the respondents and their race/ethnicity. A third victim characteristic, family class—measured by asking respondents to identify their class of origin while growing up—was included. Recent work by Ruback et al. (1999) has suggested that being under the legal drinking age and drinking alcohol (underage drinker) may influence victims' decisions to report to the police. Hence, our fourth measure, victims drinking alcohol and being under the legal drinking age when incidents took place, was also included in the analysis.

Contextual characteristics. Studies have reported that both offender use and victim use of alcohol and/or drugs prior to or at the time of the incidents may affect victims' decisions to report incidents (Pitts & Schwartz, 1993; Ruback et al., 1999). To measure the context of incidents, we employed two variables. First, because sexual victimization can transpire in various places, we included a contextual measure of the locations of the incidents. The following four locations were used in our analysis: (a) in living quarters, (b) at a fraternity, (c) on campus property but not in living quarters, and (d) all other locations. Second, we included a measure of alcohol and/or drug use on the part of victims and offenders. We included a measure that took into account if both offenders and victims drank alcohol and/or took drugs prior to the incidents, if one did and the other one did not, and if neither did.

***

Table 15.1   Descriptive Characteristics of the Incidents

Descriptive Characteristics of the Incidents of Sexual Victimization	*%*	*n*
Incident characteristics		
Type of sexual victimization		
Rape	11.9	157
Sexual coercion	16.8	221
Sexual contact	54.9	723
Threats[a]	16.5	217
Seriousness Injury		
Yes	5.5	73
No[a]	94.5	1243
Presence of a weapon		
Yes	1.7	22
No[a]	98.3	1292
Victims considered incident rape		
Yes	6.3	82
No[a]	93.7	1222
Offender characteristics		
Victim-offender relationships		
Known others[b]	7.5	99
Current or ex-intimates[c]	12.6	165
Strangers	20.9	274
Fellow students[d]	27.8	365
Friends[a,e]	31.3	411
Offender-victim race/ethnicity		
Different	20.8	272
Same[a]	79.2	1037
Victim characteristics		
Age		
Mean age	21.4	1318
Standard deviation	3.1	
Younger than legal drinking age and drinking alcohol at time of incident		
Yes	21.4	290
No[a]	78.6	1030
Races/ethnicities		
African American non-Hispanic	5.0	66
Latina or Hispanic	6.8	90
Other non-Hispanic[a]	3.6	47
White non-Hispanic[a]	84.6	1112
Family classes		
Upper class	9.2	121
Upper middle class	41.1	541
Middle class	36.6	482
Working class	12.1	159
Poor	1.0	13

(Continued)

Table 15.1 (Continued)

Descriptive Characteristics of the Incidents of Sexual Victimization	%	n
Contextual characteristics		
Locations		
Fraternity	6.5	85
Campus property	7.8	103
Living quarters	38.9	511
All other locations[a]	46.8	616
Drinking alcohol and taking drug behavior		
Both offender and victim drank alcohol and/or took drugs prior to incidents[f]	41.7	522
Offender drank alcohol and/or took drugs and victim did not do either	26.9	337
Offender did not drink alcohol and/or take drugs and victim did either or both	1.5	19
Neither offender nor victim drank alcohol or took drugs[a]	29.8	373

a. Reference group used in the multivariate models.

b. This category includes professors, teachers, graduate assistants, teaching assistants, employers, supervisors, bosses, coworkers, stepfathers, and other male relatives.

c. This category includes current and former husbands, boyfriends, or lovers.

d. This category includes classmates or fellow students.

e. This category includes friends, roommates, housemates, suitemates, or acquaintances.

f. The categorization is based on victims' responses to questions about their behavior prior to the incidents and their perceptions of the offenders' behavior.

Descriptive Characteristics of the Incidents

As a prelude to exploring the reporting behavior of the victims in the sample, we present the characteristics of the sexual victimization incidents, offenders, victims, and context in Table 15.1. As seen in this table, some of the incident-level characteristics exhibited much variation, whereas other characteristics did not. . . .

***

Results

Tables 15.2 and 15.3 present the descriptive information on victims' decisions to report the incidents. As Table 15.2 reveals, a very low percentage of victims (2.1%) reported their victimization to the police and 4.0% reported their victimization to campus authorities. Among on-campus incidents, just more than 5% were reported to campus authorities.

A cross-tabulation of the data showed that all the incidents that were reported to any police agencies were also disclosed to someone else. This is also the case for all the incidents reported to any campus authorities because all the incidents reported to any campus authorities were also disclosed to someone else (see the last two rows of Table 15.2).

Looking at Table 15.3, the results indicated that even among completed and attempted rapes, fewer than 5% were reported to the police and an even lower percentage were reported to campus authorities. Reports for most other forms of sexual victimization ranged from none to very few of the incidents being reported to the police or campus authorities. Reports to officials of threats of rape and of sexual contact with force did climb to about 10% of the incidents, but the small number

Table 15.2   Victims' Decisions to Report Incidents to Officials and Disclose Incidents to Someone Other Than Police or Campus Authorities

Victims' Decision	%	n
Reported to officials		
Reported to any police agencies	2.1[a]	27
Reported to any campus authorities	4.0	37
On-campus incidents only	5.3	27
Victims disclosed incident to people other than police or campus authorities[b]	69.9	919
Victims disclosed incident to		
Friends[c]	87.9	808
Family members[d]	10.0	92
Intimates[e]	8.3	76
Other persons[f]	3.3	30
Other authority figures[g]	1.7	16
Counseling services[h]	1.0	9
Reported to any police agencies and disclosed to someone else	2.1	27
Reported to any campus authorities and disclosed to someone else	4.0	37

a. The percentages refer to telling at least one person in the specific category.

b. Percentage may exceed 100 as respondents could give multiple responses as to whom they told. Each specific category includes telling at least one type of person who was included in that category.

c. Category includes friends, roommates, suitemates, or housemates.

d. Category includes parent, parents, or family members other than parents.

e. Category includes husbands, boyfriends, or partners.

f. Category refers to other nonspecified persons.

g. Category includes off-campus employers, bosses, or supervisors.

h. Category includes women's programs or services, victims' services hotline, clergy, rabbi, or other spiritual leaders.

of incidents involved made the percentages potentially prone to substantial fluctuation, with only a couple of incidents being reported.

In contrast, although victims were unlikely to report incidents to formal officials, they tell others about their victimization experiences. Thus, in about 70% of the incidents, victims disclosed their victimization to someone other than the police. Most often, this person was a friend (in 87.9% of these incidents). Family members and current intimates were the second and third most cited people to be told, but they were contacted in only 10% and 8.3% of the incidents, respectively. As seen in Table 15.3, the percentages of incidents reported to someone other than police and/or campus authorities differed by type of victimization. To illustrate, a larger percentage of sexual contact incidents were told to someone else compared with the other three

types of sexual victimization (74.1% compared with 66.2%, 62.9%, and 65.9%).

It is relevant that for completed and attempted rapes, approximately two thirds of the incidents were reported to someone else. Again, this was a large proportion in comparison with the percentage of incidents disclosed to the police, which was fewer than 5% for both rape categories. This pattern was evident across all the types of victimization. Again, Tables 15.2 and 15.3 reveal that most college women who are sexually victimized do not report their victimization either to the police or to campus authorities. . . . [T]he reasons for not reporting to law enforcement officials [were] explored by types of victimization. By far the most frequently given responses for not reporting were incident related reasons. Across all victimization categories, in 81.7% of the incidents, college

Table 15.3   Type of Victimization Reported to Any Police Agencies and/or Campus Authorities and Whether Told to Someone Other Than Police and/or Campus Authorities

Type of Victimization	Reported to Any Police Agencies		Reported to Any Campus Authorities		Told to Someone Other Than Police and/or Campus Authorities	
	%	(n)	%	(n)	%	(n)
Rape	4.5	(7)	3.2	(5)	66.2	(104)
Sexual coercion	0.0	(0)	.9	(2)	62.9	(139)
Sexual contact	1.4	(10)	2.8	(20)	74.1	(533)
Threats	4.6	(10)	4.6	(10)	65.9	(143)
Totals	2.1	(27)	2.8	(37)	69.9	(919)

women stated they failed to report incidents to the police because the events were not serious enough. In 42.1% of the incidents, respondents did not disclose the events to the police because they were not sure a crime or harm was intended. In approximately 30% of the incidents, respondents believed the police would not think the incidents were serious enough, whereas in about 20% of the incidents, women stated that the police would not want to be bothered and/or that they lacked proof the incidents happened. Beyond incident and criminal justice characteristics, in approximately 20% of the incidents, women expressed a reluctance to report incidents because they did not want their families (18.3%) or other people to know about their victimization (20.9%). And in 19% of the incidents, respondents said they did not report the incidents because they were afraid of reprisals by their assailants or other people.

Although some variation was present, the general pattern of reasons given for not reporting to the police was fairly consistent across types of victimization. Still, there were some tendencies in the reasons given for not reporting rape incidents that may warrant attention. Similar to other victimization categories, the reason most frequently given for not reporting was that the incidents were not serious enough. In contrast, victims of completed and/or attempted rape were more likely to link their failure to report to not wanting family members and others to know of the victimization (38.9% of the incidents), not having proof of the incidents (36.9%), and being fearful of reprisals (32.9%). For these three

reasons, the totals across all victimization incidents were, respectively, about 20%, 23.2%, and 19%.

. . . Victimization characteristics significantly affected the probability that incidents were reported to any police. First, similar to past studies, reporting to the police was more likely when the incidents were more serious (i.e., weapons were present or the victims defined the events as rape). Second, sexual contacts but not rapes were less likely than were threats of sexual victimization to be reported to the police.

Offender and victim characteristics played significant roles in determining the likelihood that victimization was reported to the police. First, incidents involving strangers were more likely to be reported than were those involving friends. Second, incidents in which the race/ethnicity of offenders and victims was not the same were more likely to be reported to the police than were incidents in which race/ethnicity was the same. Third, supportive of Bachman's (1998) results, incidents in which victims were African American students were more likely to be reported to the police than were those incidents involving White non-Hispanics or students of other races/ethnicities.

A contextual characteristic of the incidents was also important. The analysis revealed that incidents on campus property were more likely to be reported to the police than were those that occurred off campus.

The more serious incidents were significantly more likely to be reported to campus authorities (e.g., incidents that involved injuries or in which weapons were present). Victim-offender relationships were also salient as to the probability of incidents having been reported to any campus authorities. Compared with when offenders were friends, victims were more likely to report incidents in which the assailants were either strangers or known others (i.e., someone they knew but who was not a fellow student or a current or ex-intimate).

Victim characteristics were significant in decreasing the likelihood that incidents were reported to any campus authorities. Incidents involving younger and lower family class victims were significantly less likely to be reported to any campus authorities.

Two contextual characteristics of the incidents had significant impacts on reporting to campus authorities. As could be expected, incidents that happened on campus property were more likely to be reported to campus authorities. If both offenders and victims were drinking or had taken drugs, the incident was less likely to be reported to campus authorities.

As for reporting to someone other than police or campus authorities, victims' decisions to disclose their incidents were more likely for sexual contacts, when they sustained injuries, and when the offenders were known others. Notably, in contrast with the finding for campus authorities, they were more likely to tell someone of their victimization if their assailants and/or they had been drinking or taking drugs prior to the incidents.

Across all three types of victimization, it was difficult to discern any factors that clearly prompted victims' decisions to report. Reporting to the police seems structured more by the characteristics that may make the victimization seem more believable to law enforcement officials: That is, the sexual victimization involved demonstrable evidence that the incident had taken place (e.g., injury) and was committed by a stranger. As for the other forms of reporting to campus authorities and someone other than the police (mainly friends), key factors were (a) whether any injuries occurred, (b) victim-offender relationship, and (c) whether alcohol and/or drugs were present. The precise impact of these factors on the two types of reporting, however, was not always consistent.

DISCUSSION

Similar to previous research, only a low percentage of college women who were sexually victimized reported these incidents to the police. Even when the offense involved was a completed or attempted rape, supportive of Koss et al.'s (1987) findings, fewer than 1 in 20 incidents was brought to the attention of law enforcement officials. As we noted previously, not all of the incidents defined as sexual victimization would qualify as criminal acts. Even so, regardless of where one might draw the line in defining victimization as criminal, the findings of this study do not change: Incidents, including rapes, are not reported to the police or to campus authorities but are reported to others. Consistent with previous research, including the literature on classic rapes (Estrich, 1987; Williams, 1984), there was a tendency for sexual victimization to be reported to police when incidents involved the presence of weapons, were committed by strangers, and took place on campus but outside living quarters. Again, these features are likely to serve as prima facie evidence that women were sexually victimized and thus provide confidence that a report to enforcement officials would be seen as believable. In contrast, the presence of alcohol and/ or drugs made the reporting of incidents less likely, perhaps because victims perceived that their use of these substances would diminish their credibility. Finally, victims' definition of incidents as rape also increased the probability of reporting incidents to officials.

Still, the central point is that respondents refrained from contacting the police about most of their incidents of victimization. Furthermore, women in our sample also were reluctant to involve campus authorities. These authorities were notified in only 2.8% of all incidents of victimization and in 3.2% of all rapes. Why is there such a low reporting of sexual victimization incidents to the police and to campus authorities?

A feminist perspective might suggest that the extremely low proportion of incidents reported cannot be attributed simply to the general low reporting by college students of criminal events. In fact, as noted previously, college women report victimization by other violent crimes at a much higher level (Fisher & Cullen, 1999). Instead, feminists would likely maintain that patriarchal influences in society, including on college campuses, provide barriers to reporting. In our data on rape incidents, for example, one third to 40% of the sample stated they did not report incidents to the police because they lacked proof that the incident happened, were afraid of reprisals, and did not want their families or other people to know about their victimization. Reasons such as these suggest that sexual assault victims believed that proof beyond their testimony was needed to secure police action, that they would not be protected if they disclosed their assailants' identities, and that a sexual victimization was something sufficiently embarrassing or shameful that it should even be kept from their families. Our study does not have data on whether victims experienced self-blame, but the finding that alcohol limits reporting is consistent with the possibility that this may have had some influence. As noted, there is some evidence that when victims consume alcohol, they may perceive that they have contributed to their own sexual victimization. In a feminist view, however, such cognitions are a reflection of sexist cultural beliefs that create a context conducive to the continued victimization of women by men. Notably, in 7 of 10 incidents, alcohol and/or drugs were present.

The findings of our study, however, also might be interpreted by conservative commentators as reinforcing their view that most events reported as sexual victimization on surveys such as Koss et al.'s (1987) and ours are not really victimization (see Gilbert, 1997; Roiphe, 1993). In this conservative perspective, feminists are portrayed as advocacy researchers who employ survey methods that count as rape and sexual assault events that supposed victims do not define as criminal. Either implicitly or explicitly, ideology is held to trump science, with conservatives accusing feminists of interpreting shaky survey findings as showing definitively that the sexual victimization of women by men is not rare but widespread. The feminist political agenda, according to critics, is to use such claims to reinforce the notion that patriarchy's influence is extensive and in need of radical change. The real effects, say the critics, are that advocacy research creates unwarranted fears

among college women, encourages women to view themselves as oppressed, increases gender conflict, and creates sexual turmoil in intimate relationships (Gilbert, 1995, 1997).

In our data, conservatives would likely use one finding to support their position that the sexual victimization of college students is overstated: in 8 of 10 incidents, respondents stated they did not report their victimization to the police because it was not serious enough. Even for rape, this reason was given for 7 of 10 incidents. The implication of these data is obvious: If college women, arguably a bright and privileged group, did not define the incidents in question as serious, then perhaps their failure to report matters to the police reflected a rational decision that nothing of consequence really occurred. In this view, the study's methodology manufactured sexual victimization that, revealingly, the women themselves perceived as nonserious and at worst as men acting badly, not criminally.

Three considerations lead us to question the conservatives' interpretation. First, a salient research issue is what students mean when they define incidents as not serious enough to report. For conservatives, the phrase *not serious* is taken in a strictly literal sense as meaning that the incidents were unimportant. For feminists, however, such a response may merely indicate a false consciousness expressed by women acculturated to see their victimization as somehow acceptable. It may also reflect a rational assessment in which female victims decide that reporting coerced sexuality is not worth turning in fellow students when such an act may incur negative reactions from their peers and no real action from the criminal justice system. That is, the events may be appraised as lacking seriousness not according to an objective standard but relative to what reporting the incidents actually entails. In any case, before definitive interpretations can be ventured, detailed qualitative studies need to be undertaken of women's cognitive understandings of sexual victimization incidents.

Second, conservative critics often question the methodological rigor of sexual victimization studies, with the endpoint being that the estimates produced by this research are artifacts of faulty measurement strategies. We cannot claim that our study is beyond reproach, but its design was formulated to ensure that incidents would only count as victimization when respondents answered detailed questions in the incident report. That is, we did not merely rely on behaviorally specific questions to determine whether victimization transpired but confirmed or disconfirmed its occurrence through the incident report. Accordingly, it is unlikely that the events counted as victimization in our study did not really happen or that they are the inventions of distraught women. In short, we believe that we are on fairly firm ground in maintaining that most incidents, including those that legally satisfy the definition of rape, are not reported to police or campus authorities.

Third and perhaps most important, our data show that approximately 7 in 10 sexual victimization incidents apparently are not treated as trivial but are serious enough for college women to tell others about what happened to them. In the case of rape incidents, for example, there is about a 60 percentage point difference between the percentage of rapes reported to the police or to campus authorities and the percentage told to others. Although not definitive, findings such as these suggest that women counted as victims by our methodology did in fact experience sexual victimization that could have been but was not reported to law enforcement and school officials.

These findings also suggest that we need systematic research into why victims of sexual assault, including rape, do not tell the police but do tell those in their social circles about what happened to them. We suspect that one profitable line of research will be to investigate more fully how the context surrounding victimization affects how women interpret not only what happened to them but also what represents appropriate responses on their part. Most of the incidents reported by respondents in our study involved assailants that women knew, occurred when offenders and/or victims had been drinking or taking drugs, and were often located in living quarters. Sexual victimization that occurs in such contexts may leave women burdened and in need of support from friends. But such contexts may, in a number of ways, make turning to authorities unappealing. Thus, when women are alone and drinking with men in private residences, typically late at night, it is difficult to prove not only that an assault was perpetrated but also that consent was not given. Furthermore, in those circumstances, women not only may engage in self-blame but also may be unsure as to whether their assailants had the criminal intent to rape or assault. In contrast, because the victimization was real and disturbing, victims sought out help from friends and fellow students. In short, they handle the incidents informally, not formally.

Finally, college officials wishing to address the larger problem of the sexual victimization of female students might gain one important lesson from this research: Although officials are informed about only a fraction of incidents, many students on their campuses might have victimization incidents disclosed to them. We know relatively little about how disclosure of victimization affects recipients of this information and about whether these students should lend informal support, urge victims to seek counseling, and/or encourage victims to seek legal solutions by reporting the incidents to the police and campus authorities. Regardless, future research that explores these matters in more detail is needed. In a more applied domain, it would also seem prudent for campus officials charged with administering sexual assault awareness programs to provide the general population of students with guidance as to what steps they should take when sexual victimization is reported to them.

16

PATTERNS OF ANTI-GAY VIOLENCE

An Analysis of Incident Characteristics and Victim Reporting

KRISTEN KUEHNLE
ANNE SULLIVAN

Although the past decade saw a burgeoning of research investigating various aspects of victimization, few studies examined the factors related to anti-gay victimization. This research brings together available information on anti-gay victimization to gain an understanding about the type and extent of anti-gay incidents and the reporting practices of the victims.

A rich body of research presently exists on the nature and extent of criminal victimization in the general population. Studies have shown that the risk of victimization varies across different demographic groups (Cohen & Felson, 1979; Garofalo & Martin, 1993; Gottfredson & Hindelang, 1981; Laub, 1997; Maxfield, 1989). For example, the risk of victimization is greater for males. Men are more likely than women to be victims of personal crimes such as robbery and assault. Similarly, young people between the ages of 16 and 24 face a much higher risk of becoming victims than do older members of society (Garofalo & Martin, 1993; Laub, 1997). Likewise, significant racial differences exist in the risk of victimization. African Americans are much more likely to be victims of crime than members of other groups.

These findings suggest that what people do, where they go, and who they associate with affect their likelihood of victimization (Cohen & Felson, 1979; Garofalo & Martin, 1993; . . . Laub, 1997; . . .). In other words, rather than being a random event, victimization appears to be a function of the risks associated with a person's lifestyle and routine activities. Specifically, the risk of victimization is greater for males, African Americans, and young people because their activities take them into public places at night, which increases their exposure to criminals. . . .

Editors' Note: This article was originally published in *Journal of Interpersonal Violence*, Vol. 16, No. 9, September 2001, pp. 928-943. Though most of the article remains intact, we have removed two tables as well as information on coding of variables and analysis of some data.

Another frequently examined aspect of victimization is the reporting of crimes to the police. Although crime reporting is relatively independent of the demographic characteristics of victims (Block & Block, 1980; Green, 1981; Skogan, 1984), crimes committed by relatives, friends, and lovers are less likely to be reported to the police (Skogan, 1984). Whether an offense was completed or only attempted and whether there was injury or financial loss are also strong determinants of victim reporting.... Specifically, violent crimes involving injury or weapons are most likely to be reported to the police (Laub, 1997).

Historically, hate crimes have been underreported in the United States. Several studies have found that lesbians and gays are reluctant to report hate crimes to the police (Berrill & Herek, 1992; Comstock, 1989; Finn & McNeil, 1987; Gross, Aurand, & Addessa, 1988; Morgen & Grossman, 1988). Specifically, many gays and lesbians believe that the police will treat them with indifference and insensitivity if they report a hate crime. Hence, many gays and lesbians do not report hate crimes to the police for fear of an unsympathetic or even hostile response (Berrill, 1992 . . .).

Research has also found that gay males experience more extreme levels of physical violence than lesbians. Males are also more likely to be victimized in public, including gay-identified areas, whereas females are more often victimized in or near their homes (Aurand, Addessa, & Bush, 1985; Comstock, 1989; Gross et al., 1988). A few studies have analyzed racial and/or ethnic differences in anti-gay victimization. Comstock (1989) found that gay men and lesbians of color experience higher rates of anti-gay violence than Whites.

This descriptive study investigates anti-gay victimization and reporting practices. An analysis of victims and incidents and reporting practices was conducted to examine whether victimization patterns and reporting practices are similar to those evidenced in prior research.

METHOD

This non-experimental study includes a descriptive analysis of victim reports and examines the following questions:

1. Is anti-gay victimization similar to previous research on victimization, with differences in gender identity, race, and age?

2. Does lifestyle activity, such as location and the type of victim-offender relationship, affect the type of incident?

3. Is there a difference between unreported and reported incidents?

4. Are victim or incident characteristics a factor in reporting practices?

Sample

Because underreporting often occurs in formal arrest records, self-reported incidents were used for this analysis. Self-reports of victimization also present methodological difficulties; however, they can provide insight into the hidden data regarding certain types of crime. This non-probability convenience sample consisted of self-reported incidents to a victim program in a large northeastern city from January 1995 through September 1998.

Procedure

When a victim reports an incident, the agency obtains information about the victim, the offender, the incident, the criminal justice response, and the referral services. An intake worker records this data on a standardized form.

The selection criteria for inclusion in this analysis were as follows:

1. The self-reported incident met the legal criteria to be considered a criminal act in the state.

2. The victim's gender identity was male, female, or transgendered or the individual was perceived to be gay, lesbian, or transgendered.

3. The victim was 18 years of age or older.

4. The incident had a bias motive.

5. No other motives, such as domestic violence or race, were involved.

Research Hypotheses

The following were the hypotheses guiding the research.

Hypothesis 1: Differences will exist between gender identity, race, and age in types of offenses.

Hypothesis 2: Differences will exist between gender identity and incident characteristics.

Hypothesis 3: Victim characteristics will affect reporting practices.

Hypothesis 4: Incident characteristics will affect reporting practices.

***

Sample Characteristics

A total of 241 incidents were included in the analysis. Table 16.1 provides a description of the demographic characteristics. Gender identity was 74.2% male; 21.6% were female, and 4.1% were transgendered. About 94.1% of the females were lesbian, and 5.9% were bisexual; 94.9% of the males were gay, 4% were bisexual, and 1.2% were heterosexual. All of the transgendered people were male to female.

Almost 75% of the sample was 30 years of age or older. About 6.3% were in the 18-to-22 age group; 19.2% were between 23 and 29 years of age, 60.3% were between 30 and 44 years of age, and 14.3% were 45 years of age or older.

About 84% of the sample was White, 5% were Latino/a, and nearly 6% were African American. Almost 4% fell into the "other" category, which included Asian, Native American, Pacific Islander, and unidentified groups.

Almost 45% of the sample was victimized by a stranger. In relationships that could be considered more intimate, ex-lovers were offenders in 2.3% of incidents, families in 1%, roommates in less than 1%, and pickups in 2.6%. About 5.5% of the victims had a social relationship with the offender, such as acquaintance or friend, whereas 5% were involved in a workplace relationship with the offender. Another 20.2% of the offenders were residential, that is, landlord, tenant, or neighbor. About 12.4% were victimized by law enforcement/security personnel, with 5.9% being victimized by a service provider.

Nearly 50% of the incidents were serious personal offenses, whereas 39.4% were other personal offenses. About 1% of the incidents were serious property offenses. Vandalism made up about 7.3% of the offenses, and unjustified

arrest made up almost 3% of the cases. Out of the total number of incidents, 77.2% were reported to the police, which is higher than the rate found in earlier research (Berrill & Herek, 1992; Comstock, 1989; . . .).

Medical attention was not received in nearly 78% of the incidents. About 18% required outpatient medical attention. About 3% required hospitalization, and slightly more than 1% resulted in death.

Most incidents occurred in street areas or private residences. More than a quarter took place in a private residence, and 30% occurred in the street. About 12% occurred in public accommodations such as restaurants. About 8% occurred on public transportation, 5.9% in the workplace, 8% in cruising areas, 4.6% in a GLBT area, 1.3% at school, and 1.3% in police precinct, jail, or car.

FINDINGS

Victimization Patterns

The cross-tabulation analysis suggested some trends in these self-reported victimizations (see Table 16.2). Generally, the victimizations involved actions against people, either serious or other personal offenses, rather than property offenses. The incidents against males (55.3%) and against transgendered people (70%) were more serious in type of alleged offenses than the incidents against females (25%). More than one half of the incidents against females involved less serious personal offenses, such as attempted assault and harassment, in contrast to males (35.2%) and to transgendered people (30%). The comparison between age groups did not yield consistent trends. Older victims between the ages of 46 and 64 were slightly more likely to experience a serious personal offense (66%) in comparison to any other age group. Younger victims (21%) were more likely to experience vandalism than any other age group.

The comparison between race groups suggests some differences. Those individuals who identified themselves as Latino/a were more likely to be victims of an alleged serious personal offense than other race/ethnic groups. A total of 67% of Latino/a victims experienced serious personal offenses in comparison

Table 16.1   Sample Characteristics

	n	Percentage		n	Percentage
Gender identity			Relative/family	2	1
Female	52	21.6	Roommate	1	< 1
Male	179	74.2	Law enforcement/		
Transgendered	10	4.1	security personnel	27	12.4
	n = 241		Service provider	11	5.9
Sexual orientation			Stranger	97	44.5
Female			Other	1	< 1
Lesbian	48	94.1		n = 218	
Bisexual	3	5.9	**Offenses**		
Male			Serious personal	119	49.4
Gay	167	94.9	Other personal	95	39.4
Bisexual	7	4	Serious property	3	1.2
Heterosexual	2	1.2	Unjustified arrest	7	2.9
			Vandalism	17	7.3
Age					
18 to 22	14	6.3		n = 241	
23 to 29	43	19.2	**Reporting practices**		
30 to 44	135	60.3	Reported	186	77.2
45+	32	14.3	Not reported	55	22.8
	n = 224			n = 241	
Race			**Medical attention**		
African American	13	5.6	Not received	186	77.8
Latino/a	12	5.2	Outpatient	43	18
White	199	83.6	Hospitalization	7	2.9
Other	14	6	Death	3	1.3
	n = 238			n = 239	
Income			**Site**		
Less than $18,000	120	59	Police area	3	1.3
$18,000 to $28,000	30	15	Private residence	66	27.8
$28,000 or more	53	26	Public transportation	19	8
	n = 203		Street area	71	30
Victim-offender relationship			Workplace	14	5.9
Acquaintance/friend	12	5.5	Public accommodation	29	12.2
Employer/coworker	11	5	Cruising area	19	8
Landlord/neighbor/	44	20.2	School	3	1.3
tenant			GLBT area	11	4.6
Ex-lover	5	2.3	Other	2	< 1
Pickup	6	2.6		n = 237	

to African Americans (36%), Whites (50%), and other races (33%).

In contrast to past research on criminal victimization in general, these self-reported victims of anti-gay bias crimes were not young African American males. Instead, the victims were older, male or transgendered, and Latino or White. The ethnic/racial differences noted by Comstock (1989) in a similar population continue to be present for this sample.

Routine Activities and Incident Characteristics

Because the concept of lifestyle is difficult to measure, incident characteristics were used for

Table 16.2   Gender Identity, Age, and Race by Type of Offense

	Gender Identity					
	Female		Male		Transgendered	
Type of Offense	n	%	n	%	n	%
Serious personal	13	25	98	55.3	7	70
Other personal	28	53.8	62	35.2	3	30
Serious property	2	3.8	1	< 1	0	
Vandalism	9	5	9	5	0	
Unjustified arrest	0		7	3.9	0	
	n = 52		n = 177		n = 10	

	Victim's Age							
	18 to 22		23 to 29		30 to 44		45 to 64	
Type of Offense	n	%	n	%	n	%	n	%
Serious personal	7	50	19	44.2	68	50.4	21	65.6
Other personal	4	28.6	20	46.5	53	39.8	8	25
Serious property	0		1	2.3	2	2	0	
Vandalism	3	21.4	2	4.6	8	6	2	6.3
Unjustified arrest	0		1	2.3	3	2.3	1	< 1
	n = 14		n = 43		n = 134		n = 32	

	Race							
	African American		Latino/a		Other		White	
Type of Offense	n	%	n	%	n	%	n	%
Serious personal	4	33.3	8	66.7	3	36	100	51
Other personal	6	50	2	16.7	4	50	76	38.6
Serious property	1	8	0		0		2	1
Vandalism	0		0		0		17	8.6
Unjustified arrest	1	8.3	2	16.7	1	14	2	1
	n = 12		n = 12		n = 8		n = 197	

this analysis. As shown in Table 16.3, some patterns were present in the analysis between gender identity and the site of the incident, the victim-offender relationship, and medical attention.

Findings regarding the site of the incidents were similar to previous research (Aurand et al., 1985; Comstock, 1989; Gross et al., 1988), in that males were the only gender identity to be victimized in cruising areas and GLBT areas. About 50% of transgendered people reported victimizations in a private residence, compared to 36.5% of females and 23.5% of males. Both females and males were similar in reporting more victimizations in the street than did transgendered people (10%).

The relationship between the victim and offender displayed variation between gender identities. Strangers were more likely to be reported as the alleged offenders in 41.5% of the incidents with females and 46.7% with males, compared to 20% with transgendered people. Transgendered victimizations (20%) were more likely to involve a pickup than victimizations of males (1.8%) or females (2.4%).

This analysis raises questions about the combined effects of location and the victim-offender relationship. Are transgendered people more likely to be victimized in a private residence by someone they met socially there? And are strangers more likely to victimize males and

Table 16.3   Gender Identity and Incident Characteristics

| | Gender Identity | | | | | |
| | Female | | Male | | Transgendered | |
	n	%	n	%	n	%
Site						
Precinct/jail/car	0		3	2	0	
Private residence	19	36	42	23.5	5	50
Public transportation	4	8	13	7	2	20
Street/public area	17	32.7	53	29.6	1	10
Workplace	3	5.8	11	6	0	
Public accommodations	5	9.6	22	12	2	20
Cruising area	0		19	11	0	
School	3	5.8	2	1	0	
GLBT area	0		11	6	0	
Other	1	2	3	2	0	
	n = 52		n = 179		n = 10	
Relationship						
Acquaintance/friend	3	7.3	8	4.8	1	10
Employer/coworker	2	4.9	9	5.4	0	
Landlord/neighbor/tenant	10	24.4	31	18.6	3	30
Ex-lover	2	4.9	3	1.8	0	
Pickup	1	2.4	3	1.8	2	20
Relative/family	1	2.4	1	< 1	0	
Roommate	1	2.4	0		0	
Law enforcement/security personnel	2	4.9	24	14.4	1	10
Service provider	0		10	6	1	10
Stranger	17	41.5	78	46.7	2	20
Other	1	2.4	0		0	
	n = 40		n = 167		n = 10	
Medical attention						
Not received	47	90	134	75.3	6	66.7
Outpatient	5	10	37	21	1	11.1
Hospitalization	0		7	4	0	
Death	0		0		2	22.2
	n = 52		n = 178		n = 9	

females in more public areas such as the street, public transportation, or GLBT areas, as well as cruising areas for males?

Gender identity may be a factor in the seriousness of the injury. Generally, medical attention was not received for reported injuries. Females were less likely to receive medical attention than males and transgendered people. However, transgendered people had a significantly higher percentage of deaths than males or females. In particular, 22% of the incidents involving transgendered victims resulted in death compared to 2% of incidents involving lesbians and none involving gays.

REPORTING PRACTICES TO POLICE: REPORTED AND NON-REPORTED INCIDENTS

Initially, reported and non-reported incidents were compared to identify basic differences between the two. . . . Gender identity of the victim and the victim-offender relationship were similar for both reported and non-reported incidents. Some slight differences were present in medical attention and in type of offense. In non-reported incidents, medical attention was less likely to be received. Specifically, medical attention was not received in 91% of non-reported incidents, compared to 74% of the reported incidents.

Reporting Factors

Treating reporting practices as an outcome, several variables were used as predictors: namely, gender identity, race, medical attention, and type of offense. . . . The findings provide some support to prior research showing that crime severity and extent of injury are strong determinants of victim reporting (Block & Block, 1980; Green, 1981; Skogan, 1976, 1984). In this sample, gender identity did not appear to affect reporting practices, and this finding is similar to previous research on demographic characteristics (Block & Block, 1980; Green, 1981; Skogan, 1984). One difference in this study, however, was that race did appear to affect reporting practices. Latinos were less likely to report than other groups. About 33% of Latino/as did not report incidents, compared to 15% of African Americans, 23% of Whites, and 22% of other races.

Medical attention also appeared to be a factor in reporting. All of the incidents involving hospitalization and death were reported. Similarly, 88% of the incidents involving outpatient care were reported. This reporting, however, may reflect mandated reporting by other individuals, such as medical personnel or law enforcement.

The type of offense seems to affect reporting. About 81% of serious personal offenses were reported. Likewise, all incidents involving serious property damage were reported. Victims may be motivated to report serious property damage for insurance purposes. These findings are consistent with prior research showing a positive relationship between financial loss and reporting (Block & Block, 1980; Green, 1981; Skogan, 1976, 1984).

Summary

Several victimization patterns were present and warrant further investigation. Nearly half of these anti-gay incidents were serious personal offenses, including murder, robbery, sexual assault, and assault with and without a weapon. Gender identity may have an effect on both the seriousness of the offense and the extent of medical attention. In particular, transgendered individuals were more likely to sustain serious personal injuries, such as hospitalization and death. Race and ethnicity may also be factors in the likelihood of victimization. Specifically, Latino/as were more likely to suffer a serious personal crime than members of other racial/ethnic groups.

Differences were also found when gender identity and lifestyles were analyzed. Transgendered people were more often victimized in private residences, either by someone in their immediate residential area or by a pickup. Females also experienced victimization in private residences or in the street by someone in their neighborhood or a stranger. In contrast, males were victimized by a stranger in the street, in GLBT areas, or in cruising areas.

In this study, a larger percentage of victims reported incidents to the police, compared to previous research. Three characteristics appear to be linked to reporting practices: being Latino/a, receiving medical attention, and the type of offender. Latino/as were less likely to report their victimization to the police. When they did have contact with the police, Latino/as were more likely to be arrested. Incidents involving medical attention were more likely to be reported, which may be a function of mandatory reporting requirements for medical personnel. In addition, insurance may play a role in reporting to the police, because 100% of serious property crimes were reported.

Discussion

This descriptive analysis, although preliminary, provides insight into bias crimes against lesbians, gays, and transgendered individuals and those perceived to be of same-sex orientation. There are, however, some methodological limitations associated with the use of victim reports. For example, these incident reports were collected through a hotline, and there is a high turnover rate for intake workers. This could affect accuracy and consistency in completion of intake forms.

In addition, there was no way to confirm whether all of these events actually occurred by cross-referencing police reports. Moreover, some victims did not wish to reveal characteristics about themselves or their assailants.

Despite these limitations, this descriptive study provides a basis for understanding various dimensions of anti-gay hate crimes. Moreover, there were some notable similarities with previous research. Specifically, offenders were more likely to be strangers, acquaintances, friends, or pickups. Likewise, incident reporting was affected by the extent of injury and financial loss. Differences from past research were also found. In particular, victims were as likely to report an incident involving a landlord, friend, and acquaintance as an incident involving a stranger.

The present analysis also found additional characteristics that appear to affect victimization. Latinos and transgendered people were more likely to be victims of serious personal offenses. Our within-group analysis found some support for routine activities theory. For example, females were more likely to be victimized in or around a private residence by a stranger, landlord, tenant, or friend. Males were more likely to be victimized in public by a stranger, followed by a landlord or tenant. Like females, transgendered people were most likely to be victimized in a private residence, but the incident was more likely to involve an acquaintance, friend, or pickup. In terms of offenses, males and transgendered people were more likely to be victims of serious personal offenses, whereas females were more likely to be victims of less serious personal offenses.

Gender differences in the amount of serious personal victimization may result from women in general being more cautious in their routine activities. Prior research has shown that lesbians report higher levels of fear of anti-gay violence (Gross et al., 1988). As a result, lesbians may modify their behavior to protect themselves from victimization. For instance, lesbians may avoid holding hands or hugging more openly in public, whereas gays may be more demonstrative.

CONCLUSION

This non-experimental descriptive study provides results that partly support prior research on victimization and reporting practices and also presents a broader perspective by examining hate crimes committed against gays, lesbians, and transgendered individuals. Gays and transgendered people were more likely than lesbians to be victims of serious personal offenses. Reporting these incidents to police varied by race, the victim/offender relationship, the type of offense, and the injury.

Although these findings should be treated as preliminary, they have implications. For example, Latinos were the least likely to report a hate crime to the police. Latinos may be less inclined to report because of cultural barriers. Victim advocates need to become familiar with these cultural barriers to encourage more Latinos to report hate crimes to the police. In addition, future research should expand on the present study by examining the routine activities of lesbians, gays, and transgendered people to determine if the risk of victimization is related to lifestyle.

UNIT 5

PSYCHOLOGY AND THE COURTS

Introduction and Commentary

Mental health professionals can have interactions with criminal and civil courts at virtually every stage of court proceedings. We most often think of them as testifying as experts in criminal or civil trials, but they are even more likely to be involved pretrial, such as evaluating defendants, other litigants, or witnesses for competency. Additionally, their expertise is often sought at the sentencing phase of criminal trials. They participate in numerous other court-related contexts, such as aiding in the preparation of witnesses, helping attorneys select jurors, assessing an individual's capacity to make a will, or evaluating plaintiffs in an age or sex discrimination suit.

Several of the readings in this section reflect the tension that can exist between courts and the mental health experts and practitioners who consult or testify in these settings. It has been observed that testifying in court as an expert witness is not for the timid, but—as some of the selections here suggest—many of these witnesses may err in the opposite direction—that is, they may exaggerate their abilities or misapply diagnostic instruments.

The first article, an editorial by **George Palermo**, addresses the ambivalence experienced by many mental health professionals when asked to be experts in courts, particularly criminal courts. Palermo highlights the ethical tensions these professionals face as a result of the rules of procedure that limit their testimony

to facts. Unable for the most part to address motivations or possible hidden organic pathology, experts often feel they cannot present the person behind the facts. After commenting on a variety of such legal limitations, Palermo nevertheless concludes that experts can testify or participate in court proceedings and still remain true to their ethical principles.

The assessment of individuals with purported brain disorders, neuropsychological assessment, is the topic of the reading by **Tedd Judd and Breean Beggs**. In both criminal and civil courts, forensic neuropsychologists may testify about the results of their assessments of plaintiffs, defendants, victims, and in some cases other witnesses. Although the professional literature is giving increasing attention to these specialized assessments, rarely does the literature mention cross-cultural issues. Yet, as Judd and Beggs indicate, one's culture and language may well affect the outcome of a neuropsychological test. The authors review the elements of a neuropsychological assessment, offer guidelines for making it culturally sensitive, and review pertinent legal standards. The reading includes an interesting case study that illustrates many of the principles discussed.

One of the most complex and controversial practice areas for forensic psychologists is the child custody evaluation. It is such a potential minefield that the American Psychological Association (1994) has developed guidelines specifically for this purpose. As a result, it is

169

generally believed that the quality of child custody evaluations has improved over the past decade.

The reading by **James Bow and Paul Boxer** focuses on one aspect of child custody evaluations, the appraisal of possible domestic violence. Not infrequently, one or both of the parents seeking custody alleges violence on the part of the opposing parent. On the basis of their survey of custody evaluators, the authors conclude that the 115 clinicians in their sample were informed about domestic violence and were conscientious about obtaining information from a variety of sources. However, they tended not to use specialized questionnaires or instruments specifically designed to assess the risk of domestic violence. Although the article ends on a positive note, the authors emphasize that problems do exist and offer suggestions for continuing improvement of these important evaluations.

In the article by **John Edens**, we see the Hare Psychopathy Checklist—Revised (PCL-R), which was introduced in the section on criminal and delinquent behavior, discussed once again. Here, the focus is the criminal trial and the sentencing hearing. While acknowledging that the PCL-R has predictive power in some situations, Edens is concerned about its indiscriminate application across judicial settings. Using case examples, he cautions that—without further empirical research—the PCL-R should not be used to predict incest or violence in prison (and thereby to support a death sentence as opposed to life without parole).

The final article in this section highlights the importance of remaining aware of developing psychological research relevant to the legal system, in this case research on children as witnesses. Children are increasingly being called to testify in both criminal and civil courts, often as victims of crime. The assumption that testifying in open court will traumatize the child has led many jurisdictions to allow alternative modes of testimony. **Jeffrey Sandler** reviews key court cases relevant to children's testimony and provides a review of the psychological research on these alternative forms, including their effects on both children and jurors.

As a group, the above readings remind forensic psychologists and other mental health practitioners who interact with the courts to remain informed about developments in their profession and to exercise caution in their interpretations and their use of assessment methods. They also must be continually aware of and familiar with the psychological and criminal justice research that is relevant to the courtroom, such as the research on eyewitness testimony, domestic violence, and risk assessment. As increasingly more psychologists participate in courtroom proceedings, guidelines and standards of practice will likely become more necessary. Finally, as legal professionals such as judges and lawyers become more sophisticated about psychological principles and research, they also may demand more accountability on the part of the mental health professions.

17

FORENSIC MENTAL HEALTH EXPERTS IN THE COURT

An Ethical Dilemma

GEORGE B. PALERMO

During the past decades, mental health and legal scholars have debated the ethical role of psychiatrists and psychologists in the forensic setting, especially in those cases in which a not guilty by reason of insanity plea (NGRI) has been entered or competency to stand trial is an issue. The proper role of mental health professionals in the legal process certainly calls for clarification. . . . [T]he following factors should be taken into consideration: the moral values held by society and the difference, if any, between the ethics involved in the diagnostic or treatment-oriented patient/doctor relationship and those related to a forensic mental health expert examination of a defendant who is allegedly mentally ill. Also, consideration should be given to the relationship between the court of law and the forensic mental health expert.

Society upholds moral values that are accepted by the majority of its members. Those in the mental health professions abide by codes of ethics laid down by their associations (e.g., American Psychiatric Association, American Psychological Association, American Medical Association, and their respective forensic sections).

Their conduct, whatever the professional setting, should comply with specific guidelines, which basically are respect for the patients/clients and their autonomous decisions, informed consent, beneficence, and nonmaleficence. The aforementioned are basic to the ethical relationships of mental health professionals with their clients/patients. Deviation from the aforementioned guidelines rarely occurs, and any person who does not uphold them may receive some type of censure and in serious cases have their licenses revoked and legal charges instituted for whatever omission or commission in which they have been involved.

Although it is widely believed that a trial is aimed primarily at resolving a dispute, the ethical foundation of any court trial should primarily be the search for truth. After all, witnesses swear to "tell the truth, the whole truth, and nothing but the truth." It is assumed that mental health professionals who testify in a trial uphold the

Editors' Note: This article was originally published in the *International Journal of Offender Therapy and Comparative Criminology*, Vol. 47, No. 2, 2003, pp. 122-125.

truth and that they abide by the ethical guidelines of their professions. However, looking at the role of mental health experts in a trial, one is often left with the impression that at times the aforementioned is not fully taken into consideration by the triers of facts. Indeed, a certain degree of ethical tension exists in the forensic setting regarding the court testimony of mental health experts in NGRI or related cases.

It is well known that the law gives primary importance to the facts of a case. Forensic mental health experts appreciate the importance of the facts as well, but because of their training, they go beyond them. While attempting to determine whether there is any relationship between the mental condition of a defendant and his or her criminal conduct, they inquire about the motivations behind the defendant's antisocial behavior with the purpose of reaching a total understanding of him or her—the person behind the facts. The total discovery of the expert (facts, personality structure, and motivating factors) often clashes with the rigidity of the rules of law, and a state of incomplete communication between the expert and the triers of facts ensues. This brings about a limitation of the testimony that the expert can offer to the court, and his or her role appears to be truncated.

It can be argued that the nonscientific rules of a judicial proceeding may actually infringe on the defendant's rights. Because of the nature of the game, the mental health experts—pressured into playing an ambiguous role—are limited in their professional testimony to just presenting a behavioral assessment of a defendant. [They are unable to add a] psychodynamic explanation that could support a defendant's inability to comply with the requirements of the law. Rarely are they allowed to search for hidden organic pathology that may be at the basis of a defendant's behavioral manifestations, and when allowed to do so, it may not be given due importance. For example, in a fit of jealous rage, a 27-year-old man shot and killed his rejecting girlfriend. He claimed that he wanted to kill and be killed at the time of the offense, and prior to his apprehension, he was wounded by the police. At trial, he was unsuccessful in an NGRI plea even though an MRI of his brain revealed extensive multiple sclerosis plaques of a vast region of his brain involving the midtemporal

lobes and the amygdala. The court dismissed the aforementioned findings as irrelevant even though such lesions are well known to trigger impulsive, unreflective, destructive rage.

Furthermore, there is a tendency by the triers of facts to look on psychodynamic explanations for allegedly "sick" antisocial behavior as intriguing fancies or "junk science," and this attitude is often shared by juries. In all fairness, it should be noted that some judges do request a total psychological appraisal at the time of sentencing.

Limiting the testimony of forensic mental health experts not only creates identity confusion for them and an ethical quagmire but is a disservice to all: the defendant, the triers of facts, and the experts themselves. Actually, it is a negation of those ethical values that mental health experts otherwise hold in their professional practice. This may contribute to the reluctance of some mental health experts to testify in a court of law. One would expect that the ethical rules of law within a trial would reflect those of society at large. At times one wonders, however, whether the courtroom is just an arena that primarily tests the skillfulness of the triers of facts, where animosity and partisanship regulate the ups and downs of a trial, and where the search for the truth becomes a secondary issue.

Motivational factors are not so-called psychobabble but are dynamically important feelings and thoughts that may prompt the irrational behavior of alleged mentally ill people and should be part of the narrative of meaningful forensic testimony. Stressing the motivational factors in a defendant's behavior is not a proposal to return to the Durham rule in mental health cases. [Rather], it is intended to provide additional information to the triers of fact that could help them to find if not the truth, the best assessment of a defendant and the optimal solution in a case. The presentation of these factors to the court is not binding because any judge has the discretion to reject unreasonable expert testimony. We are told that forensic mental health expert testimony tends to be somewhat subjective, but a certain degree of subjectivity is present in all the participants in a trial. It is part of their human nature. Thus, all parties should exercise caution to avoid any degree of sympathy for—or antipathy toward—the defendant.

Mental health experts, in defending their reluctance to participate as experts in a trial, have claimed that the relationship between the forensic mental health experts and an alleged mentally ill defendant differs from that encountered in their professional practice outside of the legal system. Furthermore, they claim that they cannot pursue the best interests of the defendant . . . in a forensic examination of alleged mentally ill offenders. [This is] because such examinations are basically concerned with the determination of legal culpability, legal competency to stand trial, and at times, even competency to be executed in death penalty cases. All of these outcomes are viewed as maleficent versus a defendant and thus unethical. On the contrary, such examinations and eventual testimony are highly ethical in view of the consequences that the assessment might generate for a defendant who even though a miscreant may be mentally ill. It is then that the search for the truth is of the utmost importance.

Furthermore, mental health experts who in their private practice frequently diagnose their patients as persons affected by a functional or an organic illness should also recognize that many defendants can be diagnosed with personality disorders and suffer from organic or functional illnesses (e.g., schizophrenia, bipolar illness, or organic dementias). However, in the case of such defendants, their mental disorders are not self limited but have created sociolegal problems. This is one more reason why mental health experts as members of society should overcome any reluctance to become involved in the assessment of defendants who are allegedly mentally ill. Professional ethics certainly do not preclude social ethics. These defendants/patients deserve the same expertise that is given to patients in general mental health assessments or to those patients placed in isolation because they are affected by contagious diseases. A defendant seen for a forensic mental health assessment should be looked on as a possibly sick individual who because of his or her mental disorder may spread his or her sick behavior to society and its members. Bad behaviors may influence predisposed individuals to act out in an antisocial manner. If one follows the aforementioned reasoning, it is evident that potential forensic mental health experts should not consider themselves to be acting in an unethical manner when doing assessments of allegedly mentally ill defendants for the courts. Obviously, they are not there to condone an offender's behavior but only to diagnose and advise treatment. And that treatment may at times take place within confinement, confinement that is at times necessary to protect both society and the defendants themselves.

The judicial system needs more flexibility, and the testifying experts should realize that they are not infringing on their professional ethical tenets of beneficence or nonmaleficence with their testimony but instead are exercising their healing social duty and enabling the law of the land to take its therapeutic course. As members of society, they should view themselves as participants in the moral community and the moral microcosmic setting of a court trial.

18

CROSS-CULTURAL FORENSIC NEUROPSYCHOLOGICAL ASSESSMENT

TEDD JUDD

BREEAN BEGGS

I n this chapter we offer an introduction to cross-cultural forensic neuropsychological evaluation for the non-neuropsychologist. We will review the types of forensic questions a neuropsychological evaluation can address, the cross-cultural considerations that need to enter into each type of evaluation, the knowledge and skills needed to carry out such evaluations, and the impact of culture and language on neuropsychological tests. We aim to provide the users of such evaluations with the means to understand what can and cannot be determined, and a means for judging the quality of the work on a case-by-case basis.

Neuropsychological Evaluation

Clinical neuropsychology is a specialization of clinical psychology concerned with people

with brain disorders. In neuropsychological evaluation the clinician assesses the changes or impairments in thinking abilities, executive functions, emotions, behavior, and functional abilities of people with brain disorders. The evaluation typically involves review of records, interviews, and behavioral observations, but the most distinctive feature is the use of neuropsychological tests (Lezak, 1995; Mitrushina, Boone & D'Elia, 1999; Spreen & Strauss, 1998).

Forensic Roles of Neuropsychological Evaluation

Clinical neuropsychology was born in a medical setting and its primary allegiance is still to psychology and medicine. The science and practice of neuropsychological evaluation is aimed at medical and mental health diagnostic

Editors' Note: From Judd, T., & Beggs, B. (2005). Cross-cultural forensic neuropsychological assessment. In Barrett, K. H., & George, W. H. (Eds.), *Race, culture, psychology, and law* (pp. 141–162). Thousand Oaks, CA: Sage. In addition to a table and one case study, portions of material describing specific tests as well as a section on standards of proof have been deleted.

and treatment questions. Nevertheless, neuro-psychological evaluation has come to have a growing role in the forensic setting, and certain aspects of research and practice have become increasingly directed at those needs (McCaffrey, Williams, Fisher, & Laing, 1997; Murrey, 2000; Sweet, 1999; Valciukas, 1995).

The amount of damage caused by a personal injury is one of the chief forensic issues addressed by neuropsychologists. But neuropsychological evaluation is also used to help determine personal competence to manage one's own affairs, to stand trial, to give testimony, to parent, and to benefit from schooling and rehabilitation. It is used to determine level of disability with respect to disability accommodations, qualification for disability benefits, and specialized education. It is used to determine qualifications on an accused criminal's culpability and appropriate sentencing. These many different types of legal needs require the neuropsychologist to answer a variety of questions at several different standards of proof and require a variety of clinical and investigative skills.

Forensic neuropsychological evaluations are typically much more thorough than medical or mental health neuropsychological evaluations and involve distinct skills and standards of proof. They may also involve distinct tests or uses of tests.

The person with the purported brain disorder may be the defendant, the plaintiff, the victim, the client, or other roles. For this reason, in this chapter we will call the person with the purported brain disorder the focus person. . . . This chapter will be oriented primarily towards the forensic issues and legal system of the U.S., recognizing that applications in other jurisdictions may require modification.

Cross-Cultural Evaluation

We will define a cross-cultural evaluation as taking place whenever there are cultural differences among the examiner(s), the focus person, and the examination materials and/or concepts. This includes not only majority culture examiners working with immigrants or linguistic, cultural, or subcultural minorities; but also immigrant or minority examiners working with those of other cultures including the majority culture.

It also includes minority examiners working with people of their own culture, but using tests and materials from another culture.

In the arena of forensic evaluation, we also need to recognize that there are circumstances when what is at issue is the focus person's ability to conform their behavior to the norms (laws, justice system, institutional expectations) of another culture. This means that an evaluation may cross cultures between the focus person and that person's adaptive behavior within the host culture, even if the neuropsychologist, the tests, and the norms are all from the focus person's culture/language. For example, suppose an immigrant has marginal cognitive abilities due to a traumatic brain injury, a stroke or the early stages of dementia. A neuropsychologist from their culture, in their language, could examine that person with tests normed on an appropriate population. The focus person could be competent to parent, manage money, or stand trial, in their country of origin. In a new culture their cognitive limitations could render them unable to work with an interpreter, or to learn, understand, or track procedures competently in their new setting. The focus person might, therefore, be incompetent in the context of the host culture. The neuropsychologist may need to evaluate these adaptive abilities within the context of the host culture. This, too, would be a cross-cultural evaluation.

Psychologists and neuropsychologists face an ethical dilemma with cross-cultural work. They are bound by statute and professional ethics not to discriminate in the provision of services on the basis of race, ethnicity, language, or country of origin (American Psychological Association, 1993, 2002). Yet they are also bound by those same professional ethics to provide services that are ethnically, linguistically, and culturally sensitive, and to act within the confines of their competence. They cannot possibly provide services of equal quality and cultural competence to all ethnic and linguistic groups because it is not humanly possible to become equally knowledgeable of and competent in all cultures and languages. Even if a psychologist were fully bilingual and bicultural and thereby tried to serve just two cultural groups, it is likely that the service could not be of equal quality because it would not be backed by an equal body of research concerning both groups.

How does a neuropsychologist address this dilemma? In some cases, it is clear that the ethical thing to do is to refer the focus person to a clinician more skilled with that linguistic or cultural group. But at times the choice is not clear. There may be no such clinician available. The available clinician who is culturally appropriate may not have the needed neuropsychological or forensic skills. Unfortunately, ethical guidelines offer little help beyond leaving such decisions to the psychologist's judgment. We cannot offer rules to cover all such situations. But we do hope that this chapter will offer the clinician or attorney struggling with such issues some further guidelines on how to make such choices on a case-by-case basis. We also aim to demystify the forensic neuropsychological evaluation for the non-expert so that its cultural limitations can be examined.

FORENSIC EVALUATION ISSUES

The Forensic Question

The forensic question being asked has a profound influence on the way the assessment is carried out. It determines the degree to which history is relevant, whether the testing focuses on neuropsychological functions or everyday adaptive abilities, whether or not a diagnosis or a cause of handicap is relevant, the level of proof required, and the degree of cross-cultural competence required of the examiner.

Medical Versus Cultural Determinants

Neuropsychological evaluations typically describe weaknesses and impairments in cognitive abilities, peculiarities and pathologies of emotions and behavior, and limitations in adaptive skills and activities. The source(s) of these various impairments and pathologies may be the result of a brain disorder, they may represent limitations or differences in education or cultural norms of an immigrant population, or they may result from a combination of factors.

For some forensic questions it is important to determine the source of the problem. For example, in order for a child to qualify for public special education services due to learning disability, their academic impairment must be due to a medical condition. They do not qualify as learning disabled if their poor academic achievement is due to cultural factors or poor teaching in the past. . . .

For other forensic questions, the medical or cultural source of an impairment may not matter. For example, many issues of competency such as competency to stand trial, to testify, to parent, or to manage one's own funds depend only upon the person's ability to carry out the required activity correctly (Grisso, 2003). . . . It does not matter if limitations in these competencies are due to cultural and educational background, a medical condition, or a combination of factors. Such distinctions are important, however, in predicting whether or not the person may be capable of acquiring a competence that is lacking, which may then dictate the length or the extent of a guardianship, an attempt to educate a defendant into competence to stand trial, a plan to restore parental rights, and so on.

Diagnosis

In some cases a clinician may be reasonably certain that the focus person has an impairment due to a medical condition, but they may not know what medical condition caused the impairment. There may be multiple medical conditions that could have caused the impairment, or no known medical cause, but a clear impairment, nevertheless. In many instances statutes require a specific diagnosis, and the clinician may need to resort to a "generic" diagnosis such as 294.9 Cognitive Disorder Not Otherwise Specified (American Psychiatric Association, 1994). In other circumstances, the specific diagnosis may not be very relevant. For example, an immigrant applying for a waiver from the English test requirement for U.S. citizenship may have a history of an untreated childhood fever with seizures that could have been encephalitis and two traumatic brain injuries. The relevant medico-legal question is whether or not they have an impairment that prevents the learning of English, not which one of these brain insults caused the impairment.

Causality

In personal injury litigation, injured worker claims, and in certain criminal assault cases it is necessary to demonstrate not only that the focus person has an impairment due to a medical condition, but also that that impairment was caused by a specific event. Most usually this involves a trauma to the brain, a toxicity, anoxia, or medical malpractice event. Determining this cause often requires a reconstruction of the history of an impairment and evidence of pre-injury ability levels. In many other forensic settings, however, the specific cause of an impairment is much less important.

PROGNOSIS AND PREDICTION

Looking Ahead. Neuropsychological evaluation is often used to predict future behavior regarding competency, rehabilitation, education, disability accommodation, dangerousness, and compensation. For example, it can be important to know if someone is likely to recover from an incompetency, so that a trial might be postponed, or a guardianship or disability pension revisited. It is also important to know what the prognosis of a condition is in order to set realistic education and rehabilitation goals.

Looking Backwards. Neuropsychological evaluation can also be used as part of a determination of past behavior. It may play a role in reconstructing someone's past state of mind at the time of a crime, one's previous competence to give testimony, to make a confession, to stand trial, to sign a will or contract, or to let a deadline pass.

Culturally Relative Standards

The Need (or Lack Thereof) for Culturally Relative Standards. For some forensic questions it is critically important that the neuropsychological evaluation uses a culturally relative standard (Ferraro, 2002; Fletcher-Janzen, Strickland, & Reynolds, 2000; Nell, 2000). The neuropsychologist must determine if the focus person's abilities and behavior are deviant within their cultural context in order to determine if a medical condition is present. Tests used must compare the person to an appropriate population in order to have validity as measures of brain disorder. This is especially true for personal injury liability, disability accommodation, and special education.

For many forensic questions the standard is absolute and it concerns competence within a specific U.S. cultural and institutional framework rather than culturally relative standards. For example, the question of competence to stand trial is a question of the focus person's ability to understand what is going on in a U.S. court and to collaborate in their defense with a U.S. attorney. Although an interpreter is provided, the focus person is not given the option of standing trial under another legal system or of having the system simplified. . . .

Many other forensic questions stand somewhere in between. For example, competence to parent, to work, or to manage funds must take into account cultural values and typical behaviors for these activities, but there are also some expectations with regard to U.S. culture and laws that the focus person is expected or needs to manage, such as not abusing or neglecting children, or being able to manage U.S. currency.

Specific Cultural Competence in Neuropsychological Evaluation. The neuropsychologist and his or her psychometrist, intern, and other assistants need to have knowledge of the culture of the focus person in order to perform a competent and ethical evaluation. The degree of knowledge needed may depend upon the nature of the question asked, as noted above. Some degree of general cultural competence is a prerequisite for specific professional cultural competence. . . .

The aspects of specific cultures that are most relevant to neuropsychological evaluation are as follows:

- Worldview—This includes how a culture tends to view the locus of control of the individual (whether things happen to you primarily because of your own choice and initiative, because of chance, because of the actions of family or society or God, etc.), how the culture views causality (scientific, magical, religious, chance, balances, etc.), how the culture views the purpose of life, and so on.

- Values—This includes concepts of honor, shame, justice, family expectations, time sense, and the like.

- Religion and beliefs—This includes not only the formal theological belief system but also the rituals, social structures, and functions of the religion in everyday life.

- Family structures—This includes not only how the culture describes kinship, but also the expectations for participation in a family and expectations for behavior towards specific family members according to role.

- Social roles—This includes expectations for interactions based on age, gender, social class, position of authority, and so on. This also includes how members of the culture view and interact with members of other cultures and ethnic groups.

- Recent history—This includes wars, famines, epidemics, immigration trends, and so on that may give indications of likely causes of brain illnesses, emotional traumas, or other life-shaping events.

- Epidemiology—This includes local diseases, genetic disorders, toxicities, etc., that may be characteristic of a particular population.

- Responses to psychotropic medications— These have been found to vary by ethnicity (Strickland & Gray, 2000).

- Attitudes and beliefs regarding [health, illness, and disability]

- Communication and interpersonal style:

  Language (including features such as tonal languages, nature of the writing system, and use of the alphabet)

  Expectations between individuals of various social roles

  Personal disclosure (what is considered appropriate in what contexts)

  Rapport and how to establish it

  Non-verbal conventions such as interpersonal distance or eye contact

- Educational system—This includes the quality and nature of the educational system and the role of testing within that system.

***

CULTURALLY RELATIVE STANDARDS—TESTING

The Rationale of Normative Based Testing in Neuropsychology. In order to use tests to determine the degree of cognitive loss resulting from a brain disorder, it would be ideal to have neuropsychological test results from the focus person prior to the development of the brain condition. This is rarely the case (although limited cognitive testing is sometimes available from various sources). Lacking such data, neuropsychologists attempt to estimate what the focus person's test scores would have been by comparing them to a similar population. What constitutes a "similar population" can vary from test to test, as can the quality of the norming project. It is most usual to norm by age, and tests are also sometimes normed by gender, education, ethnicity, and other variables.

***

Determining the presence of brain dysfunction is only one of the roles of neuropsychological testing. These tests are also used to assist in diagnosing different types of brain dysfunction, to assist in determining various forms of competence, to predict future behavior, to predict educational and vocational potential, and other functions. Each of these functions has forensic applications, distinctive types of validation, and distinctive considerations in how norms are used.

The Myth of Culture-Fair Testing. Some naïve psychologists still believe that psychological testing is a universal phenomenon, and that it can be made culturally fair. There are even tests that incorporate "culture-fair" in their names. This myth has had an unfortunate role in advancing xenophobic and racist agendas (Fraser, 1995; Gould, 1996; Herrnstein & Murray, 1994). Psychological testing is not a universal phenomenon, and there is a great deal of cultural and individual variability in the knowledge and attitudes that people bring to the evaluation (Nell, 2000; Lonner & Malpass, 1994).

***

Some traditional cultures without formal educational systems may have no tradition of formal testing whatsoever. Others have markedly different attitudes towards testing. For example, independent thinking and making mistakes have long been regarded as dangerous in a large part of Russian culture, to the point that there is a Russian saying, "Thinking is the privilege of the intelligent" (Michael Zawistowski, personal communication, 2002). For cultural reasons, Russians will often say, "I don't know," in response to test items rather than risk an error, and may appear to be giving inadequate or even invalid effort. Similarly, although "quick" is (in some contexts) a synonym for "intelligent" in English, in many sub-Saharan African cultures, intelligence is associated with wisdom, thoughtfulness, and even taking time to make decisions (Mpofu, 2002). A common testing experience with people from these and other immigrant populations is that it is difficult to "hurry" the focus person on the tests. This can likewise give an erroneous impression of inadequate effort and malingering.

Because of these considerations, adjusting for culture is not simply a matter of new norms for the relevant cultural group or adjusting the interpretation of test scores. It involves an entire set of testing skills to understand how the focus person views the experience, to assure that the focus person understands what is expected, and to interpret the results in light of that understanding.

***

Mental Status Examination. All physicians and mental health care providers are trained in administering a mental status examination (although some maintain these skills better than others). The mental status examination is very useful for screening, but it is unstandardized, not quantified, and not normed. Its interpretation is based upon clinical judgment. . . .

Psychiatrists and other mental health professionals are often quite good at detailing specific qualitative aspects of the focus person's thought processes, such as the nature of their delusions, hallucinations, paranoia, and anxieties. They may supplement their examinations with personality tests. Behavioral neurologists are particularly skilled at teasing out mental status changes

resulting from focal lesions to specific parts of the brain.

Mental status examinations are heavily dependent upon the skills and interpretation of the individual clinician. This can be quite variable, and the research literature indicates that the mental status examination is, in general, not very reliable across clinicians (Rodenhauser & Fornal, 1991; Tancredi, 1987).

Cultural considerations are also up to the individual clinician. These can be quite astute, but horror stories also abound. To give one small example, a psychiatrist was conducting a competence-to-stand-trial evaluation of a Spanish speaker and asked him to interpret the proverb, "People who live in glass houses shouldn't throw stones." The medical interpreter, in an aside, explained to the examiner that this was not a known proverb in Spanish. The examiner insisted that the focus person ought to be able to interpret it anyhow. The interpreter afterwards made her point by asking the examiner to interpret the Spanish proverb, "A horse with a sore back will always flinch" (Sara Koopman, personal communication, 2003). (It should be noted, however, that not all professional interpreters can be counted on to be cultural brokers in this manner, and are often professionally proscribed from doing so.) Similarly, many English speakers may be baffled by the Russian expression, "to discover America" and the Spanish expression, "to discover warm water," while having no problem with the corresponding English expression, "to reinvent the wheel."

The Mini Mental State Exam is a brief exam widely used by physicians primarily to screen for level of delirium or dementia. It consists of items regarding orientation, memory, attention, drawing, reading, writing, repetition, naming, and following directions. It is scored on a 30-point scale and is normed by age and education. Many translations and cross-cultural adaptations and norms are now available (cf. Ostrosky-Solis, Lopez-Arango, & Ardila, 2000; Tang, et al., 1999), but are not always known or used. It plays a useful role in the evaluation of mental status, but can rarely stand alone as the basis of a medico-legal opinion.

Cultural differences in judgments of insanity are also well known. One need only read the headlines to find world leaders hurling accusations of paranoia, delusions, and irrationality at one another. Other chapters in this book treat this theme in more detail.

Cognitive tests. Cognitive tests, such as IQ tests, are designed to measure thinking abilities in a general population. They are usually designed to measure various components of thinking abilities in a general way as these relate to theories of cognition or to academic or life skills. The tests are not designed to measure specific brain functions. The tests are usually designed to give a "normal" distribution of scores, with most people's scores clustering around the average score (e.g., IQ of 100), with fewer and fewer people scoring farther and farther away from average. Many of the most common cognitive tests used in the U.S., such as most intelligence tests and memory tests, are normed on a population representative of the U.S. general population by census matching. Typically, only English speakers are used in the norming sample and sometimes people are excluded because of various disabilities or limited education. Norms are available for the Wechsler Adult Intelligence Scale—III and the Wechsler Memory Scale—III for subtests and indexes that have been adjusted for age, education, sex, and ethnicity (African-American, Hispanic, and Caucasian only) for individuals educated primarily in the U.S. (Taylor & Heaton, 2001). These norms are used for specific inferences, but not for IQs.

The most widely used cognitive tests, the Wechsler Intelligence Scales and others, have been widely translated and adapted and often renormed in other countries. It is less common for these tests to be revalidated. The translated and renormed versions are often relatively difficult to obtain in the U.S. because they are most typically published in the country where they were adapted (or not published at all), and may not be distributed in the U.S. Even their existence may be noted only in regional journals published in the relevant language.

Whether or not it is "fair" or appropriate to use a U.S. IQ test or other cognitive test with someone from another culture depends in large part on the use to be made of that test and even on the results obtained. Certainly,

there is potential for an egregious error to label a child as mentally retarded based upon a test administered in their second language they have not yet mastered or based upon a culture that is still foreign to them. Similarly, it can be unfair to the defense in a personal injury case to conclude that a plaintiff has brain damage on the basis of poor test results if those poor test results are actually due to cultural considerations. On the other hand, normal test results and strong performances in certain areas might be helpful in qualifying someone for educational and vocational opportunities, for establishing their competence, or for inferring good recovery from injury when other information is insufficient to allow for such conclusions. Such results may also add confidence to a conclusion to meet the standards of a certain legal level of proof. Furthermore, impaired test performances may be used to contribute to a conclusion of brain damage particularly when those impaired performances are congruent in their specifics with converging evidence from other sources (nature and location of the injury, adaptive behavior before and after the injury, etc.).

***

Neuropsychological tests. Neuropsychological tests are most often designed to measure impairments in specific brain functions such as attention, memory, executive functions (abstraction, reasoning, problem solving, decision making, self control), language, visual-spatial abilities, perceptual abilities, motor skills, and so on.

Many of these tests have a "low ceiling." Most people with intact brains will have few or no errors on such tests, but the tests will not discriminate well among normal people with strong or weak abilities in that area. However, people with specific brain impairments will usually fail the test. Some neuropsychological tests compare the focus person to him/herself by comparing sensory or motor abilities on one side of the body with the other side. For this reason, norms may be less critical for some of these tests.

Some more cognitively oriented neuropsychological tests have high ceilings and are normed by age and education so as to be able to predict more closely the expected performance of the focus person (Heaton, Grant, & Matthews, 1992; Ivnick, *et al.*, 1996).

Most neuropsychological tests in common use in the US are normed on populations with at least eight years of education. Research on groups with little or no education has suggested that the first two years of education have the greatest impact on neuropsychological test performance (Ostrosky, *et al.*, 1998). U.S. neuropsychologists must be especially careful in their interpretations when working with low education populations.

***

Functional Abilities Tests. Some tests are designed to measure functional abilities in specific skill areas. These tests are typically used to determine if the focus person is competent to exercise those skills. Such tests attempt to look as directly as possible at the area of competency. For example, the Independent Living Scales (Loeb, 1996) are designed to measure competence for community living primarily in the elderly. The focus person is actually tested on his or her ability to look up a number in the phone book and dial it, read a bill and write a check to pay it, read a clock, and so on. Measures of the competency to stand trial (Everington & Luckasson, 1992; Grisso, 2003) ask a series of questions about the functions of a criminal court, and about the person's knowledge of the alleged crime. . . .

Adaptive Behavior Rating Scales. Adaptive behavior rating scales are not tests of abilities. The focus person and/or an informant who knows that person well rate the person on the ability to carry out various everyday activities. These scales are particularly important in the diagnosis of mental retardation because the accepted definitions of mental retardation (American Association on Mental Retardation, 2002; American Psychiatric Association, 1994) require impairment not only on IQ testing but also in adaptive behavior.

***

Adaptive behavior is clearly culturally relative, and this is evident in the rating scales. For example, the referenced scales contain items referring to the use of telephones, microwaves, small electrical appliances, clothes washers and dryers, repair services, cars, seatbelts, air conditioners, thermometers, handkerchiefs, televisions, menus, dictionaries, alphabetizing, phone books, zip codes, bathroom cleaning supplies, electricity, scales, rulers, schedules, Christmas, Hanukah, forks, reading materials, ticket reservations, shoelaces, clocks, classified ads, and checkbooks. Access to these items is not universal and is related to culture, urbanization, and social class. There are no items referring to clotheslines, chopsticks, domestic animals, Ramadan, and so on.

Other items depend upon cultural norms of behavior or values that are not universal. [This includes such aspects as] looking at others' faces when talking, ending conversations, not interrupting, carrying identification, traveling independently in the community . . . obeying street signs, needing time alone, . . . punctuality, hospitality, controlling temper, "pleasant breath," saying "thank you," conversational distance, dating, and so on. Although several of these scales have been translated into Spanish (and possibly other languages) there has been minimal cultural adaptation of the items, and there are minimal instructions in the manuals concerning cross-cultural applications.

***

Adaptive behavior scales can play an important role in cross-cultural neuropsychology. At times they may help document that an individual who does not "test well" on standardized cognitive tests, perhaps for cultural reasons, nevertheless is able to function adequately and competently in this society. Adaptive behavior scales in brain injury cases can document the changes in a way that cognitive tests cannot. However, interpretation of low scores is problematic because the scales are culture bound. . . .

Symptom Validity Tests. In the last fifteen years there has been a rapid increase in the number and sophistication of forensic neuropsychology testing instruments and techniques. This is particularly true in personal injury cases where the answers to forensic questions have significant consequences for injured people and the insurance companies that pay their claims. Measures of memory and attention have become increasingly sophisticated so as to detect more and more subtle impairments resulting from mild injuries in plaintiffs. At the same time, techniques to detect inadequate effort or malingering during neuropsychological testing have also become increasingly sophisticated, and have been used to undermine plaintiff's claims (Reynolds, 1998).

***

Personality Tests. Most "personality tests" used by neuropsychologists are actually psychopathology inventories. They are designed to detect psychopathology according to psychiatric classifications, but they are less sensitive to variations in normal personality. The most common tests (Millon Clinical Multiaxial Inventory-III [MCMI-III], Millon, 1994; Minnesota Multiphasic Personality Inventory-2 [MMPI], Butcher, *et al.*, 1989; Personality Assessment Inventory, [PAI], Morey, 1991) were not designed with brain disorders or the changes in personality resulting from those disorders in mind. . . .

A new generation of neuropsychological personality tests is emerging. These are specifically designed to measure the changes in personality resulting from brain disorders (for reviews, see Judd, 1999; Judd & Fordyce, 1996). These may be normed by gender, age, and education. Their cross-cultural application is not yet validated.

***

SPECIFIC FORENSIC QUESTIONS

Personal Injury

When personal injury liability work is cross-cultural it generally requires one of the highest levels of cross-cultural competence of the neuropsychologist. Although the level of proof required is only more-probable-than-not, the neuropsychologist often has to determine whether or not there is brain injury present in cases of subtle injury. The neuropsychologist is also asked to determine if that injury is due to a specific event. This usually requires considerable

investigation beyond the testing and interview. It may require interviews of family members or others from the same cultural group as the focus person. The neuropsychologist must be very well versed in cross-cultural knowledge and skills in general as well as in the specific culture of the focus person. The neuropsychologist also needs to be familiar with any available neuropsychological knowledge specific to that culture. The neuropsychologist should also be able to describe the impact of the injury on the focus person's life and family, and this will include cultural considerations. In the case of severe injuries where there is clear impairment, the neuropsychologist's job may be simply characterizing that impairment. In such situations the need for cross-cultural competence is still present but is not as acute.

Competencies

Issues of the focus person's competence (to stand trial, to testify, to make a will, to consent to medical treatment, to manage funds, to drive, to sign a contract, to parent, and so on) require less cross-cultural skill on the part of the neuropsychologist than personal injury liability. This is because diagnosis and causality are less at issue, and also because competence is, in part, a question of functioning within the U.S. culture. Nevertheless, the neuropsychologist should be sensitive to culturally typical ways of functioning around the issue at hand. For example, U.S. mainstream culture places a much greater premium on personal independence than many other cultures. These other cultures use a more interdependent mode of functioning, especially within families. For example, the focus person may rely on family assistance with transportation, the mechanics of money management, dealing with institutions, and childrearing, much more so than is typical for mainstream U.S. culture and yet that person may be competent in their context. Many immigrants deal only in cash and do not use bank accounts, credit cards, or money orders, which some may interpret unfairly as suggesting marginal financial competence.

Many forensic competence issues require a judgment of prognosis, that is, whether the person can become competent. These questions may require more cultural sensitivity, especially when culture is a contributing component to incompetence. The neuropsychologist must be able to take into account the focus person's ability to learn in the context of brain dysfunction and usual patterns of acculturation.

Vocational, Educational, and Disability Issues

Disability accommodations in education, vocational rehabilitation, social services, and other domains require that it be established that the focus person more probably than not has a disability due to a medical condition. Unlike personal injury liability, the disability need not be attributed to one specific cause or medical condition (except in the case of worker's compensation). The disability might be the result of multiple or unknown medical conditions. Towards this end, the neuropsychologist must have cross-cultural skills to be able to determine the presence or absence of brain dysfunction as in personal injury liability.

When disability is already established, the neuropsychological evaluation may be confined to questions of reasonable accommodations. This type of evaluation has a component that concerns adaptation to the U.S. context for which cross-cultural considerations are less important. However, the neuropsychologist must be able to understand the goals and expectations of the focus person and family in their cultural context. For example, someone who's inability to learn English and cognitive impairments might render them unemployable in the open market might nevertheless play a significant helpful role in a business run by their family.

***

CRIMINAL DEFENSES

Neuropsychology can play a role in criminal defense with regard to competence to stand trial (discussed above), the insanity defense, the accused's state of mind at the time of the crime, and the mitigating and aggravating circumstances that might contribute to sentencing

considerations. Neuropsychological testing may contribute to establishing a diagnosis and a pattern of cognitive abilities and disabilities that, in many instances, can be reasonably inferred to have been present at the time of the crime. This aspect of evaluation is subject to all of the cross-cultural cautions regarding testing that have already been mentioned.

Frequently, however, what is at issue is a neurobehavioral syndrome—a change in emotions, personality, and self-regulation resulting from a brain condition. Many of these syndromes—especially those associated with damage to the frontal lobes—have few manifestations on most cognitive tests. Those cognitive tests that are somewhat sensitive to these changes are tests of executive functions (Cripe, 1996). However, these tests are among the most problematic in cross-cultural application and are among the least cross-culturally researched (Sbordone, Strickland, & Purisch, 2000). For these reasons, the cross-cultural neuropsychologist who works on these criminal issues must be particularly skilled in understanding and evaluating behavior that is incongruent for the culture, subculture, and individual. This type of evaluation will typically involve extensive interviewing of multiple sources and review of records. It may involve little or no testing (Artiloa I Fortuny & Mullaney, 1998), or the testing may turn out not to be very relevant to the case. Rather, the neuropsychologist will be attempting to construct a plausible explanation of the behavior in question based upon the accused's perception of the situation and behavioral tendencies. These tendencies must be seen as congruent with other behavior at other times and with what is known about any brain insults or dysfunctions that are present. For these reasons, this type of evaluation is particularly demanding of clinical neuropsychological and cross-cultural skills.

PUTTING IT ALL TOGETHER: COMPETENT FORENSIC CROSS-CULTURAL NEUROPSYCHOLOGICAL ASSESSMENT

To perform a competent forensic cross-cultural neuropsychological evaluation the neuropsychologist should have:

- knowledge and skills concerning cross-cultural evaluation in general (how to work with an interpreter, principles of acculturation, dimensions of cultural impact on behavior, principles of test translation and adaptation, and so on);
- knowledge concerning the specific culture/language of the focus person;
- knowledge of neuropsychological literature regarding the culture/language of the focus person;
- access to appropriate test materials and norms;
- knowledge concerning the specific forensic question(s); and
- knowledge concerning the professional ethical principles applicable to the situation.

When the neuropsychologist is not fully prepared in all of these areas, it may be possible to make up some deficiencies through research and consultation. The neuropsychological report should reflect this background through description of:

- the focus person's cultural, linguistic, and acculturation status;
- any use of interpreters;
- tests and their appropriateness and any translations and adaptations made; and
- norms used and their appropriateness.

The evaluation should include information from as wide a variety of sources as is practical and necessary to answer the questions at hand to the standard of proof needed. This diversity of data can include:

- review of medical, mental health, educational, employment, criminal, and other records;
- interviews with multiple informants;
- behavioral observations; and
- tests and scales of cognition, neuropsychological functions, personality, functional abilities, adaptive behavior, symptom validity, and personality.

These data should be integrated into one coherent and consistent account. Doubts and limitations of knowledge should be clearly stated. Where competing explanations are plausible, a competent neuropsychological report will weigh the evidence for each. Under the U.S. legal system, the ultimate standard is the ability of the neuropsychologist to convince the jury and judge of the line of reasoning that led to the conclusions. The competent cross-cultural forensic neuropsychologist, in addition to having the above-mentioned knowledge, skills, and qualifications, must be able to communicate that information convincingly to a lay and legal audience.

The U.S. legal system itself and the science and art of neuropsychology are cultural artifacts. They produce neither universal justice nor universal truth. U.S. justice may not be the same as Somalian or Mayan or Thai justice. "Disability" as defined by U.S. law and neuropsychology may be quite different from disability as perceived by the Hmong or Inuit. Causality as defined by U.S. law and neuropsychology may be perceived quite differently by the Navajo or Samoan. In many instances those from other cultures may be unaware of their rights or reluctant to pursue them. Even when cross-cultural law and neuropsychology are done "correctly" by their own standards, the result may not feel appropriate or just to those of other cultures.

The roles of professionals are many in these cases, and it is not always our job to reconcile these differences. But to the degree that we can at least recognize, understand, and respect the distinctive perspectives of those from other cultures, we can all do our jobs better. More than just that, we can work to build better systems of justice and knowledge to better serve a broader segment of human diversity.

CASE STUDY: MIGUEL

It was a clean catch. The prosecutor had a videotape of Miguel, a 27-year-old undocumented Mexican immigrant, handing the cocaine to the undercover agent through the car window and accepting the money. His companion, the driver of the car, had already plea bargained. The public defender was concerned, because Miguel did not really seem to understand what was going on in his case. He did not seem concerned, he did not ask questions, and each time she went to see him he acted almost as if they had never met. All he would say about the crime was that he had gone for a ride with his friend because he had a nice radio in his car. The psychologist she hired to determine his competence to stand trial reported that he had completed the 3rd grade in Mexico, similar to his siblings. On a translated test his Spanish word reading was at the 12th grade level, with an estimate of average intelligence. On a commercially available Spanish IQ test he was in the low normal range. When interviewed through an interpreter he was cooperative, and there were no signs of psychopathology. On a translated personality test, however, his profile was invalid because of inconsistent responses and a "fake bad" validity scale. The psychologist concluded he had normal intelligence, was malingering mental illness, and was competent to stand trial.

Although her colleagues thought she was wasting her time, the public defender hired a cross-cultural forensic neuropsychologist. He spoke with Miguel's younger sister, with whom he had lived at the time of his arrest. She reported that Miguel worked as a dishwasher at a nearby Mexican restaurant owned by friends. He knew his way to and from the restaurant, but she did not allow him to walk around the neighborhood or take a bus because he would get lost. He had never learned to drive or to ride a bike. He did not shop, and handed all of his earnings over to her. He spent much of his free time watching cartoons on TV or playing with her young children. She did not trust him to baby-sit, because he did not have enough sense to know how to manage the unexpected. As far as she knew, Miguel had always been this way. The neuropsychologist called Miguel's mother in Mexico. She cried on the phone, and begged to have her son sent back to her, promising she would never let him leave home again. She said that she had come home one day 5 years earlier and a neighbor told her that a friend had come by and asked Miguel to go to the U.S. with him

and he had left. She did not hear from him for 2 months until someone dropped him at his sister's apartment. She said that when Miguel started the 4th grade the teacher sent him home because he was not learning. After that he stayed very childlike and never learned skills like the other children. He could do only the simplest of chores. The other children made fun of him, but he did not seem to notice. He played with children much younger than himself. He always stayed close to home and never developed any romantic interests or attachments. When asked about his health she recalled that he had had fevers and chills the summer after the 3rd grade. He later had to take a bitter medicine when the government workers came through to spray for mosquitoes.

On testing Miguel had severely impaired memory and executive functions, even when compared to Mexicans with no education. The cross-cultural neuropsychologist concluded that Miguel probably had contracted childhood malarial encephalitis and was left effectively mentally retarded. He explained to the public defender that Spanish is a regularly spelled language and so word reading is not a valid estimate of intelligence as it can be in English. He also noted that the first intelligence test used was normed over forty years ago on a questionable population and has since been found to produce IQ scores that are about twenty-five points too high. On a formal test of competence to stand trial Miguel had minimal knowledge of any legal system. Attempts to educate him about specific points were unsuccessful. The public defender negotiated with the judge, Miguel, and his family to arrange Miguel's deportation to his mother's home in Mexico in lieu of a trial.

The case of Miguel is an amalgam from several cases of the first author's experience, and illustrates many of the challenges of cross-cultural forensic neuropsychological evaluation.

19

ASSESSING ALLEGATIONS OF DOMESTIC VIOLENCE IN CHILD CUSTODY EVALUATIONS

JAMES N. BOW
PAUL BOXER

Because of the complexity of custody disputes, the court is increasingly relying on expert testimony in child custody cases. Child custody evaluators are faced with a complicated task (Bow & Quinnell, 2001). This task can be made even more difficult when allegations of domestic violence by one or both parents are involved. Domestic violence in the context of child custody evaluation has been receiving increased attention in recent years, most likely because of certain legislative initiatives, judicial decision making, and enhanced public awareness. As a result, child custody evaluators are conducting an increased number of evaluations involving this issue. Custody evaluations involving allegations of domestic violence hold special challenges for evaluators because of the alleged secrecy of the parties and the frequent lack of adequate investigation and documentation to support or refute the allegations. Variations in the empirical research base of domestic violence coupled with varying legal statutes (Lemon, 2000) and definitions

lend an additional level of complexity to these evaluations.

A child custody evaluator's opinion about alleged domestic violence can have a profound impact on the ultimate custody decision. Thus, it is important to quantify and clarify the procedures followed by custody evaluators in constructing such an opinion. As prior studies of custody evaluation practices have indicated, such evaluations are typically quite comprehensive in nature, even without any special attention called to allegations of domestic violence (Bow & Quinnell, 2001, 2002). The current study was designed to examine the ways in which custody evaluators handle the critical issue of domestic violence allegations.

Domestic Violence: The Veil of Secrecy

In custody disputes, the legal system often becomes a symbolic background for the continuation of the domestic violence. Child support, visitation, and custody all become major issues

Editors' Note: This article was originally published in the *Journal of Interpersonal Violence*, Vol. 18, No. 12, December 2003, pp. 1394-1410.

of control for the perpetrator. This is particularly true, as more than two thirds of states have passed laws authorizing joint custody (Pagelow, 1993) unless evidence indicates otherwise. Perpetrators often use intimidation and harassment, and children become pawns in the legal process. Allegations and counter-allegations are common. Perpetrators of domestic violence are masters at denying, minimizing, and blaming the victim. They are also good at projecting a non-abusive image (Bancroft & Silverman, 2002), meaning they can present to the court and evaluator as calm, loving, and sensitive. The absence of a single psychological profile of the perpetrator or victim of domestic violence (American Psychological Association [APA], 1996; Guyer, 2000), along with the lack of adequate documentation of domestic violence in most cases, makes it difficult for the evaluator to ascertain the veracity of the allegation.

It can thus be quite problematic for custody evaluators to confirm the status of perpetrators. Recent improvements in documentation by law enforcement agencies, along with arrests, should assist in substantiating incidents of domestic violence. Prior to the 1980s, police departments wrote policies discouraging arrests in these cases (Lemon, 1999) as well as requiring the official documentation of police contacts. Currently, at least 24 states have mandatory arrest statutes when police are called for domestic violence (Austin, 2001). These steps have assisted in verifying incidents of domestic violence reported to the police. Even so, only a very small percentage of domestic violence incidents are ever reported (Harway & Hansen, 1994). Therefore, in most cases, direct verification is lacking, which complicates the assessment process for the child custody evaluator.

Current Status of the Empirical Research on Domestic Violence

The overall prevalence rate of marital violence between partners is about 12% (Austin, 2000). However, in high-conflict and/or entrenched custody cases, the rate is significantly higher with estimates in the 72% to 80% range (Johnston & Roseby, 1997; Newmark, Hartell, & Salem, 1995). There is also an increased risk around the time of the marital separation (APA, 1996; Pagelow, 1993).

Domestic violence in marital situations (i.e., marital or family violence) involves many dimensions including physical, sexual, property, and/or psychological violence, which range on a continuum in severity from mild to severe. It is important to note that no single definition of family violence is established or agreed upon by researchers (APA, 1996). Furthermore, much research has focused on samples drawn from clinical and domestic violence shelter samples. Generalizing from these samples is ill advised (Straus, 1990), although it is often done. In child custody cases, domestic violence research has been performed primarily by Hanks (1992), Johnston and her colleagues (Johnston & Campbell, 1993; Johnston & Roseby, 1997), and Newmark et al. (1995). In particular, Johnston and colleagues have provided the most comprehensive typology of interparental violence and its detrimental impact on children.

Domestic violence affects families in a variety of ways. First, it creates serious concerns about the safety and welfare of the victim and children. Second, children who witness domestic violence are at high risk for emotional and behavioral problems (Dalton, 1999; Holden, Geffner, & Jouriles, 1998; Johnston & Roseby, 1997). Third, children in such situations are at high risk for child abuse (Dalton, 1999; Lemon, 1999). Fourth, a history of domestic violence predicts a poor prognosis for parenting cooperation (Austin, 2000). Therefore, a thorough and accurate assessment of this area is critical, even if it is not alleged or identified as an initial concern.

Another critical issue for child custody evaluators is the possibility of interactive (e.g., bidirectional) or female-initiated violence. The vast majority of research in the past has focused on male-initiated violence. However, some research using community samples indicates the presence of wife-to-husband assaults at roughly the same rate as husband-to-wife assaults (Straus, 1990; Straus & Gelles, 1988). Then again, the injury rate for wives is about six times greater than that for husbands (Straus, 1993) because of the greater physical size and strength of men. As a result, there is a greater chance that injuries to wives will be documented. Johnston and

Campbell's (1993) typology of inter-parental violence in contested custody cases included interactive and female-initiated categories. Furthermore, 16% of the arrests for domestic violence in California in 1998 were women (Clifford's report as cited by Austin, 2001). Consequently, interactive or female-initiated violence cannot be dismissed and must be considered in the assessment process.

Domestic Violence in the Legal Arena

Recent concerns about domestic violence and its detrimental impact on the family have resulted in legislative action. The overwhelming majority of states currently have statutes that require the court to consider domestic violence in all custody determinations, and 14 states have adopted statutes creating a presumption against awarding custody to a perpetrator of domestic violence (Lemon, 2000). Professional associations such as the American Bar Association and the APA have taken strong positions against granting custody to perpetrators (APA, 1996). Consequently, a finding of domestic violence has a substantial impact on custody determination.

Given the high stakes, some parents might use false allegations of domestic violence to a strategic advantage in custody disputes. Stahl (1994) noted a rapid rise in such allegations in the late 1980s and early 1990s. Domestic violence allegations can be a powerful weapon to limit or deny custody and/or visitation in a vindictive manner. Custody evaluators should thus be aware of this possibility. This is especially important because judges tend to award primary physical custody to the parent who made the allegation of spousal abuse, even if the other parent's actions were not substantiated (Sorensen et al., 1995).

Determining Practice Standards

Child custody evaluations involving allegations of domestic violence are clearly challenging and complex with many factors that need to be investigated. Bancroft and Silverman (2002), Dalton (1999), Jaffe and Geffner (1998), and Walker and Edwall (1987) have harshly criticized such evaluations. Criticism of child custody evaluators has focused on the following:

(a) lack of basic knowledge about the domestic violence field, (b) failure to use collateral sources and record review, (c) over reliance on psychological testing, (d) failure to consider domestic violence as a major issue in custody determination by assuming that the allegations are exaggerated or fabricated, and (e) evaluators having a severe bias in favor of male perpetrators. Bancroft and Silverman (2002) claimed there is an urgent need to establish oversight and review of child custody evaluators. However, formal research on the practices and procedures for child custody evaluations involving domestic violence is lacking. Nevertheless, one state—California—requires custody evaluators to take training in domestic violence issues for court appointment.

The APA (1994) and the Association for Family and Conciliation Courts (AFCC) (1994) have developed child custody guidelines that outline preparatory and procedural steps to follow. Although not mandatory, the guidelines set parameters for professional practice in the custody evaluation field. Both guidelines mention that evaluators should have expertise in the specific area assessed (e.g., domestic violence); otherwise, additional supervision, consultation, and/or specialized knowledge or training should be sought. Neither set of guidelines offer specific procedural steps for assessing domestic violence. Also, only a few authors have specifically addressed procedures to use in assessing domestic violence allegations in custody evaluations (Austin, 2000, 2001; Stahl, 1999; Walker & Edwall, 1987).

Austin (2000, 2001) discussed a risk assessment approach within a clinical-forensic-scientific paradigm. His approach shows great promise and is comprehensive in nature. He also outlined a 6-factor test of credibility, which includes objective verification, pattern of abuse complaints, corroboration by credible others, absence of disconfirming verbal reports by credible third parties, psychological profile and past history of abusive behavior by the alleged perpetrator of marital violence, and psychological status of the alleged victimized spouse. Still, there are currently no studies documenting the actual practices of evaluators involved in child custody evaluations with domestic violence allegations.

The purpose of the present study was to assess the status of child custody evaluations involving allegations of domestic violence. Four major areas were addressed: (a) training in the domestic violence area, (b) the nature and types of abuse referred for such evaluations, (c) practices and procedures utilized, and (d) types of custody/ visitation arrangements and interventions recommended by evaluators. It is hoped that this information will inform practice and help mental health professionals better meet the needs of children, parents, and the judicial system.

METHOD

Identification of Participants

Names of doctoral-level psychologists were obtained through public access forensic referral lists, Internet searches of clinical and forensic psychologists who specialize in child custody work, and Friend of the Court (FOC) nominations. A list of master's-level child custody evaluators was obtained from the Association of Family, Court, and Community Professionals. Overall, 348 potential participants were identified.

Instrument

A comprehensive, six-page survey was developed after a thorough review of the child custody and domestic violence literature. The following areas were assessed: demographic information of the evaluator, specific training in the area of domestic violence, nature and types of domestic violence cases referred for child custody evaluations, practices and procedures used in such cases, victim characteristics that support domestic violence, importance of different risk factors in the assessment of the perpetrator, and types of interventions and recommendations typically used. A copy of the survey may be obtained by contacting the first author.

Procedure

Each potential participant was sent a packet of information including a letter outlining the purpose of the study, an informed-consent sheet, a blank survey form, a request form for results, and a stamped return envelope. The blank survey forms for doctoral- and master's-level child custody evaluators were almost identical except the doctoral-level form asked for additional credentialing information and the master's-level form inquired about tests requested or given. The latter was necessary because some of the master's level evaluators were social workers that do not administer tests but might request testing. Potential participants were informed that all data would be coded, analyzed, and reported on a group basis to protect individual confidentiality.

Potential participants were requested to complete anonymously and return the survey. If they no longer performed child custody evaluations or evaluations involving domestic violence, they were asked to return the blank survey indicating so. Results of the study were promised to those who returned an enclosed request form or e-mailed the first author requesting such information. Approximately 1 month later, reminder letters were mailed.

A total of 148 surveys were returned (43%). Of these, 115 were usable surveys, that is, completed by master's- or doctoral-level professionals currently performing child custody evaluations involving domestic violence allegations. Twenty-four blank surveys were returned indicating that recipients no longer performed custody work or declined custody evaluations involving domestic violence; 1 survey was incomplete and 8 were undeliverable.

Demographics of Participants

The gender of respondents was almost equal, with 52% female and 48% male. Almost all were Caucasian (97%), with 3% Hispanic. Sixty-eight percent were doctoral-level psychologists, 16% were master's-level psychologists or counselors, and 16% were master's-level social workers. One person from each of the latter two groups was also an attorney. The overwhelming majority worked in private practice (80%) followed by court clinics (11%). The remaining worked in other settings such as universities or community mental-health clinics. Forty-eight percent practiced in an urban area and 44% in a suburban setting, with only 8% working in rural areas. Respondents were represented from 33 states, including Washington,

D.C., with the following regional distribution: 31% West, 19% South, 27% Midwest, and 23% East. Professional experience averaged 22.09 years in the clinical area ($SD = 7.74$) and 13.84 years in the child custody area ($SD = 7.48$). The median number of evaluations completed by respondents in their career was 150. It is important to note that this sample was a highly experienced group of child custody evaluators working mostly in private practice in an urban area. Therefore, the findings may not represent the full spectrum of custody evaluators.

RESULTS

Training in Domestic Violence

The majority of respondents (68.2%) reported taking no graduate courses addressing domestic violence. The primary method for learning about domestic violence was through seminars (median = 4 seminars) and reading books and articles (median = 18 articles/books), although there was much variability ($M = 7.38$ seminars, $SD = 10.25$; $M = 43.28$ articles/books, $SD = 78.20$). Only 4.5% of respondents did not attend any seminars, and only 2.7% read fewer than 3 articles/books on the topic. Some respondents also indicated that they taught courses/seminars and/or had written articles on domestic violence.

Type and Nature of Referrals

Respondents reported that almost all child custody referrals were court ordered (93.24%). On average, they reported that 37% of their child custody referrals involved allegations of domestic violence. Forty-six percent of the cases involved domestic violence related to the separation, whereas 29% were episodic (i.e., occurring intermittently during the marriage) and 24% were enduring and chronic in nature. In terms of the alleged perpetrator, the following pattern was reported: 51% male instigator; 17% bidirectional, mostly male; 14% bidirectional, mutual; 11% female instigator; and 7% bidirectional, mostly female. Table 19.1 shows the specific types and frequency of domestic violence allegations. Emotional/verbal abuse, physical aggression, and coercion/threats were most common. In terms of physical aggression, respondents were asked to rate the severity. Fifty-one percent rated it as mild (e.g., threw something, pushed, or grabbed), 33% as moderate (e.g., slapped, bit, or kicked), and 16% as severe (e.g., hit with fist, choked, or threatened with a weapon).

Practices and Procedures Used

Table 19.2 displays the frequency of procedures typically used by respondents in these evaluations along with the average time allotted and

Table 19.1   Specific Types and Frequency of Domestic Violence Allegations

Type	Frequency Ratings						
	1	*2*	*3*	*4*	*5*	*M*	*SD*
Emotional/verbal abuse	0	3.5	9.6	19.3	67.5	4.51	0.82
Physical aggression	0	9.6	18.4	43.0	28.9	3.91	0.93
Coercion/threats	1.0	7.1	27.4	31.0	33.6	3.89	0.99
Controlling finances[a]	1.0	17.0	25.9	45.5	10.7	3.48	0.93
Destruction of property	2.6	21.1	33.3	35.1	7.9	3.25	0.96
Isolation	7.1	29.2	18.6	31.0	14.2	3.16	1.20
Stalking	6.3	62.5	17.9	10.7	2.7	2.41	0.87
Forced sex	9.6	57.0	21.1	10.5	1.8	2.38	0.87
Kidnapping children	23.5	66.1	4.3	4.3	1.7	1.95	0.78

NOTE: Value was rated on a Likert-type scale from 1 (*never*) to 5 (*almost always*). Numbers in frequency rating categories indicate the percentage of respondents indicating that value.

a. Refers to the overcontrol of finances or economic abuse as described by Harway and Hansen (1994).

value of each in the decision-making process. Multiple methods of data collection were indicated with almost all respondents using the following procedures: history gathering with each parent, interview with each child, parent-child observations, review of police and medical documents, and collateral contact with therapist(s). Psychological testing was used by three-quarters of the respondents. It is important to note that a portion of the sample involved social workers that did not administer or request testing. Conjoint sessions were infrequently used. As expected, the most time-intensive procedure was the interview with each parent. Much time was also spent reviewing police and medical documents. In terms of decision making, the greatest value was placed on the interview with the father and interview with the child along with the father-child observation. Next was the interview with the mother and mother-child observation. Police and medical documents were also seen as having high value. Interestingly, psychological testing of the parents and child was in the lower tier for value in decision making.

Only 30% of respondents indicated that they administered specialized questionnaires, instruments, or tests pertaining to domestic violence. Twenty-nine percent of these respondents indicated they developed their own questionnaires, 20% used the Spousal Assault Risk Assessment Guide (SARA), 15% used the Psychopathy Checklist–Revised, 11% gave the HCR-20: Assessing Risk of Violence, 9% gave the Conflict Tactics Scale, and 9% used the Child Abuse Potential Inventory.

Respondents were asked to list the top three signs, symptoms, or characteristics that support the contention of domestic violence during the assessment of the victim. Sixty percent of the respondents listed classic battered traits/signs such as shame and guilt, fear of perpetrator, low self-esteem, financial vulnerability, or inability to leave the relationship. Thirty-seven percent identified physical injuries or medical problems; 31% reported independent confirmation of domestic violence by eyewitness report, records, photos, or conviction; 28% identified the creditability and consistency of the report; and 21% listed Axis I symptoms such as depression, anxiety, or Posttraumatic Stress Disorder.

Respondents rated on a 6-point Likert-type scale (1 = *none* to 6 = *great*) the value

Table 19.2   Average Usage Rate, Time Allotted, and Decision-Making Value of Procedures Used in Child Custody Evaluations Involving Domestic Violence Allegations

Specific Procedure	% Using Procedure	M Hours	SD	M Weight in Decision Making	SD
Interview/history with mother	100	3.49	1.72	4.46	1.06
Interview with each child	100	1.95	1.08	4.60	1.02
Interview/history with father	99.0	3.49	1.72	4.61	1.08
Mother-child observation	98.2	1.54	1.06	4.43	1.11
Father-child observation	98.2	1.56	1.06	4.46	1.07
Review of police documents	97.3	1.26	0.80	4.40	1.07
Review of medical documents	95.5	1.54	0.95	4.25	1.13
Collateral contact with therapist	94.6	1.35	0.88	4.22	1.14
Collateral contact with physician	83.0	0.90	0.54	3.91	1.21
Collateral contact with neighbors and friends	77.5	1.68	1.41	3.35	1.10
Psychological testing of father	75.9	3.25	1.93	3.98	1.15
Psychological testing of mother	75.0	3.25	1.95	3.93	1.18
Psychological testing of children	49.1	1.95	1.25	3.65	1.25
Conjoint session with both parents	25.0	2.10	1.20	3.71	1.46

NOTE: Weight in decision making was rated on a Likert-type scale from 1 (*none*) to 6 (*great*) for those that used the procedure.

of different risk factors in the evaluation of the alleged perpetrator and importance in the decision-making process. . . . All factors, except for IQ, received a mean rating above 4. Drug usage, past use of weapons, ability to accept responsibility, power and control issues/attitudes, access to weapons, and past history of criminal behavior received the highest ratings.

Impact of Domestic Violence and Interventions/Recommendations

Of those respondents that offered an opinion on the veracity of the allegation (90%), a contention of domestic violence was supported in an average of 57% of the cases. In these cases, 76% of respondents claimed it greatly or extremely affected their recommendations. For a single perpetrator, respondents recommended sole legal/physical custody with the victim in 50% of cases and joint legal custody with primary physical custody with the victim in 39% of cases.

In cases involving bidirectional (mutual) domestic violence, there was much greater variability in custody/visitation recommendations. On average, respondents recommended joint legal custody with primary custody with the mother in 29% of the cases, joint legal and physical custody (50/50) in 18% of the cases, sole legal/physical custody with the mother in 16% of the cases, joint legal custody with primary custody with the father in 14% of the cases, third-party custody in 10% of the cases, and sole legal/physical custody with the father in 8% of the cases.

When parenting time was recommended for the perpetrator, on average, respondents reported that 40% of the cases involved supervised visits, 24% involved limited visitation, and 5% involved no visitation. The remaining 31% of cases involved regular visitations with no restrictions. When supervised visitation was proposed, respondents recommended a visitation center 40% of the time. The next most common places were a neutral party's place (15%), relative of the perpetrator (13%), and relative of the victim (12%).

Respondents also rated the frequency of recommended interventions on a Likert-type scale from 1 (never) to 5 (almost always). Individual

therapy for parties and children, domestic violence groups for the perpetrator, and parenting classes were most recommended (means > 4.0). Therapy for the perpetrator received the highest frequency rating ($M = 4.63$, $SD = 0.69$). Family therapy and the involvement of special masters or Guardians Ad Litem were less often recommended (means < 3.0), and mediation received the lowest rating ($M = 2.28$, $SD = 1.19$).

On average, respondents claimed that custody evaluations involving domestic violence took 23.9 hours to complete plus 11.5 hours for the report with a timeframe of 9.9 weeks. Respondents also reported, on average, that 25% of these cases required testimony in court.

Discussion

Even in the absence of a custody dispute, domestic violence can have a serious negative influence on the physical and psychological well being of children and adolescents exposed to it. Thus, it is critical for custody evaluators to assess the presence and impact of domestic violence regardless of whether it was raised as a specific issue at referral. Child custody evaluators have been harshly criticized in the past for their assessment of domestic violence allegations (Bancroft & Silverman, 2002; Dalton, 1999; Jaffe & Geffner, 1998). This criticism raises a concern that needs to be further explored, because domestic violence is an increasingly common allegation in child custody disputes. This study was conducted to assess the status of practice in this area.

In terms of training in domestic violence, only a minority of respondents had taken graduate courses addressing this topic. However, this is expected considering that the vast majority of respondents attended graduate school more than 20 years ago when there was less focus, awareness, and research on domestic violence. In the present study, seminars and reading articles and books were the most common training methods, but there was wide variability among the respondents in the number of seminars attended and articles and books read. Only a small number of respondents (< 5%) had done neither. The vast majority had attended numerous seminars and read many articles and/or books. Therefore, as a group, they had basic exposure to the topic and were far from uninformed, contrary to common criticism.

Respondents reported using multiple methods of data collection in evaluating domestic violence allegations in child custody cases such as interviews with each parent, interviews with each child, parent-child observations, documentation review, collateral contacts, and psychological testing as stressed in child custody guidelines (APA, 1994; AFCC, 1994). All procedures involved as much time or more time than in typical custody evaluations as found by Bow and Quinnell (2001). Furthermore, the total time involved (procedures plus report = 35.4 hrs) was significantly more than the time spent on the typical child custody evaluation (24.5 to 28.5 hours; Bow & Quinnell, 2001). Therefore, child custody evaluations involving domestic violence appear to be more time intensive than the typical child custody evaluation.

Parent-child observations were almost universally used by all evaluators. It is important to note that there is no empirical support that an observation of a child and parent will help accurately differentiate a perpetrator from a non-perpetrator, although it may provide information about attachment, parenting style, and comfort level.

Bancroft and Silverman's (2002) criticism that child custody evaluators fail to use collateral sources and record review was not supported. Respondents almost universally reported utilizing these procedures. They also reported spending considerable time contacting collateral sources and reviewing police and medical reports. Further, they rated the latter two in the upper tier in the decision-making process.

Psychological tests were administered or requested by the majority of respondents. The types of tests utilized compared favorably with typical child custody evaluations as found by Quinnell and Bow (2001). However, the average weight of psychological testing in the decision-making process was rated relatively low. Consequently, there is no indication that respondents are overvaluing or over-relying on psychological tests. One pertinent criticism might be that they are underutilizing specialized instruments for assessing domestic violence. Less than one third acknowledged using specialized questionnaires, instruments, or tests.

Of this group, 29% of respondents developed their own, which may not be legally defensible. The latter issue is also applicable for published instruments and tests that lack adequate validity and reliability. Useful, empirically derived instruments, such as the SARA (Kropp, Hart, Webster, & Eaves, 1999) and Conflict Tactics Scales (Straus, 1979; Straus, Hamby, Boney-McCoy, & Sugarman, 1996) need to be utilized more in these cases.

Although respondents indicated much value in assessing risk factors for alleged perpetrators, few of them actually used risk management inventories. However, this might reflect appropriate caution given that many of these inventories (e.g., Psychopathy Checklist) were normed on criminal or institutional populations that may not represent the perpetrator.

Only a few respondents reported using a comprehensive domestic violence model in the assessment process such as Austin's (2001) violence risk assessment. This model incorporates different components such as interview data, psychological testing, collateral information, special domestic violence instruments such as the SARA, and evaluation of static (resistant to change over time) and dynamic (situational and changeable over time) factors. This integrative model may have much applicability, but it requires empirical validation.

Respondents in this study reported that 37% of their child custody referrals involved allegations of domestic violence, which is higher than the prevalence rate of marital violence (12%; Austin, 2000) but significantly lower than researchers have found in high-conflict and/or entrenched custody disputes (72% to 80%; Johnston & Roseby, 1997; Newmark et al., 1995). In regard to the alleged perpetrator, 51% were reported to be male, 38% were bidirectional, and 11% were female. The latter two figures affirm that bidirectional and female-instigated complaints are made and need to be appropriately investigated.

In 57% of the cases, respondents supported the contention of domestic violence. In those cases, 76% of respondents claimed it greatly or extremely affected their recommendation. This finding supports previous research that found child custody evaluators rated domestic violence as one of the top factors in custody decision making (Bow & Quinnell, 2001).

In cases involving a single perpetrator, 89% of respondents reported recommending physical custody to the victim thereby supporting the trend that preference should be given to the non-violent parent whenever possible. Further, it was recommended by the respondents that the perpetrator's visitation be supervised, limited, or terminated in 69% of cases. Last, the most commonly recommended intervention was therapy for the perpetrator. These findings are fervently contrary to the contention that child evaluators do not take this issue seriously in custody determination. Also, there is no evidence of an evaluator bias in favor of the perpetrator.

In terms of interventions, as expected, family therapy and mediation were seldom recommended. Both interventions are intimidating for victims of domestic violence along with being unsafe. Most professionals argue against mediation in these cases (Hart, 1990; Jaffe & Geffner, 1998; Pagelow, 1993). Regardless, many states mandate mediation in contested custody and visitation disputes. Guyer (2000) also noted that family therapy is not the treatment of choice because of safety concerns and lack of attribution of responsibility to the perpetrator. A recommendation that was seldom used, but may have great utility, is a special master and/or case manager. This person, appointed by the court, acts as a go-between and assists in coordinating the parenting plan to hopefully help parents to resolve conflictive issues.

CONCLUSION

Although child custody evaluators are often criticized for their work in the domestic violence area, the findings of this study fail to support such an assertion. In general, evaluators reported adequate training in the field. Their custody procedures closely adhered to child custody guidelines, and the amount of time delegated for many procedures exceeded the typical child custody evaluation. A review of documents (e.g., police and medical reports) and collateral contacts were seen as valuable components in the evaluation process. Psychological testing was used, but respondents did not overvalue it in the decision-making process. However, the vast majority of respondents underutilized valid and reliable domestic violence instruments and questionnaires. Such instruments and questionnaires might be an asset in the evaluation process. In those cases that respondents supported a contention of domestic violence, it significantly affected custody recommendations.

20

MISUSES OF THE HARE PSYCHOPATHY CHECKLIST–REVISED IN COURT

Two Case Examples

JOHN F. EDENS

Psychologists and other mental health professionals frequently are called on by the legal system to conduct evaluations to address some type of psycholegal issue and to provide information to attorneys and judges (Melton, Petrila, Poythress, & Slobogin, 1997). Given the important role that expert opinion may play in the disposition of some cases, it is fortunate that there are established guidelines and standards to which mental health professionals should adhere when conducting evaluations in general (American Educational Research Association [AERA], American Psychological Association [APA], & National Council on Measurement in Education [NCME], 1999) and when working in forensic contexts in particular (American Academy of Psychiatry and the Law [AAPL], 1995; Committee on Ethical Guidelines for Forensic Psychologists,

1991). These guidelines provide instruction regarding what roles clinicians should play (e.g., what types of referral questions can be appropriately addressed), what types of general procedures and practices should be employed (e.g., what information is necessary to competently and ethically address the referral question), and what types of conclusions can be appropriately drawn based on the results of such evaluations. Ignorance of or inattention to these guidelines does a considerable disservice to all parties involved in this process and diminishes the credibility of mental health professionals working in these settings (Mossman, 1999).

Many psychologists tend to rely heavily on various types of psychometric tests and other assessment procedures to collect information relevant to psycho-legal issues. Although the relative merits of psychological testing as it

Editors' Note: This was originally published as a "Brief Notes from Practice" in the *Journal of Interpersonal Violence*, Vol. 16, No. 10, October 2001, pp. 1082-1093.

relates to forensic evaluations have been debated widely regarding both criminal (e.g., Cunningham & Reidy, 1999; Heilbrun, 1992; Pope, Butcher, & Seelen, 2000) and civil (e.g., Brodzinsky, 1993; Melton et al., 1997; Otto, Edens,&Barcus, 2000) cases, it seems clear that at least in some instances such data can provide meaningful information to the "trier of fact." Unfortunately, it is also clear that many forensic examiners inappropriately administer various psychometric measures, misinterpret their results, or both, and then attempt to introduce this flawed information into judicial proceedings, either through reports or direct testimony. Moreover, even well-intentioned mental health experts can have their data misrepresented by resourceful prosecutors and defense attorneys.

Although any test or assessment method can be misused or misrepresented, some arguably have the potential to cause greater harm than others in legal proceedings, due to the circumstances in which they tend to be used (e.g., Cunningham & Reidy, 1998; Zinger, 1995; Zinger & Forth, 1998), the stigma associated with their results (e.g., Toch, 1998), or both. This article details possible misapplications of a particular instrument, the Psychopathy Checklist–Revised (PCL-R) (Hare, 1991), which increasingly is being used in violence risk assessment. Two cases are reviewed that illustrate how the presence or absence of psychopathy can be misinterpreted and misrepresented—both by the prosecution and by the defense—as it relates to violence potential in criminal proceedings. Although the PCL-R is an instrument that may provide important information relevant to risk assessment in forensic settings (see, e.g., Borum, 1996; Edens& Otto, 2001; Fulero, 1995; Quinsey, Harris, Rice,& Cormier, 1998), the cases detailed in this article illustrate how information derived from this measure may also be misused by either naïve or, perhaps more cynically, biased examiners, attorneys, or both. One case involved an erroneous conclusion that was asserted based on the results of this test, whereas the second consisted of a more egregious series of mistakes in the administration, scoring, and interpretation of the PCL-R. In both cases, the misuse of the PCL-R might have significantly influenced the jury's decision.

Before describing these two cases, a brief overview of the PCL-R is provided, focusing in particular on its association with violence and its appropriate uses in criminal proceedings. Following each case summary, a discussion of the misapplication of the obtained PCL-R results is provided, focusing on how the conclusions being drawn were inconsistent with empirical research on the relationship between psychopathy and violence and inconsistent with ethical guidelines and standards of practice.

THE PCL-R

Psychopathy represents a distinct cluster of personality and behavioral features, including (among others) superficial charm, lack of empathy and guilt, pathological lying, irresponsibility, and poor behavioral controls. The PCL-R was designed to assess this personality construct using a combination of an extensive social history interview and a review of institutional file data. The PCL-R is based loosely on Cleckley's (1941) description of psychopathy, although the 20 items of the PCL-R are weighted more heavily with antisocial and criminal behavior items than were Cleckley's original 16 criteria— perhaps because of its initial development and validation primarily among offender samples. In terms of administration, the PCL-R manual (Hare, 1991) contains explicit instructions regarding the information needed to score each of the 20 items on a 3-point scale: 0 = *item does not apply;* 1 = *item applies to a certain extent;* 2 = *item applies.* Based on the combination of interview and file data, examinees receive a score ranging between 0 and 40, with scores greater than or equal to 30 typically being used to classify someone as "psychopathic." It is important to note that the manual also clearly states that the PCL-R cannot be scored reliably in the absence of adequate collateral information regarding an offender's history (e.g., institutional files, criminal history data, arrest reports, interviews with family members, psychological assessment data). Reliance on self-report information, particularly in adversarial settings, is likely to result in highly biased ratings.

The psychometric properties of the PCL-R are well established. Various indices of reliability (internal consistency, inter-rater) have been reported and are in the acceptable range

(Fulero, 1995; Hare, 1991). In terms of predictive validity, several studies have shown that the PCL-R is a robust predictor of general criminal recidivism and violent criminal recidivism among released offenders (for reviews, see Hemphill, Hare, & Wong, 1998; Salekin, Rogers, & Sewell, 1996). PCL-R scores have also been shown to be associated with treatment outcome in correctional settings across several studies (see Ogloff, Wong, & Greenwood, 1990; O'Neill, Heilbrun, & Lidz, 2000; Rice, 1997; Rice, Harris, & Cormier, 1992; Seto & Barbaree, 1999). In summary, the PCL-R has repeatedly been shown to be a reliable and valid measure regarding the prediction of recidivism and treatment responsiveness among correctional populations.

Given the existing database, it is not surprising that psychopathy is becoming increasingly important in the assessment of violence risk among offenders. For example, the PCL-R is a central component of recently developed risk assessment methods such as the HCR-20 (Historical-Clinical-Risk Management Model, Violence Risk Assessment Scheme) (Webster, Douglas, Eaves, & Hart, 1997) and the Violence Risk Assessment Guide (VRAG) (Quinsey et al., 1998). Moreover, the state of Texas recently passed legislation explicitly requiring an assessment of psychopathy as part of the evaluation process for sex offenders who are being assessed for possible civil commitment following the completion of their prison sentences (*Civil Commitment of Sexually Violent Predators Act,* 1999). Several other states also have passed or reenacted similar legislation that makes reference to psychopathy, "antisocial personality," or personality disorders more generally as factors to be considered in the commitment process of sex offenders, as well as of "dangerous" offenders more generally (Becker & Murphy, 1998; Heilbrun, Ogloff, & Picarello, 1999). Although highly controversial, such laws clearly indicate that psychopathy is a psychological construct with considerable public policy implications regarding the assessment and management of violent offenders.

Unfortunately, with increased usage of any assessment procedure comes the increased possibility of its misuse by unskilled, uninformed, or unethical examiners (Zinger, 1995; Zinger & Forth, 1998). The two cases that are reviewed

below illustrate two different but equally problematic misapplications of the PCL-R in the context of forensic evaluations in which examiners made claims about the association between psychopathy and violence that were not supported by the existing empirical literature. One represents misuse by the prosecution in a death penalty case, whereas the other represents misuse by the defense in a sexual assault case. Some minor details have been left out or changed to ensure the anonymity of those involved. The basic facts of the cases are accurate as presented, however.

CASE 1: PSYCHOPATHY AS JUSTIFICATION FOR THE DEATH PENALTY

The first case involved a defendant being tried for multiple capital murders who had been evaluated by a psychologist using the PCL-R (without an interview) at some point prior to the penalty phase of his trial. Based on this evaluation, Defendant X received a score (i.e., PCL-R = 36) beyond that traditionally associated with the designation of being a "psychopath" (i.e., as noted earlier, PCL-R = 30). After Defendant X was convicted, the prosecution sought to enter his PCL-R score (as well as other psychometric data) into evidence during the penalty phase. This information was to be presented as an aggravating factor and used to argue that the defendant was likely to commit further acts of violence if he did not receive the death sentence. More specifically, it was noted in the clinician's report that, because Defendant X was a psychopath, he was highly likely to engage in future acts of violence, even if he were incarcerated in a 23-hour-per-day lockdown facility for the remainder of his life.

Given the well-established association between psychopathy and violence—widely noted in various review articles addressing risk assessment (e.g., Borum, 1996; Edens & Otto, 2001; Hare, 1998b; Hemphill et al., 1998)—one might conclude that such an assertion could be supported to some extent based on the published research in this area. However, a more thorough inspection of this literature suggests that such a conclusion is in fact not consistent with the published empirical research on the

PCL-R. Although one of the earliest and most widely cited studies examining psychopathy and institutional misbehavior (Forth, Hart, & Hare, 1990) found that there was a fairly strong correlation ($r = .46$) between the PCL-R and violent disciplinary infractions, base rates of institutional violence among incarcerated, PCL-R–defined psychopaths have been shown to be marginally higher than among non-psychopaths in only a few other studies, and others have failed to find a significant difference at all (for reviews, see Cunningham & Reidy, 1998; Edens, Petrila, & Buffington-Vollum, 2001; Edens, Skeem, Cruise, & Cauffman, 2001). Moreover, none of this research has been conducted in the types of 23-hour-per-day lockdown facilities in which this defendant would be detained if he were to receive a life sentence.

Clearly, psychological or psychiatric expert testimony related to "dangerousness" in the penalty phase of capital cases has a checkered history (e.g., *Barefoot v. Estelle,* 1983) that raises issues beyond simply the possible use of the PCL-R in this context (for reviews, see Cunningham & Reidy, 1999; Ewing, 1983). However, claims that these individuals were likely to be violent were often based only on unsubstantiated clinical opinion, and the introduction of a standardized and psychometrically sound assessment procedure such as the PCL-R into this process arguably (and unfortunately) further substantiates the imprimatur of scientific credibility and accuracy of violence risk predictions where little or none exists in this particular situation.

The "Ethical Principles of Psychologists and Code of Conduct" (American Psychological Association Ethics Committee, 1992) clearly indicates that psychologists should engage in socially responsible behavior (Principle F), do no harm (§ 1.14), and attempt to prevent the misuse of their work (§ 1.16). More specific to psychological assessment, the *Standards for Educational and Psychological Testing* (AERA, APA, & NCME, 1999) note that "those who select tests and draw inferences from test scores should be *familiar with the relevant evidence of validity* and reliability for tests and inventories used and should be prepared to articulate a logical analysis that supports all facets of the assessment and *the inferences made from the assessment*" (Standard 12.13, p. 133, italics added).

More specific to forensic assessment, the "Specialty Guidelines for Forensic Psychologists" (Committee on Ethical Guidelines for Forensic Psychologists, 1991) clearly state, regarding methods and procedures employed, that "forensic psychologists have an obligation to maintain current knowledge of scientific, professional and legal developments within their area of claimed competence" (p. 661). These guidelines also assert that forensic psychologists do not "either by commission or omission, participate in a misrepresentation of their evidence" (p. 664). Although the use of PCL-R results in the context of release decision making for an offender would clearly be defensible on ethical and scientific grounds (i.e., given the established association with recidivism), allowing such results to influence what is literally a life or death decision by a jury when that information is not particularly relevant to the issue at hand (i.e., likelihood of future institutional violence) seems not only incompetent and factually misleading but also highly unethical.

CASE 2: THE ABSENCE OF PSYCHOPATHY AND (CONSEQUENTLY) THE ABSENCE OF INCEST

The second case involved an assessment conducted by a psychiatrist and psychologist on an individual who recently was charged with several counts of sexually assaulting one of his adolescent children several years ago. Defendant Y had no documented criminal history and was considered generally to be a well-respected member of his community. Retained by the defense team, the examiners administered a battery of psychometric tests (e.g., MMPI-2, Rorschach, TAT) to this defendant, conducted six 1-hour clinical interviews, and consulted with his current (third) wife—not the mother of the accuser—and a mental health professional who had seen them briefly for marital therapy.

Based on this evaluation, the psychiatrist first attempted to testify that she could conclude that Defendant Y did not commit the crimes he was accused of beyond a reasonable degree of scientific certainty. The prosecutor objected to this type of "ultimate issue" testimony and the judge instructed the jury to ignore her conclusions.

However, the psychiatrist was then allowed to testify that, because of the absence of various risk factors associated with violence and sex offending, the defendant was not likely (again, with a reasonable degree of scientific certainty) to commit acts of sexual violence such as those of which he was accused.

Although not documented anywhere in the psychologist's report or the psychiatrist's testimony, the defendant also had been administered the PCL-R (it is unclear by whom, because the examiner line of the interview protocol was left blank). Nowhere in the raw data file was a PCL-R score sheet that should have been used to summarize the results of this assessment. What was in the file, however, was a list of the aforementioned "risk factors for violence and sexual offending," coded in a present-absent format, that was compiled by the testifying psychiatrist. What factors were detailed on this list? Several variables that have some empirical connection with sexual recidivism (e.g., prior sexual offenses) were listed (Hanson & Bussière, 1998). More significantly, approximately 10 to 15 individual items from the PCL-R were noted on this list and were cited during direct testimony by the psychiatrist as evidence that the defendant did not display "sociopathic tendencies" and was unlikely to be capable of sexual violence.

Unlike Case 1, in which the only apparent misapplication of the PCL-R was in the erroneous conclusion drawn regarding the increased likelihood of institutional violence, in Case 2, there are multiple problems associated with the use of the PCL-R. Defendant Y's expert witnesses (a) did not have adequate information available to administer and score the PCL-R appropriately; (b) presented the obtained results in a highly unusual and non-standardized manner; and (c) drew conclusions that are in no way supported by the existing empirical literature regarding the relationship between psychopathy and sexual violence. The mistakes made related to Points a and b are relatively elementary and will not be detailed here (for a review of some of these issues, see the instrument's manual, Hare, 1991, and Hare, 1998a).

Related to Point c, the conclusions presented by the examiners, both in the psychologist's report and the psychiatrist's testimony, were seriously flawed regarding their connection with existing empirical literature. Although it is true that some sex offenders score quite high on the PCL-R (e.g., Edens, Hart, Johnson, Johnson, & Olver, 2000; Quinsey et al., 1998) and that the combination of psychopathy and deviant sexual arousal has been shown to be a robust predictor of sex offender recidivism generally (Rice & Harris, 1997), these factors have very little to do with the prediction of incest per se. Notwithstanding the obvious psychometric and ethical problems inherent in attempting to determine whether a specific behavior (i.e., having sex with one's own child) did or did not occur based on any kind of clinical diagnosis or psychological "profile" (Becker & Murphy, 1998; Edwards, 1998), there is very little reason to assume that PCL-R scores would be meaningful in terms of differentiating incest offenders from non-offenders even at the group level, given the relatively low scores that many incest offenders obtain on the PCL-R (Firestone, Bradford, Greenberg, & Larose, 1998; Forth & Kroner, 1994, as cited in Hare, 1998b; Serin, Malcolm, Khanna, & Barbaree, 1994). The blanket claim made by the psychiatrist in this case—that it was extremely unlikely that Defendant Y would engage in incestuous acts because of the absence of "sociopathic tendencies"—clearly lacks any scientific foundation. Furthermore, such claims specifically violate relevant practice and ethical guidelines espoused by various professional organizations such as the Association for the Treatment of Sexual Abusers (1997), as well as more general guidelines established by the American Psychological Association Ethics Committee (1992), the *Standards for Educational and Psychological Testing* (AERA, APA, & NCME, 1999), the American Psychology-Law Society (Committee on Ethical Guidelines for Forensic Psychologists, 1991), and the AAPL (1995) noted earlier (also see Melton et al., 1997).

CONCLUSION

One would be hard-pressed at this time to argue that the PCL-R is not relevant to the assessment of risk in many forensic contexts, given the extensive body of empirical research demonstrating its association with violence. However, applicability to certain situations does not translate into appropriateness for and predictive utility in all situations (Cunningham & Reidy, 1998, 1999; Hare, 1998a). Review papers addressing concerns about the potential misuse of the PCL-R have been published in reference to juvenile justice settings (Edens et al., 2001) and in relation to Canadian court proceedings (Zinger, 1995; Zinger & Forth, 1998), but no detailed accounts of its misapplication in U.S. criminal courts have been documented up to this time.

The two cases reviewed above clearly delineate how both the presence and absence of psychopathy can be misleading as they relate to violence potential in specific contexts. It is incumbent on examiners who use this measure to be familiar both with (a) the settings, circumstances, and populations in which the instrument is appropriate for use and (b) the existing research literature on which their conclusions supposedly are based. In Case 1, the examiner was not attentive to Point b, at a minimum. In Case 2, the examiners violated Points a and b. Such mistakes not only are potentially harmful (or even deadly) to those involved, but they also diminish the credibility of the mental health field more generally by increasing the likelihood that

examiners are perceived as biased in their conclusions. It is widely noted in the legal community that some clinicians have reputations for being "hired guns" (Mossman, 1999). Examples such as the preceding two, which resulted in "dueling experts" drawing contradictory conclusions, do little to ameliorate these impressions. What were the outcomes of these two cases? In Case 1, after the examiner's report was submitted by the prosecution, the defense submitted a motion *in limine* to exclude the PCL-R results and all references to "psychopathy." Following this motion, which included affidavits from several researchers that addressed the lack of a clear association between psychopathy and institutional violence in prisons, the prosecution eventually withdrew the report. The examiner did not testify in the penalty phase of the case. The defendant received life without parole rather than the death penalty. In Case 2, as already noted, the defense expert introduced several PCL-R items and the "absence" of psychopathy as part of her list of risk factors that were not evidenced by the defendant. Rebuttal expert testimony was offered that outlined the issues described above regarding the problems associated with this type of testimony and its irrelevance to the case at hand. Following several hours of deliberation, the defendant was found not guilty on all counts of the indictment.

21

ALTERNATIVE METHODS OF CHILD TESTIMONY

A Review of Law and Research

JEFFREY C. SANDLER

Almost every recent article on child witnesses or testimony begins by noting a rise over the past 25 years in the number of children being called to testify in criminal and civil courts. The articles then cite possible reasons for the rise (see, for a review, Ceci & Bruck, 1993), the most common reason being an increase in both the reporting and the prosecution of child sexual and physical abuse cases starting in the early 1980s. At this point, some articles make special mention of the corresponding increase in child-related research that accompanied the testimonial rise, while many others do not. Finally, each article eventually begins to focus on its specific area of interest regarding the use of children as witnesses. These areas of interest include such topics as the development of memory and the ability to lie, the interviewing of children, suggestibility, and identification accuracy, each of which are well-researched fields.

For example, a large body of research has been compiled on the ability of children to select suspects from various types of police line-ups (e.g., simultaneous, sequential, elimination, or show up; Pozzulo & Lindsay, 1998, 1999).

Likewise, a considerable number of articles and books have been written addressing the suggestibility of children (e.g., Ceci & Bruck, 1993), their ability to accurately recall events (e.g., Ceci, Loftus, Leichtman, & Bruck, 1994; Loftus & Davies, 1984), their competency to testify (e.g., Cordon, Goodman, & Anderson, 2003), their ability to fabricate and deceive (e.g., Ceci, Leichtman, & Putnick, 1992; Talwar, Lee, Bala, & Lindsay, 2002), and the most effective methods for the interviewing of child witnesses (Poole & Lamb, 1998; see also London, this volume).

The present article, however, focuses on research relating to the experiences of child witnesses within the criminal justice system, specifically within criminal courts. The article summarizes and reviews the accumulated literature on some alternative methods of testimony proposed to reduce the trauma experienced by children on the witness stand. As research consistently indicates that having to face the defendant is the cause of distress most often cited by child witnesses (Cashmore, 2002; Goodman et al., 1992; Spencer & Flin, 1990), several of these alternative techniques have been designed to either limit or eliminate the need for such face-to-face meetings. They include the use of closed-circuit television (CCTV), audio- or videotaped testimony, privacy screens, and allowing parents or guardians to testify as a proxy for the child (Marsil, Montoya, Ross, & Graham, 2002).

This article begins by examining some of the legal issues surrounding the use of alternative testimony methods in the United States through U.S. Supreme Court opinions and existing state statutes. Research on the impact of using alternative methods of testimony is then summarized, emphasizing the ability of these alternatives to (a) reduce child witness trauma and (b) influence jurors' perceptions and verdicts. Finally, in line with the reviewed legal writings and social science evidence, some suggestions are made with regard to child testimony procedures.

LEGALITY OF ALTERNATIVE TESTIMONY METHODS

The Supreme Court

Several U.S. Supreme Court decisions over the past 25 years have either directly or indirectly addressed the use of alternative testimony methods for child witnesses. The first of these decisions, *Ohio v. Roberts* (1980), established an exception to the hearsay rule, which states that testimony or documents quoting persons not in court are not admissible. *Ohio v. Roberts* allowed hearsay as long as (a) the testimony or documents are found to be reliable and (b) the witness from whom the testimony or documents come is unavailable to testify in court. Although the Court reached this decision on a case pertaining to check forgery, the opinion has relevance to the use of either audio- or videotaped testimony (see Table 21.1) in child abuse cases. In addition, it might open the way for adults to testify to information received from the child.

Some children's advocates have suggested allowing videotaped police interviews with children, or interviews with child protection workers, to be admitted in lieu of the children having to testify in open court (Cashmore, 2002). This type of evidence might be allowed under the *Roberts* ruling as long as it can be

Table 21.1 Hearsay and Nonhearsay Alternatives to Children Testifying in Open Court

Type of Testimony	Alternative Method of Testimony
Hearsay	Audio taped police interviews Videotaped police interviews Parent or guardian testifying as proxy
Nonhearsay	Child allowed to testify from a separate room with one-way mirrors Closed circuit television (one- or two-way) Use of a screen to shield the child from the accused

shown that (a) the interview was conducted in a manner that established the reliability of the testimony and (b) the trauma of appearing in court or facing the defendant would impair a child's ability to testify accurately. This issue was revisited by the Court 24 years later in *Crawford v. Washington* (2004), which will be discussed shortly.

While *Ohio v. Roberts* (1980) was an indirect ruling on alternative methods of testimony for child witnesses, *Coy v. Iowa* (1988) dealt with the matter directly. Specifically, the issue before the Court was whether an Iowa statute permitting a screen to be placed between victims of child sexual abuse and their alleged abuser violated the Confrontation Clause of the Sixth Amendment (i.e., the right of a criminal defendant "to be confronted with the witnesses against him"). Although both the trial court and Iowa Supreme Court ruled that use of the screen was not a constitutional violation, the U.S. Supreme Court disagreed. In a 6–2 ruling, the majority found that although the Confrontation Clause does not *necessitate* a face-to-face meeting between a defendant and his or her accuser, any exceptions to such a meeting would "be allowed only when necessary to further an important public policy" (*Coy v. Iowa*, 1988, p. 1021). The basis for this strong emphasis on a face-to-face meeting lies in the belief that witnesses are more likely to be truthful when directly confronted by the defendant. As Justice Scalia, in writing for the majority, stated, the face-to-face presence of the defendant

> may, unfortunately, upset the truthful rape victim or abused child; but by the same token it may confound and undo the false accuser, or reveal the child coached by a malevolent adult. It is a truism that constitutional protections have costs. (p. 1020)

The majority further ruled that while exceptions to a face-to-face meeting may be made on a case-by-case basis, the Iowa statute—as it was then worded—eliminated the need for judges to ever examine case-specific variables (i.e., whether a particular witness in a particular case actually needs special protection).

However, in his dissent Justice Blackmun (with whom Chief Justice Rehnquist joined), disagreed as to the main purpose of the Confrontation Clause. They did not view the right as a means of discouraging a witness from being less than honest. Rather, the dissenters believed that the essence of the right was for the defendant "to be shown that the accuser is real and the [defendant had the] right to probe [the] accuser and [the] accusation in front of the trier of fact" (*Coy v. Iowa,* 1988, p. 1026). As the use of a screen interfered with neither of these two functions, Justice Blackmun did not view its use as a constitutional violation.

Two years later, in *Maryland v. Craig* (1990), the Court once again heard a case related to the testimony of an alleged victim of child sexual assault. In this case, the trial judge, after hearing that the child would suffer serious emotional distress if forced to testify in the courtroom, allowed her to testify from a separate room via one-way CCTV. Although the defendant was convicted at trial, the State Court of Appeals reversed on the grounds that the reason given for avoiding a face-to-face confrontation between accuser and accused did not reach the high level required by *Coy v. Iowa* (1988; i.e., necessary to meet a significant public policy). Specifically, the State Court of Appeals felt an attempt should first have been made to interview the alleged victim in the presence of the accused (to observe her level of distress) before allowing the use of CCTV.

Again, the U.S. Supreme Court disagreed with the state court. In a 5–4 vote, the Court allowed the use of CCTV and reversed the decision of the Maryland State Court of Appeals. The majority's decision (written by Justice O'Connor) once again turned on the Court's interpretation of the Confrontation Clause. This time the Court took yet another step away from a guaranteed right to a face-to-face meeting between accuser and accused by enumerating four key elements to the clause: (a) physical presence of the accuser, (b) that the accuser gives his or her statement under oath, (c) the right of the defense to cross-examination, and (d) the ability of the trier of fact to observe the accuser's demeanor (*Maryland v. Craig,* 1990). The majority subsequently found the CCTV procedure designed by Maryland to meet these criteria as follows:

> The child must be competent to testify and must testify under oath; the defendant retains full opportunity for contemporaneous cross-examination; and the judge, jury, and defendant are able to view (albeit by video) the demeanor (and body) of the witness as he or she testifies. (p. 851)

The majority also ruled that the decision to use CCTV had been made on an informed, case-specific basis (thereby meeting one of the hurdles set by *Coy v. Iowa,* 1988). Furthermore, "buttressed by the growing body of academic literature documenting the psychological trauma suffered by child abuse victims who must testify in court," there existed a compelling public policy reason for the use of CCTV (p. 855; thereby meeting the second hurdle set by *Coy*). In sum, the *Craig* Court indicated that a blanket rule supporting CCTV in all cases was inappropriate. However, on a case-by-case basis, a judge could decide that a given child's inability to communicate on the witness stand in an open courtroom justified the use of CCTV.

Finally, the U.S. Supreme Court's most recent opinion to affect the admission of alternative testimony methods or hearsay evidence (which includes audio- or videotaped police interviews) was in the case of *Crawford v. Washington* (2004). This case involved a man convicted of assault and attempted murder at whose trial the audiotape of a police interview with his wife had been entered as evidence. The trial court allowed admission of the tape (and State Supreme Court upheld the decision) based on criteria for the admission of hearsay evidence set forth in *Ohio v. Roberts* (1980). Namely, the trial court found (a) the evidence to be reliable (it was of a police interview and its content nearly matched the testimony offered by the defendant himself) and (b) the witness was unavailable to testify (under spousal privilege she was barred from doing so without her husband's consent). Thus, the case was a specific test of the *Roberts* criteria.

The U.S. Supreme Court, though, did not allow the evidence. In writing for the 7–2 majority, Justice Scalia made an interesting distinction not mentioned in the Court's opinion on *Roberts,* namely the difference between testimonial and declarative statements. According to Scalia, testimonial statements are those that an objective third party would judge were made with the reasonable belief that they would later be available for use at trial. (Declarative statements, by contrast, were all nontestimonial statements.) Given their implicit legal nature, testimonial statements must be evaluated for reliability by a different, more restrictive set of criteria than declarative statements. Although Scalia left it to each individual state to decide its own method for measuring the reliability of declarative statements, he wrote that all testimonial statements must have their reliability determined in only one particular manner: through cross-examination. Because the statements obtained in the police interview were not subjected to cross-examination, they were inadmissible.

Thus, the Court's ruling in *Crawford v. Washington* (2004) represents a step away from the admittance of hearsay evidence established in *Ohio v. Roberts* (1980). More important, from the perspective of child witness advocates, it represents a significant barrier to the use of audio- or videotaped interviews in place of a child testifying in open court. So long as the taped interviews are deemed to be testimonial (which they almost assuredly would be), to be admissible they would have to include an opportunity for cross-examination. Although this precludes using either audio- or videotapes of police interviews with child victims as a method to spare the children testimonial distress (as those would almost certainly not include cross-examination), videotaped depositions might be acceptable. However, given the recent nature of the *Crawford* ruling, it remains

too early to determine the breadth of its ultimate impact (National Center for Prosecution of Child Abuse, 2004).

State Laws and Statutes

Within the constitutional limits set forth by the U.S. Supreme Court, each state is responsible for establishing its own rules with regard to the testimony of children. This includes not only the use and admittance of alternative methods of child witness testimony (e.g., audio- or videotapes, CCTV, parent or guardian as proxy), but also general issues relating to the ability of children to testify. Table 21.2 displays the current federal and state policies with regard to three important issues in child witness testimony: (a) competency to testify, (b) use of CCTV, and (c) use of videotaped testimony. (See Goodman, Quas, Bulkley, & Shapiro, 1999, for the views of prosecuting attorneys on various forms of testimony.) As can be seen in Table 21.2, the majority of states assume competence on the part of child witnesses (the same as that given to adults), while a small minority requires a special showing of competence prior to a child giving testimony (usually accomplished through judicial questioning). Likewise, the majority of states also allows for testimony via CCTV (at least for alleged victims), although the exact procedure for that testimony varies (e.g., one- or two-way, who is allowed in the room with the child, how its use is deemed appropriate for a given child). Other states, though, specifically disallow CCTV testimony on the basis that it violates confrontation clauses of their *state* constitutions. Finally, only about one third of the states have statutes allowing for the admittance of videotaped testimony (even for alleged victims), and most of those still contain passages questionable under *Crawford v. Washington* (2004) (National Center for Prosecution of Child Abuse, 2004).

IMPACT OF ALTERNATIVE METHOD
USE ON CHILDREN AND JURORS

Although most states allow children to testify by either CCTV or videotape in order to reduce the likelihood of them suffering trauma

Table 21.2 State and Federal Policies With Regard to Child Testimonial Competence, as Well as the Admissibility of Videotaped and Closed-Circuit Television Testimony

Jurisdiction	Competency[a] Assumption of	Provisional	Constitutional or Unchallenged Use of CCTV[b]	Video[c]
Federal (U.S. Code)	X		X	
Alabama	X		X	X
Alaska		X	X	
Arizona	X			X
Arkansas	X		X	
California	X		VO	
Colorado	As victim	Just as witness	VO	X
Connecticut	X		VO	
Delaware	X		X	
Florida		X	X	
Georgia	As victim	Just as witness	VO	
Hawaii	X		VO	VO
Idaho		X	VO	
Illinois	X		VO	
Indiana		X	X	VO
Iowa	X		X	VO
Kansas	X		VO	VO
Kentucky	X		X	
Louisiana	X		VO	X
Maine	X			
Maryland	X		VO	
Massachusetts	X			
Michigan	X			X
Minnesota		X	X	VO
Mississippi	X		X	
Missouri	As victim	Just as witness		VO
Montana		X		
Nebraska	X			
Nevada		X		
New Hampshire	X			
New Jersey	X		X	
New Mexico		X		
New York		X	X	VO
North Carolina	X			
North Dakota	X			VO
Ohio		X	VO	
Oklahoma	X		X	
Oregon	X		VO	
Pennsylvania		X		
Rhode Island	X		VO	VO
South Carolina	X			
South Dakota		X	X	
Tennessee	X		X	

(Continued)

Table 21.2 (Continued)

| Jurisdiction | Competency[a] | | Constitutional or Unchallenged Use of | |
	Assumption of	Provisional	CCTV[b]	Video[c]
Texas		X	X	VO
Utah		X	X	X
Vermont	X		VO	
Virginia	X		X	
Washington	X		VO	
West Virginia	X			
Wisconsin	X		X	X
Wyoming	X			

NOTE: This table was constructed using information available from the National Center for Prosecution of Child Abuse, which was retrieved on February 20, 2005, from www.ndaa-apri.org/apri/programs/ncpca/statutes.html. CCTV = closed-circuit television; X = available to both victims and witnesses; VO = available to victims only.

a. As of June 2004.
b. As of September 2002.
c. As of July 2004; only includes statutes relating to pretrial videotaped statements, not general hearsay; many of these statutes have not been tested under or modified to account for *Crawford v. Washington* (2004).

(i.e., eliminating a face-to-face confrontation with the accused), these statutes were often based on assumptions rather than empirical evidence (Nathanson & Saywitz, 2003; Wade, 2002). In fact, surprisingly few studies have been conducted on the responses of either child witnesses or jurors to alternative testimony methods, and methodological differences between these studies (e.g., how distress was measured, whether mock or videotaped trials were used) make interpreting and combining their results somewhat difficult (Clifford, 2002). However, certain trends have emerged in the research findings, which suggest that some alternative testimony methods do in fact lower the distress levels of child witnesses without biasing jurors' perceptions (of either the child or the accused).

Impact on Child Witnesses

Hill and Hill (1987) investigated the effects of both the courtroom setting and having to face the accused on child recall accuracy. The researchers had 37 children (aged 7–9 years) watch a videotaped confrontation between a father and daughter before being questioned about the encounter in either a small separate room (with one-way mirrors) or a large courtroom. Results of the study indicated a "trend toward" improved recall accuracy on responses to both free-recall and specific questions for children who testified in the small room (pp. 814–815). Hill and Hill (1987) attributed this to lower levels of anxiety and to a greater tendency by children who testified in the courtroom to answer either "I don't know" or offer no response. However, these findings should be interpreted with caution, as only the increased tendency of children in the courtroom condition to respond either "I don't know" or offer no response actually reached statistical significance. Although this could possibly be due to the study's small number of participants, the effect of the courtroom setting may also have been muted by the children being merely witnesses rather than alleged victims (or of them not being acquainted with the accused). That is, the distress experienced by alleged victims at having to testify or face the accused may be considerably more than that experienced by nonvictim witnesses, which could make the differences in recall accuracy between testimonial conditions (i.e., courtroom setting versus separate room) more pronounced for victims. This possibility is very important given the increase in the prosecution of child sexual and physical abuse cases mentioned above.

Although the influence of a courtroom setting on the testimony of alleged child victims could be gauged by observing actual trials, this method presents several problems. For example, even if similar cases could be located in which one child testified in open court and one testified through an alternative method (e.g., CCTV), accuracy of the testimonies could not be reliably compared. Not only would the facts of each case be different, but without verification the actual facts may not even be known (i.e., there would be no way to tell whether any given statement was correct). Furthermore, there would likely be no random assignment, and the child who testified via an alternative method may have been selected to do so for some preexisting reason. That is, the child who testified outside of court may have been allowed to do so only because he or she displayed higher levels of initial distress than other children.

Rather than attempting to code and compare actual trial testimony, Goodman et al. (1998)—in one of the most comprehensive and elaborate studies on the effects of alternative testimony methods to date—used live mock trials. To simulate victimization of the children (aged 5–9 years), a confederate made movies in which the child was either (a) directed to place stickers on his or her exposed skin (guilty condition), or (b) directed to place stickers on his or her clothing (not guilty condition). Two weeks later the children were randomly assigned to testify in a mock trial before a mock jury, either in open court or via one-way CCTV. This design allowed the researchers not only to compare the recall accuracy of child victims across testimonial conditions, but also to assess the suggestibility of the children in response to leading and nonleading questions (as some had been victimized, while others had not). The children were also compared on numerous measures of anxiety and legal knowledge via scales and questionnaires.

Although several age effects emerged from the analyses (with 8- and 9-year-olds generally responding more accurately and being less suggestible), no significant main effects appeared for method of testimony. However, 5- and 6-year-olds made significantly fewer errors of omission (information left out) when testifying via CCTV than in open court. This result corresponds with the findings of Hill and Hill (1987), in which children were more likely to answer "I don't know" or offer no response when testifying in a courtroom. Goodman et al. (1998) also found that children with greater legal knowledge experienced less anxiety (a finding also noted by Spencer & Flin, 1990; Wade, 2002) and answered more direct questions correctly. Furthermore, children who experienced greater court-related anxiety (e.g., feelings about having to talk to judges and lawyers, speaking in front of the defendant) before the trial were more likely to refuse to testify, as were children asked to testify in open court (with this latter result only approaching significance).

In an attempt to further explore the effects of open court testimony on child witness anxiety levels, Nathanson and Saywitz (2003) conducted a study to measure differences in physiological anxiety correlates between children (aged 8–10 years) interviewed in a courtroom setting and those interviewed in a small, private room. Results of the study indicated (a) children in the courtroom condition recalled fewer pieces of information during free recall (again supporting the findings of Hill & Hill, 1987) and experienced more variability in heart rate (indicating greater stress), (b) children with greater knowledge of the legal system performed better in open court testimony, and (c) children with higher self-perceptions and perceptions of social support experienced less anticipatory anxiety. Spencer and Flin (1990), in their thorough review of the social science research relating to child witnesses, likewise noted an inverse relationship between children's levels of social support and their levels of distress, as well as the importance of legal knowledge. Furthermore, Spencer and Flin (1990) also found the research to show the use of age-inappropriate language in the interviewing of children to be a significant cause of trauma. Finally, in a qualitative analysis, Wade (2002) interviewed 26 children aged 7–17 about their experiences testifying in the British legal system either in open court or by CCTV. In general, children indicated that a lack of knowledge concerning the court process was their greatest source of anxiety (even more so than facing the defendant). Furthermore, the children emphasized their lack of control in the process (something especially noted by victim-witnesses) and anxiety at having to be cross-examined. Although the majority of children who testified via CCTV appreciated not having to face the defendant, two of those who testified in open court said the presence of the defendant was incentive for them to tell everything they could remember.

Given the research summarized above, it seems that some alternative methods of testifying (particularly CCTV) may be effective in reducing the anxiety of child witnesses. Furthermore, results of the studies point to several other possible methods for reducing anxiety levels, including (a) educating children on the legal system and process, (b) improving children's perceptions of themselves and their social support, and (c) giving children some measure of control over the system. Although the findings listed above do not consistently show enhanced recall accuracy for children testifying by alternative methods, they do consistently show no harmful effects. Thus, alternative testimony methods do appear to improve the testimony experiences of child witnesses, without impairing their performance. However, alternative testimony methods could still have a negative effect if they unfairly bias jurors' perceptions either for or against the accused.

Impact on Jurors' Perceptions and Verdicts

As scant as research has been on the differences between the testimony of children in open court and their testimony by alternative methods, there has been even less measuring differences in jurors' perceptions of the children's testimony across techniques. Furthermore, the few available studies have generated equivocal findings (Cashmore, 2002). Swim, Borgida, and McCoy (1993) had mock jurors watch either a child witness's videotaped deposition or a videotape of the trial in which the child testified in open court. Although no significant differences were found on jurors' perceptions

of either the child's credibility or guilt of the victim across conditions, jurors who watched the child testify in open court tended to view the defendant as more guilty and the child as more accurate (although neither difference reached significance). Lindsay, Ross, Lea, and Carr (1995) found no differences in mock jurors' perceptions of defendant guilt, witness credibility, or trial fairness after watching a 2-hour trial video in which a child witness testified (a) in open court, (b) by CCTV, or (c) with a screen blocking the child from the defendant's view (see also Ross et al., 1994). However, in a study by Eaton, Ball, and O'Callaghan (2001), jurors were more likely to rate a defendant guilty when a child testified in open court than when the child testified by videotaped deposition or CCTV. Unfortunately, all of the studies listed above suffer from the same limitation: In all of them the testimony in all conditions (i.e., in open court, videotaped depositions, use of a screen, or CCTV) were presented to mock jurors on videotape. That is, the in-court testimony presented to mock jurors was not viewed live, but rather live on tape.

In an attempt to address this rather major confound, Goodman et al. (1998) recruited over 1,200 mock jurors from community voter registration lists to observe their live mock trials. The responses of jurors who observed the trials were compared across testimonial conditions (CCTV versus open court) on (a) guilt judgments, (b) perceived fairness of the trial, and (c) ability to discern accurate from inaccurate testimony. Results of the analyses revealed no significant differences in jurors' perceptions of defendant guilt, trial fairness, or accuracy discernment, although there were gender differences. Specifically, women who viewed testimony via CCTV rated the trial as more fair to the child than women who viewed the testimony live. In addition, women were more likely than men to consider CCTV testimony fairer to the children, and they were also less likely than men to indicate sympathy for the defendant. Furthermore, and rather depressingly, while "there was no indication that jurors discerned children's accuracy better in the CCTV or regular-trial condition," that may be due to the fact that jurors in neither condition were very good at discernment in general (p. 193).

When Goodman et al. (1998) then conducted a path analysis, two counteracting effects were observed. First, jurors tended to view children's testimony as less accurate or believable in the CCTV condition. Second, jurors tended to correctly believe children's accurate testimony more than their inaccurate testimony, and children tended to testify more accurately in the CCTV condition. It should be noted that prior to deliberation the judge instructed jurors in the CCTV condition that "no implications should be drawn from the use of CCTV, that it is not evidence in itself, and that it should not be considered during deliberations" (pp. 180–181). According to standard rules of criminal procedure, such a jury instruction should be issued whenever an alternative form of testimony is allowed.

The results of the studies listed above may not be uniform and conclusive, but they seem to indicate that testimonial condition (e.g., CCTV, open court, videotape) does not significantly bias jurors either for or against the defendant (although the trend appeared to favor the defendant). Jurors' perceptions of trial fairness also appeared uninfluenced by testimonial condition, as was the ability of jurors to correctly identify a child's testimony as either accurate or inaccurate. Thus, combined research on the impact of alternative testimony methods on child witnesses and jurors' perceptions indicates beneficial effects for the child witnesses (e.g., reduced anxiety levels) and a lack of detrimental effects on jurors' perceptions.

SUMMARY AND CONCLUSIONS

This chapter has reviewed some of the legal and social science literature surrounding the use of alternative methods of testimony for child witnesses. The U.S. Supreme Court has indicated a willingness to accept certain nonhearsay forms of alternative testimony (*Maryland v. Craig,* 1990), but it has been reluctant to expand the use of hearsay options (*Crawford v. Washington,* 2004). In addition, in light of the ruling in *Coy v. Ohio,* it is unlikely that screens to place a visual block between the child victim and her or his alleged abuser will be found acceptable, even with case-by-case consideration. The prosecution

would have to document the necessity of the screen to further an important public policy. Furthermore, in some states, the screen (as well as CCTV) violates the confrontation clause of the state constitution. In line with these rulings, current state statutes (see Table 21.2) tend to show a legislative preference for the use of CCTV testimony over the use of videotaped interviews or depositions. Existing social science research (e.g., Goodman et al., 1998; Nathanson & Saywitz, 2003) supports the use of alternative testimony methods as a way to reduce the anxiety of child witnesses, while at the same time posing no significant threat to (a) the quality or accuracy of the testimony, (b) jurors' perceptions of the testimony or the defendant (at least when instructed by the judge to disregard the method of testimony), (c) jurors' ratings of defendant guilt, or (d) jurors' ability to discern between accurate and inaccurate testimony. Furthermore, research has also identified other options for reducing the trauma suffered by child witnesses, including education of the legal system, use of age-appropriate language and interviewing techniques, and increased levels of perceived social support.

With all of this in mind, the use of constitutionally acceptable alternative testimony seems justified, as its benefits appear to outweigh its detriments. However, as noted by Wade (2002), not all children experience trauma at having to face the defendant. Some even find such a face-to-face confrontation motivational and cathartic. Furthermore, numerous children expressed a feeling of powerlessness within the process, which was especially acute for victim-witnesses (who may have already felt powerless due to their victimization). Thus, combining the cases and studies reviewed above, several suggestions can be made concerning child witnesses and the legal system. First, child witnesses should be (a) educated on the legal system and its processes, (b) interviewed using age-appropriate language, and (c) allowed to have some form of social support with them during the interview. Second, all constitutionally acceptable alternative testimony methods should be identified and researched. Third, child witnesses (especially victim-witnesses) should then be given their choice of the acceptable testimony methods whenever possible (with some limitations according to the age of the child). With the guidance of a parent, guardian, or legal advocate, they should be allowed to choose the method of testimony with which they are most comfortable, thereby maximizing the reduction in their anxiety as well as giving them some sense of control over the process. Although this places a great deal of responsibility upon the shoulders of young children, those same children will have already been cleared to testify in a judicial proceeding. The key to using alternative methods of testimony seems to be balancing constitutional rights with empirical research findings, which at the moment appears to be possible.

UNIT 6

CORRECTIONAL PSYCHOLOGY

Introduction and Commentary

Correctional psychology represents a broad landscape of opportunities for researchers and practitioners who operate in both institutional and community settings. Prisons and jails are in need of direct services to inmates, evaluation of programs, assessment for making classification decisions, and training of staff, among many things. In the community, psychologists and other mental health professionals provide a very wide range of services to persons on probation and parole. Additionally, there is a multitude of opportunities in the juvenile equivalents of these adult settings.

In the first reading in this section, **Jennifer Boothby and Carl Clements** report on a nationwide survey of correctional psychologists working in U.S. state and federal prisons, where the estimated psychologist to inmate ratio is 1:750. The article provides us with a glimpse into their work, such as the types of assessments they conduct and the instruments and treatments they favor. The authors also asked their respondents to describe how their workload was divided and how they would like their time to be allotted. Respondents reported that nearly 30% of their time was spent on administrative tasks, and most wanted less time there and more time for direct treatment of prisoners.

Correctional officials often have to find the balance between holding offenders accountable for their crimes and providing them with meaningful opportunities to engage in prosocial behavior after their sentences have been served.

In his article on offender rehabilitation, **Paul Gendreau** summarizes what we know about effective treatment based on evaluation research. His checklist of what does and does not work remains valid, even though this article is nearly 10 years old. Gendreau, a Canadian psychologist, decries the American criminal justice system's emphasis on punitive and justice models, arguing that neither lends itself to effective treatment. He is also very critical about the ethnocentrism that prevents theorists, researchers, and practitioners from sharing ideas and being receptive to alternative viewpoints across academic disciplines and across nations.

Michael Prendergast, David Farabee, Jerome Cartier, and Susan Henkin report on a study comparing drug treatment in a prison setting for inmates who participated voluntarily in the treatment and for those who were mandated or coerced to participate. Surprisingly, there were no significant group differences. Both groups improved significantly in psychological and social functioning, though change was most likely in the psychological arena (such as in self-esteem and decision making). The description of the substance abuse treatment program and the therapeutic community in which it is based is informative for readers who are unfamiliar with these concepts.

The great majority of individuals under correctional supervision are not in jails, prisons, or juvenile treatment centers, but rather are under community supervision. The last article in this section focuses on community corrections, specifically as it relates to juveniles. Juvenile corrections on the whole is a rapidly developing area for theory, research, and treatment.

One of the most attention-getting community treatment programs for serious juvenile offenders is multisystemic therapy (MST). This approach provides intensive treatment services to juveniles and their family, with one goal being to preserve the family unit. **Willem Martens**, however, suggests a number of modifications to MST in the case of some juveniles. For example, he suggests that additional professionals (such as a pediatrician and a neurologist) should be added to the MST team. He also advocates treatment of some youths away from the influence of their families. If all of Martens' recommendations were to be implemented, MST as it was originally conceived would hardly be recognizable. However, integration of some of his suggestions may be warranted.

As a group, the above articles support the work of correctional psychologists, but they also prompt questions about the policies of the criminal justice system in which they operate. Many psychologists find great satisfaction working in correctional facilities or consulting with a variety of correctional agencies. The challenges in these settings are often immense, but there also are numerous opportunities to contribute to significant change in practices and in the lives of individuals.

22

A NATIONAL SURVEY OF CORRECTIONAL PSYCHOLOGISTS

JENNIFER L. BOOTHBY

CARL B. CLEMENTS

Psychologists have long had distinct roles in the nation's correctional institutions. Their functions have been described as a blend of clinical and community psychology (Milan & Long, 1980). Assessment, treatment, training, and consultation functions take place in an environmental context that, itself, often calls for conflict resolution, program design and evaluation, and attention to stressful conditions. The number of persons incarcerated in the United States grows daily. . . . Also observed has been a substantial increase in the number and percentage of mentally disordered offenders in prison (Bureau of Justice Statistics, 1999a). Both traditional and emerging roles for psychologists are evident in this "growth industry." Though a number of articles have suggested functional models and specific areas of expertise in the application of psychology skills to prisons and offenders (Clements, 1987, 2000; Milan, Chin, & Nguyen, 1999), a comprehensive survey of actual contemporary practice has been notably absent.

Information with regard to the roles and duties of correctional psychologists has not been examined fully in nearly two decades

(Otero, McNally, & Powitzky, 1981). As noted, a number of changes have occurred at the state and federal levels in corrections during the past 20 years. The prison population is booming, sentencing policies have become more severe, and public attitude seems to favor punishment over treatment. How the roles and responsibilities of correctional psychologists may have changed in the context of these trends is not known. In addition to the Otero et al. (1981) report, two other studies are in limited circulation (Bartol, Griffin, & Clark, 1993, cited in Bartol, 1999; Gallagher, Somwaru, & Ben-Porath, 1999). These surveys involved, respectively, the distribution of duties of 120 correctional psychologists and the use of psychological tests in 41 state jurisdictions. In the current study, we sought both a larger sample size and greater breadth of inquiry.

METHOD

Procedure

Potential survey participants (doctoral psychologists and master's-trained psychology staff)

Editors' Note: This article was first published in *Criminal Justice and Behavior*, Vol. 27, No. 6, December 2000, pp. 716-732.

were identified through contacting state corrections commissioners or directors of prison mental health services and comparable administrative officials for the Federal Bureau of Prisons. These individuals were asked to provide either a list of all psychologists working within their system or to designate a contact person who would be responsible for distributing the surveys. Ten state systems (21%) supplied lists of their doctoral and master's level psychology staff, whereas the remaining systems chose to distribute the surveys internally. The different methods of survey distribution did not appear to influence response rates. Based on address lists and numbers of surveys requested by each system, we estimated a potential pool of some 2,000 professionals. Of note, we did not survey psychologists who work in local jails or in state juvenile justice institutions, nor other mental health professionals (e.g., social workers) employed by prison systems.

MATERIALS

A four-page questionnaire was developed specifically for this study. Survey questions addressed multiple facets of the correctional psychologist's experience. Major topics included (a) demographics, (b) job duties and responsibilities, (c) the provision of mental health services, (d) assessment practices, and (e) training recommendations. Psychologists were encouraged to include their name and address on a detachable sheet to indicate their interest in receiving a brief summary of the survey results. If not already detached, these sheets were separated from the survey on receipt to ensure anonymity of the respondents.

RESULTS

Participant Characteristics

Survey respondents included 830 psychologists (estimated response rate = 42%) working in 48 state prison systems (78% of respondents) and the U.S. Federal Bureau of Prisons (22%). Generally, the response rate was higher within the federal system and among doctoral-level personnel. Variation in response rate across the 48 state systems was not remarkable. Most respondents (59%) held either a Ph.D. or Psy.D., whereas 37% were master's level graduates. The mean age of respondents was 45 years, and an overwhelming majority (92%) identified themselves as Caucasian. Approximately 62% of respondents were male, and 38% were female.

Although most psychologists working in corrections report having degrees in clinical psychology, this specialization is not uniformly distributed across settings. Approximately 67% of psychologists employed by the Federal Bureau of Prisons have degrees in clinical psychology, and all have doctorates. State correctional systems employ psychologists with master's and doctoral degrees at approximately the same rate, and 49% of these professionals report training in clinical psychology. Table 22.1 provides additional information about training emphasis.

In recent years, an increasing number of psychologists are employed on a contractual basis by correctional facilities. Many professionals apparently prefer this type of employment as it often enables them to work fewer hours in the prison system and to continue other work activities, such as private practice. Of the survey respondents, 12% indicated that their work was contractual.

Some psychologists responding to this survey were relative novices in corrections; others were long-time career professionals. The average length of employment in corrections was 8 years, but experience ranged from a few months to 38 years. Salary was obviously related to the number of years employed, but psychologists employed for similar lengths of time by federal and state systems earned significantly different salaries. Doctoral-level psychologists employed by the federal system earned an annual income of $61,800 on average, whereas doctoral-level psychologists employed by state systems averaged approximately $53,400. In comparison, master's-level staff averaged about $40,100 in annual income.

Reflecting the gender ratio of America's prisons (93% male), most respondents (82%) reported working only with male offenders. Some (10%) work with both male and female inmates, and only 8% work solely with female offenders. Correctional psychologists appear to work with inmates representing a full range (and usually a combination) of custody levels. These include maximum custody (44%), close custody (23%), medium custody (51%), and minimum

Table 22.1 Percentage of Correctional Psychologists Reporting Training Emphasis

Training Emphasis	Federal (n = 172)	State (n = 614)
Clinical psychology	67	49
Counseling psychology	22	27
Educational/school psychology	3	5
General psychology	3	6
Other	5	11

custody (30%). It is also of interest that correctional psychologists do not appear to specialize in the treatment of any one type of offender. Few respondents indicated that they provided services aimed at only a single type of inmate or a single problem area (e.g., substance abuse, developmentally disabled, inpatient mental health). Rather, these professionals work with a variety of offenders.

Job Functions

Correctional psychologists have a wide range of responsibilities within their respective institutions. They describe a broad distribution of time across many tasks. On average, administrative tasks consume the largest percentage (30%) of work time, whereas direct treatment (26%) and assessment (18%) also occupy a substantial portion of the correctional psychologist's time. Survey respondents, on average, reported relatively little time devoted to research. We also asked how these professionals would prefer to spend their time within these same job categories. . . . [P]sychologists expressed interest in spending much less time on administrative duties. Conversely, they reported a desire to increase the amount of time spent in providing therapy to offenders and in staff training. Similarly, many expressed interest in increasing the amount of time available for research. When asked to list activities they wished they were involved in, 47% included research on their wish list. Even so, the desired amount of time for research remained low (6%), perhaps reflecting the reality of other demands and lack of institutional support.

TREATMENT APPROACHES AND PROBLEM FOCUS

Correctional psychologists spend, on average, one quarter of their time providing therapy to inmates. Respondents were asked to further describe the format of interventions offered to inmates and the theoretical underpinnings of the services provided. Despite the ever increasing number of prisoners needing mental health services, 60% of treatment continues to be provided in an individual format. This allocation of resources exists in the face of an average psychologist to inmate ratio of 1:750. In contrast, respondents indicated spending approximately 18% of therapy time on psycho-educational groups and 15% on process groups. With respect to the theoretical orientations that correctional psychologists use to guide their provision of services, most reported a combination of frameworks. An overwhelming majority (88%) use a cognitive model. A behavioral orientation was endorsed by 69%, and another 40% employed a rational-emotive approach. Though we did not specifically pose an "eclectic" option, most endorsed one or more secondary theoretical orientations, suggesting an eclectic approach to psychotherapy. Table 22.2 contains additional data on respondents' orientation.

Given the substantial proportion of time correctional psychologists spend evaluating (18%) and treating (26%) prisoners, it becomes important to understand the types of inmate problems typically being addressed. Respondents were asked to list the four inmate problems they most commonly treated. Depression was overwhelmingly cited as the most frequent problem presented by inmates. Eighty percent of psychologists cited depression within the "top four problems." Anger problems were also mentioned by many psychologists (40%). Psychotic symptoms, anxiety, and adjustment issues were frequently mentioned as well. Table 22.3 summarizes these responses.

ASSESSMENT PRACTICES

Approximately 65% of respondents indicated that they were involved, to varying degrees, in the psychological assessment of offenders. The types of evaluations described range from

Table 22.2 Percentage of Respondents Reporting Theoretical Orientations

Orientation	Percentage of Respondents
Cognitive	88
Behavioral	69
Rational-emotive	40
Psychodynamic/psychoanalytic	23
Humanistic	19
Existential	15
Systems	14
Other	13

Table 22.3 Percentage of Correctional Psychologists Indicating Various Mental Health Problems as One of Four Most Frequent Problems Treated

Problem	Percentage of Psychologists
Depression	80
Anger	40
Psychoses	25
Anxiety	24
Adjustment issues	20
Personality disorders	18
Substance abuse	17
Sexual behavior	14
Acting out/impulse control	12

NOTE: Not all respondents listed four problem areas.

Table 22.4 Percentage of Correctional Psychologists Reporting Usage of Specific Psychological Tests

Instrument	Percentage
MMPI	87
WAIS	69
MCMI	30
Bender Gestalt	23
Rorschach	20
Projective Drawings	14
BDI/BAI	13
PCL-R	11
PAI	10
WMS	8
SIRS	7
TONI	6
Trails A & B	6
MSI	6
Halstad Reitan	5
Luria Nebraska	4
Slosson	3
LSI	< 1
V-RAG	< 1

NOTE: MMPI = Minnesota Multiphasic Personality Inventory; WAIS = Wechsler Adult Intelligence Scale; MCMI = Millon Clinical Multiaxial Inventory; BDI/BAI = Beck Depression Inventory/Behavior Assessment Inventory; PCL-R = Psychopathy Checklist-Revised; PAI = Personality Assessment Inventory; WMS = Wechsler Memory Scale; SIRS = Structured Interview of Reported Symptoms; TONI = Test of Nonverbal Intelligence; MSI = Multiphasic Sex Inventory; LSI = Level of Service Inventory; V-RAG = Violent Risk Assessment Guide.

intellectual assessment to the assessment of risk (see Table 22.4). Most typically, however, psychological testing in the prison system is done to assess personality characteristics (42%). A smaller percentage of testing time is spent on intellectual assessment (19%), the evaluation of risk (13%), and symptom assessment (12%). Very little time is devoted to neuropsychological assessment (5%) or behavioral analysis (3%).

Although psychologists reported using a variety of assessment instruments, most continue to rely on very few tests. As might be expected,

the Minnesota Multiphasic Personality Inventory (MMPI, MMPI-2) continues to be the most widely used psychological instrument in corrections. Approximately 87% of respondents reported using the MMPI in their clinical work with prisoners. It is probable that many psychologists in corrections do not administer instruments themselves, but rather, use psychological data gathered during the reception and classification process. The MMPI has long been a mainstay of the intake process. Other personality instruments cited by psychologists include the Millon Clinical Multiaxial Inventory (MCMI) (30%), Rorschach (20%), projective drawings

(14%), and the Personality Assessment Inventory (10%).

With respect to intellectual assessment, most correctional psychologists use the Wechsler Adult Intelligence Scale (WAIS) (69%). Of those performing neuropsychological evaluations, 23% reported using the Bender-Gestalt. Tests used less frequently by these psychologists included the Wechsler Memory Scale (8%), Trails A&B (6%), the Halstad Reitan (5%), and the Luria Nebraska (4%). Although 13% of respondents described involvement in the assessment of risk, few professionals reported the risk instruments they were using. Of the instruments reported, the Psychopathy Checklist-Revised (PCL-R) was most commonly indicated (11%). The Multiphasic Sex Inventory (MSI) was reported by 6% of respondents engaged in risk assessment, whereas the Level of Supervision Inventory (LSI) was cited by fewer than 1%. It seems that many correctional psychologists rely on instruments such as the MMPI regardless of the referral question.

PROFESSIONAL MEMBERSHIPS

To gauge their affiliation patterns, respondents were asked to report any national or state membership in psychological organizations. Approximately 43% were members of the American Psychological Association (APA). Membership in divisions of APA was also investigated, with specific attention directed to those divisions that involve some aspect of corrections (Division 18) or forensic issues (Division 41). Only 8% reported membership in an APA division, with 1% belonging to Division 18 and 3% belonging to Division 41. Similarly, few respondents (7%) belong to the American Association for Correctional Psychology, a group specifically devoted to the issues facing psychologists in corrections.

PRIOR EXPERIENCE AND TRAINING RECOMMENDATIONS

Approximately 37% of respondents reported some type of previous forensic or correctional experience prior to employment in corrections. This background differed significantly for those with master's degrees (27%) versus those with doctorate degrees (44%). Doctoral-level psychologists in federal versus state prisons also differed in prior experience. Approximately 63% of those working in federal prisons described some type of previous correctional or forensic experience compared to only 33% of those in state prisons. The majority of those reporting previous training had completed an internship (or rotation) (62%) or practicum (43%) in a correctional setting. Others described corrections-related experience in research (23%), coursework (36%), or independent study (16%).

We solicited opinions about training for those psychologists or graduate students interested in correctional work. Table 22.5 summarizes recommendations made by correctional psychologists currently working in this field. The most frequent preparation recommended for a career in correctional psychology was to undertake an internship or practicum in a prison facility. Many respondents indicated that such experience would not only give students a better idea of the job responsibilities and opportunities but would also clarify what it was like to work with inmates in a security-oriented facility. Other training recommendations frequently cited by respondents include gaining experience in psychological testing, training in the diagnosis and treatment of personality disorders, experience with issues specific to forensic psychology such as the evaluation of competency, and criminal justice or law-related coursework. Clinical skills such as interviewing and diagnosis were mentioned by practically all respondents; therefore, these items were not included in Table 22.5.

PREDICTIONS FOR THE FUTURE

Respondents were given the opportunity to make predictions about the future of correctional psychology as a career. Although it was clearly evident from reading survey responses to prior questions that these professionals viewed their jobs as important, interesting, and challenging, their predictions about the future were not nearly so optimistic. For example, many expressed concern that the number of available jobs will gradually decrease, despite the growing need for psychological services in corrections. Those with doctorate degrees feared

Table 22.5 Percentage of Correctional Psychologists Making Specific Training Recommendations

Training Recommendation	Percentage
Practicum or internship in a correctional setting	30
Training in personality disorders	21
Training in issues related to forensic psychology	13
Criminal justice or law-related coursework	12
Training in assessment	11
Training in the detection of malingering	10
Training in crisis intervention	8
Training in substance abuse evaluation and treatment	7

their positions would be lost to master's level professionals, whereas those with master's degrees expressed concern about losing their jobs to social workers. Many (15%) also reported a continuing trend toward administrative duties replacing treatment. It may be that correctional psychologists see their positions turning into managerial or administrative positions, leaving the less well-trained or paraprofessionals to deliver the majority of treatment. Some respondents (10%) predicted an increasing presence of managed care in corrections, and others (9%) indicated concerns about privatization.

DISCUSSION AND RECOMMENDATIONS

The authors were gratified by the impressive return rate (42%) for this project. This level of response can be attributed, in part, to the encouragement of chief psychologists and other administrators in prison systems across the United States. We speculate too that eagerness for professional interchange and information were motives for many respondents. Nearly 65% requested a summary of preliminary results. By contrast, correctional psychologists are not heavily involved in national psychology organizations. Beyond membership in the APA (46% of respondents), very few had joined either of

the potentially most relevant APA divisions, Psychologists in Public Service (Division 18) or the American Psychology-Law Society (AP-LS) (Division 41). Membership in the American Association for Correctional Psychology (AACP), an affiliate of the American Correctional Association, also was sparse, even though AACP is directly targeted at these professionals. Some respondents requested more information about these organizations, and AACP and AP-LS have recently announced a joint membership initiative to attract correctional psychologists.

A number of differences emerged between our results and those of previous surveys. Several similarities were also noted. In terms of sample size and characteristics, we reached more than 800 respondents, including 172 federal psychologists. Clearly, the number of psychologists employed in corrections has risen dramatically since the survey by Otero et al. (1981). At that time, an estimated 600 masters- and doctorate-level psychologists worked in corrections in the United States and Canada. In contrast, our estimates show that number to have jumped to approximately 2,000 in the United States alone. Even so, this growth rate has not kept pace with the more-than quadrupling of the number of offenders confined in correctional institutions. Interestingly, the demographics of psychologists working in corrections are largely comparable to those of psychologists working in other areas (Kohout & Wicherski, 1999). An exception is the smaller number of women employed by corrections as compared to other settings.

Despite the growth in absolute numbers of psychologists in corrections, the estimated psychologist-to-inmate ratio (1:750) appears to be approximately half that observed in the early 1980s. The still lower ratio of doctoral-level providers (1:2,000) is even more disturbing. Although the proportion of professional time devoted to treatment has remained steady over the past two decades, the actual amount of service delivered per inmate has obviously shrunk. Commentary supplied by many respondents indicated a growing concern, and potential ethical quandary, with the imbalance of limited resources and escalating demand/need for services. Most wanted to devote more time to intervention. It would not surprise us if some providers felt the frustration reflected in Rice and Harris' (1997) observation that, "the huge problems in changing institutional and bureaucratic routines make implementing (treatment) programs with high integrity extremely difficult" (p. 432).

At the same time, management roles, sometimes called the unseen career path (Kilburg, 1984), have increased since 1981. Today, correctional psychologists spend almost one third of their time in administrative tasks. Interestingly, more involvement in core management was one of the stated wishes of Otero's sample some 20 years ago (Otero, et al., 1981). In addition, staff training activities also occupy more time than previously reported. One could argue that these management and training roles serve to extend the impact of psychological perspectives, but a certain irreducible need for assessment and treatment services cannot be finessed by delegating to others or through administering programs. Reflecting this attitude, respondents with administrative duties would, on average, like to see such time cut almost in half. In addition, some psychologists in corrections would like more time to devote to research, an activity urged by a number of writers (e.g., Andrews & Bonta, 1998; Bartol, 1999). Our observation is that such aspirations are best realized through academic partnerships and system-wide mandates (and support) to conduct evaluation studies. Such conditions are enjoyed more noticeably by our colleagues in Canada (Motiuk, 1999).

Correctional psychologists appear more likely than psychologists in general to endorse cognitive and behavioral orientations as guides to treatment (Milan, Montgomery, & Rogers, 1994). Given the adaptability and relative success of these approaches with offenders (Clements, 1987; Gendreau, 1996b; Milan et al., 1999), this finding is encouraging. Among the psychological problems of inmates most commonly dealt with by survey respondents, depression was widely seen and treated, as were anger, anxiety and adjustment issues. All are amenable to cognitive-behavioral strategies.

Pressed for time and spread so thinly, correctional psychologists nevertheless remain dedicated to one-on-one treatment. Given the daunting number of offenders in need of treatment, the failure to shift toward a framework of group treatment seems like a potentially poor use of important resources. One recent survey of group therapy providers in corrections reports an estimated effectiveness rating of greater than 5 on a 7-point scale in such areas as anger and stress management, adjustment, and cognitive restructuring (Morgan, Winterowd, & Ferrel, 1999). These writers urge the development of treatment manuals and heightened attention to "what works" outcome studies. Though group-based treatments have not been directly tested against individual therapy, those methods finding the most empirical support, cognitive-behavioral interventions (Gendreau & Goggin, 1997), are quite adaptable to group delivery. Ready examples include the aggression replacement training (ART) model developed by Goldstein and colleagues (Goldstein & Glick, 1997; Rokach, 1987), as well as programs that focus on antisocial attitudes and other "criminogenic needs" (Andrews & Bonta, 1998). Based on shrinking staff resources, creative attempts to expand service capacity through group methods seem fully warranted.

Somewhat puzzling is the relative underemphasis on treating both serious mental illness and substance abuse. Given the growing proportion of mentally disordered offenders in prison—recently estimated at 16% (Bureau of Justice Statistics, 1999a)—it appears either that few resources are being directed toward these individuals or that psychologists are playing a relatively minor role. We know that in some jurisdictions, services for the severely mentally ill are provided under contract and/or within special settings. Perhaps those providers are underrepresented in this survey. By contrast, substance abuse treatment—itself a major thrust in many prisons (see Inciardi, 1993; Milan et al., 1999)—has historically been the purview of counselors and case workers. Nevertheless, in both of these areas, psychologists clearly have a stake in treatment planning, service delivery, supervision, and program evaluation. There is also a clear need to provide services to incarcerated women whose mental health and health problems are likely to be widespread and diverse (Acoca, 1998; Bureau of Justice Statistics, 1999a). Physical and sexual victimization, parental responsibilities, depression, and patterns of drug use often distinguish women offenders (Conley, 1998). The substantial increase in the number of aging prison inmates also presents a challenge and opportunity for psychologists and other health professionals.

We are also concerned about reported assessment practices. Popularity and tradition aside, one cannot argue that any test, even the revered MMPI—used by 87% of those involved in assessment—is generically applicable to all correctional issues. Increasingly though, for instruments like the MMPI-2 and MCMI, offender norms are available. We did not assess whether these norms were being regularly employed. By contrast, some newer instruments that reportedly aid in the assessment of risk and supervision needs were minimally used. For example, the PCL-R (Hare, 1991) was used by 11% of respondents who assessed offenders. The Level of Service Inventory-Revised (LSI-R) (Andrews & Bonta, 1995), widely used in Canada, is virtually absent in the United States. These observations are consistent with Gallagher et al. (1999), who report MMPI use at high rates during intake (65% of states) and even higher (96%) for pre-parole evaluations, a logical place for instruments such as the LSI-R. More surprisingly, projective tests (drawings, inkblots) were frequently used in both samples and enjoy an even heightened popularity in prerelease evaluations (Gallagher, et al., 1999).

Attracting, recruiting, and retaining qualified professional staff remains a challenge. Recruitment of minority psychologists is especially needed, given the disproportionate representation of African Americans in the U.S. prison population. Although pay scales are now reasonably competitive, training avenues remain limited. However, evidence of growth in the field of psychology and law, including interests and research in corrections, suggests an expanding pipeline of professionals (Bersoff et al., 1997). The doctoral programs that are available are being buttressed by an increasing number of accredited internships with a strong correctional or forensic focus. Several of these are located at correctional institutions and medical centers within the Federal Bureau of Prisons. These and similar state correctional and forensic settings partially address respondents' clear call for practicum and internship training. Assessment skills, personality disorder treatment competencies, and other forensic

knowledge are also seen as contributing to the correctional psychologist's role.

To these recommendations, we would add familiarity with newer instruments specifically relevant to offenders, knowledge of cognitive-behavioral (and social learning) treatment paradigms, an orientation to applying skills to the institutional milieu, and a commitment to outcomes assessment. These recommendations apply to master's level psychology staff as well. Corrections employs more master's than doctoral staff (though the Federal Bureau of Prisons and selected states more exclusively employ doctoral level, licensed psychologists), and their preparation to carry out important assessment and treatment functions should not be left to chance.

In some state institutions, psychologists function as sole practitioners. We suspect that professional isolation and burnout are possible consequences. In addition, the opportunity for supervision and consultation with regard to ethics, case management, or myriad other issues would seem to be sacrificed at these outposts. We recommend that regional systems of professional consultation be established, including, where necessary, employing part-time consultants to enrich the working environment. Indeed, part-time employment in corrections may be a viable model for some who wish to remain connected to community, academia, or mental health agency.

Although this study examines a cross-section of the current roles of correctional psychologists working in state and federal prisons, it does not address similar roles that are being filled by other professionals nor psychologists' presence and functions within the nation's jails, juvenile institutions, and youth detention centers. Our guess is that mental health professionals in these settings are even less well-connected to fellow professionals, especially if they work full-time in remote locations. The task of identifying psychologists who practice in the hundreds of local jails and juvenile facilities in the United States will present a challenge to understanding how their roles might diverge from their prison-based colleagues. As the field of correctional psychology continues to expand, such surveys might enlighten both the profession and future practitioners.

23

OFFENDER REHABILITATION

What We Know and What Needs to Be Done

PAUL GENDREAU

The opportunity to prepare this article made me appreciate how far we have come in such a relatively short period of time regarding our knowledge about rehabilitation programs for offenders. Let me put this remark in context. I began working as a psychological intern in Canada's largest prison, Kingston Penitentiary, in 1961. It was considered, at the time, to be the flagship institution for offender treatment. The inmate count was just over 1,000; the majority of them were serious, chronic offenders. The treatment professionals consisted of a psychiatrist and his nurse, two M.A.-level psychologists, and several classification officers, most of whom did not have university training.

Program decisions were based on psychiatric interviews, social history reports, and psychological tests (e.g., MMPI, Rorschach). Treatment consisted of individual counseling and occasional group work of an amorphous nature, menial work programs, and extensive use of medication and ECT for psychiatrically disturbed inmates.

My training was typical of the times. I had not taken courses on the theory and treatment of criminal behavior. There were none to be had, nor were there any North American university-based programs of which I was aware that specialized in correctional psychology. Guidelines for professional practice did not appear until much later (Brodsky, 1972).

What scant knowledge we had was picked up along the way. The sum of it was adaptations of Freudian concepts to offenders (Abrahamsen, 1960), reformulations of Sutherland's differential association theory into operant terms (Burgess & Akers, 1966), Cleckley's (1964) classic text on psychopaths, and a few MMPI studies on offenders by a pioneering North Carolina prison psychologist named James Panton.

Our knowledge base did not expand until later, with the publication of various psychological and sociological theories of crime (e.g., Eysenck, 1964; Hirschi, 1969) and new treatment approaches to offenders (Tharp & Wetzel, 1969). We had to wait for the next decade, when evaluations of offender treatments began

Editors' Note: This article was originally published in *Criminal Justice and Behavior*, Vol. 23, No. 1, March 1996, pp. 144-161.

to appear sporadically in the literature (Jessness, 1975 . . .). The first comprehensive reviews of the treatment literature emerged shortly thereafter . . .

Ironically, although there was a zeitgeist favorable to rehabilitation 30 years ago, there never was, despite the claims of rehabilitation skeptics, a halcyon era when offender treatment flourished in practice. Indeed, just when our knowledge base was expanding and treatment professionals were being attracted to the field, Martinson's (1974) famous edict of "nothing works" appeared and turned the corrections field upside down. The aforementioned cynics eagerly embraced "nothing works" to help justify abandoning rehabilitation and redirecting American correctional philosophy and practice to the new epoch of deterrence and "doing justice" (Cullen & Gendreau, 1989). As it turned out, the despairing fact is that deterrence policies, and to a lesser extent justice proscriptions (i.e., flat sentencing), now dominate the American criminal justice landscape. It is estimated that 4 million offenders will be imprisoned in the United States by the year 2000 (DiIulio, 1991). The recent "three strikes and out" federal legislation, which also has been adopted enthusiastically by many states . . . will probably maintain the U.S. lead in incarceration rates by fivefold over comparable Western democracies (see Shapiro, 1992). In addition, boot camps, electronic monitoring, drug testing, shock incarceration, and restitution are increasing exponentially (Cullen, Wright, & Applegate, 1996; Gendreau, 1996b).

Reality, however, sometimes can be deceiving. Despite the foregoing, evidence concerning effective treatment services for offenders has continued to accumulate at an impressive pace. This evidence is contained in a variety of literature reviews published since 1980 (Andrews & Bonta, 1994; . . . Ross, Antonowicz, & Dbaliwal, 1995; Ross & Fabiano, 1985; Ross & Gendreau, 1980; Van Voorhis, 1987; Whitehead & Lab, 1989).

Tempting though it may be to revisit the old battleground and chart the course of the "nothing works" debate over the ensuing years, for the sake of parsimony, let us return to the present and summarize the voluminous literature noted above. Given that quite a few of the following conclusions are based on meta-analyses of large

databases (Andrews, Zinger, et al., 1990; Gendreau, Little, & Goggin, 1995; Gottschalk et al., 1987; Lipsey, 1992), it is fair to conclude that we know the following with a reasonable degree of certainty.

WHAT WE KNOW

Effective Assessment Strategies

At first glance, it may seem a bit curious that a treatise on effective treatment begins by insisting that assessment issues are absolutely crucial to the delivery of effective treatment programs. From my experience in corrections, assessments are used most often for security re-classifications and parole assessments. Surveys of offender treatment programs have indicated that well-conceptualized actuarial assessments for the purposes of treatment rarely occur (Gendreau, Goggin, & Annis, 1990; Hoge, Leschied, & Andrews, 1993).

The field is indebted to Andrews and his colleagues (Andrews & Bonta, 1994; Andrews, Bonta, et al., 1990) for developing an elegant risk/need/responsivity theory that intimately links assessment and treatment, which, in turn, has profound implications for reducing recidivism. The risk and need components have the most significance for assessment. The risk principle states that offenders must be assessed thoroughly on a wide range of factors that are predictive of recidivism, because it is primarily those individuals who are defined as higher risk who will benefit from intensive treatment. Second, treatment must target a specific set of risks defined as criminogenic needs, for example, antisocial attitudes and behaviors regarding authority, interpersonal relationships, leisure activities, peers, substance abuse, and work. Because criminogenic needs are dynamic (i.e., open to change), they must necessarily serve as the targets for treatment.

The effectiveness of this theory is dependent on (a) whether the assessment literature is clear as to what risk factors are predictive of criminal behavior and (b) whether any measures have been developed that have demonstrated adequate predictive validity in this regard. Gendreau et al. (1995) conducted a meta-analysis of the adult offender recidivism literature to shed light on this question. Their findings supported some obvious facts (e.g., criminal history is a potent predictor of recidivism); however, equally potent predictors were criminogenic needs, which often have been ignored or derided in the criminological literature (Andrews & Wormith, 1989). Other marginally less robust predictors were various family factors (e.g., rearing practices) and indices of educational and employment achievement. Weak predictors were social class of origin, intellectual functioning, and personal distress (e.g., anxiety, low self-esteem). The relevance of this approximate ranking becomes self-evident upon examining treatment programs that have failed to reduce recidivism. These programs often have been ones that treated low-risk offenders and/or treated non-criminogenic needs such as personal distress (Andrews, Zinger, et al., 1990; Gendreau, 1996a).

In addition, some actuarial measures predicted recidivism better than others. Recommended for clinical use with adults are the Level of Supervision Inventory (Andrews & Bonta, 1994), which samples a wide range of criminogenic needs; the Wisconsin model (Baird, 1981; see update by Bonta, 1996); and measures of antisocial personality (e.g., Hare, 1991). Unfortunately, there is a paucity of data on prediction instruments for juveniles. The most promising measure identified by Gendreau et al. (1995) was a juvenile version of the Level of Supervision Inventory (Shields & Whitehall, 1994).

As a final comment, it is worth noting a striking correspondence between the predictors of adult criminal behavior and juvenile delinquency. The rankings of the predictors for adults and for juveniles (see the meta-analyses of Loeber & Stouthamer-Loeber, 1987; Simourd & Andrews, 1994) are virtually identical.

Effective Treatment Strategies

For most recent summaries of what is known as the "principles of effective intervention literature," the reader is directed to Andrews and Bonta (1994), Andrews, Zinger, et al. (1990), Gendreau (1996a, 1996b), and Gendreau et al. (1994). Before outlining the most important principles, let me provide you with the following demographics about the treatment literature. First, if one surveys all treatment studies having

control group comparisons, as Lipsey (1992) did in his truly impressive overview of 443 programs, 64% of the studies reported reductions in favor of the treatment group. The average reduction in recidivism was 10%. Second, when the results were categorized by the general type of the program (e.g., vocational), reductions in recidivism were as high as 18%.

However, one must go beyond superficial program labels and examine exactly what was accomplished in the name of treatment. In other words, it is necessary to look into the "black box" and sort out those characteristics that differentiate between programs that reduced recidivism and those that did not. When that was done, the results became even more impressive. Reductions in recidivism routinely ranged from 25% to 60%, with the greatest reductions found for community-based rather than prison programs (Andrews, Zinger, et al., 1990; Gendreau & Ross, 1981).

The following were the characteristics associated with those programs that successfully reduced recidivism:

1. The services were intensive, usually of a few months' duration, and were based on differential association and social learning conceptualizations of criminal behavior.

2. The programs were behavioral, primarily of the cognitive and modeling type, and targeted the criminogenic needs of high-risk offenders.

3. Programs adhered to the responsivity principle, that is, they were delivered in a manner that facilitated the learning of new prosocial skills by the offenders. An example of responsivity would be the placing of impulsive, aggressive offenders in a work-token economy program and with therapists who functioned best in a structured setting.

4. Program contingencies were enforced in a firm, fair manner, with positive reinforcers greater than punishers by at least 4:1.

5. Therapists related to offenders in interpersonally sensitive and constructive ways and were trained and supervised appropriately.

6. Program structure and activities reached out into the offenders' real-world social network and disrupted the delinquency network by placing offenders in situations (i.e., among people and in places) where prosocial activities predominated.

Programs that, almost invariably, did not reduce (and sometimes slightly increased) offender recidivism were:

1. Traditional psychodynamic and nondirective/client-centered therapies

2. Sociological strategies that were based on subcultural and labeling perspectives on crime

3. "Punishing smarter" programs or those that concentrated on punishments/sanctions, such as boot camps, drug testing, electronic monitoring, restitution, and shock incarceration

4. Any program, including behavioral ones, that targeted low-risk offenders or noncriminogenic needs or did not focus on the multiple causes of offending

Those readers who wish to review some of the exemplary programs that featured most of the principles of effectiveness can consult Ross and Gendreau (1980), which is an edited volume with commentary on the studies by the editors and updates of some of the original studies by the program designers themselves. Andrews, Zinger, et al. (1990) supplied the references to 35 program evaluations designated "appropriate correctional service." Thirty-three of the 35 programs reduced recidivism rates, and 20 of these lowered offender recidivism rates, by at least 25% compared to their control groups. Since then, reports of successful interventions continue to appear (e.g., Gordon, Graves, & Arbuthnot, 1995; Henggeler, Melton, Smith, Schoenwald, & Hanley, 1993 . . .).

In summary, we have come a long way since the early 1960s. There is no excuse for feigning ignorance about the what and how of offender assessments for the purposes of delivering effective treatment programs. Nor do we have an alibi for being unaware of the type of treatment programs that should be put in place. However, an issue we addressed several years ago (Gendreau & Ross, 1987) is still being ignored, that is, how do we live up to our claims that we are the "experimenting society" (cf. Campbell, 1969) and translate our behavioral technology so that it is readily available to academics and practitioners? The barriers are daunting in this regard. The next section attempts to define the

problems, suggest what needs to be done, and point to a few small victories along the way.

What Needs to Be Done

If the concept of the experimenting society is to prosper in the rehabilitation area, three major obstacles must be removed. These impediments are the theoreticism that exists at the scholarly and policy-making level, the failure to effect technology transfer from the "experts" to the practitioners, and the dearth of suitable training programs.

Theoreticism

The practice of theoreticism involves accepting or rejecting knowledge on the basis of one's personal values and experiences (Crews, 1986). Methods of inquiry that are based on positivism and inductive reasoning are disparaged. Theoreticism is a critical problem in the criminal justice field (Andrews & Bonta, 1994), where a bewildering array of disciplines (e.g., criminology, economics, law, management, psychiatry, psychology, social work, and sociology) and occupations (academics, administrators, clinicians, and the police) are competing in an unseemly fashion for the holy grail of intellectual hegemony (Gendreau & Ross, 1979). All types of theoreticism are susceptible to a profound anti-intellectualism that takes the form of a lack of interest and/or respect for other sources of knowledge. Theoreticism may be seen as operating in three ways. These are paradigm passion and ethnocentrism, knowledge destruction, and the "MBA management syndrome."

Paradigm passion and ethnocentrism. Paradigm passion refers to the realities of our world of work, which can be quite circumscribed. First, our graduate training, by necessity, is narrowly focused. Most of us associate intimately with very few colleagues, who are mainly from the same specialty area and in agreement on various professional matters. Moreover, the mandates of our work settings often impose filters on our professional outlook. Reinforcement is rarely forthcoming for embracing ideas and activities that are in opposition or orthogonal to the accepted ways we view issues in our field of expertise. Ethnocentrism evolves out of paradigm passion. Once it is taken for granted that our disciplinary boundaries and the sociopolitical context we live in adequately define how things should be, then it is a small step to tacitly assume our reality is superior to others'.

The following are examples of paradigm passion that I have experienced in my own profession. Often I have heard psychologists express puzzlement as to why one would read sociological journals and be aware of sociological theory, thereby disregarding the fact that some sociological theories—such as differential association and social control—have major implications for the delivery of effective treatment services (Andrews & Bonta, 1994). Other theories are being revised in light of the offender treatment literature (Agnew, 1992).

As a result of reviewing some of the evidence that contributed to the American Psychological Association's Commission on Violence and Youth, I was struck by the fact that psychologists dealing with juvenile offenders disregarded the supporting literature emanating from the adult domain. In preparing the present article, I examined several reviews of the juvenile offender treatment literature and further confirmed the above observation. Similarly, drug abuse treatment evaluators have been, with few exceptions, oblivious to the corrections literature (Gendreau, 1995). All of this is unfortunate, given that the predictors of antisocial behavior and the principles of effective treatment for juvenile and adult offenders correspond highly (Andrews, Zinger, et al., 1990; Gendreau et al., 1995) and that it is almost impossible to distinguish between the clientele served by the criminal justice and drug substance abuse systems (Gendreau, 1995).

These examples also may be seen as evidence of a subtle form of ethnocentrism. More blatant examples of ethnocentrism are the fact that American reviews on treatment effectiveness almost never reference the literature from foreign countries where different approaches to the "crime problem" exist (e.g., less incarceration). Regrettably, there have been occasions where foreign contributions were dismissively referenced in order to support current policies—in this case, punishment rather than rehabilitation (Logan et al., 1991).

Paradigm passion and ethnocentrism can lead to anti-intellectual consequences of staggering proportions. As noted previously, one of the principal, ineffective strategies were punishing-smarter programs. One would think that program designers and evaluators in this area would pay some attention to these findings, and particularly to the vast experimental and human behavior modification literature on punishment and the social psychological research on persuasion and coercion, which provide a convincing rationale as to why punishing-smarter programs would not work (Gendreau, 1996a). I counted about 30,000 references on these latter two topics. Just two of these references were cited in the entire punishing-smarter literature.

Knowledge destruction. Knowledge destruction is a deliberate and conscious attempt to ignore or dismiss competing findings. This has been a longstanding problem in the offender prediction and treatment literature (see the classic review by Andrews & Wormith, 1989), because the underlying support for prediction and treatment initiatives arises more from psychobiological conceptualizations of behavior rather than from the social structure perspectives favored by the disciplines of sociology and criminology. The former has been ridiculed on moral and professional grounds. Some academics (e.g., Gibbons, 1986) have claimed that psychobiological perspectives can lead only to repression and terror; at the professional level, Hirschi and Hindelang (1977) remarked that the protection of the profession of sociology from these alternative viewpoints was the primary motive.

A number of arguments have been generated by knowledge destruction proponents to support anti-prediction and treatment views (Andrews & Bonta, 1994). There are two types of arguments in this regard (Gendreau, 1995). Methodological knowledge destruction arguments claim any study in question (a) relied on imperfect theory, (b) could not rule out all other explanations for the results found, (c) had possible errors in measurement, and (d) reported effects that either were not large enough or were due to statistical gymnastics. The second type of argument is more philosophical in nature. Three of these are: (a) social problems are intractable, and to think that the rehabilitation agenda can address them successfully is to live in a chimerical and utopian world; (b) treatment involves a monopoly of values and requires more control than absolute freedom; and (c) the results found today regarding treatment effectiveness will be irrelevant in the future because of changes in the social context. Obviously, no study can escape the above critiques unscathed. Knowledge destruction wins out every time.

The MBA management syndrome. A final form of theoreticism can be called the MBA management syndrome in criminal justice. Over the years, the criminal justice system has witnessed a new generation of high-level corrections administrators who are generalists with little or no training in the helping professions and certainly not in the prediction and treatment of criminal behavior (Gendreau, 1995; Hamm & Schrink, 1989). The primary qualification nowadays, it seems, is having some general experience as a manager. It also helps to be a political appointee. Even if a few of the new breed of administrators are well-versed in correctional issues, they rarely stay in the job for long. The "nothing works" credo has also encouraged the MBA management syndrome. Struckhoff (1978) was prescient when he predicted that, in the face of "nothing works," correctional systems without well-trained professionals would become basically fraudulent. With the demise of rehabilitation, all the system requires is content-free administrators who will bend to the political winds of the time and embrace the latest panacea. In fact, "panaceaphilia" has been endemic to corrections for years (cf. Gendreau & Ross, 1979), with the current panacea being that of punishing smarter, which has been embraced eagerly by many corrections officials (Leschied & Andrews, 1993).

Although theoreticism, in all its forms, seems to be a highly resistant virus to the goal of becoming the experimenting society, remedial action may be forthcoming from what, at face value, appear to be two more barriers.

Technology Transfer

Technology transfer means getting the necessary information into the hands of those who need it. Sadly, such information is not getting into the hands of practitioners. There are some despairing data in this regard. As a result of my fortuitous contact with the National Institute of Drug Abuse, which, for obvious reasons, is vitally concerned with technology transfer (Backer, David, & Soucy, 1995), I have learned that many substance abuse practitioners' clinical decisions are never based on reading professional periodicals. If practitioners do receive information that changes their approach to treatment, it tends to be from workshops; even then, it is a relatively small percentage who profit.

Nevertheless, there is room for hope. A few measures and intervention strategies are now available for programmers, trainers, and policymakers to better effect technology transfer (Backer et al., 1995; Backer, Liberman, & Kuehnel, 1986). As a case in point, Andrews and I have been involved in technology transfer at the organizational and practitioner levels, in prison, parole, community corrections, and police settings. In 1979, we reported on our first 19 attempts at technology transfer (Gendreau & Andrews, 1979), and presently we have 65 case studies in our files. The following guidelines are based on our retrospective and subjective judgments of the conditions associated with our successful attempts at technology transfer. Success, which we defined as having a new program still in operation 2 years after our technology transfer intervention, occurred when (a) we were action-oriented and worked "hands on" with staff until they felt secure enough to take over; (b) the agency had a senior administrator who championed the new initiatives (if not, we identified such a person and cultivated his/her interest); (c) we ensured that the sociopolitical and program values of the agency and ourselves as change agents were congruent; and (d) the new initiatives were cost-effective and sustainable.

The above activities, however, are not enough. The opportunity to directly bring about changes in service delivery demands that the knowledge has to be made accessible in the first place. The only means of which I am aware to accomplish this is to be involved in the grinding, exhausting work of providing numerous workshops, presenting at nonacademic conferences, encouraging responsible media coverage (and appearing in the media), publishing in newsletters, and using professional associations to lobby for changes with government bureaucracies, private sector organizations, and the political body. One would like to think that some of the major proposed revisions to some Canadian criminal justice legislation (cf. Leschied & Gendreau, 1994), as well as the fact that the rehabilitative ideal has flourished in some of the provinces, are to a significant degree due to the collective effort of several psychologists who have undertaken these activities.

Training

There are precious few training programs for people interested in offender treatment. None of the national-level training institutes in the United States specializes in treatment, although they occasionally contract out to experts in the area. There are no training institutes of this kind in Canada. There are several academic-based training programs in the field of law and psychology in the United States (Melton, 1987), but when I consulted the 1994 American Psychological Association graduate training guide, I could identify only two or three possibilities for extensive training in corrections clinical work.

Certainly, it does not take much in the way of training programs to have an impact. Just one program and/or the work of two or three individuals can have a meaningful effect. . . .

***

Unquestionably, the quality of offender service delivery systems will improve as a result of investing in training programs. Although it is discouraging to note that only 10% of more than 200 treatment programs we have surveyed to date (Gendreau et al., 1990; Hoge et al., 1993) were offering a level of service that was defined as adequate on the basis of a standardized, objective measure of program quality (Gendreau & Andrews, 1994), I am always heartened by the fact that most service providers are keen on upgrading their clinical skills. We must give them every opportunity to do so. Another long-term benefit of pursuing a vigorous training agenda will be, it is hoped, to produce a little more respect among scholars for evidence (collected from diverse disciplines) and better-informed administrators.

CONCLUSION

In conclusion, impressive gains have been made in the last two decades regarding our knowledge about "what works" in offender rehabilitation. On the other hand, there is the sobering reality that far too little of this knowledge is being used by practitioners, scholars, and policymakers. The major impediments in this regard—theoreticism, failure to effect technology transfer, and the shortage of appropriate training programs—are not easily overcome. In addition, in the United States at least, the arguments for more and more punishment of offenders . . . dwarf the rehabilitation agenda. The remedies suggested in this article are far from original, and they are partial solutions at best. Nevertheless, one hopes that the evidence mustered here in support of rehabilitation provides succor to those scholars, clinicians, and policymakers who respect evidence and want to advance effective services for offenders in need.

24

INVOLUNTARY TREATMENT WITHIN A PRISON SETTING

Impact on Psychosocial Change During Treatment

MICHAEL L. PRENDERGAST

DAVID FARABEE

JEROME CARTIER

SUSAN HENKIN

The number of drug abusers within the criminal justice system has increased significantly over the past 15 years (Dorsey & Zawitz, 2000). According to various estimates, the criminal justice system is responsible for 40% to 50% of referrals to community-based treatment programs (Maxwell, 1996; Price & D'Aunno, 1992; Weisner, 1987). Moreover, during 1997, approximately one third of state prison inmates and one quarter of federal prison inmates reported participation in some form of substance abuse treatment since admission (Bureau of Justice Statistics, 1999c). Given the high proportion of criminal justice treatment clients in the United States, a major policy and program issue in drug treatment is the appropriateness and effectiveness of coercing offenders to enter and remain in treatment.

Coercive treatment approaches for drug addiction have been used throughout the 20th century, beginning with the morphine maintenance clinics that operated in some cities in the early 1920s until they were shut down by the Treasury Department. Beginning in the 1930s, many of the nation's opiate addicts spent time at the federal narcotics treatment facilities operated by the Public Health Service in Lexington, Kentucky, and Fort Worth, Texas. During the 1960s, broad-based civil commitment procedures to treatment for all types of addicts were implemented in the federal system as well as in New York and California. The system of treating substance-abusing offenders today relies less on formal civil commitment procedures and instead emphasizes community-based treatment as an alternative to incarceration or as a condition of probation or parole. Treatment programs provided to substance-abusing inmates also rely on coercion. The following is a brief review of coerced treatment studies in the United States;

more comprehensive historical reviews of coerced treatment can be found elsewhere (Anglin & Hser, 1991; Inciardi, 1988; Musto, 1987).

There have been several reviews of research on coerced treatment (Anglin & Hser, 1990, 1991; Farabee, Prendergast, & Anglin, 1998; Miller & Flaherty, 2000 . . .). Farabee et al. (1998) summarized the findings of studies of coerced treatment and provided a critique of the methodological and conceptual gaps in the literature. The authors identified 11 published studies of coerced treatment (10 focused on illicit drugs and 1 on alcohol) published between 1976 and 1996 and covering a variety of treatment settings. In 5 of the studies, clients under criminal justice referral or pressure had better outcomes than clients who were under no legal pressure or who entered treatment voluntarily; in 4 studies, outcomes of the two groups did not differ; and in 2 studies, coerced clients had poorer outcomes than voluntary clients. Overall, the evidence supports the claim that coerced clients do at least as well as voluntary clients (or clients under low levels of legal pressure). But the authors also observed that a number of features in the literature on coerced treatment should lead to caution in interpreting the results and in applying them in real-world settings. Numerous conceptual issues need to be addressed to design meaningful empirical studies or to interpret existing studies appropriately. Three issues of particular importance are the terminology used to characterize coerced treatment, the interaction of coercion (external pressure) and motivation (internal pressure), and the lack of studies of coerced treatment in prison-based treatment programs.

INCONSISTENT TERMINOLOGY

Authors use a variety of terms to describe the process by which offenders with drug abuse problems are pressured or forced into treatment by some agency of the criminal justice system. (The situation is further complicated by studies of pressure from employers, welfare agencies, and families, but these sources of pressure are not considered here.) The terms coerced, compulsory, mandated, involuntary, legal pressure, and criminal justice referral are all used in the literature. Sometimes, these terms are used interchangeably within the same article. . . . Our intention in this article is not to resolve this terminological ambiguity but to use a standard set of terms in discussing the design and findings of the analysis. Hence, we define coercion in the realm of criminal justice substance abuse treatment as correctional policies in which inmates are identified and referred to a treatment program without regard for the wishes of the inmates. Those inmates who enter treatment in this manner are called involuntary participants; those inmates who agree to enter treatment are called voluntary.

MOTIVATION FOR TREATMENT

A further complication is client perception of the conditions of referral to treatment. In psychiatric populations, many patients report having entered treatment voluntarily when in fact they were under court mandate (Gilboy & Schmidt, 1971; Hoge et al., 1997). Conversely, in another study, about 50% of patients who were admitted to psychiatric treatment under involuntary conditions reported that they would have entered voluntarily if given a choice (Toews, el-Guebaly, Leckie, & Harper, 1984). None of the studies reviewed by Farabee and colleagues (1998) included a measure of the internal motivation of clients at admission. Neither did any of the studies examine changes in motivation over time. (A recent study by Knight, Hiller, Broome, and Simpson, 2000, did examine the combined impact of legal pressure and motivation—defined as treatment readiness—and found them to be independent predictors of retention.) Motivation is not a static condition; it changes in response to both internal and external events (Miller, 1985). One clinical argument for coerced treatment is that it keeps clients in treatment long enough for them to become engaged in the treatment process and for their motivation to shift from resistance to commitment (e.g., Brecht, Anglin, & Wang, 1993; De Leon, 1988). It may also be the case that offenders who want treatment and would seek it voluntarily resent being forced into a particular program. Their resentment may lead to recalcitrance and undermine their initial desire to enter treatment.

***

COERCION IN PRISON TREATMENT

Although a number of evaluations of prison-based substance abuse treatment programs have been published, all of the programs evaluated involved voluntary clients as subjects (Inciardi, Martin, Butzin, Hooper, & Harrison, 1997; Knight, Simpson, Chatham, & Camacho, 1997 . . .). That is, despite the generally coercive environment of the prison, in such research studies, inmates with substance abuse problems are informed of the availability of treatment and decide whether to participate in it (as well as whether to participate in the research study of the treatment). In recent years, some states have initiated prison-based treatment programs in which inmates are identified as needing substance abuse treatment and are then mandated to participate in the program. Notable among these are the substance abuse programs currently operating in 17 of the 33 state prisons of the California Department of Corrections.

The outcomes of these involuntary prison treatment programs may not be similar to the outcomes found in the community-based treatments summarized earlier or to the outcomes of the voluntary prison-based programs. Entering treatment under coerced conditions in prison is not the same procedurally or psychologically as entering a community treatment program. In prison, there is less concern for procedural justice, in that inmates may be given little or no information about why they are being sent to treatment or what the treatment entails, much less given the opportunity to choose an alternative, however unattractive (i.e., remaining in the general prison population). In addition, upon being sent to treatment, inmates may lose privileges and preferred living conditions, which only adds to the resentment of being forced into treatment. It is also often much more difficult to drop out of (or be discharged from) a prison-based program than a community-based program. One may be skeptical about the effectiveness of coerced treatment in prison settings based solely on findings from community-based programs that accept court-referred clients. Unlike many in-prison treatment inmates, [court-referred clients] are informed about their treatment options, have some degree of choice in the decision, and may receive some benefit from selecting treatment (e.g., a place to stay).

In summary, the studies reviewed by Farabee and colleagues (1998) apply only to treatment provided within community-based settings, not prison-based treatment. In addition, all published studies of prison-based treatment are based on subjects who have volunteered for treatment. Thus, it is by no means clear that findings on coerced treatment conducted in community programs or prisons can be generalized to prison-based treatment in which many or most of the clients are mandated to treatment.

This article attempts to address the following question: What is the impact of involuntary (compared with voluntary) admission to a prison-based substance abuse treatment program on psychosocial changes measured during treatment participation?

DESCRIPTION OF THE CALIFORNIA SUBSTANCE ABUSE TREATMENT FACILITY

The California Substance Abuse Treatment Facility (SATF) and State Prison at Corcoran, which opened in September 1997, has a total housing capacity of 6,013. The two self-contained substance abuse treatment units at the institution were specifically designed to provide housing and residential treatment for 1,056 minimum (Level I) and moderate (Level II) security risk offenders (1,478 with 40% overcrowding). The California Department of Corrections is responsible for custodial operations at the facility, and treatment services are provided under contract with two California treatment organizations (Phoenix House and Walden House).

The admission criteria for a classification assignment to treatment at SATF, which need to be considered in interpreting some of the findings of this study, are as follows:

- A history of drug and/or alcohol abuse: the history can be established through either self-report or review of documents such as probation reports, criminal history, or reports of in-custody behaviors
- An offender classification score between 0 and 27 (Level I and II inmates within the California correctional system)
- No less than 6 months and no more than 18 months left to serve at the time of the

classification committee review for placement at the SATF

- No placement in a secured housing unit during the past year for violence or weapons charges
- Not a member of a prison gang
- No active or potential felony or U.S. Immigration and Naturalization Service holds, which could possibly lengthen the inmate's sentence or result in his deportation

The SATF treatment program involves a residential in-prison phase followed by a voluntary community treatment phase. Aside from some minor differences, both the Walden House and Phoenix House programs adhere to the basic therapeutic community philosophy and structure. The in-prison treatment lasts from 6 to 18 months based on the aforementioned criteria. The inmate's length of time to serve at the time of the program admission classification hearing determines the actual length of time in treatment for any single inmate. Programs are highly structured and include a minimum of 20 hours per week of substance abuse treatment as well as 10 or more hours of structured optional activities. In the second year of operation—to address program instability caused by the constant inflow of new, involuntary, and resistant inmates into the general treatment population—Walden House and Phoenix House implemented induction units. [There] newly admitted inmates to SATF receive an intensive (7.5 hours a day) orientation to the program for up to 1 month.

The therapeutic community model of treatment used at SATF regards substance abuse as a disorder of the whole person. Rather than being construed as a disease in itself, drug dependence is perceived as a symptom of a larger disorder that affects the person's values, cognition, social skills, and general behavior. A therapeutic community provides a total environment in which transformations in drug users' conduct, attitudes, and emotions are fostered, monitored, and mutually reinforced by the daily regimen. The thrust of treatment is not to change the inmate's addictive behavior as such but to change the inmate (for a detailed discussion of the therapeutic philosophy and processes, see De Leon, 2000).

As part of a comprehensive evaluation of the SATF program, we are conducting an outcome study of the during- and post-treatment performance of inmates who have participated in treatment at SATF. The present analysis is based on data collected at baseline and just prior to release to parole. The following sections describe the study design, including subject selection, instruments, and assessment schedule, and our analytic approach to addressing the relationships among coercion, motivation, and outcomes.

METHOD

Study Design and Participants

Between June 1999 and February 2000, extensive baseline, prerelease, and post-treatment interviews (using an instrument adapted from one developed by the Institute of Behavioral Research at Texas Christian University) were conducted with 404 newly admitted SATF treatment inmates as well as a non-treatment sample. . . . Interviewers solicited study participation from SATF inmates within the first 10 days of their arrival in the program. The 404 SATF inmates in the total treatment sample represent 92.4% of the 437 inmates approached. The data for this analysis were derived from participants on whom the included measures had been collected at two points in time. The subjects used in this analysis were not a random sample of the full treatment sample of the SATF outcome study but were those for whom information on admission status was available and who completed the Self-Rating Form at baseline and prerelease.

The baseline interview form was administered as a face-to-face interview within the first 10 days of admission. This waiting period allows the inmate to acclimate to his new environment and focus on the issues that brought him there. The interview instrument is comprehensive and includes sections on sociodemographic background, family and peer relations, health and psychological status, criminal involvement, in-depth drug use history, an AIDS risk assessment, and motivation for treatment. Of particular relevance to this analysis is the inclusion in the interview of selected items from the Self-Rating Form (Simpson & Knight, 1998), which assesses the participant's psychological functioning in five domains (self-esteem, depression, anxiety, decision making, and self-efficacy) and social functioning in three domains (hostility, risk taking, and social conformity). The Self-Rating Form was administered on two occasions: at baseline (shortly after inmates entered the program) and just before their release to parole. The time between administrations of the Self-Rating Form varied from participant to participant but averaged about 8 months.

Admission status was determined from a separate questionnaire administered by Walden House as part of its intake process. The instrument was administered about 2 weeks after admission while clients were participating in the induction unit. The question was "When you first arrived on the unit, had you volunteered to be here?" The possible responses were not at all, slightly, moderately, considerably, and extremely. Because only Walden House asked this question, the present analysis is limited to those subjects in the outcome study who were enrolled in the Walden House program at SATF.

Dependent Variables

The dependent or outcomes variables examined were the eight domains included on the Self-Rating Form (as described earlier). Two additional outcome variables were discharge status (whether the inmate paroled from the program or was discharged from the program before parole) and aftercare referral (whether the inmate agreed to enter a community-based program following release to parole).

Independent Variables

The main independent variable of interest was admission status. Subjects who responded *not at all* or *slightly* to the aforementioned Walden House question about volunteering for treatment were defined as *involuntary* participants ($n = 40$), and those who responded *considerably* or *extremely* were defined as *voluntary* ($n = 60$). Subjects who responded *moderately* ($n = 7$) were not included in the analysis.

How an inmate entered the program is not the same as whether he believed that he had a substance abuse problem or whether he was motivated to receive treatment. Thus, we used the following three measures of motivation from the baseline instrument in which the responses consisted of a 5-point scale ranging from 0 (*disagree strongly*) to 4 (*agree strongly*):

- "You believe your drug or alcohol use is a serious problem" (alcohol and other drug problem recognition).
- "You believe you don't need treatment. You can stop using if you want" (desire for help).
- "You believe you would like to receive drug/alcohol treatment while in prison" (readiness for treatment).

Finally, we included a number of demographic and background variables to characterize the sample and to control for possible differences between the voluntary and involuntary groups. Continuous variables were current age, years of education, lifetime arrests, lifetime incarceration (months), and time in program (months). Categorical variables were ethnicity, marital status, employment in the 6 months before prison, non-prison-gang membership, sex offense history, any illicit drug use during the past 6 months, prior participation in treatment, and prior participation in self-help groups.

***

Results

According to the voluntary-status question described earlier, 60% of the study subjects were categorized as involuntary admissions. . . . [T]he only demographic and background characteristics on which the voluntary and involuntary groups differed significantly were education and readiness for treatment. The voluntary group had completed nearly 12 years of schooling, whereas the involuntary group had completed nearly 11 years. With regard to motivation, inmates in the voluntary group were more likely than those in the involuntary group to state that they would like to receive drug/alcohol treatment while in prison, although the actual difference in level of response was not significant. Both groups were about equally likely to indicate that they had a serious drug or alcohol problem. They also tended to disagree to the same extent about needing treatment (desire for help). In short, the fact that inmates in the involuntary group were forced into treatment did not mean that they were markedly different in their acknowledgment of drug problems or their general motivation for treatment relative to those inmates who had volunteered for treatment.

On the self-rating scales of psychological functioning (self-esteem, depression, anxiety, decision making, and self-efficacy) and social functioning (hostility, risk taking, and social conformity), both groups exhibited change (in the expected direction) on most of the scales from baseline assessment (soon after entry to the program) to prerelease assessment (just prior to release to parole). . . . Significant change . . . , however, was more likely to occur for the psychological functioning measures than for the social functioning measures. Among the voluntary group, four of the five psychological functioning measures showed significant change, whereas none of the results from the three social functioning measures were significant. Inmates in the involuntary group showed significant change on all but one of the psychological measures and on one of the social measures. Furthermore, although all but one of the measures on the magnitude of the change score were greater for the involuntary than for the voluntary group, a two-way ANOVA of time by group did not show any significant group effects. With respect to the other two outcome variables, 47.5% of the voluntary group were successfully paroled compared with 56.7% of the involuntary group, and 76.3% of the voluntary group were referred to aftercare compared with 71% of the involuntary group. Neither of these outcomes differed significantly by group.

DISCUSSION

This examination of coerced treatment differs from previous studies of the issue in several ways. First, the treatment occurred in a prison rather than in the community. More important, the nature of coercion in this prison setting differed from that which typically occurs in community-based criminal justice treatment programs. Many inmates were provided with little or no information about the treatment they were being forced into, and they had no real choice in what was an administrative decision (e.g., unlike in drug courts, where the defendant can choose between jail or treatment). Also unlike previous studies, we included measures of motivation to try to separate the formal referral to treatment from perceptions of treatment need and desire for treatment. Finally, whereas the outcomes of previous studies were usually measures of drug use and/or crime at some point following treatment, this study included more proximal self-report measures of changes in psychological and social functioning over the course of treatment.

The main finding from the study was that inmates, regardless of voluntary or involuntary admission status, exhibited significant change on most of the scales of the Self-Rating Form, although significant change was more likely on measures of psychological than on social functioning. . . . Neither were significant group differences found for the other two outcome variables (parole from program and referral to aftercare). As noted in the Results section, similar percentages of both groups (a) were paroled from treatment (as opposed to being discharged from the program prior to parole) and (b) agreed to attend community treatment. In short, for the outcome measures used in this study, it did not seem to matter whether an inmate entered treatment under voluntary or involuntary conditions. This finding is in agreement with most previous studies of coercion in criminal justice treatment, albeit in a different setting and with a different type of coercion.

Another finding of this study was that an involuntary referral status did not mean an absence of motivation for treatment on the part of the inmate. At admission to treatment, involuntary inmates were just as likely as voluntary inmates to agree that they had an alcohol/drug problem and to express a desire for help. On the measure of readiness for treatment, although the involuntary inmates scored significantly lower than the voluntary inmates, they were more likely than not to express a desire to receive treatment in prison despite the coercive manner in which they entered treatment. It should be noted, however, that although involuntary inmates might have wanted to receive treatment while in prison, they may still have objected strongly to how they arrived at the SATF program. The measures of motivation were not sensitive enough to capture their attitudes and perceptions of the coercive manner of their admission to treatment.

The findings need to be interpreted in light of several features of the study design and measurement issues. The number of subjects available for analysis was small, which could have prevented us from detecting small differences between the groups. Still, it is doubtful that small differences in outcomes between involuntary and voluntary treatment participants, even if significant, would have practical implications for policy and programming purposes.

Another limitation was that the question about admission status (voluntary or involuntary) was based on self-report and asked whether the person had volunteered to be in the program, measured on a 5-point scale from *not at all* to *extremely*. A better measure of admission status would have been to rely on official institutional records, but for the sample used in this analysis, this information was not available.

The measures of motivation on the baseline interview (problem recognition, desire for help, and readiness for treatment) were each based on a single question. Using multiple questions (statements) resulting in a scaled score would likely result in a more reliable assessment of these different dimensions of motivation. Also, in addition to the more generic measures of motivation, it would have been desirable to include measures of perceived coercion and feelings about involuntary referral to treatment.

At the time of this analysis, the 12-month follow-up interviews were being conducted, and thus, the impact of coercion on post-treatment outcomes could not be determined. Although it might be argued that the main outcomes of interest are those related to drug use and crime after the person has left treatment, such outcomes are partly mediated by changes that occur during treatment. If during-treatment change cannot be demonstrated, then it is unlikely that post-treatment change will occur. Still, the question remains as to whether the comparable performance of voluntary and involuntary inmates found in this study will in fact

hold up at the 12-month follow-up in regard to drug use and crime as well as other psychosocial behaviors. We plan to repeat this analysis once the follow-up data are available.

Finally, as stated previously, the subjects used in this analysis were not a random sample of the full treatment sample of the SATF outcome study but rather were those for whom information on admission status was available and who completed the Self-Rating Form at baseline and prerelease. Thus, the findings may not be generalizable to the full SATF study sample or to other prison treatment programs with different treatment participant characteristics.

CONCLUSION

One of the strongest predictors of successful treatment is retention—length of time spent in treatment (Hubbard et al., 1989; Simpson, Joe, & Brown, 1997; Simpson & Sells, 1982). Thus, whatever increases retention is likely, although not certain, to improve treatment outcomes. External pressure—typically from the criminal justice system but also from an employer or a family member—is likely to keep people in treatment longer than if they did not have such pressure. In particular, for drug-involved offenders, the various types of legal pressures and sanctions available to the criminal justice system can be used to "force" people into treatment and to keep them in treatment. But the effectiveness of such coercive approaches largely depends on how they are designed and implemented. . . .

Although this study found that both voluntary and involuntary admissions to a prison-based treatment program exhibited equivalent outcomes (at least when measured near the end of prison treatment), it should be emphasized that coercion per se does not lead to successful treatment. Coercion can get drug-using offenders into treatment and keep them there for a relatively long period of time. However, it is not the external pressure itself that brings about commitment to change and recovery but, rather, changes in internal pressure or motivation and in thinking, behaviors, and emotions that come from engagement in a therapeutic process. Involuntary clients change not because they are coerced into treatment but because as a result of coercion they remain in treatment long enough to become engaged in various treatment activities that help facilitate change.

Accepting the findings of this and other studies on coerced treatment, it remains true that not everybody coerced into treatment does well (any more than everybody who volunteers for treatment does well). A certain percentage of coerced clients not only shows little or no improvement, but while in treatment they are often recalcitrant, hostile, and disruptive—in general, they can make life difficult for the other clients and the counseling staff. They consume a disproportionate amount of time and resources, and their behavior may reduce the impact of the program on other clients. "Coerced treatment works" should not be an excuse for imposing unrealistic expectations on providers. If a criminal justice agency decides to implement a treatment program that includes mandating offenders into treatment, there should be some provision for discharging clients who, after a reasonable period in the program and upon agreement by both treatment and correctional staff, disrupt treatment activities to the point of interfering with the progress or safety of others.

Treatment providers, particularly those with a large percentage of coerced clients, should not assume that they can necessarily rely on their usual treatment methods and techniques. To maintain their historical level of success and to minimize the disruption of treatment, providers will likely need to modify their program to take into account the high levels of resistance of many coerced clients. These modifications could include special orientation units or motivational techniques (Farabee, Simpson, Dansereau, & Knight, 1995; Miller & Rollnick, 1991). In addition, the treatment programs and the criminal justice agencies with which they are associated should try to identify and eliminate (or at least mitigate) disincentives to treatment participation and engagement. In other terms, treatment should not be more punitive than normal prison time.

In summary, the findings from this analysis of data from a prison-based substance abuse treatment program, in combination with other studies on coerced treatment, should allay some of the concerns of those who ask whether treatment works for drug-using inmates who enter treatment involuntarily. A number of questions remain to be answered in future research, however. Do voluntary and involuntary participants in prison-based treatment do equally well when assessed 12 months following treatment, after the sanctions associated with coercion have been lifted? What is the impact of large numbers of involuntary participants on the day-to-day activities of treatment programs and on the clinical progress of other clients? Using more refined measures than were included in this analysis, in what ways do motivation and perceptions about coercion interact with formal admission status to influence outcomes? Beyond these empirical questions regarding coerced treatment, policy makers and treatment providers need to address ethical and procedural issues involved in coercing offenders into treatment. These would include attention to ensuring that due process is followed, that offenders are provided with adequate information about treatment and any options they may have, that the treatment modality to which the offender is mandated is appropriate to his or her needs, and that voluntary clients have priority for treatment slots over involuntary clients.

25

MULTISYSTEMIC THERAPY FOR ANTISOCIAL JUVENILES

Suggestions for Improvement

WILLEM H. J. MARTENS

M ultisystemic therapy (MST) is an intensive family- and community-based treatment that was developed in the late 1970s to address the mental health needs of youth who were seriously antisocial . . . and their families (Letourneau, Cunningham, & Henggeler, 2002). . . . It is based on a theory of human behavior (i.e., social ecological theory) that is strongly supported by the extant literature. Social ecological theory views individuals as nested within increasingly complex systems. Thus, problem behavior is maintained by problematic interactions within and across the multiple systems in which the child is embedded (Letourneau et al., 2002). MST treats factors that might pertain to individual characteristics of the youth (e.g., poor problem-solving skills), family relations (e.g., inept discipline), peer relations (e.g., association with deviant peers), and school performance (e.g., academic difficulties). On a highly individualized basis, treatment goals are developed in collaboration

with the family, and family strengths are used as levers for therapeutic change (Henggeler et al., 1998, 1999). Intervention strategies include strategic family therapy, structural family therapy, behavioral parental training, and cognitive behavior therapies. The use of a home-based model of service delivery (i.e., low caseloads, time-limited duration of treatment) removes barriers of access to care and provides the high level of intensity needed to successfully treat youth presenting serious clinical problems and their multineed families (Henggeler et al., 1998, 1999). Multisystemic therapy is conducted by two or four therapists and an onsite supervisor, who work together for purposes of group and peer supervision and to support the 24-7 on-call needs of the team's client families. MST staff must be highly accessible to their clients (Henggeler et al., 1998, 1999).

Rowland et al. (2000) and Borduin, Heilbrun, Jones, and Grabe (2000) believed that MST appears to be a clinically effective and

---

Editors' Note: This article was originally published in the *International Journal of Offender Therapy and Comparative Criminology*, Vol. 48, No. 3, 2004, pp. 389-394.

cost-effective alternative to out-of-home placements (e.g., incarceration, psychiatric hospitalization) for youth presenting serious clinical problems, such as antisocial behavior. Kazdin (2002), however, asserted that none of the existing intervention/treatment approaches would ameliorate antisocial disorder and overcome the poor long-term prognosis. Kazdin (2002) and Martens (1997) suggested that there is only mixed evidence for (long-term) success of current MST. The author speculates that a lack of long-lasting [effectiveness] of MST in juveniles who are antisocial might be the consequence of lack of attention to [the following]: (a) neurological treatment of neurobiological dysfunctions that correlate with core features of antisocial behavior (Martens, 2000a, 2001a); (b) specific needs, condition, and coexistent mental disorders of the patient (Martens, 1997, 2000a; van Marle, 1995); (c) specific therapeutic models that are proven effective, such as psychoanalytic or psychodynamic treatment (Kernberg, 1984; van Marle, 1995); and (d) crucial environmental (Minuchin, Montalvo, Guerney, Rosman, & Schumer, 1967) and cultural factors (Martens, 1997) that interfere with treatment affectivity. I suggest that the following important topics, which are hardly considered in current MST approaches, should be included to make this treatment approach more adequate:

• The antisocial patient's old social environment will simply not accept when the patient's behavior is transformed into harmless, social behavior (Martens, 1997; Minuchin et al., 1967). Thus, most of these juveniles who are antisocial are afraid to demonstrate a prosocial attitude because of rejection by their old environment. Moreover, many juveniles who are antisocial believe that a normal prosocial life and career is boring and only acceptable for stupid/dull people and losers. Without a solution to these problems, any intervention or prevention will have only limited success. Possible solutions could be (a) transfer of the juvenile with antisocial personality disorder (ASPD) and his or her family to a better neighborhood or structural improvement of neighborhood (Martens, 2000a); (b) creation of a more prosocial network; (c) improvement of academic skills, success, and social competence that will lead to increased possibilities for successful prosocial jobs/careers (Martens, 1997, 2000a), higher socioeconomic status, increased self-esteem, social awareness, and as a consequence, a possible decrease of impulsivity/hostility (Martens, 1997); and (d) stimulation of patient's awareness that a normal, social career and life is not necessarily boring.

• Specific treatment of coexisting mental disorders—most frequently substance abuse disorders, schizophrenia, and other personality disorders (Martens, 2000a): In addition, treatment of trauma or post-traumatic stress disorder (PTSD) (see DSM-IV, 1994) is needed, because many juveniles who are antisocial suffer from (recent) traumatic experiences as a consequence of physical/sexual abuse, neglect and rejection, homelessness, chaotic and violent family life, threatening neighborhood, and so on (Martens, 2000a, 2001/2002). Solomon and Johnson (2002) concluded in their review of outcome research that the strongest support is found for treatments that combine cognitive and behavioral techniques, and that hypnosis, psychodynamic anxiety management, and group therapies also may produce short-term symptom reduction. Because of the neurobiological correlates of PTSD, neurological treatment of these patients might be necessary (Yehuda, 2002).

• Combination of specific psychotherapeutic, neurologic, and neurofeedback treatment of ASPD traits: Antisocial features that are frequently neurobiologically determined and thus need neurobiological attention are impulsivity, aggression (Martens, 2000a), sensation seeking (Martens, 2000a; Zuckerman, 1994), poor socialization and lack of guilt or remorse (Fowles & Kochanska, 2000), poor fear conditioning and associated incapacity to learn from experiences (Lykken, 1995; Martens, 2000a), criminality (Raine, Venables, & Williams, 1996), and a lack of moral capacity (Martens, 2000b). Juvenile ADHD, CD, and ODD behavior could be treated effectively with the help of neurofeedback (Horacek, 1998).

• By means of structured fantasy therapy (Garrison & Stolberg, 1983; Giannini, 2001) children and adolescents who are antisocial might be able to transform their hostile and paranoid fantasy world into a social and trustful one.

• Possibilities to learn from aggressive behavior in a controlled setting by means of agitation therapy (Martens, 2001a): This would increase the patient's awareness of his or her core problem and the roots and consequences of his or her aggression as a result of adequate guidance and confrontation with and feedback from others and psychotherapeutic aftercare, which may lead to self-insight and increased social, emotional, and moral capacities. Impressive confrontations with fellow patients and staff members may contribute to the process of remission in ASPD (Martens, 1997, 2000a). However, this treatment approach can only be realized in in-ward settings.

• Possibility for ethical and/or spiritual development, possibly by means of ethics therapy (Martens, 2001d) and/or spiritual psychotherapy (Martens, 2003b) because remission in ASPD may be linked to ethical and spiritual activities and development (Black, Baumgart, & Bell, 1995; Martens, 1997; Robins, 1966).

• Increased responsibilities (as a consequence of parenthood, marriage, joining the armed services, getting a stable job, etc.) might be linked to remission in ASPD (Black et al., 1995; Martens, 2000a; Robins, 1996). Ideal treatment conditions will include a structural enhancement of the patient's responsibilities by means of stimulation of forming of bonds, attachments or commitments, which are characterized by important dimension of loyalty, sympathy and/or care.

• Because many children and adolescents who are antisocial are homeless or frequently gadabouts, these juveniles should be offered adequate housing and guidance (hygiene, medical treatment of physical illness; Martens, 2001c, 2001/2002). Current MST programs are hardly tailored for and directed toward homeless juveniles (or those who often run away, are left alone, or are gadabouts).

• Facilities for privacy and relaxation, which might be necessary for adequate reflection, contemplation, and preparation for change, [are needed]. The life of many juveniles who are antisocial is characterized by restlessness, lack of safety, chaos, and a lack of privacy and relaxation, which interferes with healthy development and opportunities for recovery (Martens, 1997, 2000a). Moreover, the patient may experience the facility for privacy as an expression of respect, deep understanding, and constructive attention on the part of the treatment staff.

• Therapeutic circumstances/approaches that are also targeted toward enjoying life, which may include vacations, excursions, and trips, may relate to remission in ASPD (Martens, 2000a): Important learning moments (positive experiences, contacts, refreshing changes) occur frequently and could be stimulated easily during these pleasant events.

• Cultural influences may play an important role in the development of antisocial behavior: For instance, some refugees have different moral ideation and some behavioral manifestations that are regarded in the West as socially undesirable that are in the refugees' eyes acceptable (Martens, 1997). Only therapists with an understanding of these cultural dimensions of antisocial behavior may be able to change the patient's attitude.

• To meet the psychosocial, neurobiological, and psychiatric therapeutic needs of antisocial youth and to enhance the effectiveness and positive long-term outcome of MST, I suggest that a neurologist, a forensic psychiatrist, a neurofeedback specialist, a pediatrician, a trauma therapist, and a social worker involved with the homeless worker should be added to the standard MST team.

I conclude, in contrast to others (Borduin et al., 2000; Henggeler et al., 1998, 1999; Letourneau et al., 2002), that MST is mainly appropriate for those individuals who are antisocial and their families who are motivated for it, and who are not severely (a) emotionally, socially, and morally disturbed and/or traumatized; (b) abused, rejected, and neglected by their relatives; (c) angry, hostile, and rancorous; and (d) at risk of re-offending, and who are capable of cooperating with relatives and MST staff and understanding instructions. Otherwise, a forensic psychiatric treatment community would be more suitable because it is evident that only therapeutic community treatment is effective in juveniles who are severely impaired, abused, and neglected (Martens, 1997; 2003a; Ministry of Justice, 2002; van Marle, 1995). Treatment of such juveniles should take place explicitly (at least in the initial phase) away from the influence of abusive, chaotic family and friends, even when these people are willing to change their attitudes. Only when the patient becomes strong enough and able to cope with his or her negative memories, traumas, and the impact of peers and relatives is it useful that he or she be gradually involved in the MST process.

REFERENCES

Abel, G. G., Becker, J. V., Mittelman, M. S., Cunningham-Rathner, J., Rouleau, J. L., & Murphy, W. D. (1987). Self-reported sex crimes of nonincarcerated paraphilics. *Journal of Interpersonal Violence, 2,* 3–25.

Abel, G. G., Becker, J. V., Murphy, W. D., & Flanagan, B. (1981). Identifying dangerous child molesters. In R. B. Steward (Ed.), *Violent behavior: Social learning approaches to prediction, management and treatment.* New York: Brunner-Mazel.

Abel, G. G., Mittelman, M., Becker, J. V., Rathner, J. & Rouleau, J. L. (1988). Predicting child molesters' response to treatment. In R. A. Prentky & V. L. Wuinsey (Eds.), *Human sexual aggression: Current perspectives.* New York: New York Academy of Sciences.

Abel, G. G., & Rouleau, J. L. (1990). The nature and extent of sexual assault. In W. L. Marshall, D. R. Laws, & H. E. Barbaree (Eds.), *Handbook of sexual assault: Issues, theories, and treatment of the offender.* New York: Plenum.

Abrahamsen, D. (1960). *The psychology of crime.* New York: Columbia University Press.

Acoca, L. (1998). Defusing the time bomb: Understanding and meeting the growing health care needs of incarcerated women in America. *Crime & Delinquency, 44,* 46–69.

Agnew, R. (1992). Foundation for a general strain theory of crime and delinquency. *Criminology, 30,* 47–87.

Ainsworth, P. B. (1995). *Psychology and policing in a changing world.* New York: John Wiley.

Ajaelo, I., Koenig, K., & Snoey, E. (1998). Severe hyponatremia and inappropriate antidiuretic hormone secretion following ecstasy use. *Academy of Emergency Medicine, 5,* 839–840.

Alder, C. M., & Polk, K. (1996). Masculinity and child homicide. *British Journal of Criminology, 36,* 396–412.

Aldridge, J., & Cameron, S. (1999). Interviewing child witnesses: Questioning techniques and the role of training. *Applied Developmental Science, 3,* 136–147.

Aldridge, M., & Wood, J. (1997). Talking about feelings: Young children's ability to express emotions. *Child Abuse & Neglect, 21,* 1221–1233.

Aldwin, C. M. (1994). *Stress, coping, and development: An integrative perspective.* New York: Guilford.

American Academy of Psychiatry and the Law. (1995). *Ethical guidelines for the practice of forensic psychiatry.* Bloomfield, CT: Author.

American Association on Mental Retardation. (2002). *The AAMR definition of mental retardation.* Retrieved June 1, 2003, from www.aamr.org/Policies/faq_mental_retardation.shtml

American Educational Research Association, American Psychological Association, & National Council on Measurement in Education. (1999). *Standards for educational and psychological testing* (3rd ed.). Washington, DC: American Educational Research Association.

American Psychiatric Association. (1968). *Diagnostic and statistical manual of mental disorders* (2nd ed.). Washington, DC: Author.

American Psychiatric Association. (1980). *Diagnostic and statistical manual of mental disorders* (3rd ed.). Washington, DC: Author.

American Psychiatric Association. (1987). *Diagnostic and statistical manual of mental disorders* (3rd ed. rev.). Washington, DC: Author.

American Psychiatric Association. (1994). *Diagnostic and statistical manual of mental disorders* (4th ed.). Washington, DC: Author.

American Psychological Association. (1985). *Standards for educational and psychological testing.* Washington, DC: Author.

American Psychological Association. (1994). Guidelines for child custody evaluations in divorce proceedings. *American Psychologist, 49,* 677–680.

American Psychological Association. (1996). *Violence and the family: Report of the American Psychological Association Presidential Task Force on Violence and the Family.* Washington, DC: Author.

American Psychological Association. (2002). *Ethical principles of psychologists and code of conduct.* Washington, DC: Author.

American Psychological Association. (2003). Ethical principles of psychologists and code of conduct. *American Psychologist, 57,* 1060–1073.

American Psychological Association Ethics Committee. (1992). Ethical principles of psychologists and code of conduct. *American Psychologist, 47,* 1597–1611.

Americans With Disabilities Act of 1990, 42 U.S.C.A. § 12101 et seq. (West 1993).

Amick-McMullan, A., Kilpatrick, D. G., & Resnick, H. S. (1991). Homicide as a risk factor for PTSD among surviving family members. *Behavior Modification, 15,* 545–559.

Amick-McMullan, A., Kilpatrick, D. G., Veronen, L. J., & Smith, S. (1989). Family survivors of homicide victims: Theoretical perspectives and an exploratory study. *Journal of Traumatic Stress, 2,* 21–35.

Andrews, D. A., & Bonta, J. (1994). *The psychology of criminal conduct.* Cincinnati, OH: Anderson.

Andrews, D. A., & Bonta, J. (1998). *The psychology of criminal conduct* (2nd ed.). Cincinnati, OH: Anderson.

Anglin, M. D., & Hser, Y. (1990). Legal coercion and drug abuse treatment: Research findings and social policy implications. In J. Inciardi (Ed.), *Handbook of drug control in the United States.* Westport, CT: Greenwood.

Anglin, M. D., & Hser, Y. (1991). Criminal justice and the drug-abusing offender: Policy issues of coerced treatment. *Behavioral Sciences & the Law, 9,* 243–267.

Annon, J. S. (1995). Investigative profiling: A behavioral analysis of the crime scene. *American Journal of Forensic Psychology, 13,* 67–75.

Araji, S., & Finkelhor, D. (1985). Explanations of pedophilia: Review of empirical research. *Bulletin of the American Academy of Psychiatry and the Law, 13,* 17–37.

Artiloa I Fortuny, L., & Mullaney, H. A. (1998). Assessing patients whose language you do not know: Can the absurd be ethical? *The Clinical Neuropsychologist, 12,* 113–126.

Ash, P., Slora, K. B., & Britton, C. F. (1990). Police agency officer selection practices. *Journal of Police Science and Administration, 17,* 258–269.

Ashcraft v. Tennessee, 322 U.S. 143. (1944).

Association for the Treatment of Sexual Abusers. (1997). *Ethical standards and principles for the management of sexual abusers.* Beaverton, OR: Author.

Association of Family and Conciliation Courts. (1994). Courts model standards of practice for child custody evaluations. *Family and Conciliation Courts Review, 32,* 504–513.

Aurand, S. K., Addessa, R., & Bush, C. (1985). *Violence and discrimination against Philadelphia lesbian and gay people.* Philadelphia: Philadelphia Lesbian and Gay Task Force Report.

Austin, W. G. (2000). Assessing credibility in allegations of marital violence in the high-conflict child custody case. *Family and Conciliation Courts Review, 38,* 462–477.

Austin, W. G. (2001). Partner violence and risk assessment in child custody evaluations. *Family Court Review, 39,* 483–496.

Aylward, J. (1985). Psychological testing and police selection. *Journal of Police Science and Administration, 13,* 201–210.

Babiak, P. (1995). When psychopaths go to work. *International Journal of Applied Psychology, 44,* 171–188.

Bachman, R. (1993). Predicting the reporting of rape victimizations: Have reforms made a difference? *Criminal Justice and Behavior, 20,* 254–270.

Backer, T. E., David, S. L., & Soucy, G. (Eds.). (1995). *Reviewing the behavioral science knowledge base on technology transfer* (NIDA Research Monograph No. 155). Rockville, MD: National Institute on Drug Abuse.

Backer, T. E., Liberman, R. P., & Kuehnel, T. (1986). Dissemination and adoption of innovative psychosocial interventions. *Journal of Consulting and Clinical Psychology, 54,* 111–118.

Baird, S. C. (1981). Probation and parole classification: The Wisconsin model. *Corrections Today, 43,* 36–41.

Baldwin, J. (1993). Police interview techniques: Establishing truth or proof? *British Journal of Criminology, 33,* 325–352.

the developmental model into a prevention design. In J. B. Kupersmidt & K. A. Dodge (Eds.), *Children's peer relations: From development to intervention.* Washington, DC: American Psychological Association.

Conley, C. (1998). *The women's prison association: Supporting women offenders and their families.* National Institute of Justice: Program focus (NJC 172858).Washington, DC: Department of Justice.

Conte, J. R. (1985). Clinical dimensions of adult sexual abuse of children. *Behavioral Sciences & the Law, 3,* 341–354.

Conte, J. R., Sorenson, E., Fogarty, L., & Rosa, J. D. (1991). Evaluating children's reports of sexual abuse: Results from a survey of professionals. *American Journal of Orthopsychiatry, 61,* 428–437.

Copson, G., Badcock, R., Boon, J., & Britton, P. (1997). Editorial: Articulating a systematic approach to clinical crime profiling. *Criminal Behaviour and Mental Health, 7,* 13–17.

Cordon, I. M., Goodman, G. S., & Anderson, S. J. (2003). Children in court. In P. J. van Koppen & S. D. Penrod (Eds.), *Adversarial versus inquisitorial justice: Psychological perspectives on criminal justice systems.* New York: Kluwer Academic/Plenum.

Cornell, D., Warren, J., Hawk, G., Stafford, E., Oram, G., Pine, D., Weitzner, I., & Griffiths, R. (1993, August). *Psychopathy and anger among instrumental and reactive violent offenders.* Paper presented at the annual meeting of the American Psychological Association, Toronto, Ontario.

Cortina, J. M., Doherty, M. L., Schmitt, N., Kaufman, G., & Smith, R. G. (1992). The big five personality factors in the IPI and the MMPI: Predictors of police performance. *Personnel Psychology, 45,* 119–140.

Coulton, G. F., & Field, H. S. (1995). Using assessment centers in selecting entry-level police officers: Extravagance or justified expense. *Public Personnel Management, 24,* 223–254.

Courtois, C. (1988). *Healing the incest wound.* New York: Norton.

Coy v. Iowa, 487 U.S. 1012 (1988).

Crawford v. Washington, 541 U.S. 46 (2004).

Crawford, N. (2002, November). Science-based program curbs violence in kids. *Monitor on Psychology, 33,* 38–39.

Crews, F. (1986, May 29). In the big house of theory. *New York Review of Books,* pp. 36, 41.

Cripe, L. I. (1996). The ecological validity of executive function testing. In R. J. Shordone & C. J. Long (Eds.), *Ecological validity of neuropsychological testing.* Delray Beach, FL: GR Press/St. Lucie Press.

Cullen, F., & Gendreau, P. (1989). The effectiveness of correctional rehabilitation: Reconsidering the "Nothing Works" doctrine. In L. Goodstein & D. L. Mackenzie (Eds.), *The American prison: Issues in research policy.* New York: General Hall.

Cullen, F. T., & Wright, J. P. (1996). The future of corrections. In B. Maguire & P. Radosh (Eds.), *The past, present, and future of American criminal justice.* New York: General Hall.

Cullen, F. T., Wright, J. P., & Applegate, B. K. (1996). Control in the community. In A. Harland (Ed.), *Choosing correctional options that work: Defining the demand and evaluating the supply.* Thousand Oaks, CA: Sage.

Cunningham, M. D., & Reidy, T. J. (1998). Antisocial personality disorder and psychopathy: Diagnostic dilemmas in classifying patterns of antisocial behavior in sentencing evaluations. *Behavioral Sciences & the Law, 16,* 333–351.

Cunningham, M. D., & Reidy, T. J. (1999). Don't confuse me with the facts: Common errors in violence risk assessment at capital sentencing. *Criminal Justice and Behavior, 26,* 20–43.

Dahlstrom, W. M., & Welsh, G. S. (1960). *An MMPI handbook: A guide to use in clinical practice and research.* Minneapolis: University of Minnesota Press.

Dalton, C. (1999). When paradigms collide: Protecting battered parents and their children in the family court system. *Family and Conciliation Court Review, 37,* 273–296.

Damasio, A. (1994, October). Descartes' error and the future of human life. *Scientific American,* p. 144.

Damasio, A., Tranel, D., & Damasio, H. (1987). Individuals with sociopathic behavior caused by frontal damage fail to respond autonomically to social stimuli. *Behavioral Brain Research, 41,* 81–94.

Damasio, H., Grabowski, T., Frank, R., Galaburda, A. M., & Damasio, A. R. (1994). The return of Phineas Gage: Clues about the brain from the skull of a famous patient. *Science, 264,* 1102–1105.

Damon, W. (2004). What is positive youth development? *Annals, American Academy of Political and Social Sciences, 591,* 13–24.

Davies, A. (1994). Editorial: Offender profiling. *Medicine, Science and Law, 34,* 185–186.

Davies, W., & Feldman, P. (1981). The diagnosis of psychopathy by forensic specialists. *British Journal of Psychiatry, 138,* 329–331.

Davis, G. M., Tarrant, A., & Flin, R. (1989). Close encounters of a witness kind: Children's memory for a simulated health inspection. *British Journal of Psychology, 80,* 415–429.

Davison, G. C., & Neale, J. M. (1994). *Abnormal psychology* (6th ed.). New York: John Wiley.

De Leon, G. (1988). Legal pressure in therapeutic communities. In C. G. Leukefeld & F. M. Tims (Eds.), Compulsory treatment of drug abuse: Research and clinical practice. *NIDA Research Monograph, 86.* Rockville, MD: National Institute on Drug Abuse.

De Leon, G. (2000). *The therapeutic community: Theory, model, and method.* New York: Springer.

DeGeneste, H. I., & Sullivan, J. P. (1994). *Policing transportation facilities.* Springfield, IL: Charles C Thomas.

DeKeseredy, W., & Schwartz, M. D. (1998). *Woman abuse on campus: Results from the Canadian National Survey.* Thousand Oaks, CA: Sage.

DeLoache, J. S. (1995). Early understanding and use of symbols: The model model. *Current Directions in Psychological Science, 4,* 109–113.

DeLoache, J. S., & Marzolf, D. P. (1995). The use of dolls to interview young children: Issues of symbolic representation. *Journal of Experimental Child Psychology, 60,* 155–173.

Delprino, R. P., & Bahn, C. (1988). National survey of the extent and nature of psychological services in police departments. *Professional Psychology: Research and Practice, 19,* 421–425.

Demme, J. (Director). (1991). *Silence of the lambs* [Film].

Dennison, S., & Thomson, D. M. (2000). Community perceptions of stalking: What are the fundamental concerns? *Psychiatry, Psychology and Law, 7,* 159–169.

Dennison, S., & Thomson, D. M. (2002). Identifying stalking: The relevance of intent in common-sense reasoning. *Law and Human Behavior, 26,* 543–561.

Dent, H. R., & Stephenson, G. M. (1979). An experimental study of the effectiveness of different techniques of questioning child witnesses. *British Journal of Social and Clinical Psychology, 18,* 41–51.

Derogatis, L. R. (1983). *SCL-90-R: Administration, scoring, and procedures.* Towson, MD: Clinical Psychometric Research.

Dickerson v. U. S., 530 U.S. 428 (2000).

Dietz, P. E. (1985). Sex offender profiling by the FBI: A preliminary conceptual model. In M. H. Ben-Aron, S. J., Hucker, & C. D. Webster (Eds.), *Clinical criminology: The assessment and treatment of criminal behavior.* Toronto: Clarke Institute of Psychiatry.

DiIulio, J. J. (1991). *No escape: The future of American corrections.* New York: HarperCollins.

Dionne, G., Tremblay, R., Boivin, M., Laplante, D., & Pérusse, D. (2003). Physical aggression and expressive vocabulary in 19-month-old twins. *Developmental Psychology, 39,* 261–273.

Dodge, K. A. (2002). Mediation, moderation, and mechanisms of how parenting affects children's aggressive behavior. In J. G. Borkowksi, S. L. Ramey, & M. Bristol-Power (Eds.), *Parenting and the child's world: Influences on academic, intellectual and social development.* Mahwah, NJ: Erlbaum.

Dodge, K. A. (2003). Do social information-processing patterns mediate aggressive behavior? In B. B. Lahey, T. E. Moffitt, & A. Caspi (Eds). *Causes of conduct disorder and juvenile delinquency.* New York: Guilford.

Dodge, K. A., & Pettit, G. S. (2003). A biopsychosocial model of the development of chronic conduct problems in adolescence. *Developmental Psychology, 39,* 349–371.

Doka, K. (Ed.). (1988). *Disenfranchised grief: Recognizing hidden sorrow.* Lexington, MA: Lexington Books.

Doll, B., & Lyon, M. A. (1998). Risk and resilience: Implications for the delivery of educational and mental health services in schools. *School Psychology Review, 27,* 348–363.

Dorsey, T. L., & Zawitz, M.W. (2000). *Drugs and crime facts* (NCJ 165148).Washington, DC: Department of Justice, Bureau of Justice Statistics.

Douglas, J. E., Burgess, A.W., Burgess, A. G., & Ressler, R. (1992). *Crime classification manual.* New York: Lexington.

Douglas, J. E., & Munn, C. (1992, February). Violent crime scene analysis: Modus operandi, signature, and staging. *FBI Law Enforcement Bulletin,* pp. 1–20.

Douglas, J. E., & Olshaker, M. (1995). *Mindhunter: Inside the FBI elite serial crime unit.* New York: Scribner.

Douglas, J. E., & Olshaker, M. (1997). *Journey into darkness.* New York: Scribner.

Douglas, J. E., Ressler, R. K., Burgess, A. W., & Hartman, C. R. (1986). Criminal profiling from crime scene analysis. *Behavioral Sciences & the Law, 4,* 401–421.

Dubrow, E. F., Edwards, S., & Ippolito, M. F. (1997). Life stressors, neighborhood disadvantage, and resources: A focus on inner-city children's adjustment. *Journal of Clinical Child Psychology, 26,* 130–144.

Dukes, R. L., & Mattley, C. L. (1977). Predicting rape victim reportage. *Sociology and Social Research, 62,* 63–84.

Dunn, P. C., Vail-Smith, K., & Knight, S. M. (1999). What date/acquaintance rape victims tell others: A study of college recipients of disclosure. *Journal of American College Health, 47,* 213–222.

Dunnette, M. D., & Motowidlo, S. J. (1976). *Police selection and career assessment.* Washington, DC: Government Printing Office.

Easteal, P. W., & Wilson, P. (1991). *Preventing crime on transport: Rail, buses, taxis, planes.* Canberra: Australian Institute of Criminology.

Eaton, T. E., Ball, P. J., & O'Callaghan, M. G. (2001). Child-witness and defendant credibility: Child evidence presentation mode and judicial instructions. *Journal of Applied Social Psychology, 31,* 1845–1858.

Edens, J. F., Hart, S. D., Johnson, D.W., Johnson, J., & Olver, M. E. (2000). Use of the Personality Assessment Inventory to assess psychopathy in offender populations. *Psychological Assessment, 12,* 132–139.

Edens, J. F., & Otto, R. K. (2001). Release decision making and planning. In J. B. Ashford, B. D. Sales, & W. Reid (Eds.), *Treating adult and juvenile offenders with special needs.* Washington, DC: American Psychological Association.

Edens, J. F., Petrila, J., & Buffington-Vollum, J. K. (2001, Winter). Psychopathy and the death penalty: Can the Psychopathy Checklist–Revised identify offenders who represent "a continuing threat to society?" *Journal of Psychiatry and Law, 29,* 433–481.

Edens, J. F., Skeem, J. L., Cruise, K. R., & Cauffman, E. (2001). Assessment of "juvenile psychopathy" and its association with violence: A critical review. *Behavioral Sciences & the Law, 19,* 53–80.

Edwards, C. N. (1998). Behavior and the law reconsidered: Psychological syndromes and profiles. *Journal of Forensic Sciences, 43,* 141–150.

Egger, S. A. (1990). Serial murder: A synthesis of literature and research. In S. A. Egger (Ed.), *Serial murder: An elusive phenomenon.* Westport, CT: Praeger.

Egger, S. A. (1997). *The killers among us: An examination of serial murder and its investigation.* Upper Saddle River, NJ: Prentice Hall.

Eisenberg, N. (1998). *Social, emotional, and personality development* (5th ed., Vol. 3). New York: John Wiley.

Equal Employment Opportunity Commission, ADA Division, Office of Legal Counsel. (1995). *Enforcement guidance: Preemployment disability-related inquiries and medical examinations under the Americans With Disabilities Act of 1990.* Washington, DC: Equal Employment Opportunity Commission.

Escobedo v. Illinois, 378 U. S. 478 (1964).

Estrich, S. (1987). *Real rape.* Cambridge, MA: Harvard University Press.

Everington C., & Luckasson, R. (1992). *Competence assessment for standing trial for defendants with mental retardation test manual.* Worthington, OH: IDS Publishing.

Everson, M., & Boat, B. (1990). Sexualized doll play among young children: Implications for the use of anatomical dolls in sexual abuse evaluations. *Journal of the American Academy of Child and Adolescent Psychiatry, 29,* 736–742.

Ewing, C. P. (1983). "Dr. Death" and the case for an ethical ban on psychiatric and psychological predictions of dangerousness in capital sentencing proceedings. *American Journal of Law and Medicine, 8,* 408–428.

Eysenck, H. J. (1964). *Crime and personality.* Boston: Houghton Mifflin.

Farabee, D., Prendergast, M., & Anglin, M.D. (1998). The effectiveness of coerced treatment for drug-abusing offenders. *Federal Probation, 62,* 3–10.

Farabee, D., Simpson, D., Dansereau, D., & Knight, K. (1995). Cognitive inductions into treatment among probated drug users. *Journal of Drug Issues, 25,* 669–682.

Federal Bureau of Investigation. (1992). *Killed in the line of duty.* Washington, DC: U.S. Department of Justice.

Federal Bureau of Investigation. (1997). *Crime in the United States: Uniform crime reports, 1996.* Washington, DC: Government Printing Office.

Federal Bureau of Investigation. (1999a). *Index of crime,* Table 1. Retrieved May 29, 2001, from www .fbi.gov http://www.fbi.gov/ucr/99cius.htm.

Federal Bureau of Investigation. (1999b). *Section III: Crime index offenses cleared.* Retrieved July 15, 2001, from www.fbi.gov/ucr/Cius_99/99 crime/99cius3.pdf

Feldman-Summers, S., & Ashworth, C. D. (1981). Factors related to intentions to report a rape. *Journal of Social Issues, 37,* 53–70.

Felson, R. B., Messner, S. F., & Hoskin, A. (1999). The victim-offender relationship and calling the police in assaults. *Criminology, 37,* 931–947.

Ferraro, R. (Ed.). (2002). *Minority and cross-cultural aspects of neuropsychological assessment.* Royersford, PA: Sets & Zeilinger.

Finkelhor, D., & Araji, S. (1986). Explanations of pedophilia: A four-factor model. *Journal of Sex Research, 22,* 145–161.

Finkelson, L., & Oswalt, R. (1995). College date rape: Incidence and reporting. *Psychological Reports, 77,* 526.

Finn, P., & McNeil, T. (1987). *Bias crime and the criminal justice response: A summary report (prepared for the National Criminal Justice Association).* Cambridge, MA: Abt Associates.

Fisher, B. S., & Cullen, F. T. (1999). *Violence against college women: Results from a national level study: Final report submitted to the Bureau of Justice Statistics,* March 1999. Washington, DC: U.S. Department of Justice, Bureau of Justice Statistics.

Fisher, B. S., & Cullen, F. T. (2000). Measuring the sexual victimization of women: Evolution, current controversies, and future research. In D. Duffee (Ed.), *Criminal Justice 2000: Vol. 4. Measurement and analysis of crime and justice.* Washington, DC: U.S. Department of Justice, National Institute of Justice.

Fisher, B. S., Cullen, F. T., & Turner, M. G. (2000). *The sexual victimization of college women.* Washington, DC: U.S. Department of Justice, National Institute of Justice and Bureau of Justice Statistics.

Fisher, B. S., Hartman, J., Cullen, F. T., & Turner, M. G. (1999). Making campuses safer for students: The Clery Act as a symbolic legal reform. *Stetson Law Review.*

Fisher, B. S., Sloan, J. J., Cullen, F. T., & Lu, C. (1998). Crime in the ivory tower: The level and sources of student victimization. *Criminology, 36,* 671–710.

Fisher, R. P., Geiselman, R. E., Raymond, D. S., Jurkevich, L. M., & Warhaftig, M. L. (1987). Enhancing enhanced eyewitness memory: Refining the Cognitive Interview. *Journal of Police Science and Administration, 15,* 291–297.

Fisher, R. P., & McCauley, M. R. (1995). Information retrieval: Interviewing witnesses. In N. Brewer & C. Wilson (Eds.), *Psychology and policing.* Hillsdale, NJ: Lawrence Erlbaum.

Fitch, J. H. (1962). Men convicted of sexual offenses against children. *British Journal of Criminology,* 3, 18–37.

Fivush, R., & Shukat, J. (1995). What young children recall: Issues of content, consistency and coherence of early autobiographical recall. In M. S. Zaragoza, J. R. Graham, G. C. N. Hall, R. Hirschman, & Y. S. Ben-Porath (Eds.), *Memory and testimony in the child witness.* Thousand Oaks, CA: Sage.

Folkman, S., & Moskowitz, J. T. (2000). Positive affect and the other side of coping. *American Psychologist, 55,* 647–654.

Foreman, W. C. F. (1991). Police stress response to an aircraft disaster. In J. T. Reese, J. M. Horn, & C. Dunning (Eds.), *Critical incidents in policing* (Rev. ed.). Washington, DC: Government Printing Office.

Forth, A. E., Hart, S. D., & Hare, R. D. (1990). Assessment of psychopathy in male young offenders. *Psychological Assessment, 2,* 342–344.

Forth, A. E., & Kroner, D. (1994). T*he factor structure of the Revised Psychopathy Checklist with incarcerated rapist and incest offenders.* Unpublished manuscript.

Fowles, D. C., & Kochanska, G. (2000). Temperament as a moderator of pathways in conscience in children: The contribution of electrodermal activity. *Psychophysiology, 37,* 788–795.

Frankl, V. (1969). *The will to meaning: Foundations and applications of logotherapy.* New York: World Publishing.

Fraser, S. (Ed.). (1995). *The bell curve wars: Race, intelligence, and the future of America.* New York: Basic Books.

Frederickson, B. L. (2001). The role of positive emotions in positive psychology: The broaden-and-build theory of positive emotions. *American Psychologist, 56,* 218–226.

Freeman, L. N., Shaffer, D., & Smith, H. (1996). Neglected victims of homicide: The needs of young siblings of murder victims. *American Journal of Orthopsychiatry, 66,* 337–345.

Fremouw, W. J., Westrup, D., & Pennypacker, J. (1997). Stalking on campus: The prevalence and strategies for coping with stalking. *Journal of Forensic Science, 42,* 666–669.

French, J. R. P., Jr., Rogers, W., & Cobb, S. (1974). Adjustment as person-environment fit. In G. V. Coelho, D. A. Hamburg, & J. E. Adams (Eds.), *Coping and adaptation.* New York: Basic Books.

Freudenberger, H. (1977). Burnout: Occupational hazard of the child case worker. *Child Case Quarterly, 6,* 90–99.

Freund, K. (1965). Diagnosing heterosexual pedophilia by means of a test for sexual interest. *Behavior Research and Therapy, 3,* 229–234.

Freund, K. (1967a). Diagnosing homo- and heterosexuality and erotic age preference by means of a psychophysiological test. *Behavioral Research and Therapy, 5,* 209–228.

Freund, K. (1967b). Erotic preference in pedophilia. *Behavioral Research and Therapy, 5,* 339–348.

Freund, K., & Blanchard (1989). Phallometric diagnosis of pedophilia. *Journal of Consulting and Clinical Psychology, 57,* 100–105.

Frick, P. J., O'Brien, B. S., Wooton, J. M., & McBurnett, K. (1994). Psychopathy and conduct problems in children. *Journal of Abnormal Psychology, 103,* 700–707.

Friedman, W. J. (1991). The development of children's memory for the time of past events. *Child Development, 62,* 139–155.

Frisbie, L. V. (1990). *Another look at sex offenders in California. California Mental Health Research Monograph* (No. 12). Sacramento: California Department of Mental Hygiene.

Frisbie, L. V., & Dondis, E. H. (1965). Recidivism among treated sex offenders. *California Mental Health Research Monograph* (No. 5). Sacramento: California Department of Mental Hygiene.

Fulero, S. M. (1995). Review of the Hare Psychopathy Checklist—Revised. In J. C. Conoley & J. C. Impara (Eds.), *Twelfth mental measurements yearbook.* Lincoln, NE: Buros Institute.

Gacono, C. B., Meloy, J. R., Sheppard, K., Speth, E., & Roske, A. (1995). A clinical investigation of malingering and psychopathy in hospitalized insanity acquitees. *Bulletin of the American Academy of Psychiatry and Law, 23,* 387–397.

Gallagher, R.W., Somwaru, D. P., & Ben-Porath, Y. S. (1999). Current usage of psychological tests in state correctional settings. *Corrections Compendium, 24,* 1–3, 20.

Gamma-hydroxy butyrate use—New York and Texas, 1995–1996. (1997). *Morbidity and Mortality Weekly Reports, 46,* 281–283.

Ganger, J., & Brent, M. R. (2004). Reexamining the vocabulary spurt. *Developmental Psychology, 40,* 621–632.

Garbarino, J., & Kostelny, K. (1992). *Child maltreatment as a community problem.* Chicago: Erikson Institute for Advanced Study in Child Development.

Garbarino, J., Kostelny, K. E., & Dubrow, N. (1991). What children can tell us about living in danger. *American Psychologist, 46,* 376–383.

Gardner, H. (1983). *Frames of mind: The theory of multiple intelligences.* New York: Basic Books.

Gardner, H. (1986). The waning of intelligence tests. In R. J. Sternberg & D. K. Detterman (Eds.), *What is intelligence?* Norwood, NJ: Ablex.

Gardner, H. (1993). *Multiple intelligences.* New York: Basic Books.

Gardner, H. (1998). Are there additional intelligences: The case for naturalist, spiritual, and existential intelligences. In K. Kane (Ed.), *Education, information, and transformation.* Englewood Cliffs, NJ: Prentice-Hall.

Garmezy, N. (1991). Resiliency and vulnerability to adverse developmental outcomes associated with poverty. *American Behavioral Scientist, 34,* 416–430.

Garofalo, J., & Martin, S. (1993). *Bias motivated crimes: Their characteristics and the law enforcement response. Final report to the National Institute of Justice.* Carbondale: Southern Illinois University, Center for the Study of Crime, Delinquency, and Corrections.

Garrison, S. R., & Stolberg, A. L. (1983). Modification of anger in children by affective imagery training. *Journal of Abnormal Child Psychology, 11,* 115–129.

Garrison, W. E. (1991). Modeling inoculation training for traumatic incident exposure. In J. T. Reese, J. M. Horn, & C. Dunning (Eds.), *Critical incidents in policing* (Rev. ed.). Washington, DC: Government Printing Office.

Gartner, R., & Macmillan, R. (1995). The effect of victim-offender relationship on reporting crimes of violence against women. *Canadian Journal of Criminology, 37,* 393–429.

Geberth, V. J. (1995). Criminal personality profiling: the signature aspect in criminal investigation. *Law and Order, 43,* 45–49.

Geiselman, R. E., & Padilla, J. (1988). Cognitive interviewing with child witnesses. *Journal of Police Science and Administration, 16,* 236–242.

Gendreau, P. (1995). Technology transfer in the criminal justice field: Implications for substance abuse. In T. E. Backer, S. L. David, & G. Soucy (Eds.), *Reviewing the behavioral science knowledge base on technology transfer* (NIDA Research Monograph No. 155). Rockville, MD: National Institute on Drug Abuse.

Gendreau, P. (1996a). Offender rehabilitation: What we know and what needs to be done. *Criminal Justice and Behavior, 23,* 144–161.

Gendreau, P. (1996b). The principles of effective intervention with offenders. In A. Harland (Ed.), *Choosing correctional options that work: Defining the demand and evaluating the supply.* Thousand Oaks, CA: Sage.

Gendreau, P., & Andrews, D. A. (1979). Psychological consultation in correctional agencies: Case studies and general issues. In J. J. Platt & R. W. Wicks (Eds.), *The psychological consultant.* New York: Grune & Stratton.

Gendreau, P., Cullen, F. T., & Bonta, J. (1994). Intensive rehabilitation supervision: the next generation in community corrections? *Federal Probation, 58,* 72–78.

Gendreau, P., & Goggin, C. (1997). Correctional treatment: Accomplishments and realities. In P. Van Voorhis, M. Braswell, & D. Lester (Eds.), *Correctional counseling and rehabilitation* (3rd ed.). Cincinnati, OH: Anderson.

Gendreau, P., Goggin, C., & Annis, H. (1990). Survey of existing substance abuse programs. *Forum on Corrections Research, 2,* 6–8.

Gendreau, P., Little, T., & Goggin, C. (1995). *A meta-analysis of the predictors of adult offender recidivism: Assessment guidelines for classification and treatment.* Ottawa, Canada: Ministry Secretariat, Solicitor General of Canada.

Gendreau, P., & Ross, R. R. (1981). Correctional potency: Treatment and deterrence on trial. In R. Roesch & R. R. Corrado (Eds.), *Evaluation and criminal justice policy.* Beverly Hills, CA: Sage.

Gendreau, P., & Ross, R. (1987). Revivification of rehabilitation: Evidence from the 1980s. *Justice Quarterly, 4,* 349–407.

Gentz, D. (1991). The psychological impact of critical incidents on police officers. In J. T. Reese, J. M. Horn, & C. Dunning (Eds.), *Critical incidents in policing* (Rev. ed.). Washington, DC: Government Printing Office.

Gersons, B. P. R. (1989). Patterns of PTSD among police officers following shooting incidents: A two-dimensional model and treatment implications. *Journal of Traumatic Stress, 2,* 247–257.

Gettys, V. S. (1990, August). *Police and public safety psychologists: Survey of fields of study, activities, and training opportunities.* Paper presented at the annual convention of the American Psychological Association, Boston, MA.

Getzel, G. S., & Masters, R. (1984). Serving families who survive homicide victims. *Social Casework,* 138–144.

Giannini, A. J. (2001). The use of fiction in therapy. *Psychiatric Times, 8*(7), 1–7.

Gibbons, D. C. (1986). Breaking out of prisons. *Crime & Delinquency, 32,* 503–514.

Gilbert, N. (1995). Violence against women social research and sexual politics. In R. J. Simon (Ed.), *Neither victim nor enemy: Women's Freedom Network looks at gender in America.* Lanham, MD. Women's Freedom Network and University Press of America.

Gilbert, N. (1997). Advocacy research and social policy. In M. Tonry (Ed.), *Crime and justice: An annual review of research.* Chicago: University of Chicago Press.

Gilboy, J., & Schmidt, J. (1971). "Voluntary" hospitalization of the mentally ill. *Northwestern University Law Review, 66,* 429–453.

Gillstrom, B. (1994). *Abstract reasoning in psychopaths.* Unpublished doctoral dissertation, University of British Columbia, Vancouver, British Columbia, Canada.

Gillstrom, B., & Hare, R. D. (1988). Language-related hand gestures in psychopaths. *Journal of Personality Disorders, 2,* 21–27.

of effective prevention programs. *American Psychologist, 58,* 449–456.

National Advisory Commission on Criminal Justice Standards and Goals. (1973). *Task force on police.* Washington, DC: Government Printing Office.

National Center for Prosecution of Child Abuse. (2004). *Legislation regarding the admissibility of videotaped interviews?statements in criminal child abuse proceedings.* Retrieved on February 20, 2005 from http://www.ndaa-apri.org/apri/programs/ncpca/statutes.html

National Police Chiefs and Sheriffs Information Bureau. (1996). *The national directory of law enforcement administrators and correctional agencies.* Milwaukee, WI: Author.

National Victim Center and Crime Victims Research and Treatment Center (1992). *Rape in America: A report to the nation.* Arlington, VA: National Victim Center.

Neimeyer, R.A. (Ed.). (2000). *Meaning reconstruction and the experience of chronic loss.* Washington, DC: American Psychological Association.

Nell, V. (2000). *Cross-cultural neuropsychological assessment: Theory and practice.* Mahwah, NJ: Lawrence Erlbaum.

New York Criminal Procedure Law, Section § 120.45 (1999).

Newman, J. P., & Wallace, J. F. (1993). Psychopathy and cognition. In P. Kendall & K. Dobson (Eds.), *Psychopathology and cognition.* New York: Academic.

Newmark, L., Hartell, A., & Salem, P. (1995). Domestic violence and empowerment in custody and visitation cases. *Family and Conciliation Courts Review, 33,* 30–62.

Nigg, J. T., & Huang-Pollock, C. L. (2003). An early–onset model of the role of executive functions and intelligence in conduct disorder/delinquency. In B. B. Lahey, T. E. Moffitt, and A. Caspi (Eds.), *Causes of conduct disorder and juvenile delinquency.* New York: Guilford.

Nigg, J. T., Quamma, J. P., Greenberg, M. T., & Kusche, C. A. (1999). A two-year longitudinal study of neuropsychological and cognitive performance in relation to behavioral problems and competencies in elementary school children. *Journal of Abnormal Child Psychology, 27,* 51–63.

Nix, R. L., Pinderhughes, E. E., Dodge, K. A., Bates, J. E., Pettit, G. S., & McFadyen-Ketchum, S. A. (1999). The relation between mothers' hostile attribution tendencies and children's externalizing behavior problems: The mediating role of mothers' harsh discipline practices. *Child Development, 70,* 896–909.

Norris, F. H., & Kaniasty, K. (1994). Psychological distress following criminal victimization in the general population: Cross-sectional, longitudinal, and prospective analysis. *Journal of Consulting and Clinical Psychology, 62,* 111–123.

Norris, F. H., Kaniasty, K., & Scheer, D. A. (1990). Use of mental health services among victims of crime: Frequency, correlates, and subsequent recovery. *Journal of Consulting and Clinical Psychology, 58,* 538–547.

Nowikowski, F. (1995). Psychological offender profiling: An overview. *Criminologist, 19,* 225–226.

O'Neill, M. L., Heilbrun, K., & Lidz, V. (2000, March). Adolescent psychopathy in a substance abusing cohort: Predictors and treatment outcomes. In I. Kruh (Chair), *Psychopathy among juveniles/adolescents: Part 1.* Symposium conducted at the biennial meeting of the American Psychology-Law Association, New Orleans.

O'Shaughnessy, R., Hare, R. D., Gretton, H., & McBride, M. (1994). *Psychopathy and adolescent sex offending.* Unpublished raw data.

Oglesby, T. M. (1957). Use of emotional screening in the selection of police applicants. *Public Personnel Review, 18,* 228–231.

Ohio v. Roberts, 448 U.S. 56 (1980).

Olsson, C. A., Bond, L., Burns, J. M., Vella-Broderick, D. A., & Sawyer, S. M. (2003). Adolescence resilience: A concept analysis. *Journal of Adolescence, 26,* 1–11.

Orcutt, J. D., & Faison, R. (1988). Sex-role attitude change and reporting of rape victimization, 1973–1985. *Sociological Quarterly, 29,* 589–604.

Osterburg, J.W., & Ward, R. H. (1997). *Criminal investigation: A method for reconstructing the past* (2nd ed.). Cincinnati, OH: Anderson.

Ostrosky, F., Ardila, A., Rosselli, M., López-Arango, G., & Uriel-Mendoza, V. (1998). Neuropsychological test performance in illiterates. *Archives of Clinical Neuropsychology, 13,* 645–660.

Ostrosky-Solis, F., López-Arango, G., & Ardila, A. (2000). Sensitivity and specificity of the Mini-Mental State Examination in a Spanish-speaking population. *Applied Neuropsychology, 7,* 25–31.

Otero, R. F., McNally, D., & Powitzky, R. (1981). Mental health services in adult correctional systems. *Corrections Today, 43,* 8–18.

Otto, R. K., & Heilbrun, K. (2002). The practice of forensic psychology: A look toward the future in light of the past. *American Psychologist, 57,* 5–18.

Otto, R. K., Edens, J. F., & Barcus, E. H. (2000). The use of psychological testing in child custody evaluations. *Family and Conciliation Courts Review, 38,* 312–340.

Ozer, E. J. (2005). The impact of violence on urban adolescents: Longitudinal effects of perceived school connection and family support. *Journal of Adolescent Research, 20,* 167–192.

Pagelow, M. D. (1993). Justice for victims of spouse abuse in divorce and child custody cases. *Violence and Victims, 8,* 69–83.

Palmer, T. (1994). *A profile of correctional effectiveness and new directions for research.* Paper presented at the Child Witness in Context, North Atlantic Treaty Organization Advanced Study Institute, Lucca, Italy.

Pappas, D. (2000). Stopping New Yorkers' stalkers: An anti-stalking law for the new millennium. *Fordham Urban Law Journal, 27,* 945–952.

Park, C. L., & Folkman, S. (1997). Meaning in the context of stress and coping. *Review of General Psychology, 1,* 115–144.

Parker, J. G., & Asher, S. R. (1987). Peer relations and later personal adjustment: Are low-accepted children at risk? *Psychological Bulletin, 102,* 357–389.

Parkes, C. M. (1993a). Bereavement as a psychosocial transition: Processes of adaptation to change. In M. S. Stroebe, W. Stroebe, & R. O. Hansson (Eds.), *Handbook of bereavement.* New York: Cambridge University Press.

Parkes, C. M. (1993b). Psychiatric problems following bereavement by murder or manslaughter. *British Journal of Psychiatry, 162,* 49–54.

Pathé, M., Mullen, P. E., & Purcell, R. (1999). Stalking: False claims of victimization. *British Journal of Psychiatry, 174,* 170–172.

Patrick, C. J. (1994). Emotion and psychopathy: Some startling new insights. *Psychophysiology, 31,* 319–330.

Patterson, G. R., DeGarmo, D., & Knutson, N. (2000). Hyperactive and antisocial behaviors: Comorbid or two points in the same process? *Developmental and Psychopathology, 12,* 91–106.

Patterson, J. M., & Garwick, A. W. (1994). Levels of meaning in family stress theory. *Family Process, 33,* 287–304.

Payne, D. E. (1984, June). What "bothers" the emergency dispatcher. *APCO Bulletin, 50,* 20–21.

Payne, R. W. (1985). Review of the SCL-90-R. In *The ninth mental measurements yearbook* (Vol. 2). Lincoln: University of Nebraska–Lincoln, Buros Institute of Mental Measurements.

Pelcovitz, D., van der Kolk, B., Roth, S., Mandel, F., Kaplan, S., & Resick, P. (1997). Development of a criteria set and a structured interview for disorders of extreme stress (SIDES). *Journal of Traumatic Stress, 10,* 3–16.

Pepler, D. J., Byrd, W., & King, G. (1991). A social-cognitively based social skills training program for aggressive children. In D. J. Pepler & K. H. Rubin (Eds.), *The development and treatment of childhood aggression.* Hillsdale, NJ: Erlbaum.

Peterson, M. (2000). *The search for meaning in the aftermath of homicide: A hermeneutic phenomenological study of families of homicide victims.* Unpublished doctoral dissertation, University of Minnesota, Minneapolis.

Pines, A. M., Aronson, E., & Kafry, D. (1981). *Burnout: From tedium to personal growth.* New York: Free Press.

Pinizzotto, A. J. (1984). Forensic psychology: Criminal personality profiling. *Journal of Police Science and Administration, 12,* 32–40.

Pinizzotto, A. J., & Finkel, N. J. (1990). Criminal personality profiling: An outcome and process study. *Law and Human Behavior, 14,* 215–233.

Pino, R., & Meier, F. (1999). Gender differences in rape reporting. *Sex Roles: A Journal of Research, 40,* 979–990.

Pipe, M. E., & Wilson, J. C. (1994). Cues and secrets: Influences on children's event reports. *Developmental Psychology, 30,* 515–525.

Pithers, W. D. (1990). Relapse prevention with sexual aggressors: A method for maintaining therapeutic gain and enhancing external supervision. W. L. Marshall, D. R. Laws, & H. E. Barbaree (Eds.), *Handbook of sexual assault: Issues, theories, and treatment of the offender.* New York: Plenum.

Pithers, W. D., Beal, L. S., Armstrong, J. & Petty, J. (1989). Identification of risk factors through clinical interviews and analysis of records. In D. R. Laws (Ed.), *Relapse prevention with sexual offenders.* New York: Guilford.

Pithers, W. D., & Cumming, G. F. (1989). Can relapse be prevented? Initial outcome data from the Vermont treatment program for sex offenders. In D. R. Laws (Ed.), *Relapse, prevention with sex offenders*. New York: Guilford.

Pithers, W. D., Martin, G. R., & Cumming, G. F. (1989). Vermont treatment program for sexual aggressors. In D. R. Laws (Ed.), *Relapse, prevention with sex offenders*. New York: Guilford.

Polk, K. (1994). *When men kill: Scenarios of masculine violence*. Melbourne, Australia: University of Cambridge Press.

Poole, D. A., & Lamb, M. E. (1998). *Investigative interviews of children: A guide for helping professionals*. Washington, DC: American Psychological Association.

Poole, D. A., & Lindsay, D. S. (1995). Interviewing preschoolers: Effects of nonsuggestive techniques, parental coaching, and leading questions on reports of nonexperienced events. *Journal of Experimental Child Psychology, 60,* 129–154.

Pope, K. S., Butcher, J. N., & Seelen, J. (2000). *The MMPI, MMPI-2, and MMPI-A in court: A practical guide for expert witnesses and attorneys* (2nd ed.). Washington, DC: American Psychological Association.

Porter, B. (1983, April). Mind hunters. *Psychology Today*, pp. 44–52.

Porter, S., Fairweather, D., Drugge, J., Hervé, H., Birt, A., & Boer, D. P. (2000). Profiles of psychopathy in incarcerated sexual offenders. *Criminal Justice and Behavior, 27,* 216–233.

Poythress, N., Otto, R. K., Darkes, J., & Starr, L. (1993). APA's expert panel in the Congressional review of the USS Iowa incident. *American Psychologist, 48,* 8–15.

Pozzulo, J. D., & Lindsay, R. C. L. (1998). Identification accuracy of children versus adults: A meta-analysis. *Law and Human Behavior, 22,* 549–570.

Pozzulo, J. D., & Lindsay, R. C. L. (1999). Elimination lineups: An improved identification procedure for child witnesses. *Journal of Applied Psychology, 84,* 167–176.

Prentky, R. A., & Knight, R. A. (1991). Identifying critical dimensions for discriminating among rapists. *Journal of Consulting and Clinical Psychology, 59,* 643–661.

Prentky, R. A., & Knight, R. A. (1993). Age of onset of sexual assault: Criminal and life history correlates. In G. C. M. Hall, R. Hirschamn, J. R. Graham, & M. S. Zaragoza (Eds.), *Sexual aggression: Issues in etiology, assessment, and treatment*. Washington, DC: Taylor & Francis.

Prentky, R. A., Knight, R. A., & Lee, A. F. S. (1997). Risk factors associated with recidivism among extrafamilial child molesters. *Journal of Consulting and Clinical Psychology, 65,* 141–149.

President's Commission on Law Enforcement and the Administration of Justice. (1967). *Task force report: The police*. Washington, DC: Government Printing Office.

Price, R. H., & D'Aunno, T. (1992). *NIDA III Respondent Report Drug Abuse Treatment System Survey: A national study of the outpatient drug-free and methadone treatment system, 1988–1990 results*. Ann Arbor: University of Michigan, Institute for Social Research.

Psychological Corporation. (2001). *Wechsler Individual Achievement Test* (2nd ed.). San Antonio, TX: Author.

Purcell, R., Pathé, M., & Mullen, P. E. (2001). A study of women who stalk. *American Journal of Psychiatry, 158,* 2056–2060.

Quinnell, F. A., & Bow, J. N. (2001). Psychological tests used in child custody evaluations. *Behavioral Sciences & the Law, 19,* 491–501.

Quinsey, V. L. & Chaplin, T. C. (1988). Penile responses of child molesters and normals to descriptions of encounters with children involving sex and violence. *Journal of Interpersonal Violence, 3,* 259–274.

Quinsey, V. L., Harris, G. E., Rice, M. E., & Lalumiere, M. L. (1993). Assessing treatment efficacy in outcome studies of sex offenders. *Journal of Interpersonal Violence, 8,* 512–523.

Quinsey, V. L., Rice, M. E., & Harris, G. T. (1995). Actuarial prediction of sexual recidivism. *Journal of Interpersonal Violence, 10,* 85–105.

Rabwin, P., & Caulfield, B. (Producers). (1993–2000). *The X-Files*. Los Angeles: 20th Century Fox Television.

Radzinowicz, L. (1957). *Sexual offenses*. London: Macmillan.

Rafilson, F. M., & Sison, R. (1996). Seven criterion-related validity studies conducted with the National Police Officer Selection Test. *Psychological Reports, 78,* 163–176.

Raine, A., Venables, P. H., &Williams, M. (1996). Better autonomic conditioning and faster electrodermal half-recovery time at age 15 as possible protective factors against crime at age 19. *Developmental Psychology, 32,* 624–630.

Rando, T. A. (1993). *Treatment of complicated mourning.* Champaign, IL: Research Press.

Rando, T. A. (1996). Complications in mourning traumatic death. In K. Doka (Ed.), *Living with grief after sudden loss: Suicide, homicide, accident, heart attack, stroke.* Bristol, PA: Taylor & Francis.

Rapoport, I. C. (Producer). (1996–1999). *Profiler.* Burbank, CA: NBC Studios.

Raskin, D. C., & Yuille, J. C. (1989). Problems in evaluating interviews of children in sexual abuse cases. In S. J. Ceci, D. F. Ross, & M. P. Toglia (Eds.), *Perspectives on children's testimony.* New York: Springer-Verlag.

Rasmussen, K., & Levander, S. (1994). *Symptoms and personality characteristics of patients in a maximum security psychiatric unit.* Manuscript submitted for publication.

Realmuto, G., Jensen, J., & Wescoe, S. (1990). Specificity and sensitivity of sexually anatomically correct dolls in substantiating abuse: A pilot study. *Journal of the Academy of Child and Adolescent Psychiatry, 29,* 743–746.

Redmond, L. (1989). *Surviving: When someone you love was murdered.* Clearwater, FL: Psychological Consultation and Education Services.

Redmond, L. M. (1996). Sudden violent death. In K. J. Doka (Ed.), *Living with grief after sudden loss: Suicide, homicide, accident, heart attack, stroke.* Bristol, PA: Taylor & Francis.

Reese, J. T. (1986). Foreword. In J. T. Reese & H. A. Goldstein (Eds.), *Psychological services for law enforcement.* Washington, DC: Government Printing Office.

Reese, J. T. (1987). *A history of police psychological services.* Washington, DC: Government Printing Office.

Reese, J. T., & Goldstein, H. A. (Eds.). (1986). *Psychological services for law enforcement.* Washington, DC: Government Printing Office.

Reese, J. T., Horn, J. M., & Dunning, C. (Eds.). (1991). *Critical incidents in policing* (Rev. ed.). Washington, DC: Government Printing Office.

Reisner, M. (1972). *The police psychologist.* Springfield, IL: Charles C Thomas.

Reisner, M. (1982). *Police psychology: Collected papers.* Los Angeles: LEHI.

Reiss, A. D., Ones, D. S., & Viswesvaran, C. (1996, August). *Big five personality dimensions and expatriate completion of overseas assignments.* Paper presented at the annual conference of the American Psychological Association, Toronto, Canada.

Ressler, R. K., & Burgess, A. W. (1985, August). Violent crime. *FBI Law Enforcement Bulletin,* pp. 1–32.

Ressler, R. K., Burgess, A. W., Douglas, J. E., Hartman, C. R., & D'Agostino, R. B. (1986). Sexual killers and their victims: Identifying patterns through crime scene analysis. *Journal of Interpersonal Violence, 1,* 288–308.

Ressler, R. K., & Schachtman, T. (1992). *Whoever fights monsters.* New York: Simon & Schuster.

Revicki, D. A., & May, H. J. (1985). Occupational stress, social support and depression. *Health Psychology, 4,* 61–77.

Reynolds, C. R. (Ed.). (1998). *Detection of malingering during head injury litigation.* New York: Kluwer/Plenum.

Rice, M. E. (1997). Violent offender research and implications for the criminal justice system. *American Psychologist, 52,* 414–423.

Rice, M. E., & Harris, G. T. (1997). The treatment of adult offenders. In D. M. Stoff, J. Breiling & J. D. Maser (Eds.), *Handbook of antisocial behavior.* New York: John Wiley.

Rice, M. E., Harris, G. T., & Cormier, C. A. (1992). An evaluation of a maximum security therapeutic community for psychopaths and other mentally disordered offenders. *Law and Human Behavior, 16,* 399–412.

Rice, M. E., Harris, G. T., & Quinsey, V. L. (1990). A follow-up of rapists assessed in a maximum security psychiatric facility. *Journal of Interpersonal Violence, 4,* 435–448.

Rickert, V. I., & Wiemann, C. M. (1998). Date rape among adolescents and young adults. *Journal of Pediatric and Adolescent Gynecology, 11,* 167–175.

Rinear, E. (1988). Psychosocial aspects of parental response patterns to the death of a child by homicide. *Journal of Traumatic Stress, 1,* 305–322.

Robins, L. N. (1966). *Deviant children grown up: A sociological and psychiatric study of sociopathic personality.* Baltimore: Williams and Wilkins.

Robins, L. N., & Rutter, M. R. (Eds.). (1990). *Straight and devious pathways from childhood to adulthood.* New York: Cambridge University Press.

Rodenhauser, P., & Fornal, R. E. (1991). How important is the mental status examination? *Psychiatric Hospital, 22,* 21–24.

Roiphe, K. (1993). *The morning after: Sex, fear, and feminism on campus.* Boston: Little, Brown.

Rokach, A. (1987). Anger and aggression control training: Replacing attack with interaction. *Psychotherapy, 24,* 353–362.

Rosenbaum, R. (1993. April). The FBI's agent provocateur. *Vanity Fair,* pp. 122–136.

Rosenfeld, B. (2003). When stalking turns violent: Developments in the assessment of stalking risks. In M. Brewster (Ed.), *Stalking victims and offenders: Treatment, intervention, and research.* Kingston, NJ: Civic Research Institute.

Rosenfeld, B., & Harmon, R. (2002). Factors associated with violence in stalking and obsessional harassment cases. *Criminal Justice and Behavior, 29,* 671–691.

Ross, D. F., Hopkins, S., Hanson, E., Lindsay, R. C. L., Hazen, K., & Eslinger, T. (1994). The impact of protective shields and videotape testimony on conviction rates in a simulated trial of child sexual abuse. *Law and Human Behavior, 18,* 553–566.

Ross, R. R., Antonowicz, D., & Dhaliwal, G. K. (1995). *Going straight: Effective delinquency prevention and offender rehabilitation.* Ottawa, ONT: Air Training and Publications.

Ross, R. R., & Fabiano, E. A. (1985). *Time to think: A cognitive model of delinquency prevention and offender rehabilitation.* Johnson City, TN: Institute of Social Sciences and Arts.

Ross, R. R., & Gendreau, P. (1980). *Effective correctional treatment.* Toronto: Butterworth.

Rossmo, D. K. (1995a). *Geographic profiling: Target patterns of serial murderers.* Doctoral dissertation, Simon Fraser University, Burnaby, British Columbia, Canada.

Rossmo, D. K. (1995b). Place, space, and police investigations: Hunting serial violent criminals. In J. E. Eck & D. Weisburd (Eds.), *Crime and place: Crime prevention studies* (Vol. 4). Monsey, NY: Criminal Justice Press.

Rotenberg, M., & Diamond, B. L. (1971). The biblical conception of psychopathy: The law of the stubborn and rebellious son. *Journal of History of Behavioral Sciences, 7,* 29–38.

Rotundo, M., Nguyen, D. H., & Sackett, P. R. (2001). A meta-analytic review of gender differences in perceptions of sexual harassment. *Journal of Applied Psychology, 86,* 914–922.

Rowland, M. D., Henggeler, S.W., Gordon, A. M., Pickrel, S. G., Cunningham, P. B., & Edwards, J. E. (2000). Adapting multisystemic therapy to serve youth presenting psychiatric emergencies: Two case studies. *Child Psychology and Psychiatry Review, 5,* 30–43.

Ruback, R. B., Menard, K. S., Outlaw, M. C., & Shaffer, J. N. (1999). Normative advice to campus crime victims: Effects of gender, age, and alcohol. *Violence and Victims, 14,* 381–396.

Rutter, M., & the English and Romanian Adoptees (ERA) Study Team. (1998). Developmental catch-up and deficit, following adoption after severe global early privation. *Journal of Child Psychology and Psychiatry, 39,* 465–476.

Rynearson, E. (1984). Bereavement after homicide: A descriptive study. *American Journal of Psychiatry, 141,* 1452–1454.

Rynearson, E. K., & McCreery, J. M. (1993). Bereavement after homicide: A synergism of trauma and loss. *American Journal of Psychiatry, 150,* 258–261.

Rynearson, E. R. (1988). The homicide of a child. In F. Ochberg (Ed.), *Post-traumatic therapy and victims of violence.* New York: Brunner/Mazel.

Salekin, R. T., Rogers, R., & Sewell, K.W. (1996). A review and meta-analysis of the Psychopathy Checklist and Psychopathy Checklist–Revised: Predictive validity of dangerousness. *Clinical Psychology: Science and Practice, 3,* 203–215.

Santilla, P., Alkiora, P., Ekholm, M., & Niemi, P. (1999). False confession to robbery: The roles of suggestibility, anxiety, memory disturbance and withdrawal symptoms. *Journal of Forensic Psychiatry, 10,* 399–415.

Saxe, L. (1994). Detection of deception: Polygraph and integrity tests. *Current Directions, 3,* 69–73.

Saywitz, K. J., Geiselman, R. E., & Bornstein, G. K. (1992). Effects of cognitive interviewing and practice on children's recall performance. *Journal of Applied Psychology, 77,* 744–756.

Sbordone, R. J., Strickland, T. L., & Purisch, A. D. (2000). Neuropsychological assessment of the criminal defendant: The significance of cultural factors. In E. Flechter-Janzen, T. L. Strickland, & C. R. Reynolds (Eds.), *Handbook of cross-cultural neuropsychology.* New York: Kluwer/Plenum.

Schmidt, F. L., Hunter, J. E., McKenzie, R. C., & Muldrow, T.W. (1979). Impact of valid selection procedures on work-force productivity. *Journal of Applied Psychology, 64*, 609–626.

Schwartz, I. L. (1991). Sexual violence against women: Prevalence, consequences, societal factors and prevention. *American Journal of Preventive Medicine, 7*, 363–373.

Scogin, F., Schumacher, J., Howland, K., & McGee, J. (1989, August). *The predictive validity of psychological testing and peer evaluation in law enforcement settings.* Paper presented at the American Psychological Association Convention, New Orleans, LA.

Scrivner, E. M. (1994). *The role of police psychology in controlling excessive force.* Washington, DC: National Institute of Justice.

Segal, Z. V., & Marshall, W. L. (1985). Heterosexual and social skills in a population of rapists and child molesters. *Journal of Consulting and Clinical Psychology, 53*, 55–63.

Segal, Z. V., & Marshall, W. L. (1986). Discrepancies between self-efficacy predictions and actual performance in a population of rapists and child molesters. *Cognitive Therapy and Research, 10*, 363–376.

Séguin, J., Tremblay, R. E., Boulerice, B., Pihl, R. O., & Harden, P. (1999). Executive functions and physical aggression after controlling for attention deficit hyperactivity disorder, general memory, and IQ. *Journal of Child Psychology and Psychiatry, 40*, 1197–1208.

Seligman, M. E. P. (2002). Positive psychology, positive prevention, and positive therapy. In C. R. Snyder & S. J. Lopez (Eds.), *Handbook of positive psychology.* New York: Oxford University Press.

Selye, H. (1974). *Stress without distress.* Philadelphia: Lippincott.

Selye, H. (1982). History and present status of the stress concept. In L. Goldberger & S. Breznitz (Eds.), *Handbook of stress.* New York: Free Press.

Serin, R. C. (1991). Psychopathy and violence in criminals. *Journal of Interpersonal Violence, 6*, 423–431.

Serin, R. C., Malcolm, P. B., Khanna, A., & Barbaree, H. E. (1994). Psychopathy and deviant sexual arousal in incarcerated sexual offenders. *Journal of Interpersonal Violence, 9*, 3–11.

Seto, M. C., & Barbaree, H. E. (1999). Psychopathy, treatment behavior, and sex offender recidivism. *Journal of Interpersonal Violence, 14*, 1235–1248.

Sewell, J. D. (1993). Traumatic stress of multiple murder investigations. *Journal of Traumatic Stress, 6*, 103–118.

Shapiro, A. L. (1992). *We're number one: Where American stands—and falls—in the new world order.* New York: Vintage.

Shaw, J. H. (1991). The death of a police officer: Surviving the first year. In J. T. Reese, J. M. Horn, & C. Dunning (Eds.), *Critical incidents in policing* (Rev ed.). Washington, DC: Government Printing Office.

Sheridan, L. P., & Blaauw, E. (2004). Characteristics of false stalking reports. *Criminal Justice and Behavior, 31*, 55–72.

Shields, I. W., & Whitehall, C. C. (1994). Neutralization and delinquency among teenagers. *Criminal Justice and Behavior, 21*, 223–235.

Shusman, E. J., Inwald, R. E., & Landa, B. (1984). Correction officer job performance as predicted by the IPI and MMPI. *Criminal Justice and Behavior, 11*, 309–329.

Silver, R. L., Boon, C., & Stones, M. H. (1983). Searching for meaning in misfortune: Making sense of incest. *Journal of Social Issues, 39*(2), 81–107.

Simmons, M. M., & Cupp, M. (1998). Use and abuse of flunitrazepam. *Annals of Pharmacotherapy, 32*, 117–119.

Simourd, D., & Wormith, S. (1995). Criminal justice education and training: A survey of Canadian graduate schools of psychology. *Canadian Psychology, 36*, 213–220.

Simourd, L., & Andrews, D. A. (1994). Correlates of delinquency: A look at gender differences. *Forum on Corrections, 6*, 32–35.

Simpson, D. D., & Knight, K. (1998). *TCU data collection forms for correctional residential treatment.* Fort Worth: Texas Christian University, Institute of Behavioral Research.

Simpson, D. D., Joe, G.W., & Brown, B. S. (1997). Treatment retention and follow-up outcomes in the Drug Abuse Treatment Outcome Study (DATOS). *Psychology of Addictive Behaviors, 11*, 294–307.

Simpson, D. D., & Sells, S. B. (1982). Effectiveness of treatment for drug abuse: An overview of the DARP research program. *Advances in Alcohol and Substance Abuse, 2*, 7–29.

Sinclair, H. C., & Frieze, I. H. (2000). Initial courtship behavior and stalking: How should we draw the line? *Violence and Victims, 15*, 23–40.

Skogan, W. G. (1984). Reporting crimes to the police: The status of world research. *Journal of Research in Crime & Delinquency, 21,* 113–138.

Smith, G. (1999). Resilience concepts and findings: Implications for family therapy. *Journal of Family Therapy, 21,* 154–158.

Smith, K. M. (1999). Drugs used in acquaintance rape. *Journal of the American Pharmaceutical Association, 39,* 519–525.

Snyder, J., Cramer, A., Afrank, J., & Patterson, G. R. (2005). The contributions of ineffective discipline and parental hostile attributions of child misbehavior to the development of conduct problems at home and school. *Developmental Psychology, 41,* 30–41.

Society for Industrial and Organizational Psychology. (1987). *Principles for validation and use of personnel selection procedures.* Washington, DC: American Psychological Association.

Softley, P. (1980). *Police interrogation: An observational study in four police stations.* London: HMSO.

Solomon, R. M., & Horn, J. M. (1986). Post-shooting traumatic reactions: A pilot study. In J. T. Reese & H. A. Goldstein (Eds.), *Psychological services for law enforcement.* Washington, DC: Government Printing Office.

Solomon, S. D., & Johnson, D. M. (2002). Psychosocial treatment of posttraumatic stress disorder: A practice-friendly review of outcome research. *Journal of Clinical Psychology, 58,* 947–959.

Sorensen, E., Goldman, J., Ward, M., Albanese, I., Graves, L., & Chamberlain, C. (1995). Judicial decision-making in contested custody cases: The influence of reported child abuse, spouse abuse, and parental substance abuse. *Child Abuse & Neglect, 19,* 251–260.

Soroka et al. v. Dayton Hudson Corporation, 91 Daily Journal D.A. R. 13204 (1991).

Speltz, M. L., DeKlyen, M., Calderon, R., Greenberg, M. T., & Fisher, P. A. (1999). Neuropsychological characteristics and test behaviors of boys with early onset conduct problems. *Journal of Abnormal Psychology, 108,* 315–325.

Spencer, J. R., & Flin, R. H. (1990). *The evidence of children: The law and the psychology.* London: Blackstone Press.

Spielberger, C. D. (1979). *Police selection and evaluation: Issues and techniques.* Washington, DC: Hemisphere.

Spielberger, C. D., Ward, J. C., & Spaulding, H. C. (1979). A model for the selection of law enforcement officers. In C. D. Spielberger (Ed.), *Police selection and evaluation: Issues and techniques.* Washington, DC: Hemisphere.

Spreen, O., & Strauss, E. (1998). *A compendium of neuropsychological tests* (2nd ed.). New York: Oxford University Press.

Spungen, D. (1998). *Homicide: The hidden victims.* Thousand Oaks, CA: Sage.

Stahl, P. M. (1994). *Conducting child custody evaluations: A comprehensive guide.* Thousand Oaks, CA: Sage.

Stahl, P. M. (1999). *Complex issues in child custody evaluations.* Thousand Oaks, CA: Sage.

Standards Committee, American Association for Correctional Psychology. (2000). Standards for psychology services in jails, prisons, correctional facilities, and agencies. *Criminal Justice and Behavior, 27,* 433–494.

StataCorp. (2001). *Reference guide: Release 7.0. College Station.* TX: Stata Corporation.

State v. Jackson, 304 S. E. 2d 134, N. C. (1983).

State v. Michaels, 625 A2d 489 (N.J. App. 1993), aff'd, 1994WL278424 (N.J. Spu. 1994).

Stattin, H., & Klackenberg-Larsson, I. (1993). Early language and intelligence development and their relationship to future criminal behavior. *Journal of Abnormal Psychology, 102,* 369–378.

Stephenson, G. M., & Moston, S. J. (1994). Police interrogation. *Psychology, Crime and Law, 1,* 151–157.

Sternberg, K. J., Lamb, M. E., Hershkowitz, I., Yudilevitch, L., Orbach, Y., Esplin, P. W., & Hovav, M. (1997). Effects of introductory style on children's abilities to describe experiences of sexual abuse. *Child Abuse and Neglect, 21,* 1133–1146.

Stockdale, M. S., O'Connor, M., Gutek, B. A., & Geer, T. (2002). The relationship between prior sexual victimization and sensitivity to social sexual behavior in the workplace and education: Literature review and empirical study. *Psychology, Public Policy, and Law, 8,* 64–95.

Stoolmiller, M. (2001). Synergistic interaction of child manageability problems and parent-discipline tactics in predicting future growth in externalizing behavior for boys. *Developmental Psychology, 37,* 814–825.

Stouthamer-Loeber, M., Loeber, R., Farrington, D. P., Zhang, Q., van Kammen, W., & Maguin, E.

(1993). The double edge of protective and risk factors for delinquency: interrelations and developmental patterns. *Development and Psychopathology, 5,* 683-701.

Stowe, R. M., Arnold, D. H., & Ortiz, C. (2000). Gender differences in the relationship of language development to disruptive behavior and peer relationships in preschoolers. *Journal of Applied Developmental Psychology, 20,* 521–536.

Strachan, C. (1994). *Assessment of psychopathy in female offenders.* Unpublished doctoral dissertation, University of British Columbia, Vancouver, British Columbia, Canada.

Stratton, J. G. (1984). *Police passages.* Manhattan Beach, CA: Glennon.

Straus, M. A. (1979). Measuring intrafamily conflict and violence: The Conflict Tactics (CT) Scales. *Journal of Marriage and the Family, 41,* 75–88.

Straus, M. A. (1990). Injury and frequency of assault and the "Representative Sample Fallacy" in measuring wife beating and child abuse. In M. A. Straus & R. J. Gelles (Eds.), *Physical violence in American families: Risk factors and adaptations to violence in 8,145 families.* New Brunswick, NJ: Transaction.

Straus, M. A. (1993). Physical assaults by wives: A major social problem. In R. J. Gelles & D. R. Loseke (Eds.), *Current controversies on family violence.* Thousand Oaks, CA: Sage.

Straus, M. A., & Gelles, R. J. (1988). How violent are American families? Estimates from the National Family Violence Resurvey and other studies. In G. Hotaling, D. Finkelhor, J. T. Kirkpatrick, & M. A. Straus (Eds.), *Family abuse and its consequences: New directions in research.* Beverly Hills, CA: Sage.

Straus, M. A., Hamby, S. L., Boney-McCoy, S., & Sugarman, D. B. (1996). The revised Conflict Tactics Scales (CTS2): Development and preliminary psychometric data. *Journal of Family Issues, 17,* 283–316.

Strecher, V. G. (1991). Histories and futures of policing: Readings and misreadings of a pivotal present. *Police Forum, 1,* 1–9.

Strickland, T. L., & Gray, G. (2000). Neurobehavioral disorders and pharmacologic intervention: The significance of ethnobiological variation in drug responsivity. In E. Fletcher-Janzen, T. L. Strickland, & C. R. Reynolds (Eds.), *Handbook of cross-cultural neuropsychology.* New York: Kluwer/Plenum.

Stroebe, M., & Gergen, K. J. (1996). Broken hearts or broken bonds. In D. Klass, P. R. Silverman, & S. L. Nickman (Eds.), *Continuing bonds: New understandings of grief.* Philadelphia: Taylor & Francis.

Stroebe, M., & Schut, F. (1999). The dual process model of coping with bereavement: Rationale and synthesis. *Death Studies, 23,* 197–224.

Struckhoff, D. R. (1978). Deprofessionalizing corrections is bad business. *Offender Rehabilitation, 2,* 333–338.

Stuckless, N. (1996). *The influence of anger, perceived injustice, revenge, and time on the quality of life of survivor victims.* Toronto: York University.

Sweet, J. (Ed.). (1999). *Forensic neuropsychology: Fundamentals and practice.* Royersford, PA: Swets & Zeitlinger.

Swim, J. K., Borgida, E., & McCoy, K. (1993). Videotaped versus in-court witness testimony: Does protecting the child witness jeopardize due process? *Journal of Applied Social Psychology, 23,* 603–631.

Talwar, V., Lee, K., Bala, N., & Lindsay, R. C. L. (2002). Children's conceptual knowledge of lying and its relation to their actual behaviors: Implications for court competence examinations. *Law and Human Behavior, 26,* 395–415.

Tancredi, L. R. (1987). The Mental Status Examination. *Generations: Journal of the American Society on Aging, 11,* 24–31.

Tang, M., Zou, X., Han, H., Wang, Y., Zhang, L., Tang, M., et al. (1999). Application of the Chinese version of the Mini-Mental State Exam (MMSE) in 55-year-olds and above from the districts of Chengdu City, China. *Chinese Mental Health Journal, 13,* 200–202.

Taylor, M., Esbensen, B. M., & Bennett, R. T. (1994). Children's understanding of knowledge acquisition: The tendency for children to report they have always known what they have just learned. *Child Development, 65,* 1581–1604.

Taylor, M. J., & Heaton, R. K. (2001). Sensitivity and specificity of WAIS-III/WMS-III demographically corrected factors in neuropsychological assessment. *Journal of the International Neuropsychological Society, 7,* 867–874.

Taylor, S. J., & Bogdan, R. (1984). *Introduction to qualitative research methods: The search for meanings* (2nd ed.). New York: John Wiley.

Telford, F., & Moss, F. A. (1924). Suggested tests for patrolmen. *Public Personnel Studies, 2,* 112–144.

Temple, S. (1997). Treating inner-city families of homicide victims: A contextually oriented approach. *Family Process, 36,* 133–149.

Terman, L. M. (1917). A trial of mental and pedagogical tests in a civil service examination for policemen and firemen. *Journal of Applied Psychology, 1,* 17–29.

Terr, L.C. (1991). Childhood traumas: An outline and overview. *American Journal of Psychiatry, 148,* 10–20.

Tett, R. P., Jackson, D. N., & Rothstein, M. (1991). Personality measures as predictors of job performance: A meta-analytic review. *Personnel Psychology, 44,* 703–740.

Tharp, R. G., & Wetzel, R. J. (1996). *Behavior modification in the natural environment.* New York: Academic Press.

Thomas, A., & Chess, S. (1977). *Temperament and development.* New York: Brunner/Mazel.

Thomas, G. C., III, & Leo, R. A. (2002). The effects of *Miranda v. Arizona*: "Embedded" in our national culture? In M. Tonry (Ed.), *Crime and justice: Vol. 29. A review of research.* Chicago: University of Chicago Press.

Thompson, M. P., Norris, F. H., & Ruback, R. B. (1998). Comparative distress levels of inner-city family members of homicide victims. *Journal of Traumatic Stress, 11,* 223–242.

Thompson, M. P., & Vardaman, P. J. (1997). The role of religion in coping with the loss of a family member to homicide. *Journal for the Scientific Study of Religion, 36,* 44–51.

Thompson, S., & Jangian, A. (1988). Life schemes: A framework for understanding the search for meaning. *Journal of Social and Clinical Psychology, 7,* 260–280.

Thurstone, L. L (1922). The intelligence of policemen. *Journal of Personnel Research, 2,* 64–74.

Thurstone, L. L. (1924). The civil service tests for patrolmen in Philadelphia. *Public Personnel Studies, 2,* 1–5.

Tit, Q. Q., & Huizinga, D. (2002). Dimensions of the construct of resilience and adaptation among inner-city youth. *Journal of Adolescent Research, 17,* 260–276.

Titchener, J. L. (1986). Post-traumatic decline: A consequence of unresolved destructive drives. In C. R. Figley (Ed.), *Trauma and its wake* (Vol. 2). New York: Brunner-Mazel.

Tjaden, P., & Thoennes, N. (1998). Stalking in America: Findings from the National *Violence Against Women Survey.* Washington, DC: U.S. Department of Justice, National Institute of Justice.

Tjaden, P., & Thoennes, N. (2000). *Extent, nature, and consequences of intimate partner violence: Findings from the National Violence Against Women Survey (National Institute of Justice and the Centers for Disease Control and Prevention).* Washington, DC: Government Printing Office.

Toch, H. (1998). Psychopathy and antisocial personality in forensic settings. In T. Millon, E. Simonsen, M. Birket-Smith, & R. Davis (Eds.), *Psychopathy: Antisocial, criminal and violent behavior.* New York: Guilford.

Toews, J., el-Guebaly, N., Leckie, A., & Harper, D. (1984). Patients' attitudes at the time of their commitment. *Canadian Journal of Psychiatry, 29,* 590–595.

Toglia, M. P., Ross, D. F., Ceci, S. J., & Hembrooke, H. (1992). The suggestibility of children's memory: Asocial-psychological and cognitive interpretation. In M. L. Howe, C. J. Brainard, & V. F. Reyna (Eds.), *Development of long-term memory* New York: Springer-Verlag.

Tolan, P. H., & Thomas, P. (1995). The implications of age of onset for delinquency II: Longitudinal data. *Journal of Abnormal Child Psychology, 23,* 157–169.

Tremblay, R. E. (2003). Why socialization fails: The case of chronic physical aggression. In B. B. Lahey, T. E. Moffitt, & A. Caspi (Eds.), *Causes of conduct disorder and juvenile delinquency.* New York: Guilford.

Trowbridge, B. C. (2003). Suggestibility and confessions. *American Journal of Forensic Psychology, 21,* 5–21.

Tucillo, J. A., DeFilippis, N. A., Denny, R. L., & Dsurney, J. (2002). Licensure requirements for interjurisdictional forensic evaluations. *Professional Psychology: Research and Practice, 33,* 377–383.

Tugade, M. M., & Fredickson, B. L. (2004). Resilient individuals use positive emotions to bounce back from negative emotional expressions. *Journal of Personality and Social Psychology, 86,* 320–333.

Ulman, R. B. (1988). *The shattered self: A psychoanalytic study of trauma.* Hillsdale, NJ: Analytic Press.

Umbreit, M., Bradshaw, W., & Coates, R. B. (1999). Victims of severe violence meet the offender:

Restorative justice through dialogue. *International Journal of Victimology, 6,* 321–345.

Ungersma, A. J. (1976). Fantasy, creativity, conformity. *Humanitas, 12,* 73–82.

United States v. Hall, 974 F. Supp. 1198, S. D. Ill., (1997).

Ursano, R. J., & McCarroll, J. E. (1990). The nature of a traumatic stressor: Handling dead bodies. *Journal of Nervous and Mental Disease, 178,* 396–398.

U.S. Department of Education. (1993). *Fall enrollment statistics, 1991.* Washington, DC: Government Printing Office.

U.S. Department of Justice. (1996). *Bureau of justice statistics: Local police departments.* Washington, DC: Office of Justice Programs.

Valciukas, J. A. (1995). *Forensic neuropsychology: Conceptual foundations and clinical practice.* New York: Haworth Press.

van der Kolk, B. A. (1996). The complexity of adaptation to trauma: Self-regulation, stimulus discrimination, and characterological development. In B. A. van der Kolk, A. C. McFarlane, & L. Weisaeth (Eds.), *Traumatic stress: The effects of overwhelming experience on the mind, body, and society.* New York: Guilford.

van der Kolk, B. A., McFarlane, A. C., & Weiseth, L. (Eds.). (1996). *Traumatic stress: The effects of overwhelming experience on mind, body and society.* New York: Guilford.

van Marle, H. J. C. (1995). *A closed system: A psychoanalytical framework for forensic therapeutic communities.* Ph.D. dissertation, Utrecht University, Arnhem, The Netherlands. Arnhem, The Netherlands: Gouda Quint.

Van Voorhis, P. (1987). Correctional effectiveness: the high cost of ignoring success. *Federal Probation, 51,* 56–62.

Violanti, J. M., & Aron, F. (1995). Police stressors: Variations in perception among police personnel. *Journal of Criminal Justice, 23,* 287–294.

Viteles, M. S. (1929). Psychological methods in the selection of patrolmen in Europe. *Annals of the American Academy, 146,* 160–165.

Waaktaar, T., Christie, H. J., Borge, A. I. H., & Torgerson, S. (2004). How can young people's resilience be enhanced? Experiences from a clinical intervention project. *Clinical Child Psychology and Psychiatry, 9,* 167–183.

Wade, A. (2002). New measures and new challenges: Children's experiences of the court process. In H. L. Westcott, G. M. Davies, & R. H. C. Bull (Eds.), *Children's testimony: A handbook of psychological research and forensic practice.* West Sussex, UK: John Wiley.

Walker, A. G. (1994). *Handbook on questioning children: A linguistic perspective.* Washington, DC: American Bar Association Center on Children and the Law.

Walker, L. E., & Edwall, G. E. (1987). Domestic violence and determination of visitation and custody in divorce. In D. J. Sonkin (Ed.), *Domestic violence on trial: Psychological and legal dimensions of family violence.* New York: Springer.

Walker-Perry, N., & Wrightsman, L. S. (1991). *The child witness: Legal issues and dilemmas.* Thousand Oaks, CA: Sage.

Waller, M. A. (2001). Resilience in ecosystemic context: Evolution of the concept. *American Journal of Orthopsychiatry, 71,* 290–297.

Walters, G. D. (2002). *Criminal belief systems: An integrated-interactive theory of lifestyle.* Westport, CT: Praeger.

Wandersman, A., & Nation, M. (1998). Urban neighborhoods and mental health: Psychological contributions to understanding toxicity, resilience, and interventions. *American Psychologist, 53,* 647–656.

Wang, M. C. (1997). Next steps in inner-city education: focusing on resilience development and learning success. *Education and Urban Society, 29,* 255–276.

Warren, A. R. (1992, May). *Interviewing child witnesses: some linguistic considerations.* Paper presented at the Child Witness in Context North Atlantic Treaty Organization Advanced Study Institute, Lucca, Italy.

Warren, A. R., Hulse-Trotter, K., & Tubbs, E. C. (1991). Inducing resistance to suggestibility in children. *Law and Human Behavior, 15,* 273–285.

Warren, A. R., & McCloskey, L. A. (1997). Language in social contexts. In J. B. Gleason (Ed.), *The development of language* (4th ed.). New York: Allyn & Bacon.

Warren, A. R., Woodall, C. E., Hunt, J. S., & Perry, N.W. (1996). "It sounds good in theory, but . . ." Do investigative interviewers follow guidelines based on memory research? *Child Maltreatment, 1,* 231–245.

Webster, C. D., Douglas, K. S., Eaves, D., & Hart, S. D. (1997). *HCR-20: Assessing risk for violence.* Version 2. Burnaby, British Columbia, Canada: Simon Fraser University, Mental Health, Law and Policy Institute.

Weisner, C. M. (1987). The social ecology of alcohol treatment in the United States. *Recent Developments in Alcoholism, 5,* 203–243.

Went, F. V. (1979). Death anxiety among law enforcement officers. *Journal of Police Science and Administration, 7,* 230–235.

Werner, E. E. (1987). Vulnerability and resiliency in children at risk for delinquency: A longitudinal study from birth to young adulthood. In J. D. Burchard & S. N. Burchard (Eds.), *Prevention of delinquency.* Beverly Hills, CA: Sage.

Werner, E. E. (1993). Risk, resilience, and recovery: Perspectives from the Kauai longitudinal study. *Development and Psychopathology, 5,* 503–515.

Werner, E. E. (1995). Resilience in development. *Current Directions in Psychological Science, 4,* 81–85.

Werner, E. E., Bierman, J. M., & French, F. E. (1971). *The children of Kauai: A longitudinal study from the prenatal period to age ten.* Honolulu: University of Hawaii Press.

Werner, E. E., & Smith, R. S. (1977). *Kauai's children come of age.* Honolulu: University of Hawaii Press.

Werner, E. E., & Smith, R. S. (1982). *Vulnerable, but invincible: A longitudinal study of resilient children and youth.* New York: McGraw-Hill.

Westbrook v. Arizona, 384 U.S. 150 (1965).

White, M., & Epston, D. (1990). *Narrative ends to therapeutic means.* New York: Norton.

Widiger, R. A., & Corbitt, E. (1995). The DSM-IV antisocial personality disorder. In W. J. Livesley (Ed.), *The DSM-IV personality disorders.* New York: Guilford.

Widiger, T. A., Cadoret, R., Hare, R. D., Robins, L., Rutherford, M., et al. (1996). DSM-IV Antisocial Personality Disorder Field Trial. *Journal of Abnormal Psychology, 105,* 3–16.

Wiener, R. L., & Hurt, L. E. (1999). An interdisciplinary approach to understanding social sexual conduct at work. *Psychology, Public Policy, and Law, 5,* 556–595.

Wiener, R. L., Hurt, L., Russell, B., Mannen, K., & Gasper, C. (1997). Perceptions of sexual harassment: The effects of gender, legal standard, and ambivalent sexism. *Law and Human Behavior, 21,* 71–93.

Wilkinson, G. S. (1993). *Wide Range Achievement Test 3.* San Antonio, TX: Psychological Corporation.

Williams, J. (2000, April). Interrogating justice: A critical analysis of the police interrogation and its role in the criminal justice process. *Canadian Journal of Psychology, 209–240.*

Williams, L. M., & Saunders, B. E. (2000, March) *Co-occurrence of partner violence and child abuse.* Paper presented at the Doctors for Sexual Abuse Care and New Zealand College of Clinical Psychologists, Auckland, New Zealand.

Williamson, S. E. (1991). *Cohesion and coherence in the speech of psychopathic criminals.* Unpublished doctoral dissertation, University of British Columbia, Vancouver, British Columbia, Canada.

Williamson, S. E., Hare, R. D., & Wong, S. (1987). Violence: Criminal psychopaths and their victims. *Canadian Journal of Behavioral Science, 19,* 454–462.

Williamson, S. E., Harpur, T. J., & Hare, R. D. (1991). Abnormal processing of affective words by psychopaths. *Psychophysiology, 28,* 260–273.

Wilson, J. C., & Pipe, M. E. (1995). Children's disclosure of secrets: Implications for interviewing In G. Davis, S. Lloyd-Bostock, M. McMurran, & C. Wilson (Eds.), *Psychology, law, and criminal justice: International developments in research and practice.* Berlin, Germany: Walter DeGruyter.

Wilson, J. Q. (1968). *Varieties of police behavior.* Cambridge, MA: Harvard University Press.

Wilson, M., Daly, M., & Daniele, A. (1995). Familicide: The killing of spouse and children. *Aggressive Behavior, 21,* 275–291.

Wilson, P., Lincon, R., & Kocsis, R. (1997). Validity, utility and ethics of profiling for serial violent and sexual offences. *Psychiatry, Psychology and Law, 4,* 1–11.

Wiseman, R., & West, D. (1997, January). An experimental test of psychic detection. *Police Journal, 70,* 19–25.

Wong, S. (1984). *Criminal and institutional behaviors of psychopaths* (Programs branch users report). Ottawa: Ministry of the Solicitor-General of Canada.

Woodcock, R. W., McGrew, K. S., & Mather, N. (2001). *Woodcock-Johnson III Test of Achievement.* Itasca, IL: Riverside Publishing.

World Health Organization. (1990). *International classification of diseases and related health problems* (10th ed.). Geneva, Switzerland: Author.

Wortman, C. B., Silver, R. C., & Kessler, R. C. (1993). The meaning of loss and adjustment to bereavement. In M. S. Stroebe, W. Stroebe, & R.O. Hansson (Eds.), *Handbook of bereavement.* Cambridge, MA: Cambridge University Press.

Yarmey, A. D. (1990). *Understanding police and police work: Psychosocial issues.* New York: New York University Press.

Yehuda, R. (2002). Clinical relevance of biological findings in PTSD. *Psychiatric Quarterly, 73,* 123–133.

Yuille, J. C., Hunter, R., Jeffe, R., & Zaparniuk, J. (1993). Interviewing children in sexual abuse cases. In G. S. Goodman & B. L. Bottoms (Eds.), *Child victims, child witnesses: Understanding and improving testimony.* New York: Guildford.

Zelazo, P. D., Carter, A., Resnick, J. S., & Frye, D. (1997). Early development of executive functions: A problem-solving framework. *Review of General Psychology, 1,* 198–226.

Zinger, I. (1995). The misuse of psychopathy in Canadian court proceedings. *Issues in Criminological and Legal Psychology, 24,* 157–159.

Zinger, I., & Forth, A. E. (1998). Psychopathy and Canadian criminal proceedings: The potential for human rights abuses. *Canadian Journal of Criminology, 40,* 237–276.

Zuckerman, M. (1994). *Behavioral expressions and biosocial basis of sensation seeking.* New York: Cambridge University Press.

INDEX

About the Editors

Curt R. Bartol has been a college professor for more than 30 years, teaching a wide variety of both undergraduate and graduate courses, including biopsychology, criminal behavior, juvenile delinquency, introduction to forensic psychology, social psychology, and psychology and law. As a licensed clinical psychologist, he has been a consulting police psychologist to local, municipal, state, and federal law enforcement agencies for nearly 25 years. He is also the Editor of *Criminal Justice and Behavior,* the international journal of the American Association for Correctional and Forensic Psychologists, published by Sage Publications. He has written *Criminal Behavior: A Psychosocial Approach,* now in its seventh edition (2005), and coauthored, with Anne Bartol, *Juvenile Delinquency: A Systems Approach (1989), Delinquency and Justice: A Psychosocial Approach,* 2nd edition (1998), *Psychology and Law: Theory, Research, and Application,* 3rd edition (2004), and *Introduction to Forensic Psychology* (2004). He has published extensively in the field of forensic psychology.

Anne M. Bartol earned an MA and a PhD in Criminal Justice from State University of New York at Albany. She also holds an MA in journalism from the University of Wisconsin–Madison. She has taught criminal justice, sociology, and journalism courses over a 20-year college teaching career and has worked as a journalist and a social worker in child and adolescent protective services. She has coauthored, with Curt Bartol, *Juvenile Delinquency: A Systems Approach (1989), Delinquency and Justice: A Psychosocial Approach,* 2nd edition (1998), *Psychology and Law: Theory, Research, and Application,* 3rd edition (2004), *Introduction to Forensic Psychology* (2004), and the seventh edition of *Criminal Behavior: A Psychosocial Approach* (2005). She has served as book review editor of *Criminal Justice and Behavior* and has published articles on women and criminal justice, rural courts, and the history of forensic psychology.